THE BUDDHIST UNCONSCIOUS

This work focuses upon an explicit notion of unconscious mind formulated by the Yogācāra school of Indian Buddhism in a series of texts from the third to the fifth centuries CE. These texts describe and defend this "Buddhist" unconscious through a variety of exegetical and metapsychological arguments whose rationales are analyzed in terms of their historical and contemporary context. The work thus first presents the multivalent conception of consciousness (*vijñāna*) within the early teachings of the Buddha, and then demonstrates how the Abhidharma emphasis upon momentary and conscious processes of mind was widely understood to make the continuity and multidimensionality of consciousness problematic in several crucial ways. The Yogācāra thinkers addressed these multiple problems with a new model of mind centered upon the Buddhist unconscious, whose meaning and purpose is now made accessible to Western readers for the first time.

William S. Waldron received his PhD in Buddhist Studies from the University of Wisconsin after studying extensively in India, Nepal, and Japan. He currently teaches South Asian religions and Buddhist philosophy at Middlebury College, Vermont. His research areas include the Yogācāra school of Indian Buddhism, and comparative psychologies and philosophies of mind.

ROUTLEDGECURZON CRITICAL STUDIES IN BUDDHISM

General Editors
Charles S. Prebish and Damien Keown

RoutledgeCurzon Critical Studies in Buddhism is a comprehensive study of the Buddhist tradition. The series explores this complex and extensive tradition from a variety of perspectives, using a range of different methodologies.

The series is diverse in its focus, including historical studies, textual translations and commentaries, sociological investigations, bibliographic studies, and considerations of religious practice as an expression of Buddhism's integral religiosity. It also presents materials on modern intellectual historical studies, including the role of Buddhist thought and scholarship in a contemporary, critical context and in the light of current social issues. The series is expansive and imaginative in scope, spanning more than two and a half millennia of Buddhist history. It is receptive to all research works that inform and advance our knowledge and understanding of the Buddhist tradition.

THE REFLEXIVE NATURE OF AWARENESS
Paul Williams

BUDDHISM AND HUMAN RIGHTS
Edited by Damien Keown, Charles Prebish, Wayne Husted

ALTRUISM AND REALITY
Paul Williams

WOMEN IN THE FOOTSTEPS OF THE BUDDHA
Kathryn R. Blackstone

THE RESONANCE OF EMPTINESS
Gay Watson

IMAGING WISDOM
Jacob N. Kinnard

AMERICAN BUDDHISM
Edited by Duncan Ryuken Williams and Christopher Queen

PAIN AND ITS ENDING
Carol S. Anderson

THE SOUND OF LIBERATING TRUTH
Edited by Sallie B. King and Paul O. Ingram

BUDDHIST THEOLOGY
Edited by Roger R. Jackson and John J. Makransky

EMPTINESS APPRAISED
David F. Burton

THE GLORIOUS DEEDS OF PURNA
Joel Tatelman

CONTEMPORARY BUDDHIST ETHICS
Edited by Damien Keown

INNOVATIVE BUDDHIST WOMEN
Edited by Karma Lekshe Tsomo

TEACHING BUDDHISM IN THE WEST
Edited by V. S. Hori, R. P. Hayes and J. M. Shields

EMPTY VISION
David L. McMahan

SELF, REALITY AND REASON IN TIBETAN PHILOSOPHY
Thupten Jinpa

BUDDHIST PHENOMENOLOGY
Dan Lusthaus

ZEN WAR STORIES
Brian Victoria

THE BUDDHIST UNCONSCIOUS
The ālaya-vijñāna in the context of Indian Buddhist thought
William S. Waldron

THE BUDDHIST UNCONSCIOUS

The ālaya-vijñāna in the context of Indian Buddhist thought

William S. Waldron

RoutledgeCurzon
Taylor & Francis Group
LONDON AND NEW YORK

First published 2003
by RoutledgeCurzon
2 Park Square, Milton Park, Abingdon, Oxon, OX14 4RN

Simultaneously published in the USA and Canada
by RoutledgeCurzon
270 Madison Ave, New York NY 10016

RoutledgeCurzon is an imprint of the Taylor & Francis Group

Transferred to Digital Printing 2006

Typeset in Goudy by
Newgen Imaging Systems (P) Ltd, Chennai, India

British Library Cataloguing in Publication Data
A catalogue record for this book is available
from the British Library

Library of Congress Cataloging in Publication Data
Waldron, William S.
The Buddhist unconscious: the ālaya-vijñāna in the context of Indian Buddhist thought / William S. Waldron.
p. cm. – (RoutledgeCurzon critical studies in Buddhism)
Includes bibliographical references and index.
1. ālayavijñāna. 2. Yogācāra (Buddhism) 3. Mādhyamika (Buddhism)
I. Title. II. Series.
BQ7496 .W35 2003
294.3′42042–dc21 2002036709

ISBN10: 0–415–29809–1 (hbk)
ISBN10: 0–415–40607–2 (pbk)

ISBN13: 978–0–415–29809–4 (hbk)
ISBN13: 978–0–415–40607–9 (pbk)

CONTENTS

PREFACE

Our lives in this world are prescribed in countless ways. As human beings, we have certain capabilities, such as speech, but not others, such as natural flight or sonic navigation. As males or females, we inherit obvious as well as some not so obvious biological and social conditions. As Americans, Chinese, Indians, or Russians, we are acculturated from birth into particular world-views, with all of their attendant behavioral norms, cognitive regularities, and moral imperatives. Our actions in this life have done little to create the conditions in which we are born and raised, which nevertheless strongly circumscribe the parameters of our daily experiences.

This is no less true for our capacities of mind. The range of our normal perceptions, our typical array of appetites and aptitudes, even our capacities for our highest worldly achievements – to the extent that these are species-specific – are in large part already inscribed by the time we are born as human beings. Most of us, for example, cannot choose whether or not to see the sun as yellow or to feel pain when injured, or to become fearful or angry when physically assaulted. Most of this happens automatically, without our conscious choice and relatively impervious to our conscious intentions. This "unconscious structuring of experience" has been recognized to varying degrees, and with varying degrees of sophistication, in different times and places.

The essay that follows is the story of one such time and place – fifth-century CE India – where an awareness of this area of unawareness, and the challenges it poses to conscious self-transformation, were developed to an extraordinary degree. So much so that the Indian Yogācāra Buddhists who first systematically conceptualized this awareness of unawareness, if you will, felt able to describe its dynamics and delineate its contours in considerable detail. They not only explicitly differentiated a dimension of unconscious mental processes – called "*ālaya*" *vijñāna*, the "basal, store, or home" consciousness – from the processes of conscious cognitive awareness – called *pravṛtti-vijñāna*. They also articulated a variety of experiential, logical, and exegetical arguments in support of this concept of unconscious mind, arguments which we will examine in considerable detail in the several Yogācāra chapters below, which form the core of this work.

This "Buddhist unconscious," however, did not arise out of a vacuum. The description of this "*ālaya*" consciousness, as well as the problematics driving its development and the rationales offered in its defense, all evolved within a particular intellectual and religious milieu: the sophisticated traditions of Abhidharma Buddhism (roughly 200 BCE to 600 CE). Despite their (sometimes deserved) reputation for a scholasticism "as dry as dust," Abhidharma traditions evinced great intellectual vitality. Driven by religious conviction, informed by yogic practice, and expressed in a systematic, albeit painstaking, idiom, Abhidharmic modes of analysis have indelibly influenced Buddhist thought and practices ever since. These traditions developed philosophical analyses of mind and mental processes to such a degree that its practitioners became acutely aware – experientially as well as intellectually – of the underlying conditions and constraints of ordinary, and even extraordinary, forms of conscious awareness. It was within this milieu that the complex concept of ālaya consciousness developed, and within which the intricate and interwoven rationales supporting this "Buddhist unconscious" are most intelligible. The rationales for this concept are too dense, assume too many doctrines, and are simply too technical to be fully appreciated outside of this Abhidharma context. The second chapter is therefore devoted to providing the indispensable specifics of this originating context.

The Abhidharma traditions did not develop out of a vacuum either. They represented, more or less, a systematization of the teachings passed down from the Buddha himself. In these early teachings there was no overt distinction between consciousness (Sanskrit: *vijñāna*; Pāli: *viññāṇa*) as waking, object-oriented cognitive awareness and as a persisting, underlying level of basic sentience. The single term "vijñāna" encompassed both these connotations. This distinction is discernable, however, through careful analysis of these early teachings, particularly in the light of later developments. This was, in fact, exactly how the Yogācārins justified their innovative distinction between conscious and unconscious mental processes: by examining the earlier teachings in the light of the later, more sophisticated perspectives of Abhidharmic analysis. We follow in these illustrious footsteps and turn first to the earliest teachings of the Buddha, focusing in particular on the concept of vijñana (*viññāṇa*) – rendered there equally appropriately as either "consciousness" or "cognitive awareness." This, along with materials introductory to the basic Buddhist world view for the benefit of non-specialists, comprises the bulk of Chapter 1.

Although we by no means set out to replicate or validate the Yogācāra interpretation of the early concept of vijñāna, our study of these same teachings led us to similar conclusions: the "two aspects" of vijñāna which were originally undifferentiated in the early texts became increasingly, and untenably, problematic within the Abhidharma context, eliciting in its wake various conceptions of non-conscious mental processes, only one of which was the "*ālaya*" vijñāna. We will therefore briefly examine these other responses to the same set of problems – the continuity of karmic potential and the latent afflictions, and their gradual purification along the path of liberation – together with the other Abhidharma materials in Chapter 2, before turning our attention squarely on the ālaya-vijñāna itself, as it is most systematically presented and described in key Yogācāra texts, in Chapters 3–5.

We, of course, do not work out of a vacuum either. Whatever else they may think of Freud's and Jung's other theories, most scientifically educated people readily acknowledge that many if not most mental processes take place unconsciously. Indeed, a concept of a "cognitive unconscious" is now widely accepted within cognitive science and philosophy of mind.[1] Although our study focuses exclusively upon the "Buddhist unconscious," one of our aims is to introduce this fascinating concept into current Western discussions of unconscious mind. In order to address this wider audience, the first and second chapters in particular present many basic concepts which, while well known to Indian and Buddhist specialists, serve as the indispensable building blocks for the larger argument that follows.

These early materials are central to this larger argument for another reason as well. Since our main thesis is that the ālaya-vijñāna arose in response to the Abhidharmic developments of earlier Buddhist doctrines, we need to examine those earlier doctrines, first in order to appreciate the nature of the Abhidharmic innovations and the problems they generated, and second to see exactly how the concept of ālaya-vijñāna addressed these problems by skillfully integrating the Abhidharma innovations with the earlier conceptual framework. It is this synthesis of early and Abhidharmic treatments of mind that most distinguishes the ālaya-vijñāna complex, and is the main reason, we reiterate, why it is necessary to examine this ancient background and its contemporaneous context in order to fully appreciate the ālaya-vijñāna within the context of Indian Buddhist thought.

This is thus very much a synthetic work, tying together materials spanning some one thousand years of Indian Buddhist thought. Though most of these materials are familiar to specialists, they remain widely scattered in disparate publications in a host of languages around the globe. There remains, therefore, a serious lacuna that this book strives to fill. There is still no single work in any Western language that has brought together the multiple and variegated strands comprising the complex notion of the ālaya-vijñāna and woven them into an integrated, accessible,[2] and compelling narrative. And this notion is indeed multiple and variegated. Such a bewildering array of synonyms and attributes has congealed around this "conceptual monstrosity," as Conze (1973: 133) characteristically described it, that the ālaya-vijñāna remains an abstruse topic even for those relatively well versed in related areas of Buddhist thought. We have therefore taken a chronological approach, in which the various attributes of the ālaya-vijñāna, and the problems they address, are gradually introduced and accumulated over time, ultimately resulting in a complex and richly interwoven model of mind, to be sure, but one whose structuring components have each been examined in their own right. By the time the reader reaches the Yogācāra

1 Kihlstrom (1987); Lakoff and Johnson (1999: 9–15); Flanagan (1992: 173): "There is agreement that most mental processing is unconscious and occurs in parallel."

2 We have previously addressed many of these issues for a more specialized audience, expressed nearly exclusively in their Sanskritic and Abhidharmic terms, in Waldron (1994).

chapters themselves, in Part II, the outlines of this model will have already begun to fall into place, so that the ālaya-vijñāna may ironically seem the most parsimonious way of addressing the daunting array of experiential, exegetical, and doctrinal conundrums (for which see Appendix II) generated by the innovative developments of Abhidharma Buddhism.

ACKNOWLEDGMENTS

In any study of this duration, an author accumulates a debt of gratitude to mentors, colleagues, friends, and family, many more than can reasonably be named. A few, however, must be.

Although cast in an idiom he would scarcely have appreciated, this study's deepest themes reflect my father's predominate concerns: the possibilities for, and the conditions inhibiting, human happiness and freedom.

My Buddhist teachers will more readily recognize their influences, although they are hardly responsible for the errors of commission or omission that inevitably accompany it. Geshe Lhundrup Sopa first taught me Tibetan and provided a solid introduction to Gelukpa curriculum, which was reinforced by further study with Geshe Namgyal Wangchen in Sarnath. Both are inspiring examples of the continuing and compelling vitality of Buddhism in the modern world.

I have also enjoyed exemplary mentors from the world of Japanese Buddhist scholarship, whose methodological influences subtly pervade this work like *abhilāpa-vāsanā*. My graduate advisor, Professor Emeritus Minoru Kiyota of the University of Wisconsin, encouraged me to cultivate my own intellectual interests and facilitated the financial support to follow them through. Professors Ogawa Ichijo and Miyashita Seiki of Otani University in Kyoto supervised my thesis research on the ālaya-vijñāna, past incarnations of which form the basis of this book. Professor Miyashita in particular selflessly shared his extensive philological and philosophical expertise on Indian Buddhism during several years of reading Buddhist texts together. It was he who provided the rudder with which to navigate through the limitless ocean of Abhidharma and Yogācāra literature, and the awesome Japanese scholarship concerning it. I have also benefitted by numerous discussions with, in alphabetical order, Aramaki Noritoshi, Nagao Gadjin, Odani Nobuchiya, Yamabe Nobuyoshi, and Yasutomi Shin'ya.

I wish to thank the Japanese Ministry of Education for several years of funding, as well as Otani University itself, where, under the auspices of its Shin Buddhist Comprehensive Research Institute, I enjoyed three years of productive research. This first stay at Otani was the single greatest contribution to this study, and I am delighted to be applying its finishing touches once again near old friends in Kyoto.

Middlebury College has in the interim provided an intellectually stimulating atmosphere in which to continue this work and a supportive sabbatical program through which to complete it. I enjoyed stimulating discussions with my colleagues at Middlebury, particularly Rick Arthur, Jeff Dunham, Marc Garcelon, and, whilst warding off the inevitable corruption of our perishable *nāma-rūpas*, David Stahl. I especially wish to thank John Keenan, an old friend but a new mentor, who, like Chuang Tze's giant bird, P'eng, leaps over several seemingly separate realms in a single bound.

Appreciation on the part of countless students of Buddhism must also be expressed toward the editors of the Critical Studies in Buddhism, Charles Prebish and Damien Keown, for providing the series with its originating vision and the editorial labor to bring it to realization.

Special thanks go to my dear friend David Patt, who helped separate the wheat from the chaff of a very unwieldy manuscript at a critical stage in its development.

Finally, gratitude to my wife and children who have been forced to cultivate unreasonable amounts of *kṣānti-paramitā* during the long years of my absent presence.

I dedicate whatever merit this work may accrue for the benefit of all beings.

William S. Waldron
Kyoto, Winter 2002

THEMATIC INTRODUCTION

A Buddhist critique of the construction of self and world

The Buddha offered an understanding of the actions that perpetuate the repetitive behavioral patterns called "samsara" that differed from contemporaneous Indian yogic traditions in several key respects. In the Buddhist view,[1] what keeps beings trapped in these cyclic patterns is both the deep-seated but mistaken apprehension that we are (or have) an unchanging, independent, self-subsistent entity or "self" (*ātman*), as well as the misguided activities motivated by attachment to such a self. These activities are misguided, the Buddhists assert, because no permanent and independent individuality can actually be found in our worldly existence. Instead, sentient beings are thought to consist of aggregations of ever-evolving physiological and psychological processes which arise and persist only as long as the causes and conditions that sustain them persist. Chief amongst these sustaining conditions are, paradoxically, the very *ignorance* of these basic facts of life, and the futile *desires* and *activities* to deny or overcome them through attempting to grasp onto something permanent – making actions informed by ignorance and desire the "driving forces" of cyclic existence. This view of the delusions and activities that keep beings trapped in the vicious cycle of repetitive behavior patterns was already quite clear in the early discourses of the Buddha, to which we shall return shortly. Shorn of their metaphysical dimension, however, these themes are readily understandable in modern, humanist terms, which we will briefly entertain in the next few pages.

Buddhist thought thoroughly critiques our attempts to attain permanence, independence, and self-subsistence by identifying with transient, conditioned phenomena, whether material, psychological, or conceptual. We impute intrinsic meaning and value onto these phenomena, the Buddhists assert, and imagine that their possession somehow augments our essential worth or well-being. This entails that we bifurcate our world of experience into two discrete dimensions, the objective and subjective. That is, we experience the world in terms of "objective" things – which are inevitably mediated through linguistic, cultural, and social conventions – and we imagine that they possess intrinsic power to impart happiness, health, and well-being. These "things" possess, in other words, a *symbolic value*[2] above and beyond their mere physical existence. Enthralled by these enduring yet abstract objects, we create, as it were, a life-world of seemingly solid, yet unavoidably mediated "things." Man,[3] the symbol-making creature, constructs a world of his own in which to make his home.

But this is only half the picture. We also build up an image and an idea, and a deep-seated attachment to, an equally symbolic sense of "self" which can experience and enjoy these apparently independent objects and which seems to possess equally independent, intrinsic existence. We imaginatively create a locus of subjective experience, an enduring referent to the notions of self and "I" with which we can identify and hold as our own. We imagine that we actually *are* an enduring subject which exists independently of the external objects around it, which it can possess and enjoy. Our entire world of experience is experienced in reference to this self-wrought self. Man, the "self-making" creature, constructs the subject of his own existence which may dwell within his self-constructed home.

These parallel processes of the reification of object and subject constitute the main target of the Buddhist (and particularly the Yogācāra) critique of ordinary, worldly consciousness. On the one hand, we impute the actual existence of apparently external objects, transforming them from immediate experiences into abstract objects which putatively possess inherent power and worth, constituting them within our culturally mediated, symbolic universe. On the other hand, we create an equally abstracted sense of self-identity, based upon an accumulation of experiences, memories and feelings, which possesses apparent coherence and continuity. This sense of enduring identity is the subjective counterpart of the enduring objects one apprehends and objectifies. There must be an independent "someone" in order to possess or experience a separate "something."

Now, we must ask, how does all this come about? Why do we construct reality in this way, abstracting static, symbolic modes of subjective and objective experience from the on-going continuum of living processes, bifurcating them into the twin reifications of subject and object? What purposes does such creative activity serve for us as individuals, as societies, or as a species? And what drawbacks accompany these processes?

Confronted with the transiency of experience and the ever-present physical and psychological threats to our integrity and survival, organisms with higher nervous systems such as ourselves must be able to recognize and comprehend recurrent patterns underlying our variegated forms of experience, and to construct working models capable of anticipation, predication, and premeditation. In this sense, the emergence of a "self" from the stream of inchoate experience into a relatively stable locus of self-reference and self-awareness, with all its regular and regulated cognitive and affective processes, is one of the most remarkable achievements of biological evolution and constitutes perhaps the most fundamental human technology.

The Buddhist critique of these twins constructions of "self" and "world," however, rests largely upon their deleterious consequences. We typically fail to recognize, the Buddhists contend, that the twin reifications of "self" and "object" achieved through our linguistically and culturally mediated symbol systems are simply skillful means, highly practical tools for getting a handle on the whirlwind world within and without for the purpose of serving our own relative purposes. In our constant struggle to secure a stable, predictable, and prosperous life, we mistake these pragmatic tools and provisional purposes for actualities and ultimate ends: by imagining that we actually *are* such a self, we fail to fully appreciate the evolving and constructed nature of all experiential phenomena.

Hence, while our sense of self addresses one set of problems, that of coherence and continuity, it simultaneously raises another, that of our underlying anxieties bred of transience: just because it is a product of complex interactive relationships which are continuously evolving, our culturally mediated symbolic selves are also continuously slipping away, just beyond our grasp, like an optical illusion that disappears as soon as one looks straight at it. A nagging fear of our possible non-existence, a sense of the sheer fragility of this constructed "self," is always lurking around the corner, underlying all our thoughts and actions. So we grasp all the more onto our pains, our attachments, our identities, all the while vaguely sensing that the only thing standing between us and non-existence is indeed this self-wrought self. If this were lost – or so we fear – so would be who and what we think we are. So man responds, in Ernest Becker's terms, by

> building defenses; and these defenses allow him to feel a basic sense of self-worth, of meaningfulness, of power. They allow him to feel that he *controls* his life and his death, that he really does live and act as a willful and free individual, that he has a unique and self-fashioned identity, that he *is somebody*.
>
> (Becker, 1973: 55)

But this requires that we constantly reconstruct this sense of self, rehearsing our past experiences through memory and emotion and anticipating our future experiences through desire and imagination. We must continuously endow our "selves" with a history and a future, without which, as brain-damaged patients so poignantly illustrate, we would hardly be human. Ironically, it is our very attempt to hold onto this self-wrought self, to maintain its existential integrity, that insures our unending anxieties and insecurities, and instigates our activities to perpetuate its constructed patterns. Man, the "history-making" creature, transforms the raw materials of immediate experience and constructs the solidifying structures of worldly existence.

Our constructed character, our self-identity is, in other words, a vital lie, "a *necessary* and basic dishonesty about oneself and one's whole situation" (ibid.: 55), Becker continues, which is constructed "for the precise purpose of putting it between [ourselves] and the facts of life" (ibid.: 59). This sense of an underlying subject of experience, however constructed, is so basic and so habitual as to occur mostly automatically, outside of our conscious awareness. This unconscious self-clinging underlies all conscious, intentional activities, insuring that our energies are constantly directed toward the continuation of the habitual thought patterns – the twin reifications of self and world – that produce and perpetuate their own frame of reference. In this respect, virtually all cultures, belief systems, and especially characters and habits, are

> like a comfortable web [that] keeps a person buoyed up and ignorant of himself, of the fact that he does not rest on his own center. All of us are driven to be supported in a self-forgetful way, ignorant of what energies we really draw on, of the kind of lie we have fashioned in order to live securely and serenely.
>
> (Becker, 1973: 55)

Cultures as well as characters can thus be seen as symbolic wish-fulfillments: if we cannot get what we really want – actual individual, autonomous existence – then we substitute symbols for realities and achieve our aims by surrogates means. Rather than facing the facts of impermanence and insecurity and accepting the transient and contingent nature of our lives, we attempt to avoid awareness of them by constructing enduring symbols of wealth and meaning, of life and pleasure, in reference to which our putative permanent selves exist as equally undying, and hence inevitably lifeless, subjects. If things themselves have no sustainable existence, then at least their consensually mediated symbols do. If our life itself has no apparent permanency, then at least the abstract symbol of "self" that stands for it does. We live, that is, as in a symbolic world constructed by our own imaginative powers. We are always actively, albeit unconsciously, ignoring the radically interdependent nature of our existence and setting up in its place the "false idol" of a self, the undying and therefore unliving symbol that represents our unrequited desires for permanent, personal autonomous existence.

This is, of course, no deliberate course of action. It is merely the extension of those deeply embedded cognitive and affective capacities that have otherwise proved so conducive to human survival. This is the tragic vision common to so many cultural and religious traditions. It is our very success that plagues us, for, as Becker avers, these are *necessary* and *vital* lies, providing necessary skills and serving vital, albeit worldly, interests.[4] But lies they are, clothing the world in fabricated illusions, interpreting all experience in reference to our own constructed self-view. We are as drunk with our own god-like powers of self- and world-creation, inebriated by a hubris which dares to call itself *homo sapiens*, the wise one. We have, in this way, bound the bonds of our own bounded, worldly existence.

* * *

These themes, so clearly and incisively expressed in various streams of modern thought, are strikingly similar to the ideas discussed in these pages, and we shall return to them again and again in their Buddhist guise. Indeed, they suggest an **initial working glossary** of the core concepts used throughout this text:

- *kliṣṭa-manas*, "afflictive mentation," unconscious self-grasping which occurs in every moment of worldly existence, which is itself informed by:
- *kleśa*, the afflictive cognitive and emotional attitudes that color most of our activities, in particular:
- the conceit "I am" (*asmimāna*);
- the view of self-existence (*satkāyadṛṣṭi*);
- attachment to self (*ātmasneha*);
- ignorance (*avidyā*). Activities instigated by these give rise to:
- *saṃskāra*, karmic formations, the constructed physiological and psychological structures which have been built up by past activities and reinforce their own reoccurrence, and which, in some contexts, also refers to those very activities themselves. These are often accompanied by:
- *upādāna*, appropriation or grasping, the process of taking the body, thoughts, or feelings as one's own, as well as the "objects" so taken. And these underlie or support the arising of:
- *vijñāna*, consciousness or cognitive awareness, which gives rise to our common world of reified "subjects" and "objects" – which in turn instigate the afflictions leading to further activities that reinforce the whole process, creating the vicious circle called "samsara."

In contrast with modern humanistic approaches, however, Indian religious systems consider that the processes of creating our "selves" and our "world" – the bifurcation of experience into subject and object – entail actual cosmogonic (cosmos creating) or ontological consequences. As Lama Govinda explains, in the Buddhist world-view

> it is on account of our clinging to these forms of life that again and again we produce them.... It is our will, our ardent desire which creates the world in which we live, and the organism which corresponds to it.
>
> (Govinda, 1969: 54)

This book is an extended examination of these processes and the consequences they set in motion, centering on the Yogācāra concept of the *ālaya-vijñāna*, the subliminal "base, store, or home" consciousness,[5] which is always accompanied by an unconscious apprehension of self. The ālaya-vijñāna primarily represents this persisting locus of habituated yet unconscious reifications of self and world and hence constitutes the main obstacle to liberation from the bonds of cyclic existence. Like the other yogic traditions developed in classical Gupta-era India, as Eliade described them, the Yogācāra thinkers discovered that "the great obstacles to the ascetic and contemplative life arose from the activity of the unconscious, from the *saṃskāras* and the *vāsanās* – 'impregnations,' 'residues,' 'latencies' – that constitute what depth psychology calls the contents and structures of the unconscious" (Eliade, 1973: p. xvii). Although we will not discuss at any length either the practices toward or the results of liberation from these obstacles, our examination of the ālaya-vijñāna will at least clarify exactly what, in the Yogācāra view, one is to be liberated from: the dynamic cognitive and behavioral patterns perpetuating the vicious cycle of repetitive behavioral patterns called samsara.

In order to understand the historical developments through which the ālaya-vijñāna came to represent these habitual behavioral patterns, however, we must first examine these ideas as expressed in the early discourses of the Buddha. We will find here, in incipient form, nearly all of the basic elements that would later comprise the Yogācāra model of unconscious mind, the ālaya-vijñāna. This topic is addressed in our first chapter.

Part I

THE BACKGROUND AND CONTEXT OF THE ĀLAYA-VIJÑĀNA

1

THE EARLY BUDDHIST BACKGROUND

The three marks of existence

Dissatisfaction, dis-ease, and suffering, in Pāli *dukkha* (Sanskrit: *duḥkha*),[1] that ubiquitous quality of our conditioned existence,[2] is the leitmotif of all Buddhist teaching, its cessation its overriding purpose.[3] Understanding the conditions that bring about this suffering, and undertaking the activities that lead to its cessation, constitute the contents and aims of the *buddha-dharma*, the teachings and practices passed down in the name of the Buddha.[4] The fundamental causes of this dissatisfaction and suffering are ignorance (P. *avijjā*; S. *avidyā*), a basic misunderstanding of how things actually are; craving or thirst (P. *taṇhā*; S. *tṛṣṇa*) for pleasure and for continued existence; and the unhealthy actions (*akusala-kamma*) these first two bring about. This essay on the development of a Buddhist concept of unconscious mental processes afflicted with such delusions and desires is nearly exclusively concerned with the dynamic interplay between these basic causes, which constitute the contents of the second Noble Truth, the Arising of Suffering.

Ignorance is traditionally defined as regarding what is impermanent as permanent, what is suffering as pleasure, and what is non-self as self, since, the Buddhists insist, what is impermanent, filled with disease, and devoid of intrinsic self-identity, cannot afford any independent and lasting satisfaction.[5] Ignoring these basic realities, we nevertheless attempt to escape from such transience and such suffering, and to attain permanent and pleasurable states by identifying ourselves with and becoming attached to what are ultimately impermanent and unpleasant phenomena. Clinging to their apparent solidity and stability, we bind ourselves to such phenomena, and thereby increase and perpetuate our own deluded existence. As the Buddha[6] declared:

> Whoever . . . saw anything in the world that seems lovely and pleasant as permanent, saw it as happy, saw it as good, saw it as health, saw it as safety, they made craving to grow. They in making craving to grow made the basis [of existence (*upadhi*)] to grow; in making the basis grow, they make suffering grow; in making suffering to grow, they were not

> liberated from birth, from old age, from sufferings, from sorrows, from despairs – yea, I declare, they were not liberated from ill.
>
> (S II 109. PTS)

Above all, we reify or substantialize the continuity of our lives, imagining that there is, or we are, a permanent, substantive self, an unchanging locus of experience which can enjoy permanent, pleasurable states. We mistakenly think, as the Buddha put it:

> That which is this self for me that speaks, that experiences and knows, that experiences, now here, now there, the fruition of deeds lovely or depraved, it is this self for me that is permanent, stable, eternal, not subject to change, that will stand firm for ever and ever.
>
> (M I 8 PTS)[7]

In the Buddhist view, however, no such permanent, unchanging self can be found. Instead, our ever-changing mental and physical processes are likened to a stream that arises, flows, and passes away depending upon nothing but the various conditions that create and sustain it. The processes which constitute human existence are categorized into five groups, which the Buddha called the "aggregates of grasping" (*upādāna-khandha*) since we tend to identify with and grasp onto them as our "self." These are the aggregates of form, feeling, apperception, karmic formations or volitions, and cognitive awareness or consciousness (*rūpa*, *vedanā*, *saññā*, *sankhāra*, *viññāṇa*). As the term "aggregate" indicates, however, these are not independent elements or entities in and of themselves but rather distinct classes of processes. None of them should be conceived of in relation to a permanent self (S III 46), nor should such a self be conceived of apart from these processes, for all of them are characterized by the so-called three marks of existence: impermanence, dissatisfaction, and non-self.[8]

Nevertheless, we tenaciously cling to such notions of a self, and to the objects that seem to support it, imagining they somehow secure lasting satisfaction. Ironically, it is just this preoccupation with a self, with identifying something as "I" or "mine," that, in the Buddhist view, brings about suffering, not ease, bondage, not liberation. As the Buddha observed,

> He regards feeling as self … apperception as self … volitional formations as self … consciousness as self, or self as possessing consciousness, or consciousness as in self, or self as in consciousness. That consciousness of his changes and alters. With the change and alteration of consciousness, his consciousness becomes preoccupied with the change of consciousness. Agitation and a constellation of mental states born of preoccupation with the change of consciousness remain obsessing his mind. Because his mind is obsessed, he is frightened, distressed, and anxious, and through clinging becomes agitated.
>
> (S III 16 f.)

This is, of course, a vicious circle: in craving for what is "happy, good, healthy and safe," in imagining a self that enjoys them, we inadvertently increase the conditions that lead to suffering, anxiety, and distress. For as long as there is craving for and attachment to self, the Buddha declared, so will there be further distress, in response to which there will be further actions that lead to further distress and so on. It is, in short, our misguided desires for some truly lasting, satisfactory existence within this conditioned world, along with the actions taken to secure it, that keeps us continuously bound to the repetitive cognitive and behavioral patterns called "samsara." The way out of the vicious cycle, the Buddhists suggest, comes through understanding their underlying causes – the interactive dynamics between ignorance and grasping, the actions they instigate, and the results these lead to – and gradually reversing their deleterious results. And this is the fundamental aim of the formula of dependent arising.

The formula of dependent arising

The relationship between action and mind, and mind and action, has intrigued philosophers and mystics for millennia. What is the relationship between our actions and our thoughts, our awareness and our behavior? Do thoughts always direct behavior, or is it, perhaps, the other way around? Does one have priority over the other? Is one fundamental while the other merely epiphenomenal? Early Buddhist traditions considered either of these alternatives objectionable and depicted instead a reciprocal relationship between mind and actions, a relationship in which our past actions affect our present states of mind, our present states of mind affect our present actions, and these present actions in turn affect future states of mind. This reciprocal relationship, perhaps the earliest conceptualization of what we now call feedback, is depicted in the well-known formula of dependent arising (P. *paṭicca-samuppāda*; S. *pratītya-samutpāda*), arguably the most distinctive aspect of early Buddhist thought and one whose ramifications will continue to unfold throughout the history of Buddhist thought.

In this chapter we will examine this formula and its implications at some length, not only because the notion of dependent arising expresses the core of Buddhist thought – that all phenomena arise in dependence upon other phenomena – but also because the multifarious formulations of dependent arising (in its varying lengths and alternate members) touch upon all the key concepts and problems later associated with the ālaya-vijñāna model of mind. We will therefore use this formula of dependent arising to provide the basic framework for our extended examination of the meanings and functions of *viññāṇa* (S. *vijñāna*) – as both "consciousness" and "cognitive awareness" – as well as its complex and interactive relationship with action, that is, karma, and with the cognitive and emotional afflictions (*kilesa*; S. *kleśa*) that instigate these actions.

To adumbrate our argument, *viññāṇa* (S. *vijñāna*) as described in the various formulas of dependent arising exhibits two discrete aspects or functions: as "consciousness" and as "cognitive awareness." The first refers to viññāṇa as an underlying sentience which flows in an unbroken stream of mind throughout multiple lifetimes, while the second refers to viññāṇa in terms of six modalities of cognitive awareness which momentarily arise in conjunction with discrete cognitive objects. Although the early texts evince no overt distinction, let alone discordance, between these two "aspects" of viññāṇa, such a distinction can be – and in later commentaries nearly always was – discerned through careful textual and conceptual analysis. This distinction is crucial to our reconstruction of the development of the ālaya-vijñāna for two reasons. First, subsequent Abhidharma analyses of mind focused primarily upon manifest cognitive awareness, making the aspect of viññāṇa as "consciousness" conceptually problematic – a situation to which the ālaya-vijñāna was, in large part, a response. Second, the two "aspects" of viññāṇa that are discernable in these early texts also clearly foreshadow the bifurcation of viññāṇa (*vijñāna*) in the Yogācāra school into a subsisting, subliminal, and accumulating consciousness, represented by the ālaya-vijñāna, and the momentary, supraliminal forms of awareness, represented by "manifest cognitive awareness" (S. *pravṛtti-vijñāna*). We thus find the antecedents of these later notions in the earlier Buddhist texts.

These two "dimensions" of viññāṇa are also closely related to a similar distinction among the cognitive and emotional afflictions (P. *kilesa*; S. *kleśa*), between their persisting, latent forms as underlying tendencies (P. *anusaya*; S. *anuśaya*) and their momentary, active forms as "manifest outbursts" (P. *pariyuṭṭhāna*; S. *paryavasthāna*) – a distinction that became problematic in Abhidharma discourse for much the same reasons vijñāna did. This eventually led the Yogācāra school to conceptualize a distinct strata of unconscious self-grasping called "afflictive mentation" (S. *kliṣṭa-manas*), one that roughly parallels the ālaya-vijñāna itself. We will thus also briefly examine the role that these self-centered afflictions played within the early Buddhist doctrines. Together, they articulate a vision of circular causality between consciousness, the cognitive and emotional afflictions, the activities these instigate, and the results that they collectively accrue, a vision expressed in the series of dependent arising.

* * *

The theory of dependent arising (*paṭicca-samuppāda*) seeks to understand the dynamic relationship between ignorance, the afflictions, and their ensuing actions, by analyzing the patterns through which they arise, persist, and pass away in dependence upon their supporting conditions. That is, the processes that perpetuate our conditioned existence are neither completely random nor completely determined; rather, they follow regular and discernable *patterns* of arising. It is these patterns that are expressed in the formula of dependent origination, an understanding of which was considered indispensable for reversing their deleterious consequences. The simplest expression of this arising in dependence on conditions is formulated as follows:

> When this exists, that comes to be; with the arising of this, that arises. When this does not exist, that does not come to be; with the cessation of this, that ceases.
>
> (M II 32)[9]

As we can see, this is formulated in two directions: the conditions that lead from the existence of one factor to the arising of the next (*anuloma*), and, in reverse order, the conditions that lead to their cessation (*paṭiloma*). This theory of causality is neither solely simultaneous nor exclusively sequential, it is a theory of *concomitant conditionality*: when X is, Y comes to be; when X arises, Y arises, and so on. In a text called *Nidāna-vagga* or the *Sayings on Causes*, the Buddha presents the traditional twelve-member series of dependent arising in this same fashion, first describing the conditions leading to the arising of this world of suffering, and then, in reverse order, those leading to its cessation:

> And what, monks, is dependent origination? With ignorance as condition, karmic formations [come to be]; with karmic formations as condition, consciousness; with consciousness as condition, name-and-form; with name-and-form as condition, the six sense-spheres; with the six sense-spheres as condition, contact; with contact as condition, feeling; with feeling as condition, craving; with craving as condition, grasping; with grasping as condition, becoming; with becoming as condition, birth; with birth as condition, aging-and-death, sorrow, lamentation, pain, displeasure and despair come to be. Such is the origin of this whole mass of suffering. This, monks, is called dependent origination.
>
> But from the remainderless fading away and cessation of ignorance comes cessation of karmic formations; with the cessation of karmic formations, cessation of consciousness; with the cessation of consciousness, cessation of name-and-form; with the cessation of name-and-form, cessation of the six sense-spheres; with the cessation of the six sense-spheres, cessation of contact; with the cessation of contact, cessation of feeling; with the cessation of feeling, cessation of craving; with the cessation of craving, cessation of grasping; with the cessation of grasping, cessation of becoming; with the cessation of becoming, cessation of birth; with the cessation of birth, aging-and-death, sorrow, lamentation, pain, displeasure, and despair cease. Such is the cessation of this whole mass of suffering.
>
> (S II 1)[10]

Although this twelve-member series was eventually to became the standard version, variations of it are found throughout the early Buddhist texts, many of which we shall examine below. The *Nidāna-saṃyutta* itself, however, briefly describes each of the twelve members or limbs (*aṅga*) of the series:

Ignorance (*avijjā*) is defined in terms of the four Noble Truths, as "ignorance concerning suffering, the origin of suffering, the cessation of suffering, and the path leading to the cessation of suffering" (S II 4). That is to say, one of the conditions for the arising of this world of sorrow and suffering is ignorance regarding the dissatisfactory nature of worldly existence itself, of the origins of these dissatisfactions, of their cessation, and of the path leading toward their cessation.

Ignorance conditions the arising of **karmic formations** (*sankhārā*), formative structures of body, speech, and mind. This complex concept denotes both *formations* that have been formed from past actions as well as the *formative* actions that give rise to future formations, exhibiting a "process–product" bivalence we shall further examine below.[11] Sankhārā is one of the core concepts of Indian Buddhist thought and plays a particularly important role within the ālaya-vijñāna complex of mind.

These karmic formations condition the arising of **consciousness** or **cognitive awareness** (*viññāṇa*). Although *viññāṇa* is glossed in this text as the six modes of sensory and mental cognitive awareness, in this place in the series it is usually considered[12] a rebirth consciousness which descends into, "takes up," and thereafter animates the newly forming fetus, as described in this dialogue with the Buddha:

> 'I have said that consciousness conditions name-and-form. … Were, Ananda, consciousness not to descend into the mother's womb, would name-and-form coagulate there?'
>
> 'No, Lord.'
>
> 'Were consciousness, having descended into the mother's womb, to depart, would name-and-form come to birth in this life?'
>
> 'No, Lord.'
>
> (D II 62f.; PTS)

The next limb, **name-and-form** (*nāma-rūpa*), usually refers to the psychological and physiological aspects of human experience that begin developing during the intra-uterine stage and continue throughout a single lifetime. These represent the basic processes of the human mind and body and correspond closely to the five "aggregates of grasping" (*upādāna-khandha*)[13] mentioned above.

In traditional interpretations stemming from the commentarial period, the first two factors in the series, ignorance and the karmic formations, denote karmic conditions that have carried over from a past life, while the consciousness (*viññāṇa*) which enters the womb and conditions the development of name-and-form marks the beginning of a new life. This form of consciousness will later be considered the ālaya-vijñāna by the Yogācāra school. These first three factors also represent the initial steps in the feedback relationship between afflictive factors (ignorance), the actions they influence (karmic formations), and the results they give rise to (the arising of consciousness) – a relationship we will examine at considerable length below. Succeeding steps in the series depict how consciousness, the results of previous actions, in turn conditions the arising of the further afflictions and further karmic actions (see Appendix I).

The next four factors in the series – the six sense-spheres, contact, feeling, and craving – all depend upon the presence of a living psycho-physical organism (name-and-form). Collectively, these summarize the typical perceptual process. That is, perception in the early Pāli texts is explained in relation to the **six sense-spheres** or sense-domains, those of the five senses plus mind. When something impinges upon any of these, **contact** or sensation (*phassa*) arises. This sensation is experienced as a pleasant, unpleasant, or neutral **feeling** (*vedanā*), which (if pleasant) in turn conditions the arising of **craving** or "thirst" (*taṇhā*) for that "object."[14] These factors not only epitomize the basic cognitive process, but they also lead to the important afflictive factors that, typically, instigate further karma-creating activities. Craving, as we saw above (S II 109), is one of the dynamic factors driving the cycle of death and rebirth.

Thus, conditioned by craving, **grasping** or **appropriation** (*upādāna*) arises. Although the text presents the traditional enumeration of grasping as "grasping to sensual pleasure, grasping to views, grasping to rules and observances, and grasping to a theory of 'self'" (*kāmūpādāna, diṭṭhūpādāna, sīlabbatūpādāna, attavādūpādāna*), *upādāna* has much wider connotations than mere "grasping" might suggest. It also refers to a "substratum by means of which an active process is kept alive or going" (PED 149), in this case, the process of an endless succession of rebirths. *Upādāna* thus forms a natural link with the processes of newly "becoming" (*bhava*), the next member of the series. Both of these senses of upādāna will also have important roles to play in the ālaya-vijñāna model of mind.

Becoming (*bhava*), often translated as "being" or "existence," is defined (A I 223) as "repeated rebirth in the future" (*āyatim punabbhava-abhinibbatti*) into any of the three realms of existence.[15] Becoming marks the transition to another lifetime, the third and last in the commentarial interpretation of the series into a three lifetime sequence (Appendix I). Becoming thus conditions a new **birth** (*jāti*), which our Sutta explains as:

> The birth of the various beings in the various orders of beings, their being born, descent [into the womb], production, the manifestation of the aggregates, the obtaining of the sense spheres. This is called birth.
> (S II 3)

The final member of the series, **aging-and-death**, etc., is straightforward.

There is considerable uncertainty regarding the original form and scope of this formula. It occurs in so many different formulations in the early texts that it is not at all clear what form, if any, it may originally have had.[16] What all the variations do illustrate, however, is that the arising of our phenomenal world, especially our world of dissatisfactory experience, is brought about not by any single cause alone, but by the concomitance of a number of conditioning factors arising in discernibly repeated patterns.

This picture of causality is not only concomitant, however, it is also circular. Not only does the formula as a whole recursively reinforce itself, leading to the nearly endless rounds of rebirth called samsara, but core components within the formula do so as well. As we shall see, the karmic formations (*sankhārā*) and consciousness (*viññāṇa*) can be understood to occur *twice* in this series, at first explicitly between the second and third members, and then again, implicitly and in reverse order, when the processes involved in cognition (the sense-spheres, sensation, etc., that epitomize the arising of cognitive awareness) give rise first to feeling and then to the karmically productive processes of craving, appropriation, and becoming. In other words, karmic formations first condition consciousness, which is then centrally involved in the karmic activities that give rise to yet further karmic formations, and so on. We will examine this relationship, which clearly depends upon the multivalence of the key terms involved, more closely below.

Whatever the historical origins of the formula, most Indian Buddhist schools came to use the twelve-member series (and its three lifetime interpretation) as an important teaching tool, illustrations of which, in the form of the "wheel of life," are still found in temples throughout the Buddhist world. As a heuristic device for outlining the whole of Buddhist teaching, the twelve factors succinctly summarize a broad range of doctrines whose deeper implications in any case need to be fleshed out in more specific contexts. In the following sections we will therefore analyze key components of this formula, examining how consciousness continues from one life to the next propelled by self-reinforcing cycles of karmic action and reaction. What we shall see is a complex feedback relationship between our misunderstanding of who we are, the actions this misunderstanding instigates, and the psychological and "psycho-ontological" results that these lead to. But first, we must clarify what karma refers to, and address the perennial question, if there is no real "self," who or what might be reborn?

Causation and continuity without a self

"Saṃsāra" literally means a turning, a going around. What keeps the cycle turning are the energetic processes of karma,[17] that is, intentional actions and their consequences. Put another way, what the series of dependent arising describes is the way karmic actions arise, the results they accrue, and how these in turn lead to yet further actions – in short, the vicious circle called samsara.

* * *

Although a richly textured term central to all Indian religious systems, karma is much less straightforward that it first appears. As with many other terms inherited from his Indian milieu, the Buddha reinterpreted the Sanskrit term *karman*, meaning "religious act or rite," and gave it a new, more psychological, sense:

> Monks, I say karma is intention; having intended, one does karma through body, speech, and mind.
>
> (A III 415)[18]

More specifically, karma refers to intentional actions (*sañcetanika-kamma*) which eventually bring about consequences, a stipulation that will affect all the debates that follow:

> Where there are [deeds of] the body, [speech, and mind,] Ananda, personal happiness and suffering arise as a consequence of the intention of the [deeds of] the body, [speech, and mind].
>
> (S II 39–40. PTS)

Intention (*cetanā*) then is necessary for an action to accrue results, for it to be a *karmic* action. So, for example, inadvertently crushing insects underfoot while walking down the street or unknowingly killing hair mites while scratching one's head does not accrue the karma of killing, since there is no intention to kill them. Swatting mosquitos or executing criminals does.

The meaning and use of the term karma, however, entails an unavoidable ambiguity, even in these early Buddhist texts. Karma refers to a relational complex, to "the deed with reference to both its cause and its effect" (PED 191).[19] Thus, although karma often refers specifically to an action as *cause* (in later terminology, *karma-hetu*), in other contexts it refers to the *result* of an action (i.e. *karma-phala*, "the fruit of karma," or *karma-vipāka*, "the matured result of karma"). Such distinctions, however, are not always explicitly made, sometimes causing considerable ambiguity. Leading to even more ambiguity, in other contexts karma may also refer to a *potential for karmic results*, that is, to the interim period between having performed a karmic deed (as cause) and prior to its coming to fruition (as result). In this sense, karma is said to be built up and accumulated: one "accumulates karma" or amasses "a stock of good karma." This important sense of karma eventually became as problematic as it remained indispensable.

Overcoming the influences of this accumulation of karmic potential is one of the central concerns of Buddhist practice, since cyclic existence is perpetuated by and largely defined in terms of such actions, their results, and the ever-present potential for further results. Thus the Buddha says:

> I declare, monks, that actions willed, performed and accumulated will not become extinct as long as their results have not been experienced, be it in this life, in the next life or in subsequent lives. And as long as these results of actions willed, performed and accumulated have not been experienced, there will be no making an end to suffering.
>
> (A V 292. Nyanaponika, 1999: 265)

This is no strict determinism, however, for that would lead to the fatalistic attitude so often projected onto Indian religion, but here rejected by the Buddha:

> those who have recourse to past action as the decisive factor (*sārato paccāgacchataṃ*) will lack the impulse and effort for doing this and not doing that. Since they have no real valid ground for asserting that this or that ought to be done or ought not to be done ... [they] live without mindfulness and self-control.
>
> (A I 174, III 61. Nyanaponika, 1999: 62)

A deterministic view of karma, moreover, would preclude the very possibility of liberation from karmic conditioning, against which the Buddha also cautioned:

> If one says that whatever way a person performs a kammic action, in that very same way he will experience the result – in that case there will be no (possibility for) the holy life, and no opportunity would appear for making a complete end to suffering. But if one says that a person who performs a kammic action (with a result) that is variably experienceable, will reap its result accordingly – in that case there will be (a possibility for) the holy life, and an opportunity would appear for making a complete end to suffering.
>
> (A III 110. Nyanaponika, 1999: 315, n. 70)[20]

Thus, in the early texts the Buddha taught that karmic activities *conduce* to, but do not wholly determine, results that are consonant with the motivations instigating them.

* * *

Nevertheless, one key question still remains: If there is no continuing self, who is it that experiences these karmic effects? This question is unavoidable and, as we shall see from the intra-Buddhist controversies concerning it, its answer was not as obvious as it seems.

As with many other issues, the Buddha steered a middle path here between two extremes. Portraying an individual as a continuous stream of psychophysical processes which arise and cease depending upon their causes and conditions, the Buddha declared that it is neither the *exact same* person nor a *completely different* one who experiences the results of karma. Just as one cannot step into exactly the same river twice, since the flowing water is always changing from one moment to the next, so too are we never exactly the same person, because the conditions and processes which constitute our lives are also always changing from moment to moment. On the other hand, neither are we completely different, because, like the stream whose currents fall into consistent patterns depending upon the consistency of their supporting conditions, so too the continuity of individual "mind-streams" depends upon the continuity of their causes and conditions. Thus, even if we are never *exactly* the same person we were a moment ago (or last week, or last year, or last lifetime), neither are we *wholly* different; rather, what we are is the continuously evolving result of a multitude of past actions and events, whose "heirs" we are.[21] Thus, the Buddha declared:

> This body does not belong to you, nor to anyone else. It should be regarded as [the results of] former action that has been constructed and intended, and is now to be experienced.
>
> (S II 64)[22]

Thus, instead of an autonomous subject as an unchanging locus of experience independent of this changing, conditioned world – the contemporaneous view of self (*ātman*) in ancient India – the Buddha taught that we can best understand the continuity of sentient existence in terms of the cause-and-effect relationships expressed in the concept of karma and exemplified in the recurrent patterns of dependent arising. In other words: ignorance conditions the karmic formations, the karmic formations condition consciousness, and so forth. That is to say, the workings of karma and its consequences as depicted in the series of dependent arising *is* the Buddhist theory of continuity, the continuity of the dependent relations between the karmic formations, the arising of cognitive awareness, and so on.[23]

Though there was no serious departure from this basic perspective in mainstream Indian Buddhist thought, there were innumerable disputes over its details. Indeed, one of the rationales of the ālaya-vijñāna was that – given this particular notion of selflessness – only it could account for the continuity of karmic influences. This was accomplished primarily by reformulating, within an Abhidharma framework, the relationships already expressed in the early texts between consciousness and karma (in all their senses). Since these karmic influences were thought to persist from one lifetime to the next through an unbroken stream of mind, which was closely connected with consciousness (*viññāṇa*), we must carefully examine this key relationship. For it was the multiplicity of roles and the multivalency of the concept of *viññāṇa*, we argue, that laid the groundwork for the Yogācārin idea of the ālaya-vijñāna.

Viññāṇa in the formula of dependent arising

In this key section we will analyze the reciprocal and karmically generative relationship between the karmic formations (*sankhārā*) and consciousness (*viññāṇa*) within the series of dependent arising. That is to say, the formula depicts a vicious cycle between our past actions, the forms of consciousness these actions result in, and the afflictive actions these elicit – which lead to yet further karmic formations and forms of consciousness, and so on. We must keep this larger picture in mind as we immerse ourselves in the complex but fascinating details of the relationship between consciousness and the karmic formations.

Perhaps the entire notion of the ālaya-vijñāna arose out of the ambiguities surrounding the early concept of viññāṇa, for it exhibits two distinct ranges of meaning. The Sanskrit term *vijñāna*, cognate with the Pāli *viññāṇa*, is composed of the prefix *vi-*, denoting "separation" or "division" (related to the Latin *dis-*), plus the verbal root *jña*, "to know" (cognate with the Greek *gnosis*, the Latin (*co*)*gnitio*, and the English *know*). *Vi-* together with *jñāna* thus means "the act of distinguishing, discerning, knowledge" (PED 287, 611; SED 961). Although "discernment" may be a more literal translation, "cognitive awareness" comes closer to denoting its sense as an awareness of a specific object within a specific sense-field, while "consciousness" highlights the aspect of viññāṇa as a subsisting sentience which persists from one lifetime to the next.

Two distinct senses can thus be discerned in the way viññāṇa occurs in the early texts and in the formulations of dependent arising, aspects which Pāli scholar O. H. de A. Wijesekera calls "saṃsāric viññāṇa" and "cognitive-consciousness" (1964: 254 f.).[24] This first, "samsaric viññāṇa," is consciousness per se, the basic sentience necessary for all animate life, which in Buddhist thought is always dependent upon supporting conditions and perpetuated by karmic activities. In this sense, viññāṇa descends into the incipient fetus at the time of rebirth, inhabits the body throughout life, and departs at the time of death, initiating the transition to another life. This "aspect" of viññāṇa is nearly always mentioned *without reference to cognitive objects*. In contrast, "cognitive viññāṇa" refers to the forms of conscious cognitive awareness that occur in nearly every moment of life, and which in human beings arise in six modalities, the five senses and mind. *It is nearly always defined in terms of its specific objects*, one of its requisite conditions.[25] The differences between these two are succinctly expressed in two typical formulations for the arising of viññāṇa:

> Depending on karmic formations (*sankhārā*) viññāṇa arises. (S II 2)
> Depending on eye and forms visual viññāṇa arises. (S II 73)

On further analysis, however, we can discern a deeper and unexpected relationship between these two "aspects" of viññāṇa: they virtually condition each other. On the one hand, "samsaric" viññāṇa constitutes one of the preconditions for any "cognitive" viññāṇa to occur in the first place, since sentience is necessarily concomitant with all animate life, that is, only living beings have cognitive awareness. On the other hand, viññāṇa as cognitive awareness is at the center of the various processes within which karmic activities arise. That is, cognitive processes typically lead, via afflictive intentions, to the karmic activities that ultimately perpetuate the samsaric "aspect" of viññāṇa, which, accordingly, continues in an unbroken stream throughout one's nearly infinite lifetimes. As we shall see, the complex relationship between these two "aspects" of viññāṇa – in conjunction with the karmic activities informed by craving, etc. – forms the center of a self-perpetuating feedback cycle that is largely explicable in terms of the intradynamics of mind itself. In the ālaya-vijñāna model in later centuries, these two aspects of viññāṇa will be explicitly distinguished and their relationship explicitly described in terms of their mutual and simultaneous conditionality (*anyonya-sahabhāva-pratyayatā*) – a relationship that, we believe, is best understood as a systematization of the complex interactions between the two "aspects" of viññāṇa first adumbrated in these early texts. Although these "two aspects" of viññāṇa remained largely undifferentiated in the early teachings, analyses of the distinct semantic and functional contexts within which they occur led most exegetes, both traditional and modern, to precisely these same conclusions.

In order to demonstrate this, we need to analyze viññāṇa's twin roles – as consciousness and as cognitive awareness – in the context of the formula of dependent arising, focusing in particular on the complex relationship between these forms of viññāṇa and the karmic formations, the sankhārās. In the process, we will discern three distinct but interrelated areas in which viññāṇa plays crucial roles: (1) psychological – the ordinary processes of perception, conception, intention, etc.; (2) "psycho-ontological" – the causal relationship between these psychological processes (and the karmic activities they instigate) and the long-term destiny of an individual life-stream within cyclic existence; and (3) soteriological – the cessation of viññāṇa together with the karmic energies that perpetuate such existence. We shall briefly discuss the psycho-ontological and soteriological dimensions of viññāṇa as "consciousness" before proceeding to examine its more overtly psychological aspects.

Viññāṇa as consciousness

In the early texts, viññāṇa as consciousness or sheer sentience is virtually coterminous with one's samsaric existence as a whole. It occurs uninterruptedly throughout all of one's worldly lifetimes. It "descends" into the mother's womb at the beginning of each life and "departs" at its end. And it only comes to a complete cessation with the end of samsaric existence itself, that is, with nirvana. These characteristics will all later be attributed to the ālaya-vijñāna as well.

Viññāṇa is closely associated with the continuity and perpetuation of cyclic existence in a variety of ways. First, as one of the four sustenances – along with edible food, sensation, and mental intention – consciousness "sustains" each single life as well as one's stream of lives.[26] Driven by craving, the sustenance of viññāṇa becomes one of the preconditions for rebirth itself: "if there is delight, if there is craving for the ... viññāṇa sustenance" the Buddha declared, then

> consciousness becomes established (*patiṭṭhita*) there and comes to growth. Wherever consciousness becomes established and comes to growth, there is a descent of name-and-form. Where there is a descent of name-and-form, there is the growth of karmic formations.
>
> (S II 101)[27]

Viññāṇa is thus a precondition not only for the development of a new sentient body (name-and-form) in this life but also for "the growth of karmic formations" (*sankhārā*). After birth, viññāṇa and other accompaniments of life, the "life factor" (*āyu*) and "heat" (*usmā*), continue uninterruptedly throughout that lifetime until, upon their departure, one passes away.[28] Thereafter, in dependence upon these same conditions, "consciousness being established and growing, there comes to be renewed existence in the future" (S II 65).[29] Wijesekera thus remarks:

> [T]he conclusion is difficult to avoid that the term viññāṇa in Early Buddhism indicated the *surviving factor* of an individual which by re-entering womb after womb (*gabbhā gabbhaṃ*: Sn. 278, cp. D. iii 147) produced repeated births resulting in what is generally known as Saṃsāra.
>
> (Wijesekera, 1964: 256, emphasis in original)[30]

While the processes of viññāṇa grow and increase, thereby sustaining samsaric life, they can also be calmed, pacified, and brought to an end, marking the end of the cycle of birth and death. Indeed, the destruction of viññāṇa (along with the other four aggregates) is virtually equated with liberation in one passage: "By the disgust, the dispassion (*virāgā*), the cessation of viññāṇa, one is liberated without grasping (*anupādā*) – one is truly liberated" (S III 61).[31] This cessation of viññāṇa is brought about through Buddhist practice, which counters the karmic activities perpetuating samsaric existence.[32] As a result of such practice, viññāṇa is no longer increased by grasping; on the contrary, a monk "who is without grasping [or appropriation, *anupādāna*] attains Nibbāna" (M II 265).[33] Thus, "when that consciousness is unestablished, not coming to growth, non-generative (*anabhisankhāra*), it is liberated" (S III 53).[34] A Buddha or Arhat therefore differs from a worldly being, for whom viññāṇa is still continually established in samsara, in that their viññāṇa no longer has a support in cyclic existence (*appatiṭṭhita-viññāṇa*)[35] – a notion the Yogācārins will also subsequently associate with the cessation of the ālaya-vijñāna. Upon realizing nirvana at the end of the process of karmically driven rebirth, viññāṇa, the stream of worldly consciousness which persists throughout one's countless lifetimes, also comes to an end, or is at least radically transformed. The cessation of viññāṇa is here closely identified with the destruction and cessation of the "karmic activities" (*anabhisankhāra*, S III 53) which, we shall see, are necessary for the continued perpetuation of cyclic existence.[36]

Karmic formations and craving increase viññāṇa and perpetuate samsara

It is karmic activities – actions instigated and informed by the cognitive and emotional afflictions – that cause consciousness to attain growth and become established in cyclic existence. But what are the karmic activities that do this and how do they lead to the "stationing" or persistence of viññāṇa? And what has this to do with the feedback relationship between consciousness and karma?

Although it is not obvious at first glance, the karmic formations, the *sankhārā*, serve to perpetuate the cycle in two ways in the series of dependent arising: they constitute both the *basis* for samsaric continuity as well as the *causes* of perpetuating the cycle. These twin roles are implicit in the process–product nature of the concept of *sankhārā* itself. Generally, *sankhārā* (S. *saṃskārā*) denotes intentional actions, that is, following the definition of karma noted above (A III 415), actions that generate results. But *sankhārā* also refers to what *results* from such action. Hence, while one of the most important terms in Indian Buddhism, sankhārā is also one of the most difficult to comprehend, particularly in translation. Compounded of the prefix *saṃ*, meaning "with" or "together with," and a form of the verbal root *kṛ*, "to do" or "make," *saṃskārā* literally means "put or made together" or, more simply, "formation." Like many participial nouns in Pāli and Sanskrit (and like English terms such as "painting" or "building") sankhārā demonstrates a "process–product" bivalence. That is, it has both an active sense, "the act of forming," and a nominal sense, "that which is formed." In this latter sense, sankhārā refers most broadly to the entire phenomenal world insofar as everything that exists has been formed from various causes and conditions. In the psychological sense, however, sankhārā refers more narrowly to the volitions, dispositions, and actions that constitute human activities, insofar as these are both *constructed* complexes formed from past actions, as well as *constructive* and formative influences conditioning present and future actions. Edgerton thus describes sankhārā (*saṃskārā*) as "predispositions, the effect of past deeds and experience as conditioning a new state," as both "conditionings [and] conditioned states" (BHSD 542).[37]

It may seem contradictory for something to be both a cause and result at the same time, to be both constructed and constructing, conditioned and conditioning. However, these two properties are simultaneously found in many processes, especially those of living organisms, which develop and perpetuate themselves through their own interactive feedback processes embodied in patterns of circular causality, as is now widely understood in the natural sciences.[38] We can use our analogy of a river again to illustrate how easily the results of previous actions or events may become the basis, and even the cause, for succeeding ones.

A river is gradually formed through the continuous flow of water. At first, runoff water from rain flows haphazardly, directed only by the continuous forces of gravity and inertia, the particular lay of the land, and assorted obstacles in its path. As the water flows, it gradually erodes furrows in the ground beneath it, so the water from each succeeding rainfall is more likely to flow into these furrowed channels. Over time, deeper channels are formed which guide the direction and flow of each succeeding rainfall, which in turn erodes deeper channels collecting more water, and so on; eventually these two create, and constitute, the "river" itself. But even though it is the current form of the riverbed that now directs the flow of water, this riverbed was itself primarily formed by the previous flow of water. In this way, the entire river came into being through nothing but its own interactive, feedback processes: what was formed by previous events becomes the basis for, and thereby conditions, succeeding ones.

Similarly, in the early Buddhist world-view the various kinds of bodies we inhabit, with their specific types of cognitive and sensory dispositions and apparati, are also built up over the course of countless lifetimes in the particular conditions of cyclic existence. The paths our continued embodied existence take are directed by the accumulated results of our past actions, which are continually reinforced – which increase and "grow" – by our afflictive activities in the present, which themselves are deeply informed by the underlying currents of our various dispositions. In Buddhist terms, these activities are conditioned by the powers of desire and craving, the inertial forces propelling cyclic life, while their deeply furrowed paths are the sankhārās, the riverbed constructed through countless lifetimes of previous existences, which both result from past actions and serve as the basis for present ones. These sankhārās are thus formative influences which not only continuously condition our bodily forms, but also our intentional activities, the nature and direction of our mental and spiritual energies as well. That is, contoured by these banks, our stream of consciousness continuously flows with both the bubbling surface of its swift, churning waters and the deeper, hidden currents flowing beneath its surface – both of which subtly yet continuously make their mark upon the contours of that very riverbed and its banks, scouring out pockets here, accumulating deposits there. Together, the river and riverbed constitute a continuous, mutually conditioning relationship that has been built up by nothing more than the history of their own previous, continuous interactions. Sankhārās built up from the past serve as the continuous basis for our current activities.

This is an extremely apt analogy for the basic Indian Buddhist view of mind, all the more so since it also illustrates early Buddhism's radically depersonalized view of causality. Who, after all, created the river? This question would not even be asked in any naturalistic context. Such an ill-formed question would be rephrased as: "What forces, what combination of causes and conditions, brought about this great river?" As with the river, so too it makes little sense to ask – within an early Buddhist context – "Who built the sankhārās?" "Who produced this consciousness?" "Whose body is this?" As Buddha said:

> This body does not belong to you, nor to anyone else. It should be regarded as [the results of] former action that has been constructed and intended and is now to be experienced.
>
> (S II 64)

* * *

The karmic formations (*sankhārā*) are more than just constructed complexes, however, they are also constructive factors in a positive psychological sense, and as such condition the arising of cognitive awareness in a number of ways. Although their most prominent role is near the beginning of the standard series of dependent arising, where the karmic formations from previous lifetimes serve as a basis for further existence by directly conditioning consciousness in the rebirth process, the sankhārā also more actively bring about the "growth" of consciousness in their capacity as intentional actions. In some passages, in fact, the karmic formations are virtually equated with intention (*sañcetanā*, *cetanā*) itself,[39] the defining characteristic of karma. This sense of sankhārā as *intentional actions* also conditions the arising of viññāṇa in many formulations of dependent arising.

In one short passage, for example, the Buddha depicts the processes whereby intention (*cetanā*), conception (*pakappanā*), and the underlying tendencies (*anusaya*) perpetuate consciousness within cyclic existence:

> Monks, what one intends (*ceteti*), and what one plans, and whatever one has a tendency towards (*anuseti*): this becomes a basis for the maintenance of consciousness. When there is a basis, there is a support (*ārammaṇam*) for the establishing (*ṭhitiyā*) of consciousness. When consciousness is established and has come to growth, there is a descent of name-and-form.... Such is the origin of this whole mass of suffering. ...
>
> But, monks, when one does not intend, and one does not plan, and one does not have a tendency toward anything, no basis exists for the maintenance of consciousness. When there is no basis, there is no support for the establishing of consciousness. When consciousness is unestablished and does not come to growth, there is no descent of name-and-form.... Such is the cessation of this whole mass of suffering.
>
> (S II 67)

But how could intentions, conceptions, and tendencies create a "support" for consciousness to take rebirth in the future? And how do they make consciousness "grow"? This happens because they are related to craving and the karmic activities it instigates.

As we have seen, not all of one's activities generate karma, only the activities informed by afflictions such as craving (*taṇhā*) do. Without this *afflictive* dimension, without the cognitive and emotional afflictions (*kilesa*; S. *kleśa*) to instigate actions, there would be no cyclic existence. Craving in fact is so central to Buddhist thinking that it is enshrined in the second Noble Truth, the origin of suffering:

> And what is the origin of suffering? It is craving, which brings renewal of being, is accompanied by delight and lust, and delights in this and that; that is, craving for sensual pleasures, craving for being, and craving for non-being. This is called the origin of suffering.
>
> (M I 49)

That is, it is actions motivated by desire and craving – rather common aspects of human experience – that entail psycho-ontological consequences, that is, continued rebirth.

Craving leads to rebirth in the series of dependent arising in two ways. In the standard formula, sense-impressions and feeling give rise to craving (*taṇhā*), which in turn conditions the arising of appropriation (*upādāna*); these last two are afflictive influences which instigate karmic activities, thereby indirectly conditioning the arising of "samsaric" consciousness. In other contexts, however, craving directly conditions the growth of consciousness, leading directly to further rebirth. A text that closely parallels that cited at the beginning of this section (S II 66) states that when there is pleasure in or *craving* for any or all of the four kinds of sustenances (*āhāra*) of those who are already born or who desire to come to be (*sambhavesinaṃ*), then

> consciousness becomes established there and comes to growth. Wherever consciousness becomes established and comes to growth, there is a descent of name-and-form. Where there is a descent of name-and-form, there is growth in the karmic formations (*sankhārā*). Where there is growth in the karmic formations, there is the production of future renewed existence.
>
> (S II 101)[40]

We have thus seen two forces that cause viññāṇa to be supported and grow: first, the active karmic formations of intending (*cetanā*), etc. (S II 66 cited above), provide the support (*ārammaṇa*) for establishing (*ṭhitiyā*) consciousness in this world; and here (S II 101), it is the afflictive element of craving for the nutriments such as consciousness that causes it to be established and grow. *It is these two factors – intentional actions* (karma) *and the affective, afflictive powers* (kilesa, S. kleśa) *which inform them – that generate the energies propelling consciousness and perpetuating cyclic existence.*

But how do these processes actually promote the "growth" of consciousness, leading to further rebirth? The Buddha used a series of simple vegetative metaphors to describe this, metaphors the Yogācārins will similarly use to describe the ālaya-vijñāna. In one text, he asks:

> If these five kinds of seeds are unbroken, unspoilt, undamaged by wind and sun, fertile, securely planted, and there is earth and water, would these five kinds of seed come to growth, increase, and expansion?
>
> Yes, venerable sir.
>
> Monks, four stations (*ṭhitiyā*) of consciousness[41] should be seen as like the earth element. Delight and lust should be seen as like the water element. Consciousness together with its nutriment should be seen as like the five kinds of seeds.
>
> (S III 54)[42]

A similar passage effectively glosses these fertile images:

> Karma is the field, consciousness the seed and craving the moisture for the consciousness of beings hindered by ignorance and fettered by craving to become established in the lower [intermediate, or lofty] realm. Thus there is rebecoming in the future.
>
> (A I 223, III, 76, Nyanaponika, 1999: 69)

As these vegetative metaphors illustrate, the seeds of consciousness are established or "planted" in the fertile fields prepared by karmic deeds and watered by the bountiful founts of desire and craving – in short, it is karma and *kilesa* (afflictions) that condition consciousness. This metaphorical equation of consciousness with seeds, which the Yogācārins will also use in connection with the ālaya-vijñāna, suggests a close association between karma and viññāṇa, an association which, while equivocal, merits some attention.

Consciousness and the potential for karmic fruition

Although such metaphors are certainly suggestive, they hardly indicate what the relationship between consciousness and karma actually is. It is frequently said, for example, that karma is accumulated (*upacita*) and passed on, that "beings are heirs" to their actions (A V 292; M I 390, III 203), but, in the early texts at least, it is never said exactly how. Pāli scholar Johansson concludes that viññāṇa is the "transmitter of *kamma*" (1965: 195 f.), the "collector of *kamma* effects" (1979: 61), but there are, as far as we know, no passages that explicitly state that viññāṇa receives or maintains seeds or potentials for karmic results. Nevertheless, an examination of the passages that do discuss karma and consciousness, although individually ambiguous, together suggest that they are closely connected indeed, especially if we take into account that viññāṇa is the only process that explicitly continues across multiple lifetimes.

First of all, viññāṇa itself is said to be directly affected by the quality of a karmic action: "If an ignorant man undertakes meritorious actions [his] consciousness will go to merit, and [if he] undertakes demeritorious actions, [his] consciousness will go to demerit" (S II 82).[43] These suggest that viññāṇa takes on the qualities of karmic action, whose potentials, we have seen, accumulate until they come to fruition. Viññāṇa, moreover, seems to be the only process that is explicitly described as leaving one body at death and entering another one at conception.[44] For karmic potential to adhere to an individual life-stream and persist throughout one's series of rebirths, then it seems as if it must do so in conjunction with viññāṇa – at least, in any case, during the crucial juncture between death and rebirth. Though to my knowledge this is never explicitly stated in the early Pāli texts, such conclusions were commonly drawn by later exegetes and modern scholars alike. Hence, Johansson declares, with perhaps equal license and justification, that

> it is taken for granted that our existence is accumulative ... and our present state is continually changed through the effects of the past. Viññāṇa is the carrier of these accumulations, and is conceived as a stream flowing ceaselessly in time if not made to stop.
>
> (Johansson, 1970: 66)

This crucial question, with all its ambiguities, remains unanswered in the early texts, and will return to haunt Buddhist thinkers in an era exacting more precision and rigor, that is, the era of Abhidharma and Yogācāra scholasticism.

* * *

In this section we have seen, on the one hand, that viññāṇa as consciousness accompanies all animate existence and that its repeated "stationing" in this world is coterminous with one's samsaric destiny. At the time of rebirth, consciousness is directly conditioned by the sankhārā, the constructed karmic formations projected from previous actions; and during this life the afflictive factor of craving, together with the actions it impels, propel the growth of consciousness toward a further rebirth. Consciousness is thus the result, the product, of karmic activities both at the beginning of one lifetime and in the transition to the next. Moreover, since viññāṇa is the only process explicitly said to continue during rebirth, it is closely, albeit indefinitely, related to the accumulation and transmission of karmic potential over multiple lifetimes. On the other hand, viññāṇa may also be pacified and brought to an end, a condition that is virtually equated with liberation.

Therefore, as both Johannson and Wijesekera have concluded as well, viññāṇa is a subsisting constituent of individual existence which plays a central role in the early Buddhist conceptions of samsara and nirvana. And, as we shall see, every one of these characteristics will later be predicated of the Yogācāra version of subsisting sentience – the ālaya-vijñāna – which also stands in sharp contrast to the transient, discrete functions of an object-oriented cognitive awareness, the second major aspect of the term "viññāṇa." It is to this sense of viññāṇa that we now turn.

Viññāṇa as cognitive awareness

In these early texts, viññāṇa also refers to cognitive awareness insofar as it arises in conjunction with specific objects. Whereas the "samsaric" aspect of viññāṇa is usually discussed in terms of what has resulted from past actions (i.e. *sankhārā*), "cognitive viññāṇa" is typically discussed in the context of its present objects.[45] But that is not all. "Cognitive awareness" is also directly involved with the processes that *generate* new karma, and it is this karma that, in turn, causes "samsaric viññāṇa" to continue being established in cyclic existence, thereby completing the vicious circle constituting the formula of dependent arising.

In this context, viññāṇa is better rendered "cognitive awareness," since it is an awareness that arises in conjunction with specific cognitive objects. That is, a specific form of cognitive awareness arises when an appropriate object enters into its respective sense-sphere, impinging on its respective, unimpaired sense faculty (*indriya*) and there is sufficient attention thereto.[46] Sense-object and sense-organ (or faculty) are thus correlatively defined: a visual object, by definition, is that which impinges upon the eye. These cognitive modalities are, however, distinguished and classified by their object: "Cognitive awareness is reckoned by the particular condition dependent upon which it arises," the Buddha declared. "When cognitive awareness arises dependent on the eye and forms, it is reckoned as eye-cognitive awareness . . . ," and so on (M I 259). Cognitive awareness for human beings is analyzed in terms of six specific modalities – visual-, audio-, olfactory-, gustatory-, tactile-, and mental-cognitive awareness – based upon the five senses and mind. All of these arise in dependence upon the concomitance of their respective organs with their corresponding objects.

We must note, however, the asymmetry of the sixth cognitive modality (*mano-viññāṇa*), which is based upon the faculty of mind (*mano*), for this arises in conjunction with not one, but two kinds of cognitive object. When a cognitive awareness of a sensory object occurs, it is often followed by an awareness *of* that awareness, that is, a reflexive awareness "that such and such a sensory awareness (*viññāṇa*) has occurred."[47] This is one of the "objects" of mental cognitive awareness (*mano-viññāṇa*). Mental cognitive awareness, however, also arises in conjunction with cognitive objects that occur independently of the sensory cognitive system, such as thinking, reflection, or ideas.[48] Thus, mental cognitive awareness arises in conjunction with two kinds of objects: with a previous moment of sensory cognitive awareness as an object and with its "own" kind of object, that is, mental phenomena. Insofar as these latter are mental, as opposed to sensory objects, they are termed *dhammas* (S. *dharma*) – an increasingly important term we shall further examine in the Abhidharma chapter. Generally speaking, the category of mental cognitive awareness was broad enough that other schools attributed to it many of the characteristics the Yogācāra Buddhists would attribute to the ālaya-vijñāna.

Mental cognitive awareness (*mano-viññāṇa*) is, however, no more a permanent, abiding agent or self than the other processes in the early Buddhist analysis of mind are, and for the same reasons:

> In dependence on the mind and mental phenomena (*dhamma*) there arises mental cognitive awareness. The mind is impermanent, changing, becoming otherwise; mental phenomena are impermanent, changing, becoming otherwise.
>
> (S IV 69)

This passage highlights the fact that all forms of viññāṇa are seen as dependent upon the conditions that give rise to them. They occur, rather than act. That is, when an object appears in a sense-field and impinges upon its respective sense-faculty, that specific kind of cognitive awareness automatically arises.[49] This is equally true for the sixth cognitive modality, mental cognitive awareness (*mano-viññāṇa*). When sensory phenomenon give rise to sensory cognitive awareness, a second cognitive awareness may occur which depends upon that first cognitive awareness as its object. Despite its apparently reflexive character, however, mind is not "cognizing itself." Mental cognitive awareness no more "cognizes" *dhammas* than the forms of sensory cognitive awareness "cognize" objects; neither of them are agents or faculties, nor, for that matter, actions at all.

This is as much an interpretive and philosophical question as a terminological one, for it goes to the heart of the Buddhist view of dependent arising. It is common, though misleading at this stage of Buddhist thought, to think of cognition (*viññāṇa*) as an agent that acts upon its objects by "cognizing" them. In the causal syntax of dependent arising, however, *cognitive awareness does not cognize anything* – it is simply an awareness that arises when requisite conditions come together.[50] Cognitive awareness is thus not an *act* of cognition, it simply *is* cognitive awareness itself.[51] Failure to appreciate this impersonal, passive nature of cognitive awareness – to interpret it as an act rather than an event, as listening rather than hearing, or watching rather than seeing – is to overlook the most distinctive feature of early Buddhist thought: its radically depersonalized model of mind, its understanding of experience without a subject. For if cognitive awareness is not an act that one does but an event that occurs, then there is no need for an agentive subject. In this sense, the traditional Buddhist refusal to acknowledge a substantive, independent agent who "acts" or "perceives" (*anātman*) is as much a reflection of its mode of analysis as a metaphysical position.

And since cognitive awareness (*viññāṇa*) does not act, it does not in and of itself accrue karma. Only intentional activities generate karma. Thus, even though intentional activities are almost inevitably *instigated* by the affective accompaniments of cognitive awareness – which we shall see seldom occurs without them – viññāṇa itself is not the *cause* of karma; it is conceptualized altogether separately.

It is apparent, moreover, that cognitive awareness arises depending, on the one hand, on specific objects within a particular cognitive domain, as well as, on the other hand, on karmic formations (*sankhara*) such as the sense faculties that result from previous karmic activities. Even apparently simple sensory cognitive awareness (*viññāṇa*) therefore depends upon the patterns and structures garnered from past experience at the same time that it continuously arises in conjunction with present objective phenomena (an obvious point that will be fully systematized in the ālaya-vijñāna model of mind). This is merely another way of saying that new experiences are continuously conditioned by our pre-existing physiological and psychological structures, which have themselves been formed through previous activities and experiences. And these are the very patterns described in the formula of dependent arising.

Cognitive processes and the production of Karma

While "samsaric" viññāṇa is largely a product of past karmic activities, such as the karmic formations and craving, "cognitive" viññāṇa is involved in the production of these karmic activities. In the standard series of dependent arising, it is the factors which follow the descent of consciousness into name-and-form that set these processes into motion. In fact, the first several of these – the six sense-spheres, contact, and feeling – closely parallel the factors associated with the arising of cognitive awareness itself: cognitive awareness arises in conjunction with the six sense-faculties and contact, and typically gives rise to feeling.[52] These are so closely related that one text states that feeling, along with apperception (*saññā*) both considered karmic formations of mind (*saññā ca vedanā ca cittasankhāro*, M I 301) – are virtually inseparable from viññāṇa:

> Feeling, apperception, and cognitive awareness – these factors are conjoined, not disjoined, and it is impossible to separate each of these states from the others in order to describe the difference between them. For what one feels, that one apperceives; and what one apperceives, that one cognizes.
>
> (M I 293)[53]

In the standard formula, the affective factor of feeling then typically gives rise to the *afflictive* factor of craving, so crucial for perpetuating cyclic existence. Accordingly, another text simply places viññāṇa itself at the beginning of a causal chain that leads to the "origin of the world":

> And what, monks, is the origin of the world? In dependence on the eye and forms, eye-cognitive awareness arises. The meeting of the three is contact. With contact as condition, feeling [comes to be]; with feeling as condition, craving; with craving as condition, grasping; with grasping as condition becoming; with becoming as condition birth; with birth as condition, aging-and-death, sorrow, lamentation, pain, displeasure, and despair come to be. This, monks, is the origin of the world.
>
> (S II 73)[54]

We can see here, in the direct progression from cognitive awareness to feeling, to craving (*taṇha*), and on to appropriation (or grasping, *upādāna*) and becoming, etc. the crucial relationship between the cognitive and affective dimensions of mind, the afflicted karmic activities they typically give rise to, and the deleterious results that follow. Thus, while not karmically causal itself, cognitive viññāṇa is centrally involved in the processes that are: the afflictive factors of craving and grasping and the karmic factor of becoming.[55]

In another respect, these factors can also be considered varieties of karmic formations (*sankhārā*), in their causal rather than resultant character, as processes rather than products. For without karmic activities, there is no perpetuation of cyclic existence. This is epitomized by a passage already cited, in which sankhārā serves as the *only link* between name-and-form and renewed existence – that is, sankhārā replaces all the components of the cognitive processes in the standard twelve-member formula (i.e. the six sense-spheres, contact, feeling), together with the afflictive factors that they elicit (craving and appropriation):

> Wherever consciousness becomes established and comes to growth, there is a descent of name-and-form. Where there is a descent of name-and-form, there is growth in the karmic formations (*sankhārā*). *Where there is growth in the karmic formations, there is the production of future renewed existence.*
>
> (S II 101)

This underscores the profoundly bivalent nature of sankhārā as "the effect of past deeds and experience as conditioning a new state" (BHSD 542). That is, insofar as they represent what results from past actions – the sentient body (name-and-form) with its six sense-faculties, our emotional predispositions, and so forth – the karmic formations constitute the indispensable basis for new cognitive experiences and the powerful emotions they elicit. And insofar as they themselves are intentional actions – intention being the defining characteristic of karma – the sankhārā represent the dynamic components that keep beings enmeshed in samsaric life.

The causal dynamics underlying the arising of new karma, however, still needs to be analyzed in terms of its individual components, that is, conditioned by feeling, craving arises, conditioned by craving, grasping (*upādāna*) arises, followed by becoming, which leads directly to a new birth. Since it is grasping that forms the key link leading from one lifetime and the next, we must briefly examine this core concept.

Grasping or appropriation (*upādāna*) is a complex, multivalent term, equally important in early Buddhist and Yogācāra analyses of mind. Like sankhārā, it may refer both to something produced from past actions and to an active process in the present, both a conditioned and a conditioning state. It thus not only means "fuel, supply, the material out of which anything is made," and even "substratum by means of which an active process is kept alive or going" (PED 149), but also, more actively, "appropriation, grasping, attachment, and taking up." Although as a translation, the term "appropriation" lacks the graphic immediacy of "grasping," it serendipitously encompasses both the nominal sense of "that which is taken, seized, appropriated" (an appropriations bill, for example, seizes money by exacting taxes), as well as the verbal sense of grasping or, even more suggestively, "taking as one's own" (*ad-proprius*).[56]

This appropriation, this "taking as one's own," is, in the Buddhist view, the basic attitude we take towards the aggregated material and psychological processes ("the five aggregates of grasping," *pañc' upādānakkhandhā*) which comprise our sentient existence.[57] As an attitude which colors all our actions, however, grasping is not merely a pervasive psychological process, it also entails powerful psycho-ontological consequences. In the following passage, upādāna equally denotes fuel, substratum, or grasping – all of which are deemed necessary for continued rebirth:

> Just as a fire burns with fuel (*upādāna*) but not without fuel, so Vaccha, I declare rebirth for one with fuel [or grasping (*upādāna*)] not for one without fuel . . . When, Vaccha, a being has laid down this body but has not yet been reborn in another body, I declare that it is fueled by craving (*taṇhupādānaṃ*). For on that occasion craving is its fuel.
>
> (S IV 399)[58]

Without such craving and grasping, on the other hand, one may become liberated:

> If a monk seeks delight in [visible forms (*rūpā*)], welcomes them, and remains holding to them, his consciousness becomes dependent upon them and grasps to them. A monk with grasping [or appropriation] does not attain Nibbana. . . . If a monk does not seek delight in them, does not welcomes them, and does not remain holding to them, his consciousness does not become dependent upon them or grasps to them. A monk without grasping [or appropriation] (*anupādāno*) attains Nibbana.
>
> (S IV 102; translation altered)

Thus, appropriation (*upādāna*) lays the foundation for future rebirth in two ways: by serving as the basis, the substratum or fuel, for future lives, as well as by being an indispensable afflictive (*kilesa*) component in the production of new karma. And like other core Buddhist concepts, appropriation or grasping operates both within the psychological processes of ordinary life, while also entailing "psycho-ontological" results into the future, that is, by supplying the fuel for those who have "not yet been reborn in another body." Moreover, the cessation of grasping is closely associated with Nirvana, the cessation of cyclic existence. This concept of upādāna will also later play an important part in the complex model of mind centered around the ālaya-vijñāna.

The underlying tendencies (*anusaya*)

So far we have examined the complex and reciprocal interrelationship between viññāṇa and the karmic formations (*sankhārā*), observing that the arising of viññāṇa (in its two senses) is both based upon and perpetuated by the karmic formations (in both of its senses), which it in turn also serves to elicit. That is, on the analogy of the river and riverbed, the previous interactions between viññāṇa and sankhārā lay the groundwork for those same patterns of interaction to reoccur, continuously building upon each other in a constructive and self-perpetuating process. In this sense, the relationship between mind, actions, and their results – between viññāṇa and sankhārā (and *kilesa*) in all their complexity – is the core dynamic sustaining cyclic existence. But in one sense the materials we have examined have stated rather than demonstrated how this arises. How do these interactive processes actually facilitate their own repetition? That is, why do we keep repeating the same thing over and over? Why are we bound to keep looking for freedom and happiness in the wrong places? What, in other words, are the underlying and recurrent tendencies that keep us caught in vicious circles?

In early Buddhist thought, these are discussed in terms of the *anusaya*, the "underlying tendencies" or "latent dispositions." These tendencies form the essential link between the arising of cognitive awareness, with its *affective* responses, and the *afflictive* karmic activities that these latter typically elicit. As we have seen in the formula of dependent arising, the cognitive processes involving contact (*phassa*) and feeling (*vedanā*) give rise to craving (*taṇhā*) and grasping (*upādāna*). Although this sequence is usually stated without elaboration, the close connection between feeling and these afflictive responses – so essential to the perpetuation of samsara – lies within these underlying tendencies. These latent tendencies represent the infrastructure, as it were, of the cognitive and emotional afflictions, those indispensable elements underlying the generation of new karma.

Our focus on the underlying tendencies (*anusaya*) here is inspired by the important, and problematic, role they played in later developments in Abhidharma doctrine[59] – for it was the doctrinal debates over the status of these dispositions that, in large part, inspired the Yogācārins to postulate a distinct locus of unconscious affliction roughly paralleling the ālaya-vijñāna itself. Nevertheless, these tendencies were important in early Buddhism in their own right. For insofar as they represent the potential, the tendency, for cognitive and emotional afflictions (*kilesa*) to arise, the anusaya[60] are effective in the same dimensions that viññāṇa and appropriation (*upādāna*) are: (1) psychologically, they are involved in the karma-generating activities elicited by cognitive processes; and thus (2) "psycho-ontologically" are instrumental in perpetuating samsaric existence; whereas (3) soteriologically, their gradual eradication is closely linked to progress along the path to liberation.

In their psychological dimension, these tendencies underlie our usual affective responses to ordinary cognitive processes. This is stated particularly clearly in one formulation of dependent arising:

> Monks, dependent on the eye and forms, eye-cognitive awareness arises; the meeting of the three is contact; with contact as condition there arises [a feeling] felt as pleasant or painful or neither-painful-nor-pleasant. When one is touched by a pleasant feeling, if one delights in it, welcomes it, and remains holding to it, then the underlying tendency to lust lies within one. When one is touched by a painful feeling, if one

> sorrows, grieves and laments, weeps beating one's breast and becomes distraught, then the underlying tendency to aversion lies within one. When one is touched by a neither-painful-nor-pleasant feeling, if one does not understand as it actually is, the origination, the disappearance, the gratification, the danger, and the escape in regard to that feeling, then the underlying tendency to ignorance lies within one.
>
> (M III 285)

In other words, we are disposed to respond to certain kinds of stimuli in certain habitual ways. That is, particular predispositions represent a *potentiality* for that affliction to arise in response to the specific kind of feeling with which it is associated. This close relationship between types of feeling and the types of affliction they elicit is succinctly summarized in another passage:

> The underlying tendency to lust underlies pleasant feeling. The underlying tendency to aversion underlies unpleasant feeling. The underlying tendency to ignorance underlies neither-painful-nor-pleasant feeling.
>
> (M I 303)[61]

The implications of these passages are as obvious as they are odious: our cognitive processes nearly always involve affective responses (M I 293, cited above), such as feeling or sensation, which – as long as the dispositions continue to underlie them – tend to provoke the underlying potential for the afflictive responses of lust, aversion, etc. to arise, which, in turn, typically lead to new karmic activities, which result in more sensations, and so on. These dispositions, these habituated patterns of afflictive response to everyday experience, therefore play an essential role in the perpetuation of our bounded cyclic existence.

Accordingly, these underlying tendencies evince the same psycho-ontological consequences other dynamic factors in early Buddhism do. One text, for example (similar to S II 65 above), depicts the underlying tendencies as instigating an entire chain of dependent arising all by themselves:

> If, monks, one does not intend, and one does not plan, but *one still has a tendency* towards (*anuseti*) something, this becomes a basis for the maintenance of consciousness. When there is a basis, there is a support for the establishing of consciousness. When consciousness is established and has come to growth, there is a descent of name-and-form. With name-and-form as condition, the six sense bases [come to be]. . . . Such is the origin of this whole mass of suffering.
>
> (S II 66)

One who has, on the other hand, eliminated these underlying tendencies, these dispositions to passion, anger, and ignorance, no longer responds in the time-worn, habitual ways to whatever pleasant, unpleasant, or neutral feelings may arise. And since the dispositions no longer lie latent within these feelings, one no longer generates the karmic activities that perpetuate cyclic existence. The cessation of the underlying tendencies is therefore equated in this same discourse with liberation, with the end of suffering itself:

> But, monks, when one does not intend, and one does not plan, and one does *not* have a tendency towards anything, no basis exists for the maintenance of consciousness. When there is no basis, there is no support for the establishing of consciousness. When consciousness is unestablished and does not come to growth, there is no descent of name-and-form. With the cessation of name-and-form comes cessation of the six sense bases ... Such is the cessation of this whole mass of suffering.
>
> (S II 66)

The task of the Buddhist practitioner, then, is not merely to attain right understanding of the truths of suffering, its origin, its cessation, and the path leading to its cessation, but to fully eradicate the afflicting passions such as ignorance, lust, and aversion at the deeper, more entrenched level of unconscious dispositions. As the Buddha declares:

> Monks, that one shall here and now make an end of suffering without abandoning the underlying tendency (*anusaya*) to lust for pleasant feeling, without abolishing the underlying tendency to aversion towards painful feeling, without extirpating the underlying tendency to ignorance in regard to neither-painful-nor-pleasant feeling, without abandoning ignorance and arousing true knowledge – this is impossible.
>
> (M III 285)

But, in contrast, if one were to eliminate all these underlying tendencies, then a complete end to this suffering would indeed be possible. And when this is accomplished one is said to have entered the true dhamma and attained perfect view.[62]

The underlying tendency "I am" and conceptual proliferation (papañca)

These tendencies and their associated afflictions are not only emotional, however, they are also cognitive, in the broadest sense; and the combination of the two is a potent brew indeed. Recall that ignorance is, along with craving, one of the two main conditions for samsaric existence. Foremost amongst our cognitive mistakes, in the Buddhist view, is a deep-seated tendency to identify with our bodies, our feelings, our thoughts. Each of us harbors an almost innate sense that we *actually are* one or more of the five aggregates.[63] But since this sense of self-identity occurs at the deepest levels of consciousness, it is difficult to even discern, let alone radically remove. Accordingly, even an Aryan disciple, a Buddhist saint who has already removed the five lower fetters tying him to this world, is said to have subtle remnants of the conceit "I am." As the Buddha explains:

> Suppose, friends, a cloth has become soiled and stained, and its owners give it to a laundryman. The laundryman would scour it evenly with cleaning salt, lye, or cowdung, and rinse it in clean water. Even though that cloth would become pure and clean, it would still retain a residual (*anusahagata*) smell of cleaning salt, lye, or cowdung that has not yet vanished. The laundryman would then give it back to the owners. The owners would put it in a sweet-scented casket, and the residual smell of cleaning salt, lye, or cow dung that had not yet vanished would vanish.
>
> So, too, friends, even though a noble disciple has abandoned the five lower fetters, still, in relation to the five aggregates subject to clinging, there lingers in him a residual conceit "I am," a desire "I am," an underlying tendency "I am" that has not yet been uprooted.
>
> (S III 131)[64]

Moreover, this underlying tendency to personally identify with aspects of one's existence, the tendency toward "I am," is at the center of another, even more complex set of feedback relationships between consciousness, language, and self-identity, and actions and their results: all of these give rise to an unending series of conceptual or ideational proliferation (*papañca*; S. *prapañca*). This pattern also recurs at the center of the ālaya-vijñāna model of mind.

The sense "I am" is closely connected with the reflexivity of mental cognitive awareness (*mano-viññāṇa*), the only cognitive modality not directly based upon one of the sense faculties but upon the faculty of mind or mentation (*mano*).[65] Mental cognitive awareness, as noted above, arises in conjunction with two kinds of event: the occurrence of sensory cognitive awareness, which gives rise to a reflexive mental awareness "*that* such and such a cognitive awareness has occurred," as well as its "own" objects, *dhammas*, which are associated with reflection or thinking (*vitakka-vicāra*). These latter are both considered sankhārā of speech (*vitakka-vicārā vacīsaṇkhārā*, M I 301), and arise in conjunction with *mano*, with mentation (see n. 48). The reflexivity that mental cognitive awareness provides, based on such mentation (*mano*), is thus bound up with our capacities for language, which was considered in early Indian thinking, as elsewhere, as the very medium of thought and ideas.[66]

Like language itself, however, this awareness invites endless rounds of recursivity, of *papañca*, mental or conceptual proliferation[67] – even in regard to objects of sensory awareness:

> Dependent on the eye and forms, eye-consciousness arises. The meeting of the three is contact. With contact as condition there is feeling. What one feels, that one apperceives. What one apperceives, that one thinks about. What one thinks about, that one mentally proliferates. With what one has mentally proliferated as the source, apperceptions and

> notions tinged by mental proliferation [*papañca-saññā-sankhā*] beset a man with respect to past, future, and present forms cognizable through the eye, [and so on, up to:] mind-objects cognizable through the mind.
>
> (M I 111 f.)[68]

We have already seen intimations of a close relationship between cognitive awareness, apperception,[69] and linguistic use. Cognitive awareness, feeling, and apperception, M I 293 declares, "are conjoined, not disjoined ... For what one feels, that one apperceives; and what one apperceives, that one cognizes." Moreover, A III 413 states that "apperceptions (*saññā*) result in conventional usage (*vohāra*). As one comes to know a thing, so one expresses (*voharati*) oneself, 'Thus I have apperceived.' "[70] Now, in M I 111, cognitive awareness, contact, and apperception give rise first to thinking and then to mental or conceptual proliferation (*papañca*). And, with such proliferation as the "source," further apperceptions and proliferations arise in respect to other objects of cognitive awareness. That is, what one has cognized, apperceived, and thought about becomes, via mental proliferation, a condition for further cogitation, conceptualization, and so on. Cognitive awareness, language, and thought are thus so inseparable that they give rise to a runaway recursivity in their own right. Indeed, conceptual proliferation itself is so multiply entangled in its own reciprocal relationships – (1) with contact (which sometimes conditions the arising of cognitive awareness)[71]; (2) with apperception (which always accompanies it)[72]; and (3) with thought itself[73] – that it is often a synonym for phenomenal, cyclic existence as a whole.[74]

The most deeply entrenched source of these recursive possibilities, which also doubles back to generate its own recursivity, is no doubt our reflexive sense of self-existence, the sense "I am" (which is always expressed as speech, *iti*). As one text declares, the notion " 'I am' is a proliferation; 'I am this' is a proliferation; 'I shall be' is a proliferation" (S IV 202 f.; Bodhi, 2000: 1259). Not only is "the label 'I,' " as Bhikkhu Ñāṇananda puts it, an "outcome of papañca" (Ñāṇananda, 1971: 11), but the thought " 'I am" is also, in the early Pāli text the *Sutta-nipāta*, the very root of proliferation. In other words, as long as the thought "I am" persists – this thought whose residual underlying tendency lasts until far along the path to purification (S III 131, cited above) – so long will the feedback cycle between cognitive awareness, apperceptions, conceptual proliferation, and further apperceptions, etc. continue, thereby perpetuating cyclic existence. Accordingly, the *Sutta-nipāta* declares:

> With what manner of insight, and not grasping anything in this world, does a monk realize Nibbāna? Let him completely cut off the root of concepts tinged with the prolific tendency (*papañca*), namely, the thought 'I am.'
>
> (*SN* 915–16)[75]

These subtle remnants, "the residual conceit 'I am,' a desire 'I am,' an underlying tendency 'I am' " (S III 131) will, however, be uprooted when the disciple rightly contemplates the arising and ceasing of the five aggregates and clearly sees the futility of identifying "I am this" with any internal or external phenomena whatsoever.[76] Thus,

> Monks, as to the source through which perceptions and notions tinged by mental proliferation beset a man: if nothing is found there to delight in, welcome and hold to, this is the end of the underlying tendency to lust, of the underlying tendency to aversion ... to views ... to doubt ... to conceit ... to desire for being ... to ignorance.
>
> (M I 109)

The debate over latent versus manifest

The persistence of the latent tendencies until far along the path to liberation, however, immediately raises a number of questions that will challenge later Buddhist analyses of mind. If they are so persistent that one continuously harbors such tendencies until reaching liberation – which is implicit in the foregoing and explicit to differing degrees in succeeding schools – then why would they not affect all of one's activities, making *all* of them afflictive, karmic activities (and, in the process, making liberation impossible)? But if they do not, then how do they exist when they are not actively affecting one's activities? Although such questions were not raised, and hence went unanswered, until Abhidharma analyses forced the issue, the outlines of the problem are evident enough in the early texts.

While many texts are ambiguous on these points, one at least, the *Mahāmāluṅkya-sutta* of the *Majjhima-nikāya*, is more suggestive. The Buddha is depicted here correcting the misguided views of his disciple Malunkyaputta, who thought that one is only bound by the afflicting dispositions when they are patently manifest, but not otherwise.[77] The Buddha first responds by declaring that the underlying tendencies exist even in a baby boy, although in a latent state, suggesting that these underlying tendencies may be innate[78] to human beings:

> For a young tender infant lying prone does not even have the notion 'personality' so how could personality view (*sakkāyadiṭṭhi*) arise in him? Yet the underlying tendency to personality view (*sakkāyadiṭṭhānusayo*) lies within him. A young tender infant lying prone does not even have the notion 'teachings,' so how could doubt about teachings arise in him? Yet the underlying tendency to doubt lies within him. A young tender infant lying prone does not even have the notion 'rules,' so how could adherence to rules and observances arise in him? Yet the underlying tendency to adhere to rules and observances lies within him. A young tender infant lying prone does not even have the notion 'sensual pleasure,' so how could sensual desire arise in him? Yet the underlying

> tendency to sensual lust lies within him. A young tender infant lying prone does not even have the notion 'beings,' so how could ill will towards beings arise in him? Yet the underlying tendency to ill will lies within him.
>
> (M I 433)

The Buddha (M I 434) then contrasts this situation with that of the "untaught ordinary person ... [who] abides with a mind obsessed and enslaved by personality view" (*sakkāyadiṭṭhi-pariyuṭṭhitena cetasā viharati*) [doubt, etc.]. "When that personality view [etc.] has become habitual and is uneradicated in him," the Buddha warns, it serves as a fetter tying him to this world (*orambhāgiyaṃ saṃyojanaṃ*). The learned monk, on the other hand, well practiced in the Buddha's teaching and well trained in meditation,

> does not abide with a mind obsessed and enslaved by personality view [doubt, etc.]; he understands as it actually is [*yathābhūtaṃ*] the escape from the arisen personality view, and personality view *together with the underlying tendency to it* [*sānusaya*] is abandoned in him.
>
> (M I 434, emphasis added)[79]

These passages certainly seem to distinguish between the afflictions in a subsisting, latent state (*anusaya*) and the state of being overwhelmed by their outbursts (*pariyuṭṭhāna*). While the underlying tendencies subsist in the infant only in latent form, in adults they have developed into an abiding capacity to "obsess and enslave" us, tying us to this world. The advanced monk or nun, however, has rid themselves of the overwhelming manifest appearances of these afflictions, *together with* their deeper, more trenchant form as underlying tendencies. These tendencies persist throughout one's lifetime and for as long as one exists within samsara, until they are gradually eliminated along the path and only fully eradicated upon final liberation. As we shall see, later schools will disagree about the differences between the latent afflictions (*anusaya*) and the active outbursts (*pariyuṭṭhāna*),[80] drawing opposite conclusions from texts such as these, which remain, in any case, somewhat equivocal.

What is clear though is why these underlying tendencies were so important in early Buddhist thought: they connect the results of previous karma with the causes of new karma, constituting a third crucial dimension to our vicious cyclic existence, this one centered upon the cognitive and emotional afflictions. That is, feelings or sensations result from previous karma (A II 157),[81] within which the underlying tendencies lie ever ready, as it were, to be triggered into activity. Thus, when certain feelings arise they tend to elicit the underlying tendencies associated with them, causing their respective afflictions – such as the three unhealthy roots of lust, aversion, and ignorance – to burst forth (see Table 1.1). The actions that are instigated or informed by these afflictions create more karma, which in turn lead to further results, such as feeling, and so on. Insofar as

Table 1.1 The relation between feeling (*vedana*) and the underlying tendencies (*anusaya*)

M III 285		
Cognition → sensation → feeling → underlying tendency		
viññāṇa → *phassa* → *vedanā* → *anusaya*		
M I 303		
Pleasant feeling (*sukha-vedanā*)	→	tendency to lust (*rāgānusaya*)
Painful feeling (*dukkha-vedanā*)	→	tendency to aversion (*paṭighānusaya*)
Neither-painful-nor-pleasant feeling (*adukkamasukha-vedanā*)	→	tendency to ignorance (*avijjānusaya*)

they represent the potential to repeat afflictions that already "have become habitual and uneradicated," the underlying tendencies are therefore both *conditioned*, that is, constructed by past actions, as well as *conditioning*, that is, conducing to present actions. In this sense, they constitute the indispensable *afflictive* link to the dependent arising of "this whole mass of suffering," without which actions could not accrue karmic results.

Reciprocal causality between the two aspects of viññāṇa

In the introduction to this section, we argued that there is a mutually reinforcing relationship between the "two aspects" of viññāṇa (summarized in Table 1.2). That is, for as long as the cognitive processes give rise to feeling, from which follows craving, grasping, and the activities that create and sustain the "samsaric viññāṇa," so long will the cycle of rebirth be perpetuated – at the center of which is the continuity of viññāṇa itself. And for as long as this samsaric viññāṇa persists, so long will it provide the ground or basis for the continued occurrence of those very cognitive processes, with all of their attendant affective and afflictive responses.[82] In this sense, there is – clearly but implicitly – a reciprocal, yet temporal feedback relationship between these two aspects of viññāṇa in the series of dependent arising. They are, in this temporal sense, causal conditions of one another.

We drew these conclusions, however, only through inference and analysis, since there are no extant passages in the early Buddhist texts that explicitly differentiate these two, nor relate them in this fashion.[83] It is, however, sufficient for our purposes – to understand the background and context of the Yogācāra concept of the ālaya-vijñāna – to be able to delineate two *regularly occurring and consistently distinct contexts* in which these "aspects" of viññāṇa appear in the materials which later thinkers drew upon in formulating their own innovative theories of mind. All the major Abhidharma schools drew upon roughly the same materials and came to roughly the same conclusions (with some important differences, as we shall see) regarding these "two aspects" of viññāṇa. Only

Table 1.2 The relationship between the "two" viññāṇas in the formula of dependent arising

First step: Factors 2–4: past actions condition a new life beginning with consciousness. Conditioned by the sankhārā (karmic formations), samsaric viññāṇa descends into a new body (*nāma-rūpa*).
Second step: Factors 5–7: conscious body (*saviññāṇakāya*) conditions cognitive processes. Samsaric viññāṇa supports the arising of cognitive viññāṇa, which only occurs in living bodies. (Cognitive viññāṇa is recapitulated in the six sense-spheres, sense-impression, feeling).
Third step: Factors 8–10: cognitive processes collectively condition samsaric consciousness. Cognitive viññāṇa instigates the affective and afflictive karmic activities that perpetuate rebirth (*bhava*), whereby samsaric viññāṇa goes onto future existence.
Whole cycle: conditioned by the sankhārā, viññāṇa is reborn in a new body; samsaric viññāṇa conditions cognitive viññāṇa, which in turn leads to karmic activities that lead samsaric viññāṇa to further existence.

the Yogācārins formalized this distinction into a complex model of mind in which these two "aspects" were systematically distinguished and the relationship between them characterized in terms of their reciprocal and simultaneous conditionality. We will take up these developments soon enough in succeeding chapters.

But first we wish to briefly discuss the studies of at least one modern scholar, Rune Johansson, who (along with Wijesekera) came to many of the same conclusions later Buddhist thinkers did regarding these "two aspects" of viññāṇa. In contrast to our approach, however, which focuses on the systemic relations between these aspects of viññāṇa in the various formulations of dependent arising, Johansson cites a number of texts which suggest these two aspects of viññāṇa in the very same passage. And, in spite of his judicious reluctance to speak of two "aspects" of the singular term "viññāṇa," careful exegesis, he concludes, compels it.

Both aspects of viññāṇa seem to occur together in several rather similar passages. The first occurs in a discourse where the Buddha is recommending that a dying disciple relinquish attachment to anything that could serve as a support for viññāṇa to be reborn into this world, enumerating a long list of such phenomena within which viññāṇa also occurs, first as a form of cognitive awareness: "I will not cling to eye-viññāṇa (etc.) and my viññāṇa will not be dependent on eye-viññāṇa (etc.)" (M III 260).[84] This is then repeated for all five aggregates (*khandha*), ending with consciousness (*viññāṇa*): "I will not cling to consciousness, and my consciousness will not be dependent on consciousness."[85] Johansson interprets the second consciousness in both these passages as "viññāṇa in its rebirth-aspect" (1965: 198).

The next passage makes a similar point: desire for the five aggregates of grasping, the last of which is viññāṇa, provides a "support" for viññāṇa, which, however, disappears along with that desire:

> If a monk has abandoned lust for ... the consciousness (*viññāṇa*) element, with the abandoning of lust the basis is cut off: there is no support for the establishing of consciousness.
>
> When that consciousness is unestablished, not coming to growth, nongenerative, it is liberated. By being liberated ... he personally attains Nibbana.
>
> (S III 53, Bodhi, 2000: 891)

Johansson interprets this similarly:

> This could mean that through freedom from the sense-perception-viññāṇa (together with the other *khandhā* [aggregates]), viññāṇa (in its rebirth-aspect) is without support and – as the text continues – becomes *anabhisankhāra* (free from *kamma* accumulation) and *parinibbāyati* (attains *parinibbāna* [Nirvana]).
>
> (Johansson, 1965: 199)

Both of these passages suggest that viññāṇa has two distinct aspects and that its cognitive or "sense-perception" aspect is central to the perpetuation (or conversely, the cessation) of its samsaric or "rebirth-aspect."

This causal dependency also works the other way around. Not only do the activities associated with cognitive viññāṇa bring about the renewal of samsaric viññāṇa, but the presence of samsaric viññāṇa is also a precondition for any cognitive processes to arise. That is, all of one's previous actions and experiences serve – through the medium of the constructed forms of body and mind – to influence one's immediate cognitive processes. A specific occurrence of viññāṇa, in other words, is not only conditioned by its present cognitive object, which is just one of its conditions. It is also informed by the whole complex of conditions (S II 2: "Depending on karmic formations viññāṇa arises") bearing on that particular moment, for all of our physical, sensory, and mental apparati, constructed and conditioned from past actions, contribute to the range and content of experience in this life. As we have suggested, all our inherited physiological and psychological structures, the sankhārās as well as "samsaric viññāṇa," condition the forms in which "cognitive viññāṇa" currently arises.[86]

Buddhist analysis of mind, therefore, even at this early stage, is no simple empiricism in which some autonomous cognitive faculty cognizes external objects pre-existing "out there" in time and space. Rather, the theory of dependent arising suggests that mind and object dependently arise. A visual cognitive awareness, for example, only arises in response to something "visible," which is defined by the capabilities of the eye-faculty, and so on. As Johansson points out, "if we did not have the power of experiencing, the power of forming mental images [*saññā*], then the object, seen through the eye, would not produce its conscious counterpart"

(1979: 85). Our sankhārā are therefore a "necessary condition for viññāṇa to function at all" (ibid.: 139). In other words, our experience of cognitive objects is a result of constructive[87] activities whose enabling structures have been built up through the processes of countless lifetimes and which continuously condition our present forms of experience.

Johansson emphasizes this in his interpretation of a passage in which viññāṇa depends upon feeling born of contact, rather than the other way around (M III 260: *cakkhusamphassajā vedanānissitaṃ viññāṇaṃ*):

> Perception is produced through the confrontation of a neural message with memories stored in the nervous system. The information supplied through the senses can be interpreted only by being compared with this stored information; this information can from a Buddhist point of view be envisaged as provided by viññāṇa and therefore present before the stimulus; it is activated only through the contact, *phassa*. Viññāṇa is ... a precondition of perception. ... The *dimension* of consciousness is the condition of sensation, and the concrete *content* is the result of it.
>
> (Johansson, 1979: 92 f., emphasis in original)

This is hardly surprising. How else but through some ongoing "dimension" of mind could the mass of memories, the accumulation of karmic potential, and (perhaps) the afflictive dispositions which constitute samsaric continuity, persist when the momentary cognitive processes of seeing, hearing, feeling, etc. are otherwise preoccupied with their own object-specific operations?

On the other hand, how else could these potentials for karmic accumulation, these underlying tendencies, etc. be generated, strengthened, and increased, except through the fateful cognitive and afflictive activities within which cognitive *viññāṇa* plays a central role? Johansson suggests this very reciprocity while fleshing out his metaphor of the "dimension" of consciousness:

> *Viññāṇa* refers mainly to the stream of conscious processes which characterizes the human mind, but it is also ... responsible for the continuity both within this life and beyond. [I]t is probably more adequate to call it the dimension of consciousness. ... It is by nature dynamic and continually changing. ... It may become more and more dependent on the stimuli from the external world and may be stuffed with contents and memories, which transform *viññāṇa* to the new personality of the next birth. ... In the former type of context [the 'dimension' of *viññāṇa*], it is more of an inner functional unit, inner space, store-room; in the latter, more of concrete, conscious processes which are the inhabitants of this inner room.
>
> (Ibid.: 63 f.)

These are precisely the two aspects of viññāṇa we have delineated above: a continuous "dimension" of samsaric viññāṇa, which "preconditions" the second, momentary object-oriented, cognitive viññāṇa, which, in turn, "stuffs it with contents."

These aspects of mind, moreover, not only reciprocally condition each other in the extended temporal range of samsaric continuity (the "psycho-ontological" sense), but their reciprocity would seem to function within the momentary processes of immediate cognition as well – that is, they ought to condition each other *simultaneously*. If, as the metaphors of a "dimension" of mind and its "contents" suggest, cognitive viññāṇa is a particular, transient and object-specific occurrence of an otherwise unceasing, accumulative, and relatively non-intentional sentience, then why should all those accumulated potentialities, memories, and impressions associated with this sentience, this samsaric viññāṇa, simply cease when some object-specific form of cognitive viññāṇa arises? And what would happen to samsaric continuity if they did? Though the early texts nowhere say so, Johansson for one does not shrink from the simplest and most straightforward answer to these questions. There are, "according to the early Buddhist analysis, two layers of consciousness: what we called the momentary surface processes, and the background consciousness. The latter is an habitual state ... *always there*" (1970: 106 f.)[88] (emphasis added).

Johansson has thus summed up the diverse functions of viññāṇa within the early Pāli texts. In his analysis viññāṇa is characterized as:

1 a continuously flowing process ...
2 principally conscious, but with a subconscious component, because most of the content is not always present ...
3 transmitter of karmic effects, modifiable by experiences,
4 a free-moving force (e.g., connected with dreams and free imagination),
5 an explanation of rebirth in terms of consciousness,
6 a process that can be stopped, and thereby end the whole karmic process.

(Johansson, 1965: 192)

As we shall see, the Yogācāra writers will attribute every one of the characteristics of viññāṇa listed above to ālaya-vijñāna, with the explicit and obvious exception of (2), which refers to "cognitive" viññāṇa. Both the mass of textual materials we have examined, and important contemporary studies concerning it, lead to the same conclusions, motivated perhaps by similar syncretic aims, that we shall later find in the complex concept of ālaya-vijñāna.

We must admit, however, that these conclusions, in fact this entire mode of analysis, are far from the spirit and tenor of the early texts. They reflect a systematic perspective, a style of thinking more properly belonging to the scholastic period of Buddhist thought which followed. These ideas lay latent like seeds in the earliest traditions, waiting to be grasped and sown in the fertile fields of later minds where they would, watered by not a little sectarian contention, eventually bear fruit in the multi-dimensional model of mind centered upon ālaya-vijñāna. We have examined the background of this model; now we must examine its context, the context within which these simple metaphors of streams and seeds and fruits, and even the very term "viññāṇa" itself, would become problematic indeed.

2

THE ABHIDHARMA CONTEXT

> Religio is false without philosophy, in just the same way as philosophy is false without religio.
>
> (St Augustine, *Epitome*)

The Abhidharma project and its problematic

We have examined the important role of *vijñāna* (P. *viññāṇa*; note: hereafter we will use primarily Sanskrit terminology, reflecting the original language of our sources) within the series of dependent arising, as both the subsisting dimension of individual samsaric existence, and as a core component of the cognitive processes that typically lead to actions perpetuating such existence. This is not the whole picture, however, for the samsaric round would come to a halt if there were no afflictive passions (*kleśa*) instigating karma-inducing activities. Thus, as essential as vijñāna may be for the *continuity* of samsaric existence, it is the pernicious influences of the afflictions (*kleśa*), together with the karmic actions they inform, that are essential for its *perpetuation*.[1] In other words, while samsaric vijñāna may be the product of one's past actions, it is the presence of the afflictive energies (*kleśa*) in one's present activities that creates new karma. And since these are only activities that one can affect, religious effort is necessarily oriented towards controlling one's motivations and directing one's activities in the here and now.

The early Buddhists thus concentrated upon an analysis of one's present actions and the motivating intentions behind them, relying upon the relatively simple analyses of mind we surveyed in the first chapter. In the centuries following the Buddha's lifetime, these analyses developed into increasingly explicit and systematic methods of discerning the underlying motivations, and hence the karmic nature, of each and every intentional action. Over time, the Buddhists transformed what was originally a straightforward and largely descriptive psychology into a highly complex, systematic, and self-conscious *meta-psychology* – still with the explicit aim of eliminating the afflictive, karma-creating energies that perpetuate cyclic existence. This is, in brief, the Abhidharma project.[2]

In this approach, the Abhidharma emphasis upon the active processes of mind seemed to overshadow the subsisting yet subtle influences from the past – particularly the underlying tendencies toward the afflictions (*anuśaya*) and the accumulation of karmic potential (*karma-upacaya*). To grossly simplify the situation, these subsisting influences came under the purview of Abhidharma analysis only insofar as they overtly affected immediate processes of mind. But these subsisting influences could not, by their very nature, all be active, or even discerned, within one's mental processes at any given moment; they were by definition latent or potential for most of the time, and hence unavoidably obscure. Thus, two main factors that were indispensable to the Buddhist view of samsaric continuity across multiple lifetimes – the persistence of the latent afflictions and the accumulation of karmic potential – were not easily ascertained in an analysis which focused exclusively on present and active processes of mind. The existence of these subsisting factors, their patterns of arising, and their possible influences on all one's mental processes until attaining liberation – all these became problematic within the Abhidharmic analytic.

And they became problematic, we shall argue, because of the inherent tension between Abhidharma's ultimate *aim* and its immediate *method*; between the overriding religious aim of stopping the inertial energies of samsaric life altogether, and the means to that end – the systematic description of the momentary and present processes of mind. The unavoidable distinction between the persisting influences from the past and the active processes in the present would eventually bring about an explicit recognition of the kinds of influences that underlie and enable every action yet which remain inaccessible to analyses limited to immediate mental processes – it brought about, in short, a recognition of unconscious mind.

Both "aspects" of vijñāna which we analyzed in the first chapter – vijñāna as "consciousness" and vijñāna as "cognitive awareness" – were central to these problems. It was the fateful disjunction between these two originally undifferentiated aspects of *vijñāna* – with exclusive validity accorded to momentary cognitive processes at the expense of subsisting consciousness – that eventually led to the postulation of a distinct category of vijñāna, a "repository" or "base" consciousness, an "*ālaya*" vijñāna, to represent those subsisting aspects of mind which had become marginalized within the new Abhidharma analytic.

We focus on the Abhidharma project at such length because it was within the historical and conceptual context of Abhidharma scholasticism that the Yogācāra school arose, and within whose terms the notion of the ālaya-vijñāna was expressed. An understanding of this context, of its technical terms, and of the problematic issues it gave rise to is thus indispensable for untangling the interwoven logical and exegetical arguments for the ālaya-vijñāna, which, we shall see, are almost wholly products of the "Abhidharma Problematic."

Background of the Abhidharma

We must first briefly sketch the historical background to Abhidharma Buddhism. The doctrines we examined in Chapter 1 belonged to the *Sūtra-piṭaka*, the

Collection of Discourses, purported to be the words of the Buddha himself.[3] Almost all later traditions of Indian Buddhism descended from these early teachings, either directly or indirectly, and most of them have sought validation for their distinctive doctrines by recourse to this or that passage in these early *sūtras*. These discourses have thus served as a counterbalance by which divergent doctrines were weighed and judged, lending South and Southeast Asian Buddhism, despite its huge historical, geographic, linguistic, and cultural variety, a certain unity of thought and practice.

But just because the Buddha's teachings were given at different times, to diverse audiences, and in varying circumstances, the discourses preserved many teachings that were not readily reconcilable with each other, did not expound a topic in a complete or systematic fashion, or were not of equal benefit to those most assiduously practicing the Buddhist path. Consequently, possibly even during the Buddha's lifetime, the Buddha's followers began composing more consistent and systematic presentations of his teachings. The initial attempts in this direction are preserved in a collection of texts, some of which are considered to be the Buddha's words, called the *Abhidharma-piṭaka*, the Collection of Higher Doctrine.[4]

As it was several centuries before any of the three Collections (including the Collection of Discipline, *vinaya-piṭaka*) were actually written down, these "texts"[5] were transmitted orally in typical Indian fashion, with different groups of monks committing different Collections to memory. In such circumstances, divergent versions of the early discourses tended to increase as the centuries passed and as various implications of the teaching continued to be drawn out. This was particularly true in the case of the Abhidharma texts, which were constantly undergoing a process of systematization and refinement. Moreover, and just as important, there was no central authority to determine exactly what was or was not orthodox doctrine. This process of diverging interpretations and their proliferating implications was instrumental in the gradual rise of different schools of doctrine and practice.

Though it is certain that these processes – the gradual divergences of doctrine, the composition of new Abhidharma texts, and the formation of different schools of interpretation – were well under way in the centuries following the Buddha's demise, the available documentary evidence gives us only the barest outline of its early history.[6] The processes through which the various schools, traditionally numbering eighteen, came into existence are largely lost in the mists of Indian history.[7] We possess extensive textual materials from this period only from the Sthaviravāda/Theravāda school,[8] predominant in present-day Sri Lanka and Southeast Asia, and from the Sarvāstivādins, the predominant Abhidharma school in classical India (but whose texts are primarily extant only in Chinese translation).[9]

We reach surer historical ground only in the first few centuries CE, the second half of Buddhism's first millennium, when we are blessed with a large body of Abhidharma texts from a variety of schools. Outstanding in terms of its comprehensive scope, systematic organization, and continuing influence through the centuries, is the work of the fourth-to-fifth century CE Buddhist philosopher Vasubandhu, the *Treasury of Abhidharma* (*Abhidharma-kośa*).[10] With a few major exceptions (the early Theravāda text, the *Kathāvatthu*, and some of their distinctive doctrines) we will limit our examination of Abhidharma to the viewpoints expressed in the *Abhidharma-kośa*. These are traditionally thought to represent those of the Sautrāntikas, the "Followers of Sūtra," as well as those of the Sarvāstivāda, the "All-Exists" school. We focus upon the *Abhidharma-kośa* for two reasons. First, Vasubandhu was, with his half-brother Asanga, one of the two founding figures of "classical" Yogācāra. His corpus of work, his recurrent religious and philosophical concerns, even his technical vocabulary, bridge both of these traditions. Moreover, the relationship between the Yogācāra and Sautrāntika schools is currently being re-examined, leading one scholar to wonder whether "Vasubandhu's so-called Sautrāntika opinions are, in fact, Yogācāra *abhidharma* in disguise" (Kritzer, 1999: 20). Both of these make the *Abhidharma-kośa* an exceptional contemporaneous witness to the wider problematics surrounding and leading to the conceptualization of the ālaya-vijñāna.

Although it might seem strange for those concerned with the disjunction between the Hīnayāna and Mahāyāna schools of Buddhism to contextualize the "Mahāyāna" Yogācāra school in terms of "Hīnayāna" Abhidharma, the continuity and overlap between them, in India at any rate, is larger than their differences. The Yogācāra school should, in fact, be considered one of the "Abhidharma" schools, as it produced a corpus of Abhidharma literature[11] parallel to and contemporaneous with that of the other Abhidharma schools, chiefly the Theravādins and Sarvāstivādins. Although these three bodies of Abhidharma literature differed in many of their details, they nevertheless shared the same basic presuppositions, carried out their analyses in a similar fashion, and expressed themselves in nearly the same terminology. They belonged, in short, to a single intellectual milieu. And they were all, accordingly, troubled by much the same systemic problems; it was primarily their solutions to these problems that differed.

In order to understand the rationale and arguments used to defend and describe the alaya-vijñāna, it is therefore essential that we look at this common basis of doctrine in the Abhidharma traditions – their most important concepts, the problems those led to, and the various solutions the different schools offered for them. Only then will we be able to fully appreciate the complex set of arguments put forward by the Yogācāra thinkers themselves.[12] And we shall see that, in important respects, the ālaya-vijñāna is quite the most original solution to the Abhidharmic Problematic – a solution that, while remaining faithful to the presuppositions of the Abhidharma analytic, also harks back to, or rather self-consciously resuscitates, the two dimensions of vijñāna first found undifferentiated in the early teachings of the Pāli texts.

The aim and methods of Abhidharma: *dharma* as irreducible unit of experience

There is little doubt, as Stcherbatsky (1956) suggested long ago, that the central notion of Abhidharma is the concept of *dharma*. There is considerable doubt, however, as to what this elusive term actually refers to. We will suggest a synthetic, and slightly idiosyncratic, interpretation of the term, which we believe usefully elucidates the Abhidharma materials, fully aware of the diversity of interpretations concerning this central, yet – after twenty centuries – still hotly debated notion.

The Abhidharmists took the early Buddhist idea that the beings and things of the world are impermanent, selfless, and dependently arisen and extrapolated it to apply to all phenomena whatsoever. They argued that referring to anything in terms of entities or wholes (e.g. tables, persons, or even thoughts) is merely a conventional way of designating continuing yet provisional collocations of simpler, more fundamental elements or factors, which alone could be said to truly exist. Accordingly, the Abhidharmists, when speaking technically at least, supplanted the everyday conventional expressions found in the early discourses with descriptions of experienced things "as they really are" (*yathābhūtam*). That is, elaborating upon the term used to denote the objects of the sixth, mental mode of cognitive awareness, they described experience in terms of their irreducible *dharmas*. Formulating the doctrine in terms of *dharmas* was of cental importance in Abhidharma, because, as the *Abhidharma-kośa* claims, "apart from the discernment of the dharmas, there is no means to distinguish the defilements (*kleśa*), and it is by reason of the defilements that the world wanders in the ocean of existence" (AKBh I 3).[13] Those topics of the traditional discourses that were not formulated in, or could not be transposed into, dharmic terms were considered to be merely provisional or conventional truth (*saṃvṛtisatya*), whereas the doctrine (*dharma*)[14] as formulated in purely dharmic terms was considered to be the "higher doctrine," the "*abhi*" dharma, because it is turned toward the ultimate *dharma* (*paramārtha-dharma*), that is, towards Nirvana.[15] This analysis of experience in terms of its irreducible constituents, its dharmas, was to irrevocably alter the style and content of Buddhist doctrinal discourse.

Among the many subjects discussed in the Abhidharma literature, particular attention was paid to the analysis of mental processes and their associated activities, since it is these that generate karma. What had begun in the early discourses as a relatively simple if insightful "folk psychology" was gradually transformed into a systematic analysis of the entire world of experience in terms of its momentary and discrete constituents. This involved systematically formalizing the terms used in earlier analyses of mind, such as feeling, apperception, cognition, desire, and so forth, by defining their distinguishing characteristics, specifying the circumstances that condition their arising, and delineating their complex interrelationships. In this way, the ongoing processes of mind were exhaustively analyzed into momentary and discrete units or constituents of experience, discernable through the trained eye of higher insight – they were analyzed, that is, into *dharmas*.

Abhidharma thus became, in Bhikkhu Bodhi's words, a "phenomenological psychology" whose "primary concern ... is to understand the nature of experience, and thus the reality on which it focuses is conscious reality, the world as given in experience" (*Compendium*, 1993: 4). But what does a "phenomenological psychology" mean? And what is a "unit or constituent of experience"? And how is all of this related to vijñāna, the central concept of this book? Consonant with the analytic tenor of the Abhidharma traditions, we must systematically reformulate our earlier approach to cognitive awareness.

One of the standard definitions of cognitive awareness (*vijñāna*) is that it arises as "the discrete discernment [of objects]" (AKBh I 16, *vijñānaṃ prativijñaptiḥ*). Two important implications follow from this. The first is articulated well enough in early Buddhism: that all conditioned phenomena appear impermanent and changing. The second is brought out more clearly in the Abhidharma traditions: that cognitive awareness is not only conditionally arisen, but it arises as a function of discerned distinctions. If we examine the implications of this definition, we can more deeply appreciate the nature of the Abhidharma project, the status of its dharmas, and the entire series of theoretical problems that followed from this innovative mode of analysis.

As we have seen, cognitive awareness arises when a stimulus appears within an appropriate sense domain, impinges upon the sense-faculties (or mind), and there is attention thereto. Cognitive awareness would not arise without the occurrence of this stimulus, without some impingement upon the sense organs and faculties. To speak of the arising of cognitive awareness is therefore to speak of an event, a momentary interaction between sense organs and their correlative stimuli. To say that "everything is impermanent," then, is not so much a declaration about reality as it is, as a description of cognitive awareness as it arises. Cognitive awareness is thus – by definition – temporal and processual.

It is also discriminative. Gregory Bateson makes a suggestively analogous point:

> our sensory system ... can only operate with *events*, which we can call *changes* ... it is true that we think we can see the unchanging ... the truth of the matter is that ... the eyeball has continual tremor, called *micronystagmus*. The eyeball vibrates through a few seconds of arc and thereby causes the optical image on the retina to move relative to the rods and cones which are the sensitive end organs. The end organs are thus in continual receipt of events that correspond to *outlines* in the visible world. We *draw* distinctions; that is, we pull them out. Those distinctions that remain undrawn are *not*.
>
> (Bateson, 1979: 107, emphasis in original)

Without an awareness of such distinctions, without such stimuli, there would be no discernment of discrete objects, no separate "things." This is arguably already implied in the term *vi-jñāna*, whose prefix, *vi-*, imparts a sense of separation or division (cognate with Latin "dis"), suggesting a "discerning or differentiating awareness" (PED 287, 611; SED 961). Cognitive awareness, in other words, necessarily arises as a function of discernment (*prati-vijñapti*).[16] As Bateson observes: "perception operates only upon difference, all receipt of information is necessarily the receipt of news of *difference*" (1979: 31 f., emphasis in original). That is to say, that unless some distinctive stimuli – marked off from others in terms of temperature, brightness, intensity, and so forth – impinges upon the sense faculties and organs, there will be no arising of cognitive awareness.[17] This is not to say that "discrete objects are actively cognized" (see Ch. 1, n. 51), but rather, more subtly, that *the contextual distinctions that make stimuli distinct are themselves constitutive of cognitive awareness in the same way that change is.*

Thus, just as a moment of cognitive awareness arises as a temporally distinct event, so too does it arise in response to contextually distinct phenomenon. These distinctive events are therefore – by the very logic of this mode of analysis – momentary *and* discrete. And it is these events, we suggest, that are called *dharmas*. A *dharma* refers to each of these momentary[18] and distinct events insofar as they give rise to, or perhaps more precisely co-arise with, a moment of cognitive awareness.

An awareness of differences, we see, does not arise outside of a context, since differences are only meaningful between phenomenon. "Objects", that is, give rise to cognitive awareness only insofar as they stand out within a surrounding context. But a distinction is not a "thing." "Difference," as Bateson points out, "being of the nature of relationship, is not located in time or in space… Difference is precisely *not* substance… difference… has no dimensions. It is *qualitative*, not *quantitative*" (Bateson, 1979: 109 f., emphasis in original). This applies, we submit, to dharmas as well. That is, dharmas are neither substances nor "things" in and of themselves. As Piatigorsky points out:

> a *dharma*, in fact, 'is' no thing, yet a term *denoting* (not being) a certain relation or type of relation *to* thought, consciousness or mind. That is, *dharma* is not a concept in the accepted terminological sense of the latter, but a purely *relational notion.*
>
> (Piatigorsky, 1984: 181, emphasis in original)

These distinctive events, these dharmas that co-arise with cognitive awareness, are relational in yet another, more reflexive, sense as well: while dharmas may ultimately refer to experiential phenomena, what *counts* as a dharma in any system of description must itself be distinguished from other dharmas. That is, individual dharmas only occur within a larger context which functions not only cognitively, in conjunction with the forms of sensory cognitive awareness, but – even more importantly – conceptually, within a system of interrelated yet mutually distinctive definitions. In other words, although we can, and must, speak of the definition of each single dharma, we cannot speak of what a dharma "truly is" outside of a given system of analysis wherein such definitions are meaningful.[19]

The meaning and function of any particular dharma is, in other words, dependent on all the other dharmas with which it is contrasted.

Each dharma is therefore defined in terms of, or perhaps more precisely *as*, its own distinguishing mark or identity, its *svalakṣaṇa*,[20] which sets it off from other dharmas. These do not represent unchanging substrates possessing specific attributes, since dharmas are "relational notions," not substances; rather, the distinguishing characteristic (*svalakṣaṇa*) of a dharma is inseparable from the dharma itself.[21] Like the spaces on a chessboard, each dharma thus marks off a notional, logical, and psychological space within a system of description which, in theory, encompasses the entire domain of relevant experience.

And it is this notion of dharmas – as discrete events which carry their own "mark" in conjunction with the arising of cognitive awareness – that became the basic "unit" with which Abhidharma philosophy outlined and analyzed the processes of mind.

This thus entails one further level of reflexivity: an awareness of *doing* analysis. That is to say, extrapolating from dharmas as the second kind of object that gives rise to a moment of mental cognitive awareness, dharmas here also refer to objects of thought and reflection inasmuch as they too impinge upon mind. That is, insofar as the discrete factors that condition the arising of cognitive awareness themselves become objects of thinking *about* cognitive awareness, then these too become dharmas.[22] This is the sense in which Piatigorsky calls Abhidharma a "metapsychology," a system of thought that self-consciously "deals with the various concepts and categories of consciousness as the primary objects of investigation" (1984: 8). This is what we, and we presume Bhikkhu Bodhi, mean by a "phenomenological psychology."

In sum, Abhidharmic discourse expressed in terms of dharmas has several distinct and interrelated characteristics:

(1) it depends upon a *phenomenological* analysis of experience in descriptive terms;
(2) it is *metapsychological* in the sense of being a self-conscious, systematic analysis of experience;
(3) it is a comprehensive description of experience in *systemic* terms, that is, in which all of its items are mutually defined and distinguished from one another; and
(4) finally, Abhidharma thinkers considered an analysis of experience in terms of dharmas as the *only ultimate* account of "how things really are" (*yathā-bhūtam*).

This "dharmic discourse" provided a common language, a shared outlook, for an entire era of Buddhist thinking in India. For while different schools held radically different positions regarding the ontological status of dharmas, their distinctive definitions, and the interrelationships between them, it was only because they shared more or less these same basic assumptions that they could even hold such debates in the first place. This is why, for example, the Yogācārins, who are usually considered idealists, could argue with the Sarvāstivādins, who held to a realist position, or with the Sautrāntikas, who were akin to nominalists.[23] For despite all their differences, they inhabited a shared universe of discourse based upon the primacy and privileging of this specific mode of existential analysis.

Although this notion of dharma may be considered merely an elaboration of traditional Buddhist teachings on impermanence and selflessness, it entails a radically different set of implications. As Stcherbatsky provocatively describes this brave new dharma world:

> The elements of existence [*dharmas*] are momentary appearances, momentary flashings into the phenomenal world out of an unknown source. Just as they are disconnected, so to say, in breadth, not being linked together by any pervading substance, just so are they disconnected in depth or in duration, since they last only one single moment (*kṣaṇa*). They disappear as soon as they appear, in order to be followed the next moment by another momentary existence. Thus a moment becomes a synonym of an element (*dharma*), two moments are two different elements. An element becomes something like a point in time-space. . . . Consequently, the elements do not change, but disappear, the world becomes a cinema. Disappearance is the very essence of existence; what does not disappear does not exist. A cause for the Buddhists was not a real cause but a preceding moment, which likewise arose out of nothing in order to disappear into nothing.[24]
>
> (Stcherbatsky, 1956: 31)

Strange as it may seem, these are precisely the consequences of a phenomenological psychology so construed: the "differences that make a difference," as Bateson famously puts it, that are "not located in time or in space" (1979: 110), that exist only disjunctively and hence relationally, and only insofar as they are transitory events, as they momentarily impinge upon the various sense faculties – these dharmas are, as the *sūtras* continuously state, evanescent like a "dew drop, a bubble, a dream, a lightning flash or a cloud."

As an explanatory system, however, this analysis of experience in terms of such momentary dharmas raises a number of difficult conceptual problems. If dharmas are "disconnected in breadth," to whom or what do they apply? And if they are "disconnected in duration," how can causal conditioning function over time? These became major explanatory challenges for the Abhidharmists, topics that shall be addressed in one form or another throughout the remainder of this book. The Abhidharmists only discussed the first question, that of the referent of personal identity, in fairly limited ways, since it is so largely subsumed within the second question, that of causal continuity. Stcherbatsky suggests the basic Abhidharma approach to this problem, however, when he states above that "a cause is not a real cause but a preceding moment." For although dharmas are insubstantial, discrete, and last no longer than an instant, some of the causal and conditioning influences operating between them, both simultaneously and over succeeding moments, necessarily have longer-lasting effects. Some dharmas, that is, are more equal than others. It is to these sets of problems that we now must turn.

The basic problematic: two levels of discourse, two dimensions of mind

This notion of dharmas as momentary, discrete, and ultimately real constituents of experience created a powerful analytic for ascertaining the characteristics and components of our mental processes; accordingly, Abhidharma theory analyzed the processes of mind and body almost exclusively in these terms. For, as Vasubandhu claims (in AKBh I 3), there is no other way of pacifying the afflictions (*kleśa*) than through the discernment of dharmas, the sole purpose for which Abhidharma was taught.[25] Abhidharma is thus the systematic analysis of the phenomenal world in terms of such discrete and momentary dharmas, directed by the overriding soteriological aim of discerning and eradicating the afflictive emotions (*kleśa*) and thereby abandoning the karmic actions they instigate.

For all its analytic power, however, this analysis of mind in terms of dharmas inadvertently created a host of systemic problems. Although they are complex and tightly interwoven, we will group the problems pertinent to our concerns into two sets:[26] (1) those pertaining to the analysis of momentary, overt processes of mind, enshrined in "dharmic discourse" itself, and (2) those pertaining to the subsisting aspects of the mental stream, which, being nearly inexpressible in dharmic discourse, remained more or less couched in traditional terms.[27] These two sets of doctrinal issues – and their respective discourses – correspond roughly to the two senses of vijñāna discerned in the first chapter: that of momentary cognitive awareness, and that of a subsisting samsaric sentience. We shall return to this point soon enough. But first we must briefly outline these two problematic areas.

First, dharmic analysis dissects experience into discrete components in order to discern how they co-operate, that is, how they operate together within a single moment of mind. This enables one to ascertain whether or not that moment of mind is influenced by the cognitive and emotional afflictions (*kleśa*). This is the paramount aim of analysis because, we remember, it is the afflictions that influence the karmic nature of an action, making it karmically skillful or unskillful. We shall call this analysis of the dharmic factors discernable at any particular moment *synchronic analysis* or *dharmic analysis*, and its doctrinal expressions *synchronic* or *dharmic discourse* – a discourse expressed exclusively in terms of dharmas which last merely a moment and interact only with other simultaneously existing dharmas, or with those of immediately preceding and succeeding moments. The problems that synchronic discourse raises for our purposes primarily concern the ongoing status of the underlying tendencies and the accumulation of karmic potential, and the compatibility of both of these with karmically divergent moments of mind – issues that become particularly acute in connection with the gradual nature of the path to liberation. In other words, the strictures of dharmic discourse created severe problems in accounting for all the pertinent aspects of the mental stream at any given moment.

The second set of problems is in effect the inverse of the first: since only dharma discourse describes "how things truly are," it is only the strictly momentary dharmas that are ultimately real at any given moment. But the indispensable relationship between causal conditioning and temporal continuity, of how the past continues to effect the present, becomes nearly inexpressible in a discourse in which only momentary, currently effective, dharmas are considered to be truly real. Again, this was particularly problematic for such traditional continuities as the accumulation of karmic potential and the persistence of the afflictions in their latent state – continuities whose elimination was the stated purpose of Abhidharmic analysis in the first place. The Abhidharmists, in other words, had from the beginning contextualized their ultimate, dharmic analysis within a larger framework of conventional terms and expressions. In particular, they relied upon such conventional referents as "persons," "mind-streams" (*citta-santāna*), or "bases" (*āśraya*), in order to refer to the ongoing "subjects" of samsaric continuity, all the while recognizing that these could not themselves be considered dharmas,[28] momentary and discrete factors of experience which carry their own mark. We shall call this continued reliance upon traditional continuities *diachronic* or *santāna discourse*. The persistence of these modes of expression in the face of Abhidharmic claims to ultimate discourse represents more than mere vestiges of pre-Abhidharmic thinking, however; it also reflects the inherent difficulties of the Abhidharma project as a whole.

This created a dilemma for Abhidharmic theory. On the one hand, the active influences of the afflictions and the type of actions they instigate are expressible in ultimate dharmic terms only to the extent that they are immediate factors of experience. As Piatigorsky rightly observes, "the Abhidhamma is a 'theory of consciousness'" (1988: 202, n. 17); anything outside of the arising of conscious awareness is inexpressible in dharmic terms. On the other hand, the continuity of the factors constituting individual samsaric existence *in toto* can only be described in the more conventional, non-dharmic terms of the diachronic mental stream. But by its very method, Abhidharma explicitly privileges the first discourse at the expense of the second. *And this exclusive validity accorded to the synchronic analysis of momentary mental processes threatened to render that very analysis religiously vacuous by undermining the validity of its overall soteriological context – the diachronic dimension of samsaric continuity and its ultimate cessation.*[29] This is, in short, the Abhidharmic Problematic.

We shall examine the development of the synchronic analysis of mind-moments, its continued reliance upon the diachronic discourse of samsaric continuities, and the multiple problems provoked by the fateful disjunction between them. We shall find that this disjunction became more untenable as the implications of the exclusive adherence to synchronic, dharmic analysis became more fully realized. And we shall see that here too, vijñāna is not only central to both of these discourses, but that these discourses correspond closely to the two aspects of vijñāna we discerned in the early texts. In contrast to materials in the Pāli texts, however, their differentiation in the Abhidharma was explicit, the problems it raised were recognized, and some kind of solution to those problems was proposed by nearly all of the schools we have sufficient knowledge about (see Appendix II).

Although the various Abhidharma schools acknowledged and addressed these problems, they were understandably loath to forego the analytic power of dharmic discourse. It was, roughly speaking, this continued disjunction – entailed by a dogged adherence to the exclusive validity of dharmic discourse in the face of the acknowledged and obvious dependence upon diachronic, santāna discourse – that, in our analysis, generated the Abhidharmic Problematic toward which the ālaya-vijñāna was addressed. To appreciate this, however, we must examine the specific systems of mental analysis and particular terms in which these issues were couched.

Analysis of mind and its mental factors

Abhidharmic analysis focuses upon *citta*, roughly "mind," and the mental processes that occur simultaneously with it at any given moment. The term *citta*, "thought" or "mind,"[30] has an ancient pedigree in the earliest Buddhist texts, denoting the basic process of mind[31] which can become contaminated or purified by the nature of one's actions, and, for some at least, eventually liberated.[32] It is what we might loosely call the "subject" of samsara. The karmic nature of each moment of *citta* is determined by the particular kinds of mental processes or factors (*caitta* or *cetasika*, derived from *citta*, meaning "mental") that occur with and accompany it. As with *citta* itself, all of these mental factors (*caitta*) are dharmas, that is, momentary events arising in conjunction with cognitive awareness and discerned in analytic insight. Most of them, such as sensation, intention, feeling, apperception, etc., were already used in earlier Buddhist doctrine.

These mental factors, these *caitta*, play an especially important role in Abhidharmic analysis because it is the particular kind of relationship they have with the central locus of mind, with *citta*, that determines the karmic quality of that mind-moment.[33] Generally speaking, a moment of *citta* and its concomitant mental factors (*caitta*) stand in reciprocal relation with each other,[34] a relationship which is karmically neutral; that is, they simply co-occur. However, when particular mental processes arise in reference to the same cognitive object and through the same perceptual faculty, they so closely follow and envelop (*anuparivartana*) that central locus of mind (*citta*) that that moment of *citta* as a whole takes on the karmic qualities of the factors accompanying it (Stcherbatsky, 1956: 25–6). This close relationship is called "conjoined" or "associated" with mind (*citta-saṃprayukta*).[35] In other words, it is the processes that are "associated" with a moment of *citta* that determine the karmic nature of the actions in that moment. For example, when afflictive emotions such as anger or lust arise, they are "associated" with that moment of *citta*, karmically coloring whatever actions (including mental actions) they accompany. Consonant with the earlier definition of karma as intentional action, it is therefore the *intention* (*cetanā*, one of the primary mental factors) which accompanies and motivates an action that determines its karmic nature,[36] that determines what effects it will accrue for the future.

Accordingly, these moments of mind and their associated mental factors, together with the actions they instigate, are classified in terms of the results they lead to: actions that produce pleasant or desirable results are called "skillful" or "healthy" (*kuśala*); actions that produce unpleasant or undesirable results are "unskillful" or "unhealthy" (*akuśala*);[37] and actions which produce neither are considered neutral or indeterminate (*avyākṛta*). In this fashion, all moments of mind were categorized according to their motivating intentions, the actions they accompany, and the results they potentially lead to.[38]

The complete Abhidharma analysis of mind and its processes, which quickly becomes extremely complicated and technical,[39] is beyond the scope of this study. The main point for our purposes is that the karmic quality of each mind-moment as a whole is determined by, and hence categorized in terms of, the particular relationship between the *citta* and the mental factors that accompany it. That is, its karmic quality is determined by whether those accompanying processes influence and envelope that *citta* in the karmically significant relationship called "associated" (*citta-saṃprayukta*), or whether they accompany mind in one of several less influential, and hence karmically neutral, relationships such as being simultaneous (*sahabhū*) with, or being "disjoined" or "dissociated" from mind (*citta-viprayukta*). This last is particularly noteworthy.

While most ordinary active mental processes directly influence that moment of *citta*, and are therefore "associated with mind" (*citta-saṃprayukta*), the Abhidharmists realized that there are many other processes which co-occur in a moment of *citta* that are much less obtrusive and thus have little or no karmic influence. Some of these were categorized as "karmic formations dissociated from mind" (*citta-viprayukta-saṃskāra*),[40] a category consisting primarily of such anomalous factors as "life power" (*jīvitendriya*), or the very nature of dharmas to arise, abide, and fade away (*jāti-*, *sthiti-*, *jarā-lakṣaṇa*). This indeterminate category was flexible enough to encompass dharmas of various kinds and often on radically different grounds. It comprised, in effect, whatever processes were needed to give a coherent account of the continuity of experience, but not influential enough to affect it in a karmically determinate manner; hence they were called karmically "indeterminate" (*avyākṛta*). The very existence of such a category already suggests some of the difficulties a purely synchronic analysis of mind entails. For an analysis of the overt and obvious activities of mind alone necessarily neglects many factors that are essential to, and constitutive of, experience at any given moment. It was for this reason that the ongoing influence of the underlying tendencies (*anuśaya*) and accumulated karmic potential, for example, were often discussed in connection with this category. Indeed, these particular topics became the focus of considerable debate in the *Abhidharma-kośa*, a debate in which an underlying, karmically neutral basis of mind called "ālaya" vijñāna eventually participated as well.

The initial formulation of the problematic in its synchronic dimension: the accumulation of karmic potential, the presence of the underlying tendencies, and their gradual purification in the Kathāvatthu

By asserting that the ultimate account of "how things actually are" comprises only the processes discernable at the moment, synchronic dharmic analysis not only renders individual continuity problematic (to which we will return shortly), but it undermines the integrity of the individual mind-stream at any particular moment. For it precludes any ultimate account of the very factors that define one's samsaric existence: the presence of accumulated karmic potential (*karmopacaya*) and the persistence of the underlying tendencies, both of which – by definition – are not fully active in every single moment. Following the strictures of dharmic analysis, however, they must be ascertainable in the moment-to-moment analysis of mind in terms of dharmas in order to be considered ultimately true.

Clearly, the present, active, and overt processes of mind, with all their associated and karmically determinative mental processes, cannot comprise the entirety of any individual "mental stream." If they did, this would lead to either of two equally unacceptable consequences. On the one hand, if even a single moment of mind arose that was associated with skillful mental factors, this would, in and of itself, sever the continuity of the accumulated karmic potential and the latent afflictions – and this would virtually constitute liberation. But if, in order to uphold their continuity, one held that the persisting accumulation of karmic potential and latent afflictions were continuously active, karmically, then *all* moments of mind would have to be afflicted and karmically skillful processes would never be able to occur. This raises several vexing questions: if these potentialities were not active, then in what way could they still be present, in order to accord with the Abhidharmic criteria for dharmas? But if they were present, then why would they not influence that *citta* in a karmically effective way? Moreover, how could the latent tendencies together with both skillful and unskillful accumulated karmic potential co-exist in the same moment of mind, if that moment is to be characterized as exclusively skillful, unskillful, or neutral? The answer seems clear enough: the present and active processes of mind described in dharmic analysis simply cannot comprise the entirety of mind at any given moment. These issues were raised earlier in our discussion of the latent tendencies in the early Pāli texts, but here they are couched in terms of the Abhidharma analytic, which renders them particularly problematic.

These problems were recognized at a very early stage in the Abhidharma literature and were crucial in the development of the concept of the ālaya-vijñāna.

We can trace the debate over these three specific issues – the persistence of the latent tendencies toward the afflictions, the persistence of accumulated karmic potential, and the gradual elimination of these afflictions along the path to liberation – as far back as the *Kathāvatthu* (*Disputed Matters*), the fifth book of the Pāli *Abhidhamma-piṭaka*, still associated with the present-day Theravādins. As its name suggests, the *Kathāvatthu* is a compendium of disputes with various opponents, presented from the Sthaviravāda/Theravāda point of view and ostensibly dating from the second–third century BCE. The fact that these issues were recognized as problematic at such an early date[41] demonstrates their centrality for Abhidharma dogmatics: for they are framed in the *Kathāvatthu* in nearly the same fashion, and discussed in nearly the same technical vocabulary, as they are in the *Abhidharma-kośa*, some seven centuries later. Nothing so clearly illustrates the common parameters of the Abhidharma Problematic throughout the early Indian Buddhist world as the continuity, ubiquity, and specificity of these debates, from the *Kathāvatthu* to the *Abhidharma-kośa* to the Yogācāra texts on the ālaya-vijñāna. The *Kathāvatthu* provides us, therefore, with a brief preview of these issues.

* * *

First, the accumulation of karmic potential. In the *Abhidharma-kośa* Vasubandhu distinguishes between an action that is fully accomplished and its mere accumulation (*upacaya*).[42] Accumulation is defined there as the accumulation, until their fruit ripens, of those intentional actions which necessarily give a result.[43] That is, it refers to the *potentiality* for the results of some specific karmic action to come to fruition at some time in the future. The distinction between karmic action and its accumulated potential, as well as the way this accumulated potential may persist, can be traced to such early passages as seen in Chapter 1: "I declare, monks, that actions willed, performed and accumulated will not become extinct as long as their results have not been experienced" (A V 292). The extent of this distinction, however, and the precise status of this accumulated karmic potential within both the momentary processes of mind and the continuity of the mental stream, were "disputed matters." The *Kathāvatthu* (XV 11, *Kammūpacayakathā*) preserves an interesting debate on just this question: How can there be a distinct accumulation of karma within the mental stream which does not simultaneously influence the moment-to-moment processes of mind?

The interlocutors who are heterodox from the Theravādin perspective respond with two innovative suggestions. First, they suggest that, in contrast to action (P. *kamma*; S. *karma*) itself, its mere accumulation (*upacaya*)[44] occurs simultaneously (*sahajā*) with, but not conjoined to, active processes that are karmically incompatible with it – on the grounds that the nature of the accumulation is not determined by the nature of the actions with which it co-exists. And, also unlike action, which is bound to the present moment of *citta*, the accumulation of karmic potential does not cease when each moment of *citta* with which it co-occurs does. Therefore, this karmic accumulation is neither *associated*

(P. *sampayutta*; S. *samprayukta*) with that *citta*, nor does it arise in conjunction with an epistemic object (*anārammaṇo*).[45] According to the commentary, the accumulation of *kamma* is therefore karmically neutral.[46] In other words, in these schools' view at least, the influences from past actions persist relatively independently of other overt processes of mind.[47]

Much the same conclusions are found in discussions (IX. 4; XI. 1) concerning the nature, persistence, and eradication of the latent afflictions. The underlying tendencies to the afflictions (*anusaya*) are said to be dissociated from mind (*citta-vippayutta*), without an epistemic object (*anārammaṇo*), and karmically neutral; they too are therefore compatible with present mental processes with which they are karmically heterogeneous.[48] It thus follows, according to the heterodox position, that these latent dispositions should be distinguished from their more active, manifest counterparts, the "outbursts" of the afflictions (*pariyuṭṭhāna*),[49] a distinction we saw was intimated in the early Pāli texts and which will be explicitly made in the *Abhidharma-kośa*.

The latent and manifest afflictions were distinguished not only for these reasons, but also due to the inability of synchronic analysis to account for their gradual purification along the path toward liberation, the third major conundrum of Abhidharma synchronic analysis. Consider, for example, the case of an Aryan, one who is well on the way to liberation and has already largely eradicated the afflictions, but who has a momentary relapse, an outburst of an ancient affliction. From what causes could this relapse arise, the interlocutor asks, if that outburst were not conditioned by the underlying tendency to that affliction? The question implies that if no distinction were made between their latent and manifest conditions, then the latent afflictions should have been completely eradicated at the same time as the Aryan eradicated the manifest afflictions. In other words, if there were no difference between the manifest and latent afflictions there could be no partial eradication; and if there were no such partial eradication there could be no backsliding and a true Aryan would therefore never be able to have such an unskillful moment of mind.[50] But, all the schools seem to agree, this is not the case – relapses happen.

As we can see, even at this early stage problems arose from the exclusive validity accorded to the analysis of manifest activities at the expense of the latent influences from the past and their continuing potential to influence present and future experience. How could actions performed in the distant past continue to affect the present and future if the only truly real dharmas are those discernible in an analysis of momentarily discernible processes of mind? Conze has aptly summed up the entire problematic created by the synchronic analysis:

> The fact that a mental state is definitely abandoned or definitely established lies outside the momentary series of states, and so does permanent ownership or potential ownership of a spiritual skill. ... It looks as if not only actualities but also potentialities must be accepted as real. People not only do things but have the 'power' to do or not to do them.

> A person can call upon such powers, in the same way in which one is said to 'know' French, although no French word may occur in the present moment of consciousness. It is very hard to maintain the view that a person should at any given time be identified with just the one [set of] dharma[s] which is in him from moment to moment.... the dogmatic assertion of instantaneousness could be made credible only by introducing a number of pseudo-permanencies.
>
> (Conze, 1973: 138)

In short, this system had to be modified. Either it must be admitted that each moment of mind is comprised of multiple processes encompassing mutually contradictory factors, some latent and some active, some skillful and some unskillful, such as the heterodox schools in the *Kathāvatthu* suggest; or else it should be admitted that the synchronic analysis of mind expressed solely in terms of present, manifest processes is unable to account for all the pertinent aspects of one's mental stream. That is, either some of the presuppositions of analysis must be fundamentally altered, or else dharmic analysis alone must be seen as inadequate and its claims to be an ultimate account of "how things really are" (*yathābhūtam*) must be compromised or complemented by non-dharmic elements. We shall see examples of both of these strategies in the approaches of different schools below.

To compound the problem even further, the claims for the exclusive validity of synchronic analysis not only made the *presence* of the underlying tendencies and accumulated karmic potential difficult to account for, but it also rendered their *persistence* over time problematic as well – which in turn rendered samsaric continuity in general problematic. But to understand why these became problematic in diachronic as well as synchronic terms, we must look more closely at the categories the Abhidharmists developed to describe the causal and conditioning influences that permeate and guide the continuous flow of dharmas from one moment to the next. For it was the difficulties of combining this doctrine of radical momentariness with the strictures of conditioned succession over time that generated the specifics of the Abhidharma Problematic.

The problematic in its diachronic dimension: immediate succession versus the continuity of karmic potential

It is apparent that the synchronic analysis based upon dharmic discourse is, by itself, an incomplete account of samsaric existence, since it is necessarily embedded within the larger temporal context of samsaric continuity (and cessation) wherein it finds its ultimate meaning and purpose. It is, for example, only within the context of the ongoing continuity of mind that our responses to stimuli develop into the habits that keep us bound to cyclic existence. These entrenched "habits of the heart" can be neither fully described nor even fully discernible in terms of an analysis that limits itself to strictly transient, momentary phenomena. An angry reaction to a moment of pain, in other words, may readily be seen as a dharma, but the *disposition* to get angry, an angry temperament, may not; it belongs to a different level of discourse. Specifically, it is only over the long term that the inertia of accumulated karmic potential, the persistence of the ingrained afflictive dispositions (*anuśaya*), and their gradual elimination along the path to liberation, become fully discernible. The ultimate soteriological aim of the synchronic analysis, its very *raison d'être*, is thus established only in reference to the diachronic stream of mind (*citta-santāna*) coursing through samsaric existence. A snapshot of our status quo reveals neither the direction nor the intensity of our karmic trajectory. This requires a longer view.

The synchronic analysis of mind depends upon the diachronic dimension in deeper and more specific ways as well. Insofar as it represents the relationship between cause and effect, karma has no meaning outside of this extended temporal dimension, for the karmic nature of an action is established only by reference to its (expected) future result.[51] Even more crucially, the continued functioning of karma (as this relation between cause and effect) requires not just continuity in general but, in Abhidharma dharmic discourse, *an unbroken stream of causal links until their fruit ripens of the potential to give rise to future results.*[52] This simply follows from the constraints of the system: since dharmas last for only an instant, they neither endure nor change into other dharmas; rather, as with the formula of dependent arising, they condition the arising of succeeding dharmas. As Stcherbatsky pointed out above, "a cause ... [is] not a real cause but a preceding moment" (1956: 31). Therefore, it was imperative for dharmic discourse to be able to explain how the ongoing processes of mind could continuously condition the arising of succeeding processes – to explain, that is, how our accumulated potentials and behavioral tendencies are able to continuously perpetuate themselves in terms of moment-to-moment patterns of succession. For, in the context of dharmic discourse, our world of experience must be sufficiently explicable in terms of the moment-to-moment succession of one configuration of dharmas after another in order for us to fulfill the stated purpose of "discerning the dharmas in order to extinguish the afflictions."

As we observed in the first chapter, describing the patterns of causal or conditional arising is exactly what the series of dependent arising is all about. It outlines the conditions under which concomitant factors typically give rise to certain phenomena, that is, "visual cognitive awareness arises dependent upon the eye organ and a visual form," and so on. As with other doctrines inherited from the early discourses, the Abhidharmists analyzed these simple patterns of conditional arising and categorized the causal relationships between them into complex systems of causes, conditions, and results (*hetu*, *pratyaya*, *phala*).[53] By this means, the Abhidharmists described the patterns and processes which continuously condition the evolving stream of momentary phenomena that constitute our worldly experience. These articulated relationships of causal arising – the interrelations between the causes, conditions, and results – are the woof that threads the warp of momentary processes into the recurrent patterns of everyday experience.

In general, then, the totality of dharmas of each moment must not only reflect the entire trajectory of the mental stream from moment to moment and from life to life, including the persistence of the latent dispositions and the karmic accumulation that accompany it. The dharmas must also arise in an unbroken stream or chain of causal links that proceeds from moment to moment, conditioned by nothing other than these discrete, instantaneous, yet exclusively ultimate dharmas themselves. In other words, the Abhidharma project must not only account for how these latent processes can be continuously *present*, in terms of the synchronic analysis of mind examined above, but also how they can be uninterruptedly *continuous* in this larger diachronic sense. This is, roughly, what the system of causes, conditions, and results sets out to do.

Although any comprehensive account of causal conditionality within Abhidharma theory needs to examine the entire system of the causes, conditions, and results, we can only focus upon those that were crucial to the development of the concept of the ālaya-vijñāna, particularly those underlying the arguments presented in its defense. These primarily involve incompatibilities between the "homogeneous and immediately antecedent condition" (*samanantara-pratyaya*), on the one hand, and the crucial relationship between the cause and result of karmic maturation (*vipāka-hetu* and *-phāla*) on the other hand. The homogeneous and immediately antecedent condition designates the conditioning influences that a particular dharma exerts upon an immediately succeeding dharma of the *same type*; a moment of anger or apperception, for example, conduces to the arising of another moment of anger, and so on. The relationship between the cause and effect of karmic maturation, by contrast, refers to the fundamental relationship in which karmic causality is thought to operate over extended periods of time. As the very kernel of karmic theory, this relationship is crucial to the entire Abhidharma system and, in one way or another, to every Buddhist system.[54] But it also conflicts with the characteristics of the "homogeneous and immediately antecedent condition," for the results of maturation are neither homogeneous nor immediately antecedent.

A "cause of maturation" (*vipāka-hetu*) is an intentional action which eventually leads to a "ripened" or "matured fruit," a "result of maturation" (*vipāka-phala*).[55] Unlike their originating causes, these results are not intentional actions and are therefore karmically indeterminate (*avyākṛta-dharma*), that is, they are neither unskillful (*akuśala*) nor skillful (*kuśala*), and thus entail no karmic fruit of their own. The matured fruit differs from its cause in this way: it is karmically "heterogeneous" to it (the sense of the prefix *vi-* here). Moreover, and most importantly, this fruit reaches maturation neither simultaneously with nor immediately succeeding its initiating cause, but only after an intervening period.[56] In order to connect these events of cause and effect – in order for karma to work – there must be an unbroken stream of karmic potentiality, a stream of dharmas, flowing between its initiating cause and its final fruit, *regardless of the nature of the other dharmas that arise in the meantime*. The fruit of karmic maturation is thus both heterogeneous to and temporally distinct from its cause. These two characteristics together raise some serious problems.

Generally, mental processes tend to give rise to succeeding processes of a similar kind; a karmically skillful (*kuśala*) process gives rise to another karmically skillful one rather than an unskillful one (*akuśala*). This is the kind of succession that the homogeneous and immediately antecedent condition refers to.[57] For heterogeneous fruition to work, however, that is, *for karma to work*, succession cannot be both "homogeneous" and "immediately antecedent" at the same time.[58] The fruit of karmic maturation comes to fruition after an intervening period of time, following dharmas that are typically of a different karmic nature (since the fruit of karmic maturation is always karmically neutral). This raises two now familiar sets of problems – synchronic and diachronic.

First, if these heterogeneous results (*vipāka-phala*) were not conditioned by their immediately antecedent homogeneous conditions, then they must be conditioned by causes that occurred at some earlier time. But the original action, the cause of karmic maturation (*vipāka-hetu*), would have already disappeared. So how could actions that occurred in the distant past be capable of conditioning the occurrence of resultant dharmas in the present?[59] In other words, in order for these resultant dharmas to arise there must be some present dharma which conditions their present arising. And this dharma is itself the present link of that unbroken chain of links that continues from moment to moment between the cause of karmic maturation and its effect. But where or how can this present causal influence be accounted for in the momentary analysis of mind based upon present, discernable dharmas? What is its exact status?

The second question is that of succession. Not only must there be a continuous stream of dharmas linking the cause and effect of karmic maturation, but the effect of maturation comes to fruition mediately, not *im*mediately, after its cause. It thus arises immediately after some other dharma which is karmically unrelated to it. Karmic maturation, in short, typically occurs by means of heterogeneous succession – the immediate succession of dharmas of divergent natures. But, if this maturational fruit is not brought into fruition by the immediately preceding dharma, what exactly is the cause of its current arising?

In sum, not only is the presence of these forces problematic in the synchronic sense, as we first observed, but so is their continued persistence in the diachronic sense. These are, in effect, two sides of the same coin, since continuity requires moment-to-moment links in the present in order to persist, while present existence, even in a latent state, requires continuous antecedent conditions in order to exist.

Such were the problems dharmic discourse raised for karmic theory. The same kinds of question were also raised by the long-term persistence of the latent dispositions: how can they continue in an unbroken series if they are not present in each moment? Yet how could they be "present" if they were not somehow effective? This also raised corollary questions concerning the graduated nature of the path to liberation: Can a simple, karmically skillful state ever be *completely* free of the latent dispositions? If so, then their continuity would be cut and they would no longer have any immediately antecedent conditions for their future arising. And if the continuity of the latent dispositions was totally severed in this way during a moment of karmically skillful mind, then why would one not immediately become liberated? A corollary to this question is that, if only momentary mental processes are ultimately true, the continuity of attainments acquired along the path – some of which would not reach full fruition until many lifetimes later[60] – could hardly be maintained during the diverse types of mental processes that occur in the meantime.

All three of these – the relationship between maturational cause and effect, the persistence of the latent afflictions, and the graduated path to purification – necessarily concern potentialities rather than actualities. They belie the consonance between the exclusive reliance on the dharmic analysis of momentary states and the inescapably temporal dimensions of samsaric continuity, and betray the dissonance between synchronic and diachronic levels of discourse. That is, even though the synchronic dharmic analysis was considered the only ultimate discourse, Abhidharma could not dispense with the diachronic context that provided its larger soteriological framework. For, as stated in the *Abhidharma-kośa* and consonant with the traditional themes of Indian Buddhist thought, the ultimate purpose of this synchronic analysis was to ascertain the underlying motivations, and thus the karmic nature, of one's actions, in order to diminish the overpowering influence of the afflictions, cease accumulating karmic potential, and thereby gradually progress along the path toward liberation. And all of these are only intelligible in terms of diachronic discourse – in terms, that is, of continuities within one's own mental stream.

Moreover, like traditionalists everywhere, Abhidharma authors were loath to dispense with these traditional teachings; so they also faithfully preserved and transmitted the teachings that contextualized their innovative dharma discourse. It was the continuing validity, nay the necessity, of just these traditional doctrines that, when juxtaposed with the newer analytic, raised so many controversial questions and propelled so many doctrinal disputes.

Abhidharma doctrine had thus reached an impasse. What was needed was a single system of dharmic analysis that could overcome these contradictions by either incorporating elements of diachronic discourse into the newly authoritative, synchronic analysis; or, conversely, by modifying Abhidharma's claims for exclusive ultimacy and acknowledging the equal authority of traditional diachronic discourse. Each of these approaches was taken by the two opposing schools represented in the *Abhidharma-kośa*. The first strategy was attempted by the "pan-realist" Sarvāstivādins, who posited both the atemporal reality of dharmas in the past, present, and future (hence, their name, the "All-Exists School"), as well as an ad hoc dharma called "possession" (*prāpti*) which, appropriately enough, held everything together. The Sautrāntikas, on the other hand, took the second tack and sidestepped dharmic exclusivity altogether (consistent with their name, "Those Who Followed Sūtras" instead of Abhidharma). They introduced the avowedly provisional, non-dharmic concept of "seeds" (*bīja*) as a metaphor for both the potential of karmic fruition and the underlying dispositions. This fertile metaphor was not only an offshoot from canonical vijñāna theory, but also became the seminal notion around which the ālaya-vijñāna system of mind grew and developed. The ālaya-vijñāna system in turn represents the third, and in some senses most innovative, approach to the Abhidharma Problematic: by combining aspects of the other two, the Yogācārin thinkers created a single, integrated model which fully embraced the synchronic analysis of momentary dharmas, while at the same time incorporating the diachronic elements describing the continuity of the karmic potential and the persistence of the latent dispositions symbolized by the metaphors of seeds and scents (*vāsanā*).

Before we approach these developments, however, we need to examine how much Abhidharma doctrine continued to rely upon diachronic discourse for its larger metaphysical context, and how this too helped shape the various responses to the Abhidharma Problematic. For the notion of ālaya-vijñāna developed both in dialogue with, and by building upon, these other particular responses.

The persistence of traditional continuities: karma and *kleśa* in the *Abhidharma-kośa*

We have introduced important parts of the newer synchronic analysis of mind and discussed some of its tensions with the more traditional continuities equally preserved and revered by the Abhidharma writers. These traditional doctrines, and the discourses of the Buddha through which they were transmitted, were constantly cited in Abhidharma texts as the basis for this or that particular idea or interpretation. Abhidharmic ideas were typically presented, not as the innovative departures they often were, but as a more systematic and precise interpretation of the discourses upon which they commonly drew.[61] We will now examine some passages of the *Abhidharma-kośa* that preserve these traditional doctrines, particularly concerning the key issues we have been discussing: the persistence of the underlying tendencies, the accumulation of karmic potential, and the gradual nature of the path to liberation. These issues were, however, interpreted quite differently by the two schools represented in the *Abhidharma-kośa*, the Sautrāntikas and the Sarvāstivādins.[62] Since they epitomize in so many ways the diachronic and synchronic discourses, respectively, their approaches well illustrate the general parameters of the Abhidharma Problematic. What, then, does the *Kośa* have to say about karma and *kleśa*?

As in early Buddhism, the afflictions (*kleśa*) remain indispensable for the perpetuation of samsaric existence. According to the *Kośa*, it is the actions performed, permeated and influenced by the afflictions, that increase the mind-stream and propel the wheel of life:

> In accordance with the projective [cause] (*ākṣepa*-[*hetu*]) the mental stream (*santāna*) increases gradually by the afflictions and karma and goes again into the next world.... Such is the circle of existence without beginning.
>
> (AKBh III 19a–d)[63]

And what is it that gives rise to the afflictions and the karmic actions they inform? As we found discussed in the Pāli texts many hundreds of years earlier, and in the *Kathāvatthu* in between, it is the underlying dispositions (*anuśaya*) that play this critical role. "From what causes do the afflictions arise?" the *Kośa* asks:

> The affliction with complete causes [arises] from non-abandoned underlying dispositions, from the presence of an object, and from incorrect comprehension (*ayoniśo manaskāra*).
>
> (AKBh *ad* V 34)[64]

That is, the circle of birth and death would not continue without the underlying dispositions giving rise to active cognitive and emotional afflictions, arising in conjunction with specific objects and (mis)informed by ignorance. Amongst these conditions, it is the underlying dispositions that are paramount. Indeed, they are given an astoundingly important cosmogonic role[65] in the *Kośa*:

> It is said [AKBh IV 1] that the world in its variety arises from action (*karma*). It is because of the underlying dispositions that actions accumulate (*upacita*); but without the underlying dispositions they are not capable of giving rise to a new existence. Thus, the underlying dispositions should be known as the root of existence (*mūlaṃ bhava*).
>
> (AKBh *ad* V 1a)[66]

The underlying dispositions are the "root of existence" because it is they that give rise to the afflictions which, with the actions they inform, propel "the circle of existence without beginning." The *Abhidharma-kośa* thus preserves the same cyclic pattern – of action, results, afflictive reaction to these results, leading to further afflicted action and so on – that we found in the early Pāli texts, but it elaborates upon this, particularly on the relationship between the underlying dispositions and the manifest afflictions, in an interesting and compellingly modern way.

Actions, we have seen, are analyzed into the kind of results they lead to: skillful (*kuśala*) actions lead to agreeable results, ease and well-being; unskillful (*akuśala*) actions lead to disagreeable results, dis-ease and ill-being; and neutral actions to neither. In other words, actions are categorized by whether they conduce to (*-nīyam*) a pleasant feeling (*sukhavedanīyam*), an unpleasant one (*duḥkhavedanīyam*), or neither, since, as in the Pāli texts, one of the predominant (*pradhānaḥ*) results of actions, is feeling (*vedanā*).[67] And closely connected with the particular feelings that results from these actions, also in accordance with the early texts, are the latent dispositions – that is, the latent disposition toward "passion underlies (*anuśete*) pleasurable feeling, aversion underlies unpleasant feeling, and ignorance underlies neutral feelings" (AKBh V 45).[68]

The *Abhidharma-kośa* analyzes these processes, however, in considerably more detail than in the early texts. What is particularly suggestive is its elaboration of the relationship between these underlying dispositions and the conditions, the particular "objects," that provoke them. A disposition to sensual desire, the text states (nearly tautologically), is activated whenever a dharma that provokes an outburst of sensual desire (*kāmarāga-paryavasthānīya-dharma*) appears in the appropriate sense field and one has not abandoned or correctly understood the latent disposition thereto (*rāgānuśaya*) – all of this, of course, being rooted in ignorance.[69] Why is it, though, that certain phenomena (*dharma*) provoke an outburst of a particular affliction as long as one has not abandoned the disposition toward that affliction? In a passage closely resembling psychoanalytic conceptions of "invested" (*besetzen*, usually "cathected") objects, the *Kośa* says that "the latent disposition of a certain person is disposed toward a certain object; he is *bound* to it by that [disposition]."[70] That is, each type of affliction, even in its latent state, reacts to certain objects in certain habitual ways because, the text continues, "that [disposition] which is associated (*saṃprayukta*) with that [dharma] is attached (*saṃprayoga*) to it."[71] When one abandons an affliction and its latent disposition, however, one is no longer attached to these objects (dharma) and that affliction does not arise depending upon them.[72] This is brought about through the complete understanding that is progressively realized along the Buddhist path toward liberation.[73]

The close and productive relationship between karma, the afflictions (*kleśa*), and the continuous turning of the wheel of death and rebirth is now painfully clear: karma that is instigated by the afflictions accumulates the potential for results to be experienced in accordance with their originating intentions. These results (*vipāka*) are experienced as pleasant or unpleasant feelings or sensations (*vedanā*), since feeling is the predominant result of karma. Underlying these particular feelings are particular tendencies, so that whenever these feelings arise, as a result of past karma and in connection with dharmas that provoke their related afflictions (*kāmarāga-paryavasthānīya*), these feelings tend to provoke the underlying afflictions, which in turn are necessary for creating fresh karma. In short, karmic action creates results which are experienced as feelings, which evoke the active counterparts (*kleśa*) of the afflictions underlying them, which then lead to more karmically productive activities, which produce more results, and so on, ensuring the perpetuation of cyclic existence.

No wonder the latent dispositions are considered the root of existence. They permeate the mental stream and increase it through the accumulation of projective karma, setting up an energetic (*vipacyate*)[74] process that creates its own momentum, perpetuating the circle of life in endless cycles of action–results–reaction–more action. These two factors – the mass of accumulated potential karma ready to come to fruition, and the latent afflictions predisposed to flare up when it does – constitute the underlying energetic potential that perpetuates, indeed virtually constitutes, individual continuity within samsara. Though this mass of accumulated karma and affective habits is nothing more than what has been constructed out of previous afflicted activities, it has momentum, energy, and inertia. It persists, moreover, in a latent or potential fashion, constantly conditioning and provoking manifest mental processes. These manifest processes, informed by past experience and driven by the inertia of habitual responses played out in the patterns of dependent arising, in turn reinforce that very inertia, those very patterns, just as the ongoing current of water creates and deepens its own stream-bed, while the stream-bed in turn influences the direction and flow of current. This stream-bed of constructed behavioral patterns directing the flow of the mind-stream, which in combination with external conditions also gives rise to the surface waves of mental activity, will be made quite explicit in the Yogācāra model of mind centered around the ālaya-vijñāna.

This much, however, can be considered more of an elaboration of the dynamics underlying dependent arising than any real departure from its earlier expressions. But it raised serious problems for Abhidharma dogmatics by bringing to center-stage those processes that were least expressible in terms of the synchronic analysis of mind. The status of the accumulation of karmic potential and the persistence of the underlying dispositions were thus hotly debated in the *Abhidharma-kośa*. While the debates remained largely within the parameters (and even the vocabulary) adumbrated centuries earlier in the *Kathāvatthu*, the positions presented in the *Kośa* offer two distinctive and instructive approaches to the persisting Abhidharma Problematic.

Abhidharmic responses to the problematic

This connection between the underlying tendencies, their manifest afflictions, and the accumulation of karmic potential, clearly continued to play a fundamental role in the metapsychology and soteriology of Indian Buddhist thought. These became problematic, however, once there was any serious attempt to describe these processes in terms of the synchronic dharmic analysis. Limited to momentary dharmas, Abhidharma discourse seemed unable to account for these ongoing continuities of samsaric existence. In response to this situation, the two schools represented in the *Abhidharma-kośa*, the Sarvāstivādins and Sautrāntikas, each postulated some mode of mental continuity that could subsist without being karmically involved with the overtly active processes of mind (i.e. without being "associated with mind," *citta-saṃprayukta*). The particulars of these responses take us well beyond the positions, though hardly the issues, we first saw in the *Kathāvatthu*, and in so doing introduce two important new approaches.

The Sarvāstivādins gave priority to Abhidharma analysis. Consonant with the orthodox position in the *Kathāvatthu*, they simply equated the underlying tendencies (*anuśaya*) with the manifest afflictions (*kleśa*), reflecting their strong commitment to dharmic discourse and a corresponding reluctance to course in any mental factors, dispositions, or potentialities inexpressible in those terms. Distinguishing between the active and latent conditions of the afflictions is, in their view, simply mistaken. The Sautrāntikas, on the other hand, citing scripture, insisted upon the distinction between the latent dispositions (*anuśaya*) and their manifest counterparts (*kleśa*). This not only reflects their loyalties to "*sūtric*" teachings over Abhidharmic theory, but also calls upon their major innovation, the concept of seeds (*bīja*) as a metaphorical or "nominal entity" (*prajñapti-dharma*) representing the continuity of the latent afflictions and accumulated karmic potential. In succeeding chapters we will see how the Yogācārins built upon this metaphor of seeds and wove it into the Abhidharma analysis of the six modes of cognitive awareness. But first we will examine the grounds of the dispute.

The controversy over the latent versus manifest (*kleśa/anuśaya*) nature of the afflictions ranges over several pages in the *Abhidharma-kośa* (V 1–2), centering on the proper interpretation of the compound "underlying disposition of sensual desire" (*kāmarāga-anuśaya*) – whether one should interpret this phrase according to a passage cited from a *sūtra*, or whether one should follow an Abhidharmic reading of it. The discussion can be paraphrased as follows:

> Does this Sanskrit compound "*kāmarāga-anuśaya*" mean "the underlying disposition which *is itself* sensual desire" (*kāmarāga* *eva* *anuśayaḥ*), or is it "the underlying disposition *of* sensual desire (*kāmarāgasya anuśayaḥ*)"? In other words, is the underlying disposition (*anuśaya*) just a different name for that particular affliction (*kleśa*), or is it something distinct from the active outburst (*paryavasthānaṃ*) of that affliction?
>
> The Sarvāstivādins argue that the compound should be understood appositionally (*karmadhārya*), that is, that the two members are equated, just as the expression "the city of New York" simply means "the city which *is* New York." This supports the first interpretation, "the underlying disposition which *is itself* sensual desire." But this would contradict a *sūtra* passage (*sūtravirodhaḥ*), like that cited in the first chapter, which states that the outburst of sensual desire (*kāmarāga-paryavasthānaṃ*) is "eliminated *along with* its underlying disposition" (*sānuśayaṃ prahīyate*)[75] – a passage which seems to distinguish between the latent afflictions and their manifest counterparts and upon which the Sautrāntikas, in contrast, rely for their interpretation. Yaśomitra, the main commentator of the *Abhidharma-kośa*, remarks that this is because the Sautrāntikas take *sūtra* (scripture) as more authoritative than *śāstra* (scholastic treatise)[76] – as their name, "Those Following Sūtra," would suggest.
>
> If, on the other hand, the compound were interpreted as "the underlying disposition *of* sensual desire" (a genitive *tatpuruṣa*), this means that it is clearly distinguished from its active outburst, which would entail that the underlying dispositions are also dissociated from mind (*viprayukta*). This, however, would contradict an Abhidharma passage (*abhidharmavirodhaḥ*) that states that the dispositions are associated

(*samprayukta*) with the three feelings.[77] The Sarvāstivādins call upon this Abhidharma passage to interpret the scriptural passage, and so are able to maintain that the latent and manifest afflictions are simply two names for the same thing.[78]

The Sarvāstivādin theory of possession (prāpti)

Having equated the latent dispositions with the active afflictions, the Sarvāstivādins[79] had to directly respond to the Abhidharmic Problematic: how could the dispositions and the accumulation of karmic potential persist in the mental stream without also negatively influencing every moment of mind? Their attempt to reconcile the dharmic analysis of mind with the diachronic phenomena of karma, kleśa, and their gradual removal along the path, is closely related to the doctrine from which they get their name: those who hold that all dharmas exist (*sarva asti*). They proposed that dharmas throughout the three times, past, present, and future, are always existent, only their temporal condition changes. They argued for this, among other reasons, on the grounds that if past causes did not in some sense actually exist, they could not lead to current karmic results. In other words, if past actions were absolutely non-existent, then, since they were no longer present at all, they could not give rise to present results.[80] But if all dharmas always exist, how can one account for the arising of karmic results at one time rather than another?

To explain the appearance of karmic results after extended periods of time, the Sarvāstivādins proposed a mediating dharma called "possession" (*prāpti*), which, unlike past actions, persists in the mental stream by continuously replicating itself. When the fruit of past action arises, or, as they put it, "falls into its own mental stream" (*svasantāna*),[81] it does not arise directly from that past causal dharma, since its efficacy no longer exists; rather, it arises due to the *present possession* of that dharma,[82] which continuously maintains its casual efficacy. That is to say, rather tautologically, that the karmic efficacy of a past cause maintains a presence in the mental stream in the guise of its "possession." In this way, the potential for karmic fruition continuously persists in an ongoing stream of its own present dharmas, that is, as "possession." The dharma of possession, however, is not entangled in the active mental processes with which it simultaneously occurs. It is a karmically neutral dharma that is considered to be, as we would expect, "dissociated from mind" (*citta-viprayukta*); accordingly, it is able to coexist with either skillful or unskillful states of mind.[83] By exploiting the ambiguity inherent in the category of dharmas "dissociated from mind," possession is able to describe the continuous presence of the accumulated karmic potential in terms of the synchronic discourse of momentary dharmas.

The Sarvāstivādin used this same approach to address the problem of the persistence of certain afflictions until far along the path. The potential for these afflictions to arise is signified by the presence of their "possession." The problematic status of their latency – how they can have unbroken continuity without undue influence – has effectively shifted to the problem of the status of possession, so there was no need to distinguish between the active afflictions (*paryavasthāna*) and their latent counterparts. The Sarvāstivādins simply equated the two, claiming they were two names for the same thing and that all references to the latent dispositions found in the *sūtras* were actually references to "possession" by another name[84] – a prime example of prioritizing Abhidharma theory over *sūtric* teaching.

This concept of possession could also address problems raised by the gradual nature of progress along the path, particularly in cases where Aryans, Buddhist saints who have realized certain supramundane attainments, may nevertheless experience decidedly mundane states of mind, that is, by "backsliding." What distinguishes an Aryan in such a mundane moment from an ordinary being (*pṛthagjana*) whose state of mind appears equally mundane is their respective "possession" of the appropriate dharmas. The two are distinguished by the complete absence in the one case, or the continuing presence in the other, of the "possession" of the afflictions in their respective mind-streams.[85]

In this way, the concept of possession allowed the Sarvāstivādins to describe in dharmic terms the two indispensable doctrines – kleśa and karma – that presuppose, indeed require, reference to some kind of continuity outside the Abhidharmic analysis of momentary mental states. The concept of possession seems, in fact, to have been devised for the express purpose of providing such an explanation. In effect, however, this simply moved the onus of explanation away from the systematized scheme of cause, condition, and result (*hetu*, *pratyaya*, *phala*) – whose specific strictures brought about the problematic – and placed it onto a concept that was not fully integrated into that scheme, suggesting its ad hoc nature and inviting Vasubandhu's open disdain.[86] Thus, despite its ascribed status as a real dharma in the Sarvāstivādin analysis of mind, its explanatory value remained questionable. As the ultimate arbiter of the presence of karmic accumulation, the afflictions which instigate it, and their gradual eradication along the path, "possession" remained remarkably indeterminate, prompting Conze to conclude, "the prāpti theory thus proved to be a dead end."[87]

The Sautrāntika theory of seeds (bīja) *in the mental stream* (santāna)

The Sautrāntikas took a radically different approach to these same issues, utilizing the explicitly metaphorical notion (*prajñapti-dharma*) of seeds (*bīja*) to represent both the latent afflictions and the accumulation of karmic potential within the mental stream. In effect, the Sautrāntikas expressly sidestepped the dharma discourse advocated by the Abhidharmists and relied instead upon more traditional expressions drawn from the earlier texts, such as we saw in Chapter 1. This turned out to be a very suggestive metaphor indeed, leading, as we will see, to the model of mind centered on the ālaya-vijñāna. We will therefore examine several key passages in the *Abhidharma-kośa* which introduce the metaphor of seeds and its related concepts.

Addressing conundrums first outlined in the *Kathāvatthu*, the Sautrāntikas used the metaphor of seeds to signify the latent dispositions, and thus to maintain a distinction between the latent and the manifest afflictions:

> The affliction (*kleśa*) which is dormant is called a 'latent disposition' (*anuśaya*); that which is awakened, an 'outburst' (*paryavasthāna*).
>
> And what is that [affliction] which is dormant?
>
> It is the continuity (lit.: 'bound along with,' *anubandha*) in a seed-state (*bīja-bhāva*) [of that affliction] which is not manifest.
>
> What is awakening?
>
> It is being present.
>
> What is called a 'seed-state'?
>
> It is the capacity (*śakti*) of that individual (*ātmabhāva*) for an affliction to arise born from a [previous] affliction, as is the capacity for memory to arise born from experiential knowledge (*anubhava-jñāna*), and the capacity for sprouts, etc., to produce a grain (*phala*) of rice bred from a [previous] grain of rice.
>
> (AKBh *ad* V 1d–2a)[88]

In apparent agreement with the *sūtra* materials examined in the first chapter, and in sharp contrast to the Sarvāstivādins, the Sautrāntikas distinguish between the latent afflictions and their manifest outbursts, crediting the dispositions in their "seed-state" with the capacity or power (*śakti*) to give rise to new afflictions. The metaphor of seeds stems, of course, from the early texts and is here explicitly equated with the latent dispositions (*anuśaya*). The seeds are also explicitly continuous, being "bound along with" (*anubandha*) the mental stream.[89]

The Sautrāntika concept of seed is also used to represent the potential for karmic result:

> What is called a 'seed'?
>
> Any psycho-physical organism (*nāma-rūpa*) that is capable of producing a fruit, either mediately or immediately, through a specific modification of the mental stream (*santati-pariṇāma-viśeṣajāt.*).
>
> What is called a 'modification'?
>
> It is the mental stream being in a different state.
>
> What is called the 'mental stream'?
>
> It is the karmic formations (*saṃskārā*) of the three times existing as cause and effect.
>
> (AKBh *ad* II 36d)[90]

For the Sautrāntikas, both karma and kleśa, or more precisely their underlying presence as potential factors, are represented by "seeds" persisting in the mental stream. The expression mental stream (*santāna*) is glossed here as "the karmic formations (*saṃskārā*) of the three times existing as cause and effect," or, in another suggestive passage, as the "continued production of *citta* from earlier action (*karma*)."[91] A seed, then, is whatever brings about a fruit through a modification or change in the mental stream, in the karmic formations "existing as cause and effect."

We must stress that this is not adding any new concept to Buddhist doctrine. *The metaphor of seeds is simply another way of talking about the karmic relationship between cause and effect.* All intentional actions, if unimpeded, bring about some result, "some modification in the mental stream." Therefore, there are virtually no intentional actions that are not involved in the production and eventual fruition of seeds, that is, which do not involve some kind of modification of the basic structures of one's mind and body (*saṃskārā*). This is obviously a constant, ongoing process. It is, in fact, one way of talking about growth and development (i.e. the growth and development of cyclic existence) which not only takes time, but, like seeds, often produces fruit only after long periods of imperceptible gestation and maturation.

And since the growth and development of individual samsaric existence is largely equated with this mass of accumulated karmic potential (*karmopacitam*), the inertia of the latent predispositions, and their influences upon the behavioral and cognitive patterns of karmic formations (*saṃskārā*), liberation is conversely defined as the eradication of the seeds. Thus, in further agreement with the teachings of the early texts,[92] the Sautrāntikas express the eradication of the afflictions with the image of seeds rendered infertile by fire, here by contrasting the mundane and supramundane paths:

> The basis (*āśraya*) of the Aryan has been transformed due to the force of the [supramundane] Path of Seeing, so the destroyed afflictions (*kleśa*) will not be able to sprout again. It is said that the basis is without seeds, the afflictions having been destroyed [by the supramundane Path of Seeing] like [seeds] burned by fire, whereas the seeds are [merely] damaged by the mundane path.
>
> (AKBh *ad* II 36c–d)[93]

The Sautrāntikas describe the state of having fully eliminated the afflictions, not in Sarvāstivādin terms of having eliminated the "possession" of those afflictions, but rather in terms of having eliminated the "seeds" of those afflictions, seeds which are nothing but "the capacity ... for an affliction to arise born from a [previous] affliction." In this case, not only are the active afflictions absent from present processes of mind, but the very possibility of them arising again from their seeds has also been eliminated.

The Sautrāntikas thus use the metaphor of seeds for the same purposes the Sarvāstivādins use the concept of possession for – to express the capacities for the latent dispositions and karmic fruit to arise.[94] But the similarities end here, and in a very telling way. For, in contrast to the concept of possession, neither the seeds, nor for that matter even the mental stream, refer to dharmas, to "real existents" (*dravya*) in and of themselves. Rather, the seeds are explicitly considered mere designations (*prajñaptisat*) for the power or capacity (*śakti*) for the fruit of karma or the manifest afflictions to arise.[95] We must not be misled by the substantiality of the metaphor. A "seed" merely designates the potential for karmic results to occur, for the dispositions of the afflictions to arise. As "potentials" and "dispositions," the commentary points out, these are not ultimately true factors, not "real dharmas" at all. They are merely nominal entities established through designation, convention, or common usage.[96] They are, in short, not part of dharma discourse at all.

In contrast to the Sarvāstivādins, the Sautrāntikas have in effect responded to the Abhidharma problematic by simply opting out of the dharma system (on these issues at any rate). In so doing they have highlighted, in the opposite way from the concept of possession, the basic tensions between these two distinct levels of doctrinal discourse. For ultimately, in order to be a ultimate account of "how things really are" (*yathābhūtam*) – for the purpose of discerning the dharmas in order to extinguish the afflictions – the synchronic, dharmic discourse requires what it cannot accept: some way of ultimately describing, in terms of dharmas, the conventional continuities of the underlying afflictions and potential for karmic fruition represented by the metaphors of the mental stream and its accompanying seeds. These tensions, therefore, to that extent remain unresolved.

Questions raised by consciousness, seeds, and the mental stream

As attractive as the metaphor of seeds may have been, it did not resolve the Abhidharma Problematic. Of course, as a metaphor it was never meant to be a real dharma; it evaded rather than addressed the underlying problematics of Abhidharma doctrine. But as soon as this explicit metaphor was taken as an explanatory concept, that is, as soon as the interrelationships between the seeds, the mental stream, and consciousness (*vijñāna*) were used as if they were dharmic terms, other, more demanding questions came uncomfortably to the fore. These issues initially concerned the continuity of mind, but soon enough broadened into wider questions concerning the two "aspects" of vijñāna and their relationship with the two types of discourse. For, insofar as the continuities that the seeds represented were primarily associated with the diachronic dimension of consciousness,[97] their ambiguous relationship with the synchronic dimensions of vijñāna became problematic as well. The disjunction between these two aspects of vijñāna – both of which were equally essential in the *Abhidharma-kośa* – had not yet been sufficiently bridged, leading to some vexing questions.

The diachronic dimension of consciousness (*vijñāna*) is as essential to samsaric continuity in the *Abhidharma-kośa* as it is in the early Pāli texts: continued occurrence of vijñāna is considered concomitant with continued existence in samsara. As the continuous basis (*āśraya*) of sentient life, vijñāna is considered the "common element" (*sādhāraṇabhūtāḥ*) which persists, along with heat and vitality, throughout one's lifetime from the moment of "reconnection" (*pratisandhi-citta*) and descent into the womb at rebirth until its departure from the body at the moment of death.[98] In between, vijñāna (or *citta*) is thought to take up or appropriate (*upatta* or *upādāna*) the body and its sense organs throughout one's lifetime.[99] Vijñāna, moreover, is coterminous with sentient life in its cognitive aspect as well: it arises at any time when the sensory organs or mind of a living body are impinged upon – and the constant motion of our eyes and of our circulatory and nervous systems alone ensure that their associated faculties are being stimulated at every moment. There are thus almost no moments when the sense organs and mind are not being impinged upon in some way and when cognitive awareness does not arise accordingly.[100] In both senses, therefore, as "consciousness" and as "cognitive awareness," vijñāna is inseparable from the sheer processes of living and is virtually equated with sentient life itself.

In certain places in the *Kośa* vijñāna is also closely connected with the potency of the seeds to perpetuate cyclic existence. One brief passage depicts the close relationship between the generation of seeds from intentional karmic activities, their "infusion" into consciousness (*vijñāna*), and their subsequent power to project continued existence. As in the early teachings, vijñāna is the result of the sustaining and propelling energies of karma and craving, but is now, in addition, their explicit medium as well. The text is discussing the four nourishments (*āhāra*) that sustain samsaric existence – edible food, sensation, mental intentions, and consciousness. The first two sustain this present existence, the text states, while the latter two, mental intentions and consciousness, are

> for projecting and producing another existence, respectively.... Mental intention (*manaḥsañcetanā*) projects (*ākṣepa*) renewed existence; that [existence] which is projected is, in turn, produced from the seed (*bīja*) of vijñāna which is infused (*paribhāvita*) by karma. Thus, these two are predominant in bringing forth the existence which is not yet arisen.
>
> (AKBh III 41c–d)[101]

Echoing similar metaphors from the early Pāli texts ("Karma is the field, consciousness the seed and craving the moisture for... rebecoming in the future," A I 223), Vasubandhu explicitly portrays the continuity of samsaric existence in terms of the relationship of the seeds – representing the latent potencies of karma and the kleśa – and consciousness. That is to say, mental intention (which is mental karma[102]) "infuses"[103] consciousness with seeds and thereby lays the basis for further rebirth and continued existence – a process parallel to that found in series of dependent arising where the effects of intentional activities propel vijñāna into the next life. In this way, the *Kośa* states, "the series of consciousness (*vijñāna-santatis*) goes into such and such a realm of rebirth because of the power of the projection of action."[104]

Consciousness is therefore essential to samsaric continuity in the *Kośa*, as it is – allowing for the differences regarding causal mechanisms – in Abhidharma in general. But equating the series of vijñāna (or the mental stream and its seeds) with samsaric continuity as a whole, as the Sautrāntikas suggested, generated its own set of problems. For if the seeds are more than a simple metaphor, that is, if they are to be taken as a concept with *explanatory power* in the dharmic sense, then they must be systematically integrated into other parts of the doctrine. In other words, as soon as the Santrāntikas tried to transpose the underlying continuities traditionally couched in diachronic discourse into ultimate dharmas couched in synchronic discourse, more exacting questions were asked and more precise answers were demanded.

What, for example, is the relationship between this continuous "series of vijñāna" with its seeds and the momentary aspect of vijñāna as cognitive awareness analyzed in synchronic dharmic discourse? Are they the same vijñāna? If these were *exactly* the same, if the mental series were just one moment of vijñāna following another, as Vasubandhu suggests (see n. 97), then what is the relationship between the continuity of accumulated karma and the latent afflictions represented by the seeds and the six momentary modes of cognitive awareness? But if the mental stream were *not* simply metaphorical, and referred to some heretofore unspecified level of mind distinct from these six modalities, then what is the relationship between them? Are these just two distinct phenomena, separately but equally described by diachronic and synchronic discourses, respectively? In either case, this would not lessen the need to delineate the precise relationships between the continuity of the mental stream and all its seeds and the ongoing, moment-to-moment processes of mind. Systematic thought, the essence of the Abhidharma method, required that these two distinct discourses, centered around these two essential dimensions of samsaric life – consciousness and cognitive awareness – should somehow be reconciled within a single, all-encompassing framework. They needed, in short, to explicitly integrate the diachronic and synchronic discourses.

These issues were brought to a head in discussions surrounding certain forms of meditative absorption in which all overt mental activities were thought to cease, a condition which called the continuity of mind as a whole into question. In Indian Buddhist traditions this condition was thought to occur during two distinct states of deep meditation: the "attainment of non-apperception" (*āsamjñika-samāpatti*) and the "attainment of cessation" (*nirodha-samāpatti*).[105]

Such cessation raised several thorny theoretical problems, and generated some suggestive responses. In orthodox Abhidharmic analysis, continuity consists of nothing more than the moment-to-moment conditioning influences between immediately succeeding moments. In these absorptions, however, all mental activities come to a halt so that the continuity of the mental stream appears to be completely broken. The first moment of mind that arises on emerging from these meditations would therefore not have an immediately preceding mind-moment that could serve as its immediately antecedent and homogenous condition (*samanantara-pratyaya*). That is, if the mind-stream were completely cut during these meditative states, it would lack all the conditions necessary for it to reoccur, since its "mind support" (*mana āśrayaḥ*), its immediately antecedent mental cognition,[106] would be absent.[107]

Moreover, since in the Sautrāntika point of view the seeds also follow along (*anubandha*) with the mental stream (as *citta/vijñāna*) in some still undefined way, their continuity would also cease along with the cessation of all mental activity. But if the seeds actually disappeared during these attainments, then all of the accumulated karma and the latent afflictions they represented would also be destroyed, never to rise again – and this would be tantamount to liberation. What then would ensure the continuity of karmic and afflictive potential following these meditative states even though all mental activities had ceased within them?[108]

And third, since vijñāna is considered the support of existence and the common element (*sādhāraṇabhūtāḥ*) from the time of conception until death, its cessation within the body ought to result in death. But the body remains intact and alive during and after these meditative states. What kind of mental process, then, keeps the body alive during these absorptions in which all ostensible mental activities come to a halt? What prevents the practitioner from dying?

Standard Abhidharma doctrine did not have a ready answer to these questions, and was forced, in one way or another, to either modify some of its basic postulates about the relations between samsaric continuity and the mental stream, or to redefine some of its key terms and suppositions. As we shall see, these responses, despite their variety, all share a common search for a dimension of mind that could subsist in some fashion independently of the traditional six modes of cognitive awareness, yet remain consistent with the basic assumptions of dharmic discourse. The positions of these schools were discussed in a long exchange in the *Abhidharma-kośa* (*ad* II 44d), which we shall paraphrase:[109]

> Since mind is interrupted for a long time in these two kinds of attainment, how can the moment of mind (*citta*) that emerges from this absorption have a past moment of mind as its homogeneous and immediately antecedent condition, since it has already ceased for a long time?
>
> The Sarvāstivādins hold that the first moment of mind which arises upon emergence from the attainment is directly conditioned by the last moment of mind immediately preceding that meditative attainment, regardless of its duration, since for them all past dharmas currently exist insofar as their 'possession' (*prāpti*) currently exists. Consequently, it is the *citta* prior to the meditative attainment, that is, the *citta* that enters into that state, which serves as the homogeneous and immediately antecedent condition for the *citta* that emerges from that state.[110] Immediacy, in other words, need not be strictly *immediate*.
>
> The Sautrāntikas reject the notion that the first *citta* that emerges from the mindless attainments has the *citta* immediately prior to that state for its antecedent condition. They suggest instead that that newly

emerging *citta* arises *from the body* together with the material faculties (*sendriya-kāya*) as its support (*āśraya*). Vasubandhu quotes unnamed "ancient masters" (*pūrvācāryāḥ*) to the effect that, "two dharmas are the seed of one another (*anyonyabījaka*): these two dharmas are the *citta* and the body together with its material organs."[111] That is to say, the mind and body contain the seeds of each other, 'carrying' each other along when one of them temporarily ceases.[112] Homogeneity, in other words, need not be wholly *homo*geneous.

The last position suggests an entirely different approach: one master, Vasumitra, maintained that since one would die if vijñāna completely ceased, there must be a subtle form of mind (*sūkṣma-citta*) that subsists without *apparent* functioning during the attainment.[113] Thus the fully functioning manifest *citta* which arises upon emergence from the attainment of cessation directly arises from the never wholly suspended subtle *citta*, thereby fulfilling both the required conditions of being immediate *and* homogeneous (since a moment of mind, however subtle, still directly conditions another moment of mind). But, here too, the cessation of all mental activities need not mean they *completely* cease.

As Yaśomitra, one of the commentators of the *Abhidharma-kośa*, points out, this last position corresponds closely to the Yogācāra conception of the ālaya-vijñāna,[114] which in a sense combined the Sautrāntika's and Vasumitra's notions into a continuous and subtle level of *mental* processes which maintains the seeds of both body and mind together.

In sum, there were three responses to this problem: (1) to reject immediate succession in favor of atemporal causality, via the Sarvāstivādin notion of possession (*prāpti*); (2) to reject homogeneity (mind to mind, body to body) via the Sautrāntika notion of mind/body non-dualism;[115] and (3) to reject the standing definition of cessation – that is, that *all* mental processes strictly come to a halt – in order to accommodate subtle forms of mind that continuously maintain the seeds of karmic accumulation and latent afflictions. This last position is, of course, most consistent with the aspect of vijñāna as a simple sentience closely connected with living bodily processes. In effect, these various solutions represent sophisticated and systemic answers to the same questions – posed in nearly the same terms and couched in nearly the same vocabulary – which were first posed in the *Kathāvatthu* some seven centuries earlier. Without any real change in the underlying presuppositions of the system, however, the Abhidharma Problematic, in both its synchronic and diachronic dimensions, seemed relatively resistant to resolution.

There was, however, one more systemic approach to these issues, and that was the "life-constituent mind" (*bhavaṅga-citta*) of the Theravādins, which displays some surprising similarities with, as well as distinct differences from, the ālaya-vijñāna. We will examine this last alternative before turning our attention to the development of the ālaya-vijñāna itself.

The Theravādin theory of life-constituent mind (*bhavaṅga-citta*)

Although the most systematic revision of the traditional Buddhist model of mind is to be found, we shall argue, in the ālaya-vijñāna complex, the concept of the *bhavaṅga-citta* revises that model far more than either the Sarvāstivādin notion of "possession" (*prāpti*) or the Sautrāntika metaphor of seeds. While these latter appear as ad hoc solutions directed toward a particular set of problems, the concept of *bhavaṅga-citta* recasts the entire Theravādin theory of continuity and perception.[116]

First of all, the *bhavaṅga-citta*, a form of *citta* considered the "life constituent" or "factor of existence" (*bhava-aṅga*), demonstrates the same conditioned/conditioning bivalence found in many other Buddhist concepts, such as the karmic formations (*saṃskārā*), appropriation (*upādāna*), perhaps even *citta* itself (see n. 30). That is, this "factor of existence" is a conditioned, resultant form of mind (*citta*) that is reborn conditioned by past karma, and which consistently reoccurs in the same form throughout a particular lifetime. And as a conditioning state of mind, it serves as the basis or condition (*paṭicca*) upon which each momentary occurrence of perception arises.[117] In this way, it addresses a number of metapsychological issues in interesting and innovative ways.

Most Abhidharma schools, for example, considered the mind which reconnects (*pratisandhi-citta*) at rebirth (*upapatti*) to be a moment of mental cognition (*manovijñāna*). The Theravādins emended this with the idea that this "mind as factor of existence" (*bhavaṅga-citta*)[118] takes on a particular character at the time of rebirth, to which it naturally and repeatedly reverts whenever active, perceptual processes come to a rest. Since it is a product of the generative karma (*janaka kamma*; i.e. past *saṃskārās*) that ripens at the moment of rebirth, each moment of the *bhavaṅga-citta* which subsequently occurs throughout that lifetime also enjoys the same karmic character – it is a resultant (*vipāka*) and thus karmically neutral state – and is accompanied by the same associated factors (*sampayutta-dhammā*) and cognitive objects (*ārammaṇa*).[119]

The continuity of the *bhavaṅga-citta*, however, is interrupted whenever cognitive objects enter the range of the sense fields (and mind) and give rise to a specific type of cognitive awareness. When this occurs, the *bhavaṅga-citta* serves as one of the conditions for that new cognitive awareness to arise. The classic Theravādin Abhidhamma text, the *Visuddhimagga*, thus emends the standard formula for the arising of cognitive awareness with the addition of this previous moment of mind, declaring that, for example, a "mental cognition arises dependent on bhavaṅga-mind, a mental object [*dhamma*], and attention."[120] And since the *bhavaṅga-citta* is a karmically neutral form of mind which immediately conditions each moment of cognitive awareness, it also serves as a "buffer-state" between karmically incompatible states, thereby directly addressing the problem of heterogeneous succession.[121] Thus in its role in the rebirth process, during objectless sleep, and as an intermediary buffer state during ordinary cognitive processes, "the *bhavaṅga* functions quite literally as a 'stop-gap' in the sequence of moments which constitutes mental continuity" (Collins, 1982: 245).

The *bhavaṅga-citta* in the *Visuddhimagga*, however, is not an independent, continuous stream of mind that underlies the active cognitive processes, nor does it arise concurrently with those processes whose occurrence it conditions.[122] The *bhavaṅga-citta* and the forms of manifest cognitive awareness are mutually exclusive: the former ceases when the latter arises.[123] The English translator of the *Abhidhammatthaa-sangaha*, Shwe Zan Aung, therefore warns:

> it must not be supposed that the stream of being [*bhavaṅga-citta*] is a sub-plane from which thoughts rise to the surface. There is juxtaposition of momentary states of consciousness, subliminal and supraliminal, throughout a life-time and from existence to existence. But there is no superposition of such states.
>
> (*Compendium*, 1979: 11–12)

Unlike the ill-defined relation between the mental stream and the six modes of cognitive awareness in the *Abhidharma-kośa*, this seems to be patently clear. What remains unclear, however, are questions about the continuity of the latent dispositions and karmic potential. For their continuity to remain unbroken, they must also be associated in some fashion with the *bhavaṅga-citta* – at least during those intervals in between manifest active cognitive processes. This has led several scholars to interpret the *bhavaṅga-citta* from a broader perspective. Cousins, for example, states:

> We may interpret its continuance throughout life as the natural mode to which the mind continually reverts as indicating its role of 'carrying' the essential features of the individual – those tendencies which remain apparently unchanged in a particular individual throughout a given life.... Evidently it is seen either as storing past experience or as having direct access to the past (or future). In the first case we might understand it as an unconscious storehouse. The mind as a whole is certainly envisaged as accumulating tendencies, but it is not clear how far this would include experiences.
>
> (Cousins, 1981: 28–30)

In discussing this possible relation between the *bhavaṅga-citta* and past karma, Nyantiloka departs even further from its classical textual descriptions. The *bhavaṅga-citta*, he explains,

> is in the Abhidhamma commentaries explained as the foundation or condition (*kāraṇa*) of existence (*bhava*), as the *sine qua non* of life, and that in form of a process, lit. a 'flux' or 'stream' (*sota*), in which since time immemorial all impressions and experiences are, as it were, stored up, or better said functioning, but as such concealed to full consciousness, from where however they as subconscious phenomena occasionally

> emerge and approach the threshold of full consciousness, or crossing it become fully conscious. This so-called 'subconscious life-stream' or undercurrent of life, which certain modern psychologists call the Unconscious or the soul, is that by which might be explained the faculty of memory, the problem of telekinesis, mental and physical growth, karma and rebirth, etc.
>
> (Nyantiloka, 1980: 27–28)

This latter passage contradicts Shwe Zan Aung's conclusion that the *bhavaṅga-citta* is not "a subplane from which thoughts rise to the surface." There is obvious disagreement over a number of other points as well, points which, since they resemble characteristics of the ālaya-vijñāna in many ways, require some clarification. These are:

(1) the extent to which the *bhavaṅga-citta* is a basis from which or upon which cognitive awareness arises;
(2) the extent to which the *bhavaṅga-citta* is closely connected with the accumulation of karmic potential and the latent dispositions;
(3) the extent to which the *bhavaṅga-citta* is related to motivation and intention – that is the performance of active karma;
(4) the extent to which the *bhavaṅga-citta* is simultaneous with cognitive awareness (i.e. as Nyantiloka puts it, "all impressions and experiences are, as it were, stored up, or better said *functioning*, but as such concealed to full consciousness").

From our investigation, we see that the classical doctrine of *bhavaṅga-citta* is unambiguously characterized only by point (1); perhaps necessarily, but only intermittently, by point (2) (and that no more so than the manifest forms of cognitive awareness); and not at all by (3) and (4). The question of karmic potential is the most crucial. Certainly, the *bhavaṅga-citta* can be thought in some way to "carry the essential features of the individual," since these are fixed for a particular lifetime at the time of conception. But for that very reason, it is not portrayed as directly receiving or accumulating impressions or tendencies. Moreover, since the *bhavanṅga-citta* is intermittent and occurs only when the other cognitive processes are inactive, it cannot – in and of itself – afford unbroken continuity of these features.

Questions about the persistence of latent dispositions and accumulation of karmic potential thus remain: once the cognitive processes are activated, are they transmitted through the six modes of cognitive awareness? If so, why do they not influence these forms of mind? If not, how do they persist from one moment of *bhavaṅga-citta* to the next without some contiguous conditioning medium? The *bhavaṅga-citta* does not directly address these persisting questions, adumbrated in the *Kathāvatthu* so many centuries before. Nor, to my knowledge, do subsequent Theravādin Abhidhamma traditions discuss these questions in *dhammic* terms.

For this reason, Collins is circumspect about characterizations such as Nyanatiloka's. He cautions that while the bhavaṅga-citta should be considered as a separate, subliminal level of mental functioning, it should be done so "only in relation to a systematic account of perception, and not of motivation." Because,

> while many aspects of the Buddhist attitude to motivation do resemble some Freudian themes, they are nowhere related systematically to the *bhavaṅga* in the *Theravāda* tradition before modern times. Accordingly, the modern comparison between *bhavaṅga* and the psychoanalytic unconscious must be developed as part of what one might call 'speculative' or 'creative' Buddhist philosophy, rather than by historical scholarship.
> (Collins, 1982: 244)

Neither, he warns, should we consider the bhavaṅga mind as the "connecting thread" of karma, since it is intermittent and ceases to function whenever the overt cognitive processes occur. Rather, Collins concludes, karmic continuity in the Theravāda "is simply a string of beads ... which have no underlying connecting thread, save the overall force of *karma* which creates them" (ibid.: 248) – a force transmitted, we might note, through nothing but the unbroken succession of "a juxtaposition of momentary states of consciousness, [alternately] subliminal and supraliminal" (*Compendium*, 1979: 11–12, cited above), or, during the mindless absorptions in which all mental activities cease, through the material life-faculty itself.[124]

This notion of the "force of karma," however, does not answer the Abhidharma Problematic either. The concept of *force* as effective energy is certainly implicit in much of early Indian Buddhism, and becomes quite explicit in the Abhidharma era. Indeed, it is one of Vasubandhu's favorite metaphors for the notion of karma: the concepts of seeds and the "specific modification of the mental stream" (*santati-pariṇāma-viśeṣa*) are regularly glossed as *śakti* and sometimes as *samartham*, both roughly "power, force, capacity."[125] But, by itself, force has no systemic definition in Abhidharma, and hence no explanatory power; it remains, like the other responses to the Abhidharma Problematic we have examined, ambiguously metaphorical.

The continuity of karma, in any case, is not directly related to the *bhavaṅga-citta*, save for (possibly) during its short tenure as a "stop-gap" between successive moments of mind. To this extent, Theravādin Abhidhamma has not followed some of the other schools in attempting to connect karmic potential with the overt processes of mind in a systemic, that is, dharmic manner. Rather, like the Sautrāntikas, they make do with the imagery of vegetative metaphors. Collins contrasts these unsystematized "live" metaphors with the "deadened" terminology of the Yogācāra and Mahāsāṃghika schools:

> In these ideas, the original metaphor inherent in the use of such imagery becomes deadened, and the words take on the character of dry technical terms. In Theravāda, on the other hand, the imagery of seeds

> and fruit is never regularized to the extent of becoming technical terminology built into the ultimate account of continuity; correspondingly, the metaphor remains more alive. *Theravāda* tradition does speak of a type of mental phenomenon which assures continuity – the *bhavaṅga*-mind; and it does have a preferred metaphor to represent it – the image of a stream or river.
>
> (Collins, 1982: 224)

There is no doubt much truth to this – despite the obvious incompatibility between the intermittent occurrence of the *bhavaṅga-citta* and the continuous flow of a stream or river – and Collins has skillfully demonstrated how such metaphors for continuity in the Theravādin tradition both pre-dated and coexisted with the more technical *dhamma* discourse. There are, as well, several passages in the *Abhidharma-kośa* in which the living processes whereby seeds gestate, develop, and mature into final fruition are also used to describe the path of karma from its inception to its final fruit – passages in which the "seed" is used primarily metaphorically.[126] And as Collins also rightly points out, this contrasts with the more technical usage of seeds in both the kleśa/anuśaya controversy and the definition of karma in terms of the specific modification of the stream (*santati-pariṇāma-viśeṣa*) – passages in which the seeds appear with a systematic meaning and function. However, despite this transformation into a technical term in the Sautrāntika-leaning sections of the *Abhidharma-kośa*, the metaphorical nature of the seeds is never far removed, for whenever the Sarvāstivādins pressure them to explain how exactly seeds work, the Sautrāntikas fall back on straightforward vegetative analogies. The Abhidharmic Problematic, therefore, still remains effectively unresolved.

Conclusion

Collins's observation that in Theravāda "the imagery of seeds and fruit is never regularized to the extent of becoming technical terminology built into the ultimate account of continuity," points directly to the issues raised by the Abhidharma analytic as a whole. Since all dharmas are momentary, Abhidharma does not readily attribute ultimate validity to descriptions of any mental phenomena outside the momentary and manifest processes of mind.[127] But the doctrines referring to the continuity of karma and kleśa examined above *all* depend upon their relation to concepts – mental stream, basis, name-and-form, and individual existence (*citta-santāna*, *āśraya*, *nāma-rūpa*, *ātmabhāva*)[128] – that only have currency outside of dharmic discourse, that is, in diachronic discourse. And the seeds were arguably never intended to be part of dharmic discourse in the first place, since they were not real existents (*dravya*) but simply metaphors for the underlying capacities (*śakti* or *samartham*) of mind expressed in terms of the life-processes of insemination (*paribhāvita*), growth (*vṛddha*), and eventual fruition (*vipāka-phala*). The fact that every school found it necessary to juxtapose systematic technical language with such conventional and naturalistic metaphors in order to account for the most basic and fundamental doctrines of their traditions testifies not just to the systemic limitations of purely dharmic discourse, but to the ubiquity of the Abhidharma Problematic.

Nyanaponika Thera, unwittingly no doubt, displays remarkable agreement with this conclusion in a passage in his *Abhidhamma Studies*. After discussing what he calls "breadth," the simultaneous relations (*sahajāta-paccaya*) between dharmas, and "length," the "sequence of observed, consecutive changes stretching forward in time" (*anantara-paccaya*) (which correspond roughly to our synchronic and diachronic discourses, respectively), he also speaks of a third dimension, "depth":

> The spatial world of qualified analysis is limited to the two dimensions of breadth and length. Bare or qualified analysis dare not admit those conditioning and conditioned phenomena which are bound up with the third dimension, that of depth. ... By 'depth' we understand that subterraneous flow of energies (a wide and intricate net of streams, rivers and rivulets) originating in past actions (kamma) and coming to the surface unexpectedly at a time determined by their inherent life rhythm (time required for growth, maturing, etc.) and by the influence of favourable or obstructive circumstances. The analytical method, we said, will admit only such relational energies as are transmitted by immediate impact (the dimension of breadth) or by the linear 'wire' of immediate sequence (the dimension of length). But relational energies may also arise from unknown depths opening under the very feet of the individual or the object; or they may be transmitted, not by that linear 'wire' of immediate sequence in time-space, but by the way of 'wireless' communication, traveling vast distances in space and time. ...
>
> (Nyanaponika, 1976: 29f.)

Our question here is not whether this third dimension is adequately, or even eloquently, expressed in terms of such metaphors as "depth," "flow," "growth," or even "energy," but rather, to what extent they are compatible with the stated aims and expressible within the circumscribed range of Abhidharma discourse.[129] If the Abhidharma is the ultimate account of "how things truly are" (*yathābhūtam*) that it claims to be, then how, even contemporaneous critics asked, could such a philosophic discourse express these "subterraneous flow of energies" from whose "unknown depths" they arise through "wireless" transmission? If such living metaphors are necessary in order to describe this transmission of karmic energy, then they too should be expressed, from the Abhidharmic perspective, in terms of ultimately real, albeit momentary, dharmas; if not, then they are either irrelevant to the aims or inexpressible in the terms of Abhidharma discourse. In either case, on this set of issues at least, Abhidharma seems to be – on its own terms – either inadequate or incomplete.[130] Thus, a modern commentator like Nyanaponika recognizes the same limitations of Abhidharma analysis that were intimated some twenty-odd centuries ago, at first vaguely in the *Kathāvatthu*, then more specifically by the Sautrāntikas, and finally explicitly and systematically by the Yogācārins themselves. Nyanaponika himself lays bare the embedded tensions that "bare ... analysis dare not admit."

Central to these tensions lies the concept of vijñāna, with its two temporal aspects seen from the earliest times: as momentary cognitive awareness, and as a continuous, bare sentience accompanying all animate life. To the extent that Abhidharma represents the exclusive validity of synchronic analysis over diachronic discourse, it so removes its dharmas from any greater temporal context as to be nearly ahistorical – for anything more than the immediate succession of momentary dharmas was literally indescribable, only nominally or figuratively true; in fact, even immediate succession itself was problematic, since issues such as heterogeneous succession are ultimately inseparable from those surrounding the fruition of past karma, the persistence of latent dispositions, and the emergence from the absorption of cessation. Abhidharma analysis by its very method undermined its own soteriological aims, within which alone it was meaningful and coherent.

The Abhidharma project as a whole is thus at stake here. And it is at stake because Abhidharma theory cannot fully account for all the unmanifest factors "bound along" (*anubandhu*) in the mental stream that virtually constitute individual samsaric existence. It was this tension between these two levels of analysis and discourse, focused upon the momentary and continuous processes of mind, respectively, that foreshadowed and – in large part – stimulated the conceptualization of the ālaya-vijñāna. For it is the *stream* that carries all the seeds and thereby insures doctrinal as well as empirical coherence.[131] Yet this stream cannot constitute any "ultimate account of continuity" (Collins), since ultimate validity is preserved exclusively for momentary dharmas. To overcome these problems, while simultaneously preserving the synchronic analysis of momentary and discrete dharmas developed by generations of scholars and adepts, the metaphors of the stream and its seeds needed to be systematically worked into dharmic discourse, so that together they might more comprehensively and consistently describe the persistence and continuing influences of the afflicting passions, the accumulation and fruition of karmic potential, and the gradual nature of purification along the path to liberation.

And for this a wholly new model of mind was called for, one that could articulate the simultaneous existence of both of these temporal dimensions, that could perform all of those functions of the traditional vijñāna of the Pāli texts, but still retain all of the analytic detail and systematic rigor of Abhidharma thought; that is, a model that would integrate the diachronic discourse exemplified by "samsaric" vijñāna with the newer dharmic discourse exemplified by "cognitive" vijñāna. Of all the notions proffered, only the ālaya-vijñāna attempted to explicitly and systematically integrate – or rather reintegrate within the context of the Abhidharma analytic – these sharply differentiated aspects of mind originally undifferentiated in the early discourses. And this is what was first achieved in the momentous *Saṃdhinirmocana Sūtra*.

Part II

THE ĀLAYA-VIJÑĀNA IN THE YOGĀCĀRA TRADITION

3

THE ĀLAYA-VIJÑĀNA IN THE EARLY TRADITION

> Whoever would maintain the idea of pure observation... might collect thousands of things which could be verified but he would not for that reason be able to understand what is actually happening in the present. One is enabled to speak of that which is most vital in the present, of that which makes the present a generative force, only insofar as one immerses oneself in the creative process which brings the future out of the past.
>
> (Paul Tillich)

The origins of the ālaya-vijñāna

Before we enter into the Yogācāra materials themselves, presenting the ālaya-vijñāna in the complexity of its textual history, the profusion of its associated concepts, and the rationales underlying its explanation, we should reiterate the aims of this essay. Our primary aim is to understand the ālaya-vijñāna within the context of Indian Buddhist vijñāna theory, first by outlining its background and context in the early Buddhist and Abhidharma traditions, respectively, and then by examining the set of Yogācāra texts that most thoroughly and systematically espouse this intricate theory of unconscious mind.[1] Neither the concept of the ālaya-vijñāna itself, nor its elaborate defense – a complex blend of exegetical, logical, and phenomenological arguments – can, we believe, be adequately understood without reference to this larger historical context. It is only in the light of the Abhidharma Problematic as a whole, arising out of the discrepancies between the newer dharmic analytic and the traditional doctrines preserved in the early Pāli texts, that we can understand why the questions of the latent affective dispositions, the nature of karmic potentiality, and the gradual progress along the path to liberation became problematic at this point in Indian Buddhist thought – and, even more importantly, why they came to be addressed in terms of the two "aspects" of vijñāna first found in those early texts. Most of the responses to these questions either implicitly or explicitly pointed toward some kind of multi-dimensionality of mind, a "common interest in the deeper strata of conscious life ...," Guenther observes, which "reflects the collective spirit or Zeitgeist of this epoch in Indian Buddhist thought" (1989: 19).[2] In this respect, the concept of ālaya-vijñāna can be seen as merely the most comprehensive and systematic of the many innovative ideas proffered within the intellectual milieu of fourth–sixth centuries CE Buddhist India.

The origin or even first occurrence of the term *ālaya*-vijñāna is unclear. The *Saṃdhinirmocana Sūtra* is traditionally regarded as the first Yogācāra *sūtra*, announcing the advent of the special doctrines associated with that school and receiving, at least from their fellow Mahayanists, the veneration due to the sacred words of the Buddha. Most of the early Yogācāra literature dates from the second or third to the fifth centuries CE,[3] but establishing firmer dates for Indian Buddhist texts is notoriously difficult. We shall not, however, attempt our own chronology of the Yogācāra school or of the minute developments within each stage of the ālaya-vijñāna, but will roughly follow Lambert Schmithausen's careful reconstruction,[4] which, if debatable on this or that particular point, is persuasive enough in its basic outline to serve our more general purpose of introducing the doctrinal developments and demonstrating the psychological and philosophical significance of the concept of the ālaya-vijñāna in the context of Indian Buddhist metapsychology.[5]

The beginnings of the ālaya-vijñāna and of the Yogācāra school as a whole are closely connected with the voluminous *Yogācārabhūmi*, attributed to (though likely only compiled by) Asanga. He was the half-brother of Vasubandhu, the author of the *Abhidharma-kośa* and, following his own "conversion" to Mahayana Buddhism, many major Yogācāra texts as well. In all probability parts of the *Yogācārabhūmi* pre-date the *Saṃdhinirmocana Sūtra*, while other parts were composed or compiled afterwards.[6] We shall be drawing most heavily upon selected sections of the *Saṃdhinirmocana Sūtra* and the *Yogācārabhūmi* in the first chapter of Part II, before proceeding in the succeeding chapters to developments of the ālaya-vijñāna in the *Mahāyāna-saṃgraha*, also written by Asanga.

It is in the Basic Section of the *Yogācārabhūmi* (the *Saptadaśabhūmika*) that the term *ālaya-vijñāna* seems to have been first used. In what Schmithausen takes to be its *initial* occurrence,[7] the ālaya-vijñāna is portrayed as a kind of basal consciousness which persists uninterruptedly within the material sense-faculties during the absorption of cessation (*nirodha-samāpatti*). Within this form of consciousness dwell, in the form of seeds, the causal conditions for manifest forms of cognitive awareness to reappear upon emerging from that absorption. In its most important terminological innovation, these modes of manifest cognitive awareness are now collectively called forms of "arising," or "manifesting [forms of] cognitive awareness" (*pravṛtti-vijñāna*), insofar as they intermittently arise or become manifest in conjunction with their appropriate objects, and in contrast to the abiding, uninterrupted stream of sentience newly called "ālaya" vijñāna. The distinction we discerned as merely implicit within the early Pāli concept of vijñāna – between an object-specific cognitive awareness on the one hand and an abiding sentience on the other – is now terminologically explicit. It represents the Yogācārins' basic departure from earlier Buddhist models of mind.

The newly coined terms "ālaya-vijñāna" and "pravṛtti-vijñāna" are telling in themselves. The term *ālaya* conveys two distinct semantic ranges serendipitously united in Pāli and Sanskrit. *Ālaya* means "that which is clung to, adhered to, dwelled in," and thus derivatively "dwelling, receptacle, house." Yet it also retained an older sense from the early texts – whose nuances will resurface in due time – of "clinging, attachment, or grasping."[8] This new kind of vijñāna, which dwells in or sticks to the material sense-faculties, contrasts with the traditional six types of "manifest cognitive awareness" (*pravṛtti-vijñāna*) insofar as they "arise, come forth, manifest, issue, originate, occur, commence" (*pra-vṛt*, SED 693) in conjunction with objects impinging upon their respective sense-fields.

In this initial passage, ālaya-vijñāna is closely connected with bodily existence, as we would expect for any kind of process which persists during a meditative state in which all mental processes are said to come to a halt. Even in its most complex formulations, ālaya-vijñāna never entirely loses this somatic dimension. This reflects one of the roles attributed to vijñāna in both the Pāli and Abhidharma texts we have already examined: for as long one as is alive, consciousness (*vijñāna*) takes up or "appropriates" (*upādāna*) the body, the material sense-faculties, thereby preventing death; in this sense, it constitutes, along with heat (*uṣma*) and the life-force (*āyus*), one of the indispensable concomitants of any sentient being.[9]

At this stage, the conception of ālaya-vijñāna seems to be little more than a combination of the Sautrāntika view that the body is the carrier of the seeds during the absorption of cessation[10] with Vasumitra's position that a subtle form of mind (*sūkṣma-citta*) subsists at that time without apparent functioning. In effect, as Schmithausen (1987: 30) puts it, it transforms the notion of "the Seeds of mind lying hidden in corporeal matter to a new form of mind proper." As a simple "hypostatization" of the seeds, this depiction of ālaya-vijñāna is not yet a distinct vijñāna, nor is it systematically related to the traditional six modes of cognitive awareness; its status outside of the absorption of cessation, moreover, remains undefined.[11]

Thus, questions remain. On emerging from the attainment of cessation, how do these six forms of "arising cognitive awareness" arise again from the seeds that are within this "ālaya" vijñāna? And where or how does this ālaya-vijñāna function outside of that attainment of cessation? Is it a discontinuous kind of cognitive awareness that, like the *bhavaṅga-citta*, only occurs when the manifest modes of cognitive awareness do not, or does it continuously occur throughout all states of mind? If the latter, then how are the seeds that are associated with this new kind of vijñāna related to the traditional six kinds of cognitive awareness? And in what way might this ālaya-vijñāna function as a vijñāna itself, as a distinct species of cognitive awareness? In other words, if ālaya-vijñāna were to be more than a hypostatization of the seeds, if it were to become a new genre of consciousness in its own right, it would have to be related to traditional conceptions of mind in much more specific detail. These kinds of questions were not asked in the earliest sections of the *Yogācārabhūmi*, but responses to them were effectively outlined in the momentous developments found in the *Saṃdhinirmocana Sūtra*.

The new model of mind in the *Saṃdhinirmocana Sūtra*

The *Saṃdhinirmocana Sūtra*[12] addresses these questions in a few succinct passages which fundamentally restructured the Buddhist model of mind around the notion of ālaya-vijñāna. It accomplished this by combining the diachronic characteristics already associated with the "samsaric" aspects of vijñāna in the early Pāli texts (and in Abhidharma as well), designating them "ālaya" vijñāna, and then initiating their gradual integration into the synchronic discourse expressed in purely dharmic terms. While the *Saṃdhinirmocana Sūtra* presents only the outlines of this model, later developments will gradually draw out its deeper implications, slowly but systematically reintegrating the diachronic and synchronic treatments of mind found within the first millennium of Indian Buddhist metapsychology.

Adding significantly to its physiological dimension as a basal consciousness sticking closely to the body, the ālaya-vijñāna also takes on a distinctly psychological character in the *Saṃdhinirmocana Sūtra*: based upon the accumulated seeds and predispositions (*vāsanā*) with which it is associated, the ālaya-vijñāna concurrently *underlies and supports* the six types of manifest cognitive awareness, so that all forms of awareness now occur *simultaneously* rather than sequentially. The implications of this reformulation of traditional Buddhist models can hardly be overstated, and will take several centuries to be fully drawn out. The presentation of the ālaya-vijñāna in the *Sūtra* thus deserves our close attention.

In the fifth – and for our purposes most important – chapter, the *Saṃdhinirmocana Sūtra* introduces the ālaya-vijñāna as the "mind with all the seeds" (*sarvabījakam cittam*), describing its organic processes of growth and development in terms resonant with the descriptions of vijñāna in the early Pāli texts and the mental stream (*santāna*) in the *Abhidharma-kośa*. As with these earlier conceptions of mind, the ālaya-vijñāna "descends" into the mother's womb, "appropriates" the gestating fetal materials, and increases and develops in a newly re-embodied existence:

> In samsara with its six destinies (*gati*), such and such beings are born as such and such a type of being. They come into existence (*abhinirvṛtti*) and arise (*utpadyante*) in the womb of beings. …
>
> There, at first, the mind which has all the seeds (*sarvabījakaṃ cittam*) matures, congeals, grows, develops, and increases[13] based upon the two-fold appropriation (*upādāna*); that is,
>
> 1 the appropriation of the material sense-faculties along with their supports (*sādhiṣṭāna-rūpīndriya-upādāna*);

2 and the appropriation which consists of the predispositions toward profuse imaginings in terms of conventional usage of images, names, and concepts (*nimitta-nāma-vikalpa-vyavahāra-prapañca-vāsanā-upādāna*).

Of these, both of the appropriations exist within the realms with form, but the appropriation is not two-fold within the Formless Realm.

(*Saṃdhinirmocana Sūtra* V. 2)[14]

These terse passages call for careful explication. The text first indicates the indispensable relationship between the animate body and the ālaya-vijñāna; that is, continued samsaric existence (except in the Formless Realm) depends upon some form of cognitive awareness taking up or appropriating the sense-faculties "in the womb of beings." This effectively extends the physiological functions of the ālaya-vijñāna, which initially pertained only during the absorption of cessation, to (it appears) one's entire lifetime, identifying it with the traditional notion that vijñāna descends into the womb and "grows, develops, and increases."

This passage also connects the ālaya-vijñāna with the karmic, affective, and cognitive endowments from previous lives, represented here in the form of the seeds and the appropriation (*upādāna*) of the predispositions (*vāsanā*).[15] *Upādāna*, we recall, evinces a bivalent "process–product" character: it has both an active, affective sense of "grasping, holding on, attachment," as well as a resultant sense of "fuel, supply, substratum by means of which an active process is kept alive or going." Together they convey the sense of "finding one's support by or in nourished by, taking up" (PED 149). This "home" (*ālaya*) consciousness thus finds its support in the material sense faculties to which it clings, and is nourished by the predispositions toward profuse imaginings (*prapañca*) of names, images, and so on, both of which it in turn "takes up" and appropriates. As a dependently arisen form of cognitive awareness, in other words, the ālaya-vijñāna "grows, develops, and increases" based upon the two appropriations – the material sense-faculties with their physiological supports, and the mass of cognitive and affective conditionings persisting from the past – which serve as the substratum or fuel upon and by which the whole process is kept going. Conversely, these two appropriations persist only insofar as the ālaya-vijñāna continuously "appropriates" *them*, reflecting the basic interdependence of body and mind, object and consciousness, found throughout Indian Buddhist thought.

This relationship is brought out more clearly in the next section of the *Saṃdhinirmocana Sūtra* (V. 3), which presents three synonyms (*paryāya*) of this new conception of mind, along with "etymological" explanations of their characteristics:

> This vijñāna is also called the "appropriating consciousness" (*ādāna-vijñāna*) because the body is grasped (*gṛhīta*) and appropriated (*upātta*, or *ātta*) by it. It is also called the "*ālaya*" consciousness because it dwells in and attaches[16] to this body in a common destiny (*ekayogakṣema-arthena*).

> It is also called mind (*citta*) because it is heaped up (*ācita*) and accumulated (*upacita*) by [the six cognitive objects:] visual forms, sounds, smells, flavors, tangibles, and dharmas.
>
> (*Saṃdhinirmocana Sūtra* V. 3)[17]

Although the first two verses here primarily focus upon the ālaya-vijñāna's presence as a kind of basal consciousness appropriating and dwelling within the body (the etymological emphasis of *ādāna* and *ālaya*, respectively), their affective nuances of grasping and attachment remain ever close at hand. It is the third synonym, however, that most directly suggests the productive relationship between the accumulating form of mind that "grows, develops and increases," now designated the "ālaya" vijñāna, and the transient object-oriented, cognitive processes, now considered "manifesting" vijñānas. Although still embryonic in the *Saṃdhinirmocana Sūtra*, we can discern the basic outline clearly enough.

The first passage we cited (V. 2) states that the "mind with all the seeds" (*sarvabījakaṃ cittam*) grows, develops, and increases based upon the appropriation of the material sense faculties as well as "the predispositions toward profuse imaginings in terms of conventional usage of images, names, and concepts." The last passage we cited (V. 3), suggests how the "mind with all the seeds" actually increases: the objects of manifest cognitive awareness "heap up" and accumulate in the ālaya-vijñāna. Together these constitute an initial picture of the dynamic interaction between the ālaya-vijñāna and the manifest forms of cognitive awareness: (1) the ālaya-vijñāna arises based upon physiological and psychological structures (*saṃskārā*) built up over many lifetimes, the sense-faculties and predispositions toward images, names, concepts, and so on,[18] (2) which themselves largely determine the specific forms that manifest cognitive awareness may take by providing the requisite conditions by which (3) cognitive objects "heap up" and accumulate in the ālaya-vijñāna.

But how do they "heap up"? What is the link between the conditioning forces of the past and the generating activities of the present that makes the "mind which has all the seeds ... grow, develop, and increase"? The short answer – the simultaneous presence of the afflictions in a latent or quiescent form – developed only gradually through the later texts. But it was built upon the ideas of the simultaneity of multiple mental processes, as well as their innocuous but indispensable presence, that were first developed in terms of the relations between the different forms, the "two aspects," of cognitive awareness itself.

In a passage that departs even further from the somatic nature of the ālaya-vijñāna in the initial *Yogācārabhūmi* passage, the *Saṃdhinirmocana Sūtra* states that the ālaya-vijñāna arises in conjunction not only with its bases, which we have just seen, but also with its own kind of object. That is, the ālaya-vijñāna is now characterized as a *cognitive* form of awareness in its own right. But what kinds of object are there that are constantly present, so as to continuously give rise to this persisting, accumulating "ālaya" vijñāna, which, we remember, must be continuously present to insure bodily life and without which one would die? The *Sūtra* (VIII 37.1) states that the appropriating consciousness (*ādāna-vijñāna*) arises as an *imperceptible or unrecognizable perception of the stable external world* (*asaṃvidita-sthira-bhājana-vijñapti*).[19] Whether we are aware of it or not, the external world is always impinging upon our sense faculties or mind, constantly giving rise to a subliminal form of cognitive awareness, an "imperceptible" awareness of the world within and without.

From this follows the *Sūtra*'s next major development. If this imperceptible awareness of the external world is always present, then it must also occur simultaneously with any other object-specific forms of manifest cognitive awareness (*pravṛtti-vijñāna*) which happen to be occurring. This is only possible, as the debates in the *Kathāvatthu* had recognized some seven centuries before, if it neither eclipses their specific cognitive functions nor overrides their particular karmic nature – and this is possible only because it is imperceptible or subliminal. Therefore, in perhaps its most significant departure from traditional Buddhist models of mind, the six modes of manifest cognitive awareness are no longer thought to occur solely in conjunction with their respective sense bases and epistemic objects, but are in addition *supported by* and *depend upon* the subliminal form of awareness called "ālaya" vijñāna (see Table 3.1). Hence, these modes of cognitive awareness no longer occur only sequentially, they also occur *simultaneously*.[20] *Saṃdhinirmocana Sūtra* (V. 4–5) states:

> The six groups of cognitive awareness (*ṣaḍ-vijñāna-kāya*) ... occur supported by and depending upon (*saṃniśritya pratiṣṭhāya*) the appropriating consciousness (*ādāna-vijñāna*). Of these, visual cognitive awareness occurs supported by (*niśritya*) visual forms and the eye furnished with consciousness (*savijñānaka cakṣus*). A discriminating mental cognitive awareness (*vikalpaka manovijñāna*) with the same sense object occurs at the same time (*samakāla*) along with the visual cognitive awareness....
>
> If the conditions for a single visual cognitive awareness occurring simultaneously are present, then supported by and depending upon the appropriating consciousness only a single visual cognitive awareness occurs simultaneously. If the conditions for up to all five groups of [sensory] cognitive awareness occurring simultaneously are present, then all five groups of cognitive awareness occur simultaneously.[21]
>
> One can compare this to a large stream of water: if the conditions for the arising (*utpatti-pratyaya*) of a single wave are present (*pratyupasthito*) then only a single wave arises (*pravartate*). If the conditions for the arising of two or many waves are present, then many waves arise, but the stream of water is neither interrupted nor exhausted in its current.
>
> (*Saṃdhinirmocana Sūtra* V. 4–5)

Table 3.1 The dependent arising of cognitive awareness in the *Saṃdhinirmocana Sūtra*

Traditional model of the arising of vijñāna	
(1) Depending on karmic formations (*sankhārā*) viññāṇa arises (S II 2)	
(2) Depending upon: Material sense faculty + Sense object + attention	cognitive awareness (*viññāṇa*) arises
New model of the arising of vijñāna	
(1) Depending upon two *upādānas*: Appropriation of material sense faculties + Appropriation of predispositions, etc.	ālaya-vijñāna grows, increases, etc.
(2) Depending upon: Ālaya-vijñāna (with two appropriations) + Sense object + attention	manifest cognitive awareness (*pravṛtti-vijñāna*) arises
Diachronic conditioning between two aspects of vijñāna in the Saṃdhinirmocana Sūtra	
First step: Depending upon: Appropriation of material sense faculties + Appropriation of predispositions, etc.	ālaya-vijñāna grows, increases, etc. (V. 2)
Second step: Depending upon: Ālaya-vijñāna (with two appropriations) Sense object + attention	manifest cognitive awareness arises (V. 4–5)
Third step: Depending upon: Manifest cognitive awareness	(seeds) heap up, accumulate in *citta* (ālaya-vijñāna) (V. 3)
Fourth step: Depending upon: Ālaya-vijñāna with accumulated (seeds) and two appropriations + Sense object + attention	cognitive awareness (*pravṛtti-vijñāna*) arises
Whole cycle: Depending upon: Ālaya-vijñāna with seeds and two appropriations + Sense object +	→ cognitive awareness arises, which in turn → heap up and accumulate (seeds) in the ālaya-vijñāna
Ālaya-vijñāna arises with more seeds, two appropriations, and so on.	
In terms of dependent arising Saṃskārā conditions (ālaya-)vijñāna; Vijñāna is a precondition for development of mind-and-body; Mind-and-body appropriated by ālaya-vijñāna gives rise to manifest cognitive processes; Manifest cognitive processes heap up and accumulate in the ālaya-vijñāna; Ālaya-vijñāna with all the seeds is reborn.	

It is this simultaneity of all the modes of cognitive awareness, subliminal and supraliminal alike, that allows the characteristics of the passages cited above to be related to each other:

1. The ālaya-vijñāna, which "grows, increases, and develops," arises based upon the appropriations of the body and the predispositions of previous experiences (V. 2), while
2. it simultaneously supports the occurrence of new cognitive processes (V. 4–5),
3. the results of which, their cognitive objects, in turn heap up and accumulate in the ālaya-vijñāna (V. 3).

This pattern explicates the implicit diachronic feedback process between vijñāna and saṃskārā (in both their aspects) which we discerned in the formula of dependent arising in Chapter 1: (1) Vijñāna is first a resultant process that arises conditioned by the results of past actions (saṃskārās condition the arising of "samsaric" vijñāna), whose (2) cognitive processes are pre-eminently involved in the very activities that eventually bring about its own perpetuation ("cognitive" vijñāna conditions the arising of karmic activities (*saṃskārā*)), which (3) in turn make that "samsaric" vijñāna "grow, develop, increase" (S III 54).

The *Saṃdhinirmocana Sūtra* thus not only outlines this important diachronic relationship, but it also intimates – not quite explicitly – a synchronic conditioning process wherein the results of one's past experience simultaneously condition one's momentary cognitive processes, while these processes in turn simultaneously "heap up" in the ālaya-vijñāna. These implications, as we shall see, will be drawn out more fully in succeeding texts.

The ālaya-vijñāna as mental stream

It may be helpful at this point to reflect again upon the relationship of actions, mind, and the mental stream within early Indian Buddhist thought. Recall the analogy of the river we used when discussing the karmic formations (*saṃskārā*): a river comes into being through a steady stream of water flowing in (more or less) the same place over an extended period of time. The current continues to flow (provided regular rainfall) in its particular course dependent upon the stability of the riverbed, for whose formation the current itself was largely responsible. The riverbed and the current have thus mutually arisen in a temporal feedback process, so that their present existence is the long-term result of this continuous past interaction. Neither one has wholly produced the other, nor could one exist without the other – they are interdependent in their historical development, as well as in their present patterns of interaction.

In a similar way, Buddhists posit an interdependence between mind, as a mental stream, and the constructive results of karmic activity, of behavior. The continuity of one's existence depends not only upon the body, but also, and even more importantly, upon the influences that constitute samsaric existence – the accumulation of karmic potential and the afflictive and cognitive predispositions – for it is these that provide the constant push, the built-up inertia, that propels the mental stream. The configuration of one's current mental stream is thus largely a function of the material and psychological structures (the *saṃskārās*) that have been constructed and propelled by past actions instigated by the cognitive and emotional afflictions. In this sense, the mental stream is said to be "built up," "heaped up," "accumulated," and to "attain growth and increase," for ultimately the forms of our current existence result from these past activities. Indeed, like the inseparability between the river current and riverbed, the mental and physical streams (vijñāna and saṃskārā) simply *are* samsaric existence. We are, like a river, the results of all that we have thought, felt, and done. As the Buddha said:

> This body does not belong to you, nor to anyone else. It should be regarded as [the results of] former action that has been constructed and intended and is now to be experienced.
>
> (S II 64)

It is only upon the basis of such long conditioning processes that our present mental activities can operate at all. And they operate in the particular ways they do because they are based upon the specific structures and dispositions that have been built up from past experiences and activities (such as the two "appropriations" above). Our minds as well as our bodies are, in this sense, "enstructured" karma,[22] structures built up from past activities. Each moment of mind therefore brings with it in its entirety – in its current configuration and its diverse capacities – its own past history of action and experience.[23] We are no *tabula rasa* and never have been. This suggests a different approach to the concept of the ālaya-vijñāna, particularly to the many complexities associated with it – those causing Conze to characterize it as a "conceptual monstrosity" (1973: 133).

We should recall that the Yogācārins, like their contemporaries, were aiming to understand our immensely complex capacities of mind by analyzing their underlying conditions and their dynamic interrelationships for the ultimate purpose of positively redirecting their maleficent influences upon our current activities. It is due to the sheer complexity of the phenomena to be understood – the multifarious physiological and mental structures and processes subserving emotion, perception, language, memory, and so on – that the conception of the ālaya-vijñāna takes on such a long train of synonyms and characteristics. For what the ālaya-vijñāna effectively represents, in these classical Yogācāra texts at least, is *all aspects of vijñāna excluding supraliminal cognitive processes*. And since the functions and characteristics of subliminal mental processes are extremely complex and manifold, the ālaya-vijñāna is more appropriately understood as the *conceptual rubric* under which they are categorized than as a singular process of its own. It comprises, in other words, the totality of the mental stream minus whatever conscious processes happen to be arising on its surface. From this perspective (in basic agreement with early ideas on mind and *contra* later attempts to substantialize the ālaya-vijñāna), it can hardly be construed as a singular entity, much less an unchanging one. It represents rather – in its own terms – an unending stream of mind with all of its currents, eddies, and backwaters, disturbed by debris deposited on its riverbed perhaps, stirred up by windswept waves on its surface, to be sure, but nevertheless still *conceptualized* separately from the transient rising and falling of the surface waves of arising cognitive awareness. As the *Saṃdhinirmocana Sūtra* declares, no matter how many waves arise upon its surface, "the stream of water is neither interrupted nor exhausted in its current."

These metaphors, we have seen, were by no means unique to the Yogācāra tradition, nor were the issues they addressed. What *was* unique was the way the Yogācārin school responded to them: by postulating the kind of vijñāna it did – an "ālaya" vijñāna – with its own particular characteristics and qualities. For the notion of the ālaya-vijñāna was just one way, arguably the most Abhidharmic way, of analyzing and conceptualizing the complex conditions, and their equally complex interconnections, which constitute what Indian Buddhists euphemistically called persons, that is, a "mental stream."

* * *

Questions, of course, still remain. How exactly is mind "built up"? What is it that is "accumulated"? What are the energies that perpetuate the mind-stream? All these questions involve the complex interrelationship between the subliminal presence of ālaya-vijñāna and the supraliminal forms of cognitive awareness whose objects "heap up" and accumulate within it. The key connection between these two processes – the simultaneity of the resultant and hence karmically neutral ālaya-vijñāna with the active and karmically creative processes associated with manifest cognitive awareness – is still ill-defined. Karma is, after all, only accumulated when it is informed and instigated by the afflictions (*kleśa*). Nevertheless, the afflictive tendencies of "attachment" and "clinging" that accomplish this, and which were already implicit in the very terms *ādāna* and *ālaya* themselves, are clearly indicated in the famous verse which closes chapter 5 of the *Saṃdhinirmocana Sūtra*:

> The appropriating consciousness, profound and subtle,
> Like a violent current, flows with all the seeds;
> I have not taught it to the ignorant,
> Lest they should imagine it as a self.[24]
>
> (*Saṃdhinirmocana Sūtra*, V. 7)

The *Alaya Treatise* of the *Yogācārabhūmi*

The text that most systematically develops the concept of the ālaya-vijñāna in Abhidharma terms is found in a section of the *Yogācārabhūmi* entitled the

Viniścaya-saṃgrahaṇī, composed for the most part after the *Saṃdhinirmocana Sūtra*. This text portion, which we shall refer to as the *Ālaya Treatise*, is itself comprised of two distinct sections: the *Proof Portion* and the *Pravṛtti* and *Nivṛtti Portions* (all following Schmithausen's nomenclature).[25] All of these are essential for any understanding of the ālaya-vijñāna, and we shall carefully analyze their major ideas and developments.

The *Ālaya Treatise* develops the concept of the ālaya-vijñāna by expressly characterizing it in Abhidharmic terms, such as those in the previous chapter, and by systematically describing its interactive relationship with the six modes of manifest cognitive awareness (*pravṛtti-vijñāna*). Not only does it transpose the traditionally diachronic processes of "samsaric" vijñāna into synchronic dharmic terms, something barely begun in the *Saṃdhinirmocana Sūtra* itself, but it also describes those processes in terms of the categories of Abhidharma dogmatics – fully acknowledging, on the one hand, their accumulating and subsisting properties, without, on the other hand, compromising their Abhidharmic character as momentary and discrete dharmas. The systematization of the ālaya-vijñāna found in these chapters thus effectively completes the integration of the diachronic and synchronic dimensions of vijñāna along the lines first suggested in the *Saṃdhinirmocana Sūtra*.

In addition, the *Ālaya Treatise* refines the conception of latent afflictions subsisting within the mental stream, an idea we already found in the *Abhidharma-kośa*, by conceiving of these underlying dispositions as a set of continuous yet subliminal processes operating in parallel with the ālaya-vijñāna itself. These cognitive and emotional afflictions are of course essential to the generation of karmic activities, but adequately accounting for their continuing yet unobtrusive presence had been problematic since the time of the *Kathāvatthu*. By describing the subsisting influences of accumulated karmic potential and the latent afflictions in dharmic terms – that is, in terms of the ālaya-vijñāna and the afflicted *manas*, respectively – and then conceptualizing these as two distinct kinds of subliminal process which simultaneously occur with and underlie all supraliminal processes, the Yogācārins will have fundamentally redrawn the formal model of mind in Indian Buddhist thought. This constitutes, in our view, a definitive response to the Abhidharmic Problematic.

The Proof Portion

Although the conception of the ālaya-vijñāna in the *Proof Portion* is not as fully developed as in the latter two sections of the *Ālaya Treatise*, which we will examine shortly, it displays marked development from either the *Basic Section* of the *Yogācārabhūmi* or the *Saṃdhinirmocana Sūtra*.[26] In sharp contrast to the latter, the *Proof Portion* provides argued rationales for differentiating the two kinds of vijñāna, begins to delineate their mutually interactive relationship, and then addresses problems either already raised within Abhidharma doctrine, or stemming from the new model itself. In particular, it addresses the question of the immediate succession of heterogeneous dharmas, the related problem of "mutual seeding" between heterogeneous types of vijñāna, and the conditions necessary (in terms of its own conceptual framework) to account for multi-sensory experience. Moreover, it also broaches the topic of the persistence of certain afflictions throughout one's samsaric existence.

The *Proof Portion* offers "proofs" or arguments – all couched in terms of dharmic discourse – as to why the mental processes represented by the ālaya-vijñāna must be considered a distinct dimension of mind. These are argued chiefly on the grounds that: (1) the continuous, diachronic functions traditionally attributed to vijñāna cannot be fulfilled by the six modes of cognitive awareness; and that (2) even such synchronic processes as immediate cognitive awareness itself are not fully tenable unless a form of mind such as the ālaya-vijñāna simultaneously underlies and supports them. There are six such proofs. Proof 1 argues that vijñāna should be differentiated into two kinds, the subliminal processes of the ālaya-vijñāna and the forms of manifest cognitive awareness, in accordance with their divergent conditions and disparate characteristics. We shall paraphrase these arguments (citing the complete texts in the notes).

1 The ālaya-vijñāna continuously arises in an unbroken stream because it occurs conditioned by the continuous effects of past saṃskāras.[27] It is therefore a resultant state which is karmically indeterminate (*avyākṛta-vipāka*); and, unlike the other modes of cognitive awareness which arise in conjunction with specific sense organs, the ālaya-vijñāna arises throughout the entire body.
2 The forms of manifest cognitive awareness (*pravṛtti-vijñāna*), on the other hand, are momentary and discontinuous, since they arise due to present conditions (the sense-faculties, sense objects, and attention); they are experienced as either skillful or unskillful and are thus karmically determinate;[28] and since they only arise in conjunction with their respective physiological bases they cannot appropriate the body as a whole.[29]

For these reasons, the text argues, none of the forms of momentary cognitive awareness (*pravṛtti-vijñāna*) could be the vijñāna that traditional doctrine claims appropriates the entire body from birth until death. There must, therefore, be another kind of vijñāna, that is, the ālaya-vijñāna.

These characteristics establish an *explicit dichotomy* between the ālaya-vijñāna and the six modes of manifest cognitive awareness (*pravṛtti-vijñāna*) – a dichotomy that most later discussions tend to assume rather than re-argue. The ālaya-vijñāna has now become a distinct category of mental processes described in more or less standard dharmic terms.

Having established this dichotomy, the *Proof Portion* then proceeds to address several problems that, in its view, require two distinct kinds of vijñāna. Of these, we will first examine the problem of the immediate succession of divergent states of mind and the possibilities for seeds to be transmitted between them, and then, the question of the simultaneous occurrence of multiple cognitive functions and experiences – all of which are thought to require a form of mind like the ālaya-vijñāna.

The difficulties surrounding the succession of dharmas of divergent karmic natures, which we observed in the Abhidharma literature in terms of *vipāka-phala*, the maturation of karmic fruit heterogeneous to its cause, is discussed in Proof 4 insofar as it relates to the transmission of seeds from one moment to the next. How, the text asks, can a karmically skillful dharma (*kuśala-dharma*), associated with equanimity, for example, be succeeded by a karmically unskillful one (*akuśala-dharma*), associated with anger? If the succeeding dharma of anger arose conditioned by the immediately preceding dharma of equanimity, this would entail that a dharma could arise conditioned by another dharma of a completely different nature. This, however, would conflict with the "homogeneous and immediately antecedent condition" (*samanantara-pratyaya*) which requires a greater degree of homogeneity between succeeding dharmas. But if the succeeding dharma were not conditioned by that particular immediately preceding dharma, then what immediately preceding dharma was it conditioned by? The problem of the succession of heterogeneous dharmas was, we remember, one of the contexts in which various responses to the Abhidharma Problematic were raised – for the Sautrāntika metaphor of seeds (*bīja*), the Sarvāstivādin concepts of "possession" (*prāpti*), and, less directly, the Theravādin concept of the life-constituent mind (*bhavaṅga-citta*) all addressed this issue.

But the problem here is reversed: the concept of seeds is not being considered as a response to the problem of the succession of heterogeneous dharmas, but rather the succession of heterogeneous dharmas in being raised as a problem for the continuous succession of seeds. The mere introduction of the concept of seeds – without a distinct dimension of mind to support them – remains problematic, since the continuous transmission of the seeds from moment to moment in association with one specific form of mind or another still has to be explained in strictly dharmic terms,[30] with all its temporal limitations and causal qualifications. That is, moments of cognitive awareness with all their disparate conditions and divergent karmic natures routinely succeed each other, and no single one of them is continuously present in order to serve as the continuous support for the seeds. So, if no single form of cognitive awareness is continuous enough to serve that function, and neither is there sufficient continuity between diverse forms of cognitive awareness, how – or more precisely, *through what medium* – could these seeds succeed one another? Thus, just as the seemingly innocuous question of the immediate succession of heterogeneous dharmas challenged the entire edifice of karmic theory in Abhidharma doctrine (i.e. *vipāka-phala*), so here too the seemingly insignificant question of the immediate succession of heterogeneous *vijñānas* challenges the viability of the "seeds in the stream" theory of karma. In other words, the problem of karmic influences proceeding through succeeding moments of heterogeneous dharmas is expressed in terms of the problem of "mutual seeding" (*bījatvam* ... *anyonyam*) between succeeding moments of heterogeneous forms of vijñāna. Thus Proof 4 asks:

> For what reason is it impossible for the six groups of cognitive awareness to be each others' seeds? Because an unwholesome [*dharma*] occurs immediately after a wholesome one, a wholesome one immediately after an unwholesome one, an indeterminate one immediately after both of these.... These [six groups of cognitive awareness] cannot properly be seeds [of each other] in this way. Moreover, the mental stream occurs after a long time, having long been cut; for this reason too [the mutual seeding of the six groups of cognitive awareness] is not tenable.[31]
>
> (*Proof Portion*, Proof 4)[32]

In order to avoid this conundrum, Asanga argues, there must be a continuous and neutral type of mind which can receive and transmit seeds of various natures uninterruptedly, but one that also arises *simultaneously* with the six types of manifest cognitive awareness so that it (or rather, its seeds) can immediately condition their arising. What is needed, in other words, is a type of mind endowed with all the seeds, that is, the ālaya-vijñāna.

This new genre of mind which "possesses" the karmic and dispositional potentialities, does not only address the problems surrounding heterogeneous succession. It also gradually became the cornerstone of a new model of mind built upon the simultaneous, moment-to-moment arising of distinct kinds of mental processes. As with the question for mutual seeding, the *Proof Portion* again turns the argument around the other way and claims that if the ālaya-vijñāna and the six forms of manifest cognitive awareness do *not* arise simultaneously the mental cognitive awareness (*mano-vijñāna*) would not be able to function clearly. Traditionally, a moment of mental cognitive awareness arises in conjunction either with its own cognitive object, a dharma, or with another form of cognitive awareness as its objective support.[33] In the latter case, the object is an immediately preceding moment of sensory cognitive awareness; that is, technically speaking, a mental cognitive awareness arises when a previous occurrence of sensory cognitive awareness impinges upon its particular cognitive range, the *manas*. The Yogācārins argue, however, that if this mental cognitive awareness only arose subsequent to that moment of sensory awareness, not simultaneously with it, then that mental awareness would not in fact have cognitive clarity:

> Because, when one remembers an object which has been perceived in the past then the mental cognitive awareness which takes place is unclear; but the mind which takes place in regard to a present object is not unclear in this way. Thus, either the simultaneous occurrence [of the cognitive awarenesses] is correct or [there is] a lack of clarity of the mental cognitive awareness.
>
> (*Proof Portion*, Proof 3)[34]

Taking its cue perhaps from the *Saṃdhinirmocana Sūtra*, the *Proof Portion* (Proofs 2a, 6) also combines the arguments for clarity and simultaneity by citing the example of multi-sensory experience, in which we see, hear, and think all at the same time. There would be no clarity between the various forms of cognitive awareness, with all of their diverse bases, objects, and appropriated faculties, the text argues, if they were to arise serially rather than simultaneously. There must therefore be a simultaneous form of mind underlying all of them which enables a multiplicity of diverse cognitive processes to arise and function at the same time without confusion; there must be, in other words, what we call "parallel processing."[35]

The *Proof Portion* thus uses two examples – clear mental cognitive awareness and multi-sensory experience – to argue that for even the traditional six kinds of cognitive awareness to operate effectively they must arise simultaneously rather then sequentially and that this simultaneity is possible only when there is a distinct dimension of vijñāna which simultaneously appropriates the entire body and underlies and supports the various forms of manifest cognitive awareness, that is, only when a notion such as an ālaya-vijñāna is acknowledged.

This idea that diverse kinds of cognitive processes occur simultaneously had enormous implications for the Yogācāra model of mind, whose picture of a multiplicity of processes continuously occurring in every moment of mind would continue to be elaborated in increasingly Abhidharmic terms. The *Proof Portion* adumbrates this fuller picture in its most complex argument for the ālaya-vijñāna.[36] Experience, Proof 5 argues, is fourfold:

> the perception (*vijñapti*) of the world, the perception of the [physiological] basis, the perception "[This is] I," and the perception of the sense objects. These perceptions are experienced as occurring simultaneously moment to moment. It is not tenable for there to be diverse functions like this within a single moment of a single cognitive awareness.[37]
>
> (*Proof Portion*, Proof 5)

This succinct passage recapitulates previous concepts while portending further developments. As for the first perception, the *Saṃdhinirmocana Sūtra* (VIII 37.1) had already declared that the "appropriating consciousness" (*ādāna-vijñāna*) has a continuous, though all but imperceptible, perception of the enduring external world (*asaṃvidita-sthira-bhājana-vijñapti*). Second, as a form of embodied mind, the ālaya-vijñāna continuously arises in conjunction with the ceaseless sensations which accompany bodily processes, that is, "the perception of the basis." At the same time, *Saṃdhinirmocana Sūtra* V. 7 warned that the ālaya-vijñāna tends to be "imagined as a self." And last, this passage declares that all of these perceptions arise together along with manifest cognitive awareness of the external sense objects.

This short passage thus offers us the first inkling of the complete Yogācāra model of mind which will be fully elaborated in the following texts: depending upon both one's body and one's predispositions (*à la* the *Saṃdhinirmocana Sūtra*), the ālaya-vijñāna arises as a subliminal perception of the world, thereby serving as the locus of the dispositions toward self-grasping and self-identity (the thought "I am"), and based upon which various forms of manifest cognitive awareness (*pravṛtti-vijñāna*) arise as objects impinge upon their respective sense-fields. And all of these, the *Proof Portion* (Proof 5) declares, "are experienced as occurring simultaneously moment to moment." The picture is nearly developed, only the finer Abhidharmic details have yet to come into focus. This was accomplished in the extraordinary text, the *Pravṛtti Portion*.

The *Ālaya Treatise*, *Pravṛtti Portion*: analyzing the ālaya-vijñāna in Abhidharmic terms

The next stage in the systematization of the ālaya-vijñāna, and in many respects the most remarkable, is represented by the second section of the *Ālaya Treatise*, whose two parts address the continued arising (*pravṛtti*) and cessation (*nivṛtti*) of the ālaya-vijñāna – hence dubbed the *Pravṛtti* and *Nivṛtti Portions* by Schmithausen.[38] This text, less than twenty pages in translation (appended as Appendix III, below), is particularly noteworthy as it represents the most sustained attempt to describe the ālaya-vijñāna and its relation with other mental processes, particularly the forms of manifest cognitive awareness (*pravṛtti-vijñāna*), in purely Abhidharmic categories. In the process, the text also amplifies and accentuates the cognitive aspects of the ālaya-vijñāna itself. At the same time, the text portrays the ālaya-vijñāna within the larger framework of Buddhist soteriology in much the same way vijñāna had been depicted in the early Pāli texts and the *Abhidharma-kośa*: the continuity and cessation (or ultimate transformation) of the ālaya-vijñāna is equated with the continuity and cessation (*pravṛtti* and *nivṛtti*) of individual samsaric existence. This conception of the ālaya-vijñāna thus fully and finally integrates in synchronic dharmic terms the two distinct dimensions of vijñāna we first discerned in the early Pāli materials: the diachronic aspects of a subsisting "samsaric" vijñāna, and the synchronic aspects of momentary modes of "cognitive" vijñāna.

All this is clearly reflected in the structure of the text. The first part, the *Pravṛtti Portion*, describes the ālaya-vijñāna as a fully cognitive form of awareness in straightforward Abhidharmic terms: its moment-to-moment arising (*pravṛtti*) is conditioned by its distinct bases, its specific cognitive objects, and its concomitant mental factors, all of which, however, are too subtle for any but advanced practitioners to apprehend, that is, they are subliminal. This text also finally articulates the complex relationship between the ālaya-vijñāna and the forms of manifest cognitive awareness: these not only occur simultaneously (*sahabhū*) with each other, but they also provide the conditions for each other's continued arising (*pravṛtti*) in much the same way we discerned between the two "aspects" of vijñāna in the series of dependent arising. In the Yogācāra understanding, however, this relationship now occurs, like waves on a river, between two distinct yet simultaneously interactive dimensions of the same mental stream. The *Pravṛtti Portion* also further elaborates the conception of a distinct mode of mentation (*manas*) in order to denote the ongoing, yet unobtrusive, presence of the afflictions, a notion first hinted at in the *Saṃdhinirmocana Sūtra* and prefigured in the *Proof Portion* just above.

With the addition of this mode of mentation (*manas*), the Yogācārins finalized a radically new model of mind in Indian Buddhism, one in which subliminal cognitive, affective, and even afflictive, processes interact and co-exist with supraliminal processes. The problems of accounting for the continuity of karma and kleśa within a mental stream comprised solely of momentary dharmas, that is, the Abhidharma Problematic, were virtually resolved by this transposition into dharmic terms of the diachronic phenomena pertaining to the mental stream. This is, we suggest, the ultimate import of this model of mind. And with these developments, Indian Buddhist thinking about the nature of mind and the causal relationships between one's activities, one's passions, and the conditions of consciousness itself reached a new level of understanding, an understanding we may take for granted today, a century after Freud's *Interpretation of Dreams*, but one that was conceived fifteen centuries earlier in a radically different metaphysical and cultural context.

It is the second section, the *Nivṛtti Portion*, that describes the ālaya-vijñāna in terms of this larger metaphysical context. The ālaya-vijñāna not only addresses the conceptual problems reflected in the Abhidharma Problematic, but it also articulates its important soteriological dimension which harks back to the vijñāna (*viññāṇa*) of the early Pāli texts. In this respect, the ālaya-vijñāna is much more similar to the traditional notions of vijñāna than is often appreciated. Vijñāna, we remember, played a major role in the cycle of birth and death in the early Pāli literature. It was one of the essential concomitants of life whose "descent" into the womb at conception and "departure" from the body at death marked the beginning and end of a single lifetime. As the only process explicitly stated to continue from one lifetime to the next, it was the continued advent or "stationing" of vijñāna in this world that constituted samsaric existence (and thus was implicitly linked with the continuity of accumulated karmic potential). Moreover, vijñāna persisted throughout numerous lifetimes until its final eradication (or fundamental transformation) during the processes of purification and liberation. Though described in more contemporaneous terms, the ālaya-vijñāna in the *Nivṛtti Portion* is characterized along largely the same lines, reflecting the continuing multivalence of vijñāna from the earliest strata of Buddhist thought right into the Yogācāra tradition. But to understand how and why the ālaya-vijñāna must be radically transformed in the processes leading toward liberation, we must examine the specific processes through which it is continuously re-created, expanded, and perpetuated – along with all of the ill-fated consequences that such activities entail. This is the theme of the *Pravṛtti Portion*. We shall follow the structure of the text rather closely in this chapter, to whose translation in Appendix III the reader is again referred.

The ālaya-vijñāna's subliminal objective supports and cognitive processes

More than any other Yogācāra text, the first section of this text characterizes the ālaya-vijñāna as a subliminal mode of cognitive awareness. Although it is said to arise in conjunction with its own objective supports (*ālambana-pravṛtti*) and in association with other mental processes (*samprayukta-caitta*), just as the manifest forms of cognitive awareness (*pravṛtti-vijñāna*) do, all of these are said to be "undiscerned" (*aparicchinnākāra*), imperceptible "even for the wise." This conception of subliminal cognitive awareness, when combined with the rest of the ālaya-vijñāna complex, becomes the basis for a distinctively Buddhist form of depth psychology.

* * *

As in the *Saṃdhinirmocana Sūtra*, the ālaya-vijñāna here arises with two objective supports. The first consists of two "inner appropriations" (*adhyātman upādāna*), the body, that is, the sense faculties with their material supports (*sādhiṣṭhānam indriya-rūpam*), and the mass of dispositions, attitudes, and thought constructions accumulated from past experience and activities, that is, "the predispositions toward attachment to the falsely discriminated (*parikalpita-svabhāvābhiniveśa-vāsanā*)."[39] This last refers to the predispositions (*vāsanā*) toward particular cognitive and affective patterns – attachment to false understanding – insofar as they inform[40] and support the arising of the subliminal form of awareness called the ālaya-vijñāna.

These underlying structures of mind in turn subtly influence the ālaya-vijñāna's second, "outer" objective support, similarly echoing the *Saṃdhinirmocana Sūtra* (VIII37): "the ālaya-vijñāna arises by means of… the outward perception of the receptacle world whose aspects are undiscerned" (*bahirdhā-aparicchinnākāra-bhājana-vijñapti*).[41] The *Pravṛtti Portion* proceeds to gloss this expression, explaining that

> "the outward perception of the receptacle world whose aspects are undiscerned" refers to a continuous, uninterrupted perception of the continuity of the receptacle world based upon that very ālaya-vijñāna which has inner appropriation as an objective support.[42]
>
> (*Pravṛtti Portion* (1.b)A.2)

We need to analyze this dense but deeply significant passage piece by piece.

First, it is clear that the text is concerned to establish the ālaya-vijñāna in traditional terms as a genre of cognitive awareness that arises moment to moment in conjunction with its own specific objects. This is, in fact, the outline heading of this first section of the *Pravṛtti Portion* (*ālambana-pravṛtti-vyavasthāna*). Hence, the "continuous, uninterrupted perception of the continuity of the receptacle world" means that the ālaya-vijñāna continuously arises in conjunction with (and, arguably, only in conjunction with) an objective support, that is, the "receptacle world," and it is continuous because its "objective support is always present; it is not sometimes this and sometimes that" ((1.b)B.2). However, the text warns:

> It should be understood that the ālaya-vijñāna is momentary regarding its objective support, and though it arises continuously in a stream of instants, it is not unitary (*ekatva*).[43]
>
> (*Pravṛtti Portion* (1.b)B.3)

Second, the text states that this "continuous perception of the continuity of the external world" is *based upon* the ālaya-vijñāna with its inner appropriations, the sense-faculties together with their material bases and the cognitive and affective predispositions – which in effect represent the physiological and psychological structures necessary for any cogent moment of cognitive awareness to arise. In other words, this indistinct yet uninterrupted perception of the external world continuously arises whenever the bodily faculties are sufficiently impinged upon for some form of cognitive awareness, however subtle, to arise, *and* the shape and content of this cognitive awareness are continuously informed by the predispositions, the impressions instilled by past experience.

The text uses the analogy of a lamp flame to illustrate how "outer" perception depends upon the "inner" conditions of mind:

> Thus, one should know that the way the ālaya-vijñāna [arises] in regard to the objective support of inner appropriation and the objective support of the receptacle [world] is similar to a burning flame which arises inwardly while it emits light outwardly on the basis of the wick and oil.[44]
>
> (*Pravṛtti Portion* (1.b)A.3)

We take this to mean that the ālaya-vijñāna arises as an indistinct perception of the external world based upon its physiological substratum (the wick) and its psychological "fuel" (*upādāna*).[45] This combination of conditions is largely consistent with most analyses of vijñāna in Indian Buddhism, which typically include the sense-faculties and a sensory or mental object plus attention, while some schools also mention predispositions or the "life-constituent mind" (*bhavaṅga-citta*) as well. These are common conditions for the arising of cognitive awareness. Here, however, they are *all* subliminal.

Thus, third and perhaps most important, the entire complex of processes the ālaya-vijñāna represents is said to be subtle, indistinct, beyond the ken of ordinary mortals: the perception of the external world is "undiscerned,"[46] "the objective support [of the ālaya-vijñāna] is subtle (*sūkṣma*)" and "difficult to discern (*duṣpariccheda*) even by the wise ones of the world."[47] The subliminal cognitive processes of the ālaya-vijñāna do not produce a clear perception of their objects, but rather give rise to a vague, subtle, virtually imperceptible form of awareness.

Accordingly, the mental processes (*caitta*) that arise in conjunction with the ālaya-vijñāna, the topic of the next section of the *Pravṛtti Portion* ((2.b)B.2), *saṃprayoga-pravṛtti-vyavasthāna*), are equally subtle. These are the five so-called "omnipresent factors associated with mind" (*citta-saṃprayukta-sarvatraga*): attention, sense-impression, feeling, apperception, and intention (*manaskāra, sparśa, vedanā, samjñā, cetanā*). This also agrees with standard Abhidharmic doctrine in which each moment of mind (*citta*) arises accompanied by a set of specific processes (though they vary from school to school).[48] The processes occurring in conjunction with the ālaya-vijñāna, however, are so subtle and difficult to perceive (*durvijñānatva*), "even for the wise," that they do not overwhelm or interfere with the supraliminal processes of mind. They are purely resultant states (*vipāka*) and are thus karmically indeterminate (*avyākṛta*) (even intention!), their emotional tone is neither painful nor pleasurable (*aduḥkhāsukha*), and, like the supraliminal associated mental factors, they all function in regard to a single object (*ekālambana*).[49] This object, of course, is the subliminal object of the ālaya-vijñāna, not of the supraliminal manifesting forms of cognitive awareness from which it is explicitly distinguished (*asamālambana*). Hence, all the various processes associated with the subtle arising of the ālaya-vijñāna (*sūkṣma-pravṛtti-saṃprayukta*) are compatible with all types of supraliminal processes, since their respective objects, feeling tones, and karmic natures are quite distinct ((4.b)B.1).[50] The ālaya-vijñāna is, as has been stated in the *Proof Portion* and elsewhere, a second, distinct stream of mind.[51]

In sum, this first part of the *Pravṛtti Portion* portrays the ālaya-vijñāna as a distinct dimension of truly cognitive processes with three specific conditions for its continuous arising: (1) as a kind of basal consciousness, it arises dependent upon the material sense-faculties; (2) as a mind informed by "the predispositions to attachment to the falsely discriminated," its arises conditioned by various affective and cognitive dispositions and impressions accumulated through previous experience; and, based upon these first two; (3) as a subliminal mode of cognitive awareness, it arises as an indistinct perception of the external world. These processes are accompanied by roughly the same set of "omnipresent factors connected with mind" found in standard Abhidharma theory. Yet all of this is subliminal, occurring beneath the threshold of conscious awareness (*sūkṣma-pravṛtti*), imperceptible "even for the wise." This is, in short, an explicit and systematic conception of subliminal mental processes developed within the phenomenological metapsychology of Abhidharma Buddhism expressed exclusively in terms of momentary and discrete dharmas.

With this development, we must note, the Abhidharma mode of analysis has been applied to areas well beyond its original domain: the *discernment* of dharmas for the purpose of their pacification. Dharmic analysis has been extrapolated to "*undiscernable* processes" in order to address the serious conceptual and religious problems raised by its own success. Analysis had demonstrated that immediate supraliminal mental processes could never be understood completely without reference to the longer-term conditioning processes that support and facilitate their operation, or, to put it in Buddhistic terms, without taking into account the persisting influences of past karmic actions and the continuing presence of the cognitive and emotional afflictions. These influences, though, are never really past; as Faulkner once put it, "the past is not dead, it's not even past." For not only do they persist, they also simultaneously influence all our supraliminal processes, both conditioning and being conditioned by them in a constant, uninterrupted feedback process that – although implicit in the early Pāli materials, and certainly intimated in the *Saṃdhinirmocana Sūtra* – is only fleshed out in full Abhidharmic detail in the next major section of the *Pravṛtti Portion* of the *Yogācārabhūmi*: the reciprocal relations between the two distinct forms of vijñāna.

The ālaya-vijñāna's mutual and simultaneous relationship with manifest cognitive awareness (pravṛtti-vijñāna)

The complete (re)integration of the diachronic and synchronic dimensions of vijñāna – undifferentiated in the early Pāli texts, but rent asunder in Abhidharma discourse – is finally accomplished in this section of the text. It articulates a fully interdependent and simultaneous relationship between the subliminal forms of mind of the ālaya-vijñāna and the supraliminal forms of manifest cognitive awareness. This is achieved primarily through extrapolating the Abhidharmic relationship of mutual and simultaneous (*sahabhū*) conditionality, which was otherwise understood to pertain between mind (*citta*) and its concomitant mental factors (*caitta*),[52] to the relationship between the two distinct types of vijñāna, the ālaya- and pravṛtti-vijñānas. The *Pravṛtti Portion* states that the *sub*liminal as well as *supra*liminal processes arise both simultaneously (*sahabhāva-pravṛtti*) and mutually conditioning one another (*anyonya-pratyayatā-pravṛtti*) – a notion assuming their dichotomous, disjunctive nature while emphasizing their inseparable interaction.[53] The mutual conditionality between the two "aspects" of vijñāna, implicit in the multifaceted nature of vijñāna in the early series of dependent origination, has now been made explicit. The text begins with the ālaya-vijñāna conditioning the forms of manifest cognitive awareness.

First of all, cognitive processes can only occur in a body that is living, one in which some mental processes, however subtle, are already occurring. And, as we have seen, the ālaya-vijñāna has nearly since its inception been considered that form of mind (*vijñāna*) which "dwells" in and appropriates the body, keeping it from dying. In this sense, as the *Pravṛtti Portion* puts it, the ālaya-vijñāna "provides a support" (*āśrayakara*) for the manifesting cognitive awarenesses by "appropriating" the sense-faculties upon which they are based. This is the first of two ways the ālaya-vijñāna conditions the arising of manifest cognitive awareness.[54]

The second way is by "being the seed" (*bīja-bhāva*) for their arising. Each moment of cognitive awareness is itself a resultant state, an effect of past karma, in other words, a fruition of a seed. The ongoing and underlying processes that comprise the ālaya-vijñāna continuously condition the arising of supraliminal cognitive processes insofar as they store or "preserve" the specific causal conditions, the seeds, for these resultant processes to arise.

It might be helpful to reiterate what "being a seed" or "the mind possessing all the seeds" (*sarva-bījakam ālaya-vijñānam*) means in this school of Buddhist thought. As noted above, many mental processes occur automatically, they are resultant states that arise due to past causes, to karma. This much is standard Buddhist doctrine. Taking their cue from the Sautrāntikas perhaps, the Yogācārins have expressed the relationship of cause and effect with the metaphor of seeds and have closely associated them with subliminal mental processes, extrapolating upon notions, such as Vasumitra's, of a subtle form of mind (*sūkṣma-citta*) that persists during the attainment of cessation. Hence, to say that the ālaya-vijñāna is a condition for the arising of the manifesting cognitive awarenesses because it possesses all the seeds is to speak in much the same terms their contemporaries spoke in: (1) that the connection between cause and effect (karma) recognized by all schools of Indian Buddhism can be conveniently designated by the metaphor of the seed; (2) that these seeds in turn are most appropriately conceived of in relation to the mental stream; and – in what truly is a Yogācāra innovation – (3) that this mental stream with all the seeds needs to be considered a distinct form of subliminal mind, which, although distinct, nevertheless simultaneously conditions the moment-to-moment arising of the supraliminal form of cognitive awareness.

The statement that the "ālaya-vijñāna conditions the manifesting cognitive awarenesses by possessing their seeds" is, therefore, an abbreviated way of saying that the processes of mind that arise from moment to moment occur in large part due to the conditioning of karmic influences from the past, and that, upon coming to fruition, these influences themselves become dynamic factors in the ongoing processes of mind. Therefore, since every moment of mind includes multiple events that result from past karma – cognitive awareness itself as well as many of its associated mental factors – *there are virtually no moments in which multiple seeds are not coming to fruition*. By the same token, however, there are also virtually no moments in which the ālaya-vijñāna is not simultaneously "being seeded" by the processes of manifest cognitive awareness, the other half of its mutual and reciprocal conditionality.

Manifest cognitive processes produce karma and increase the ālaya-vijñāna

We have already glimpsed how this may occur. As early as the *Saṃdhinirmocana Sūtra* (V. 3) it was stated that:

> It is also called mind (*citta*) because it is heaped up (*ācita*) and accumulated (*upacita*) by [the six cognitive objects:] visual forms, sounds, smells, flavors, tangibles, and dharmas.
>
> (*Saṃdhinirmocana Sūtra*, V. 3)

This section of the *Pravṛtti Portion* ((3.b)B) elaborates upon this, describing how forms of manifest cognitive awareness serve as conditions for the arising of the ālaya-vijñāna. First, the six types of manifest cognitive awareness condition the ālaya-vijñāna by "nurturing" and "infusing" the seeds within it, which lead to several kinds of fruit:

> "Nurturing seeds in this life" means that insofar as [karmically] skillful, unskillful and indeterminate [moments of] manifest cognitive awarenesses arise based on the ālaya-vijñāna, their simultaneous arising and ceasing, supported by their own supports, infuses the impressions (*vāsanā*) into the ālaya-vijñāna.
>
> (*Pravṛtti Portion* (3.b)B.1)

Once these impressions are "infused" and their seeds nurtured within this uninterrupted, subliminal stream of mental processes, the text continues, they will eventually give rise to various fruits, amongst which are of course further moments of cognitive awareness:

> By that cause (*hetu*) and that condition (*pratyaya*), through being skillful, etc., the manifest cognitive awarenesses will arise again successively more well-nurtured, well-tempered and quite distinct.[55]
>
> (*Pravṛtti Portion* (3.b)B.1)

In this way, momentary cognitive activities condition further cognitive experiences in this life by increasing and "fattening the seeds"[56] for their own future arising. Moreover, they also bring about the continued reproduction of the ālaya-vijñāna, the virtual medium of samsaric existence, in the future ((3.b)B). In this way, the forms of arising cognitive awareness help perpetuate (*pravṛtti*) the vicious wheel of cyclic existence.

Moreover – and most profoundly – these two processes occur *simultaneously*. This is articulated in the next section of the text, "establishing the arising [of the ālaya-vijñāna] by simultaneity" (*sahabhāva-pravṛtti-vyavasthāna*), which describes how the ālaya-vijñāna arises simultaneously with any or all of the six forms of manifest cognitive awareness, as well as with the new kind of mentation (*manas*) (to be discussed below).

The ālaya-vijñāna co-arises with the mental factors (*caitta*) associated with the forms of manifest cognitive awareness, with their various feelings (*vedanā*), etc. as well as their diverse karmic natures ((4.b)A.3, 4). The ālaya-vijñāna, however, is not directly affected by any of these, the text states, because it arises only simultaneously (*sahabhāva*), not associated (*saṃprayukta*) with them. This is because mental factors are "conjoined" or "associated" with a moment of mind (*citta*) only when, among other things, they are directed toward the same object. But since the ālaya-vijñāna arises in conjunction with its own objective supports and associated mental factors, it is not associated with those of the supraliminal cognitive processes; it only arises simultaneously with them, just as other factors, such as the eye-faculty do ((4.b)B.1). Although not expressed in Abhidharmic terms, this was arguably implicit in the *Saṃdhinirmocana Sūtra* (V. 5) when it stated that no matter how many waves may arise, "the stream of water is neither interrupted nor exhausted in its current."

Hence, these two mutually conditioning processes occur simultaneously and (nearly) uninterruptedly. That is:

1 The ālaya-vijñāna provides two of the essential conditions for supraliminal cognitive processes to arise: "by being a seed (*bīja-bhāva*), and by providing a support" (*āśraya-kara*).
2 Conversely, these same cognitive processes infuse and nurture the seeds within the ālaya-vijñāna, causing them to arise in the future as well as the ālaya-vijñāna to grow and mature, thereby perpetuating samsaric existence into the future.

The largely diachronic feedback relationship between the two aspects of vijñāna we first observed as implicit in the Pāli materials is now, in the *Pravṛtti Portion*, seen to occur simultaneously between explicitly differentiated forms of vijñāna, portraying a dynamic synergy that propels and perpetuates the vicious cycle of existence.

To make all this more tangible, it may be worth revisiting our analogy of the river current and the riverbed. Earlier we discussed the interactive relationship between the flow of water and the riverbed itself, how neither one independently "created" the river, but that the river came into being through the continuous interaction between the two, each continuously effecting and conditioning the other – for, as all readers of Mark Twain know, the riverbed too is constantly changing, the sandbars shifting, the banks eroding, and so on, continuously being formed by as well as forming the direction and flow of the river current. We used this metaphor to depict the simultaneous and reciprocally conditioning relationship between vijñāna and saṃskārā, between consciousness and the physical and mental substructures that largely govern the form and content of cognitive awareness.

Here the simultaneous and reciprocally conditioning processes take place between two levels or dimensions of vijñāna itself: the deep, underlying currents "carrying all the seeds," which is closely contoured by both the shape of its hidden banks and the powerful inertia of its invisible streams (i.e. its two "appropriations"), and the superficial, arising awarenesses, rising like waves propelled by these underlying currents and buffeted by every gust of wind. The waves, of course, are a phenomena of the stream itself; they do not exist apart the stream of water which continuously supports, indeed comprises, their every rise and fall. For although the waves on the surface respond more immediately and to different kinds of forces (especially in strong weather) than do the deeper, more powerful and steadier streams below, they nevertheless remain an inseparable part of the stream itself. Every passing wave is *simultaneously* a passing change in the stream itself. At no time are they ever truly separate; they are constantly effecting each other in myriad told and untold ways – and all of this happens in every single moment.

Similarly, this picture of mind centered on the ālaya-vijñāna portrays a constant, simultaneous, and reciprocal feedback relationship between the ālaya-vijñāna and the six types of manifest cognitive awareness. While the ālaya-vijñāna supports the waves of the mind by both supporting its underlying structures and by providing the seeds, the causal conditions, for their arising, the modes of manifest cognitive awareness in turn are constantly affecting the contents of the underlying stream of mind, the ālaya-vijñāna. Or, to switch metaphors, there is virtually no time in which the seeds are not coming into fruition (because resultant states of mind such as cognitive awareness and feeling occur nearly every moment), just as there is virtually no time in which the seeds are not being infused into the ālaya-vijñāna (because intentions, *cetanā*, also occur in every moment of active mind). That is, the processes of seeding and being seeded, like the waves and the stream, are continuously, simultaneously, and reciprocally affecting each other in a dynamic whole that is greater than the sum of its parts. This is the import, and indeed the image, of the Yogācārin model of mind described as "arising by means of reciprocal conditionality" (*anyonya-pratyayatā-pravṛtti-vyavasthāna*).[57] The *Pravṛtti Portion* thus echoes the analogy from the *Saṃdhinirmocana Sūtra*:

> As there is no contradiction in a wave arising simultaneously with the stream, and there is no contradiction in the reflected image occurring simultaneously with the bright surface of the mirror, so one should understand that there is no contradiction in the manifest cognitive awarenesses also arising simultaneously with the ālaya-vijñāna.[58]
>
> (*Pravṛtti Portion* (4.b)B.2)

* * *

But, as before, there is still something missing. Cognitive awareness is merely a result of past karma and, as a non-intentional resultant state, it cannot by itself generate new karma. This requires the energetic activity of the afflictions, for it is only when one's actions are accompanied and instigated by the afflictions that karma is built up and the cycle of rebirth perpetuated. Thus, in order to account for the continuing presence of these afflictions within the mental stream, the *Pravṛtti Portion* delineates another distinct genre of mental processes, a continuous but subliminal level of mentation (*manas*) which, we shall see, is said to always arise "associated with the four afflictions … a view of self-existence (*satkāya-dṛṣṭi*), the conceit 'I am' (*asmimāna*), self-love (*ātmasneha*), and ignorance (*avidyā*)," and to be constantly "conceiving the ālaya-vijñāna as 'I am [this]' and '[this is] I.'" This idea of apprehending the ālaya-vijñāna as a self echoes both at the end of *Saṃdhinirmocana Sūtra* V, where the Buddha hesitated to teach the ālaya-vijñāna (*ādāna-vijñāna*) lest fools imagine it a self, as well as in the *Proof Portion*, which observes that "The perception '[This is] I' ... is experienced as occurring simultaneously moment to moment." Its roots, of course, go back considerably further.

The ālaya-vijñāna's simultaneous arising with (afflictive) mentation

We have already discussed the general question of how the afflictions (*kleśa*) might persist in the mental stream without determining the karmic nature of each particular moment. This was clearly foreshadowed in the latent versus manifest discussion in the early Pāli materials, was one of the core components of Abhidharma Problematic we first identified in the *Kathāvatthu*, and then became the focus of the *kleśa/anuśaya* controversy in the *Abhidharma-kośa*. The Yogācāra approach to this question is suggested in the passages from the *Saṃdhinirmocana Sūtra* and the *Proof Portion* just cited: there arises a continuous, simultaneous, but ultimately afflictive apprehension of the ālaya-vijñāna as a self. This only begins to be systematized, however, as a distinct form of mentation (*manas*) here in the *Pravṛtti/Nivṛtti Portions* of the *Yogācārabhūmi*, reaching its most elaborate development (in Indian texts at least) as the afflictive mentation (*kliṣṭa-manas*) in the *Mahāyāna-saṃgraha*, to be examined in the following chapter. We will briefly review the development of this crucial concept, for it also marks a shift of emphasis in the character of the ālaya-vijñāna itself – a shift from a somatic consciousness that pervades and maintains bodily life and preserves the karmic seeds and cognitive dispositions that influence conscious processes, to a consciousness which serves as the very locus of the defilements, afflictions, sufferings, and spiritual corruptions (*saṃkleśa, kleśa, saṃskārā-duḥkhatā, dauṣṭhulya*) that constitute cyclic existence. We will examine the continuity of these latent afflictions in general before addressing their apprehension of the ālaya-vijñāna as a self in particular.

* * *

We observed in the Pāli texts that the conceit or pride of "I am" or "I-making" and "mine" or "my-making" (*asmimāna, ahamkāra, mamaṅkāra māna*), as well as the view of self-existence (P. *sakkāyadiṭṭhi*, S. *satkāyadṛṣṭi*), were, along with their latent counterparts (*anusaya*), closely connected to continued samsaric existence, while their complete elimination accompanied if not defined perfect view (*sammādiṭṭhi*) and the end of suffering.[59] These dispositions persist, in the early Buddhist view, throughout all of one's existences until they are finally abandoned upon the higher stages of the path.

These afflictive dispositions were therefore as problematic in the Abhidharma context as the accumulation of karmic potential, and for similar reasons.

The view of self-existence and other afflictions are not abandoned until the state of an Aryan is attained, yet they must persist in a continuous chain of dharmas from each moment of mind to the next throughout these multiple lifetimes; but if they were active in each of those moments, karmically skillful states free of such afflictions could never arise,[60] and liberation would therefore be impossible.

Accordingly, some texts, such as the *Abhidharma-kośa*, divided this afflictive self-view into two kinds: an innate view of self-existence (*sahajā satkāyadṛṣṭi*), such as occurs in birds and animals, and which is karmically indeterminate and thus able to co-exist with skillful states, and a deliberated (*vikalpita*) view which is karmically effective and thus conducive to unskillful actions.[61] It is this innate view of self-existence which persists until far along the path, when all traces of it, together with its latent disposition, are finally eliminated. Until then it must subsist in some sense "within" the mental stream, from whence it is ever capable of arising and negatively influencing the activities of sentient beings, keeping them trapped in samsara. But the question is, in what exact sense does it subsist in the mental stream?

The Sautrāntikas, we recall, used the metaphor of seeds to represent both the accumulation of karmic potential and the existence of the latent afflictions. In the Yogācārin texts we have examined heretofore, however, the concept of seeds had only referred to the relation of cause and effect, to karma; they were not directly associated with the latent dispositions. Nevertheless, just as both the Sautrāntikas extended the metaphor of the seeds (*bīja*), and the Sarvāstivādins the concept of "possession" (*prāpti*), to represent the persistence of the latent afflictions as well as the accumulation of karma, so too the Yogācārins came to address the problem of the latent afflictions in the same way they addressed the accumulation of karmic seeds: by positing a continuous, subliminal stream of dispositions simultaneous with, but not contradictory to, supraliminal processes of various karmic natures.[62]

This did not come all at once. In our discussion of the *Saṃdhinirmocana Sūtra*, we mentioned that although the resultant, karmically neutral ālaya-vijñāna and the active cognitive processes (*pravṛtti-vijñāna*) arise simultaneously, the karmically causal connection between them was not completely articulated. That is to say, although the potential for the results of karma (represented by seeds in the ālaya-vijñāna) were seen to occur simultaneously with the active, karma-generating mental processes, the causal link between these two *in synchronic dharmic terms* had not yet been delineated. The simultaneous influences between the "accumulated" and "accumulating" aspects of vijñāna had not yet included that crucial afflictive link that is so essential to the Buddhist conception of samsara. The model of mind centered around the ālaya-vijñāna would only be fully completed in synchronic, dharmic terms with the addition of a continuous, though latent, locus of self-grasping which provides the ever-present potential to generate more karma – with the addition, that is, of this mentation (*manas*) which always arises "associated with the four afflictions ... a view of self-existence, the conceit 'I am,' self-love and ignorance."

This link between the influences of past actions and the generation of new karma was clear enough in the conventional diachronic terms of the series of dependent arising: the results of past actions tend to elicit the underlying afflictions, which stimulate the karmic activities – within which "cognitive" vijñāna plays a central role – that lead on to "samsaric" vijñāna being reborn in another lifetime. These earlier formulations thus depicted a dynamic but vicious feedback cycle of action, result, and reaction. That is, habitual activities typically evoke the patterns of afflictive response to the results of similar past activities, which in turn tend to instigate more of the same. This is the basic sense of samsara as a self-reinforcing cycle of compulsive behavioral patterns:

1 *Actions* (*karma*) that are instigated by the afflictions (*kleśa*) accumulate the *potential* for specific results.
2 These *results* are experienced as pleasure, suffering, and so forth, since *feelings* are the predominant result of karma.[63]
3 In *re-action*, these feelings provoke and activate (*paryavasthānīya*) the latent afflictions (*anuśaya*) which, once manifest, *instigate* further actions that accrue more karma and so on.

This older diachronic formulation is now transformed into an explicitly synchronic, and for the most part subliminal, one. The new bottles for this old wine thus appear as follows:

1 *Actions* instigated by the afflictions accumulate the *potential* for specific results, which persist in the form of karmic seeds moment to moment within the stream of mind called ālaya-vijñāna.
2 These *results* are experienced as pleasure, suffering, and so forth, since *feelings* are the predominant results of karma and are experienced in (nearly) every moment of mind.[64]
3 In *re-action*, these feelings provoke and activate the latent afflictions which always "occur simultaneously moment to moment" with the other processes of mind, and which, once manifest, *instigate* further karmic activity, the results of which "accumulate," "build up," and "infuse" the seeds of karma in the ālaya-vijñāna, and so on.

Thus, the earlier, more or less diachronic analysis of the vicious cycle of action, result, and reaction, of karma, fruit, and affliction (*karma, phala, kleśa*), is now replicated *intra-psychically*, and largely subliminally, in the synchronic relationships between distinct processes within a singular model of mind. In effect, this model encompasses all three components of the evocative passage cited in the first chapter:

> Karma is the field, consciousness (*viññāṇa*) the seed, and craving (*taṇhā*) the moisture.
>
> (A I 223)

It is in this last dimension, that of affliction, that the emotional nuances of the term *ālaya* come to the forefront, a term whose ancient connotations of "grasping" or "attachment" are emphasized in another of its "etymological definitions," this one appearing in the *Yogācārabhūmi* immediately preceding the *Proof Portion*:

> Because dharmas dwell (*ālīyante*[65]) there as seeds, or because beings grasp it as a self, it is the 'ālaya'-vijñāna.[66]
>
> (ASBh, 11. 9–14)

With this new form of mind called *manas*, which is constantly "conceiving and taking the ālaya-vijñāna as 'I am [this]' and '[this is] I,' " the dimension of afflictive intent enters decisively into the picture, with its uninterrupted power to perpetuate cyclic existence until finally being severed at the root through sustained spiritual practice.

This idea of grasping to aspects of one's samsaric existence as a self also has strong antecedents in earlier Buddhist traditions, as does its association with the term *manas*, or "mentation."[67] In the early Buddhist view one of the main factors keeping beings trapped in the vicious cycle of compulsive behavioral patterns was taking the five aggregates of grasping as a substantive "self" (*ātman*), as if they constituted or included a permanent, independent, and ultimately unitary entity. And in the *Abhidharma-kośa* it is *citta*[68] (which the Yogācārins tellingly equate with the ālaya-vijñāna) that unenlightened beings (mis)take for the self. In the Yogācāra tradition, this process of grasping to self-identity came to be thought of as a distinct level of mentation (*manas*) which conceives of its object, the ālaya-vijñāna, as a self – exactly what the *Saṃdhinirmocana Sūtra* warned against at the end of chapter V: "I have not taught it [the appropriating consciousness] to the ignorant lest they should imagine it a self."

This is natural enough. As the part of our consciousness most closely associated with our embodied existence, persisting dispositions, and continuing karmic effects – our bodily experience, emotional traits, and personal histories – the ālaya-vijñāna is near and dear, exhibiting the most continuity and most consistency of any of the mental processes in our lives. For even though the ālaya-vijñāna is explicitly "momentary regarding its objective support, and though it arises continuously in a stream of instants," and therefore "is not unitary" (*Pravṛtti Portion* (1.b)B.3), nevertheless,

> from the first moment of appropriation [of the body at the time of conception and] for as long as life lasts (*yāvaj jīvam*) its perception (*vijñapti*) always arises homogeneously (lit.: "having one flavor," *ekarasatvena*).[69]
>
> (*Pravṛtti Portion* (1.b)B.2)

Accordingly, the text states:

> The mind (*manas*) whose mode (*ākāra*) is conceiving (*manyanā*) "I-making" (*ahaṃkāra*), the conceit "I am" (*asmimāna*), always arises and functions simultaneously with the ālaya-vijñāna in states with

mental activity (*sacittaka*) and even in states lacking mental activity (*acittaka*). That [mind] has the mode of taking the ālaya-vijñāna as [its] object and conceiving [it] as "I am [this]" (*asmīti*) and "[this is] I" (*aham iti*).[70]

(*Pravṛtti Portion* (4.b) (a))

This conception of *manas* extrapolates upon traditional relations between mind (P. *mano*) and the conceit (*māna*) "I am," in order to posit a continuous, simultaneous, yet afflictive sense of self-identity as an essential component of each and every moment of mind. This level of mentation (*manas*) thus represents the ongoing sense of self-existence which taints all one's mental processes and activities until one realizes liberation. As the last part of this section of the *Pravṛtti Portion* (4.b)B.4) declares:

the *manas* ... always arises and functions simultaneously with the ālaya-vijñāna. One should know that until it is completely destroyed it is always associated with the four afflictions which by nature arise innately (*sahaja*) and simultaneously: a view of self-existence (*satkāya-dṛṣṭi*), the conceit "I am" (*asmimāna*), self-love (*ātmasneha*), and ignorance (*avidyā*). One should see that these afflictions arise without impeding (*avirodha*) the [karmic quality of] skillfulness (*kuśala*), etc., in states of collectedness (*samāhita*) or non-collectedness, and are obscured-indeterminate (*nivṛtāvyākṛta*).[71]

(*Pravṛtti Portion* (4.b)B.4)

In sum, with this additional distinct dimension of mental processes, the ālaya-vijñāna model of mind has now responded to the second core component of the Abhidharma Problematic: since these afflictions persist until far along the path toward liberation, they are continuously present in each moment without, however, preventing karmically skillful states of mind (*kuśala-dharma*) from ever arising; yet at the same time they are now able to serve as an ever-present basis upon which further afflicted and ill-informed thoughts, feelings, and actions can arise. Thus, this new kind of mentation (*manas*), like the ālaya-vijñāna, persists even during periods devoid of mental activity and occurs even in higher meditative states without contradicting their karmically skillful nature. In other words, the underlying level of afflictive processes called "manas" came to be conceived of along the same lines, and for much the same reasons, as the ālaya-vijñāna: as a separate, subliminal, and karmically neutral dimension of afflictive mentation which occurs in each moment simultaneously with all other forms of manifesting cognitive awareness.

* * *

But, of course, there is more to it than this. Although this further emendation to the synchronic conception of mind clearly recognizes the deleterious effects these processes impart to every moment of cognitive functioning – effects that further perpetuate the endless cycle of samsaric existence – nevertheless, since these processes are themselves karmically neutral, they can only indirectly affect the karmic nature of the actions they subtly influence. Something else, in other words, has to bring these latent afflictions into active manifestation. This is brought about, in this scheme at any rate, through the mediating graces of mental cognitive awareness (*mano-vijñāna*).

Mental cognitive awareness is an awkward category for Buddhist thought. In the standard analysis of mind, we recall, each of the five types of sensory cognitive awareness arises in conjunction with an appropriate object within its respective sense-field and based upon its respective sense-faculty and organ. Mental cognitive awareness, however, is different. In the sequential view of the arising of cognitive awareness, a moment of mental cognitive awareness arises either (1) conditioned by a previous moment of mind (i.e. of a sensory cognitive awareness) or (2) in conjunction with a mental dharma which occurs within its own cognitive field, that is, mind (*mano*) itself.[72] There is an asymmetry in the first case in that, unlike the five types of sensory cognitive awareness, this mental cognitive awareness lacks a physical organ or sense faculty as its *present* basis; its only basis is a past moment of mind (or, in some schools, an anomalous "mental faculty").[73] The *Pravṛtti Portion* ((4.b)A.2) therefore suggests that the simultaneous support of mental cognitive awareness is this new form of mentation (*manas*) associated with the four afflictions.

This adds, we see, another layer of influence to the arising of ordinary consciousness. Insofar as mental cognitive awareness arises in dependence upon this afflicting mentation, it is informed by the misguided cognitive processes and afflictive influences this form of mind represents. Thus, the *Pravṛtti Portion* declares:

> the mental cognitive awareness (*mano-vijñāna*) is said to be based on mentation (*manas*), because as long as that mentation has not ceased, that [*mano-vijñāna*] is not freed from the bondage of perception in regard to phenomena (*nimitta*); if the [mentation] has ceased, then the [*mano-vijñāna*] will be freed [from that bondage].[74]
>
> (*Pravṛtti Portion* (4.b)A.2)

We see here the beginning of a shift in the source of the cognitive and emotional afflictions. The predispositions for discrimination about and attachment to phenomena, which were initially part of the "psychic endowment" (*upādāna*) of the ālaya-vijñāna in the *Saṃdhinirmocana Sūtra* (i.e. as the predispositions toward profuse imaginings in terms of conventional usage of images, names, and concepts, *nimitta-nāma-vikalpa-vyavahāra-prapañca-vāsanā-upādāna*), are increasingly associated with this newer level of mental activity, the *manas*. From here they are able to more directly influence manifest forms of cognitive awareness.

This passage is suggesting that as long as mental cognitive awareness is conditioned by the *manas* – comprising the afflictive dispositions toward attachment to a sense of "I am," and so on – then its perception in regard to phenomena will always be construed in those terms. In other words, to the extent that they are always accompanied by this deep-seated, even unconscious, self-centeredness, then moments of mental cognitive awareness will never be entirely freed from the bonds of conceiving things in terms of self and other, subjects and objects, and so on, inviting all the erroneous and deluded actions that such self-centeredness fosters. It is only when this form of mentation (*manas*) has finally come to an end that mental cognitive awareness itself will be "freed from the bondage of perception in regard to phenomena." In other words, only when the latent afflictions are finally and fully eradicated at their basic, subliminal level will they cease adversely affecting our perceptions of the world and thereby cease instigating the afflictive activities that continue to perpetuate samsaric existence.

This ambitious project – tantamount to emptying out or utterly transforming the contents and structures of the unconscious mind – reflects how deeply those Gupta-era "yogic practitioners," the Yogācārins, had understood that "the great obstacles to the ascetic and contemplative life arose from the activity of the unconscious" (Eliade, 1973: p. xvii). It is this topic – the complete cessation of the ālaya-vijñāna itself – that is the final theme of the *Ālaya Treatise*.

The *Ālaya Treatise, Nivṛtti Portion*: equating the ālaya-vijñāna with samsaric continuity

This unfolding conception of mind centered on the ālaya-vijñāna, we have argued, represents a gradual reformulation of classical Buddhist notions of vijñāna. This process was instigated by the multitude of problems entailed by the Abhidharmic analytic, particularly its marginalization of the "samsaric" aspects of vijñāna, those associated with the continuity of samsaric existence, in favor of its "cognitive" aspects, those involved in immediate object-oriented cognitive awareness. Particularly problematic was the union of two assumptions, first, that the cognitive functions of mind are singular, in the sense that mind and its mental factors (*citta/caitta*) all arise in conjunction with a single, common object at any given moment;[75] and second, that the totality of its pertinent processes have to be – or even could be – ascertained and described exclusively in synchronic dharmic terms, which alone were considered to be an ultimate account of things "as they really are" (*yathābhūtam*). To the extent that these two assumptions were held simultaneously there would always be problems describing in ultimate terms the continuity of the key diachronic constituents of the mental stream. No one claimed, to our knowledge, that an analysis of the processes that were overtly active at any one time constituted a completely comprehensive account of the individual, but they lacked the conceptual tools to effectively analyze, and hence ameliorate, what remained inexpressible in terms of that discourse – a lacuna that became particularly acute as they increasingly realized that "the great obstacles to the ascetic and contemplative life arose from the activity of the unconscious."

The first step toward resolving those problems was to question the implicit assumptions about the singularity and transparency of the major processes of mind,[76] which the early Yogācārins did by distinguishing conceptually and terminologically between two dimensions of vijñāna: the subsisting and subliminal ālaya-vijñāna and the momentary and manifest cognitive awarenesses (*pravṛtti-vijñāna*). This is one of the model's basic insights. The ālaya-vijñāna system was not devised, however, to solve a conceptual puzzle, but to understand these divergent aspects of vijñāna in order to free beings from the entrenched and maleficent influences of karma, kleśa, and their results. Discerning two distinct dimensions of vijñāna was only a step toward articulating their intricate, interdependent – and ultimately samsaric – relationship, a step that was carried out most systematically in those sections of the *Pravṛtti Portion* we have just examined which describe the ālaya-vijñāna in standard Abhidharmic terms.

At the same time, however, their very success in this reformulation radically changed the issues at hand. For, once the ālaya-vijñāna came to be described in more Abhidharmic terms – as a momentary and discrete, if subliminal, dimension of cognitive functioning in its own right – then these two kinds of vijñāna no longer corresponded to the "cognitive" and "samsaric" aspects of vijñāna. For in the *Pravṛtti Portion* the "cognitive" aspects of the ālaya-vijñāna are just as prominent as its "samsaric" aspects. In this sense, one could say that the fault-line between the cognitive and samsaric aspects of vijñāna no longer lay *between* the two kinds of vijñāna, but now fell between these two aspects *within* the ālaya-vijñāna itself.[77] In this light, we can see that what the *Pravṛtti* and *Nivṛtti Portions* are respectively addressing are the cognitive and samsaric aspects of the ālaya-vijñāna itself. Whereas the *Pravṛtti Portion* is concerned primarily with describing the synchronic, cognitive dimensions of the ālaya-vijñāna and its relations with manifest cognitive awareness in Abhidharma terms, the *Nivṛtti Portion* is devoted to describing the ālaya-vijñāna in straightforward diachronic terms, that is, in terms of the perpetuation of samsaric existence and, most importantly, its final cessation. We should not forget that this latter aim never ceased to be considered the ultimate purpose of Abhidharmic systematic psychology (including the Yogācāra school).[78]

Accordingly, the last section of the *Ālaya Treatise* is entitled "Establishing the cessation (*nivṛtti*) of the root of the defilements" (*saṃkleśa-mūla-nivṛtti-vyavasthāna*), hence the *Nivṛtti Portion*. The ālaya-vijñāna is virtually equated here with the roots of the defilements (*saṃkleśa-mūla*) and the mass of accumulated karmic seeds, appropriations (*upādāna*), and spiritual corruptions (*dauṣṭhulya*) that keep beings entrapped in the vicious cycle of death and rebirth. The ālaya-vijñāna thus comprises those very processes, kleśa and karma, that both constitute and perpetuate (*pravṛtti*) samsaric existence, and whose cessation (*nivṛtti*) is tantamount to liberation – becoming, for all intents and purposes, the central locus of one's spiritual destiny. This is also in substantial agreement with those aspects of vijñāna we discerned in the early Buddhist texts, wherein vijñāna was both the product of past samsaric existence as well as the basis for its continued perpetuation, but whose cessation or radical transformation constituted liberation from that cycle.

The ālaya-vijñāna is similarly the result of past causes. It is not only brought about by past karmic formations (*saṃskārā*) itself – which, we remember, condition vijñāna in the series of dependent arising – but it also comprises all the seeds generated from past karmic actions which have yet to come to fruition. The ālaya-vijñāna is therefore considered in the *Nivṛtti Portion* to be "the root of the coming-about of the animate world (*sattva-loka*) because it is what brings forth (*utpādaka*) the sense-faculties with their material bases and the [forms of] arising cognitive awareness;"[79] hence it constitutes the "Truth of Suffering (*duḥkha-satya*) in the present" ((5.b) A.4a). And insofar as the ālaya-vijñāna possesses all the seeds, it is also "that which brings about (*utpādaka*) the Truth of Suffering in the future, and ... the Truth of the Origin [of suffering] (*samudaya-satya*) in the present" ((5.b)A.4b, c).[80]

And insofar as the ālaya-vijñāna is "accompanied by the appropriations (*sopādāna*) and spiritual corruptions (*dauṣṭhulya*)" that coincide with samsaric existence, it is also called "root of all the defiled [dharmas]" ((5.b)A) and the "cause of the continuance of the afflictions" (*kleśa-pravṛtti-hetu*) ((5.b)C.2(c)).[81]

These twin engines that perpetuate samsaric existence – karma and kleśa – have thus come to be so closely identified with the processes comprising the "ālaya" vijñāna that its abandonment is understood to be tantamount to the cessation of samsaric existence itself:

> As soon as [the ālaya-vijñāna] is eliminated, the two aspects of appropriation are abandoned and the body remains like an apparition (*nirmāṇa*). [Why is that?]
>
> Because the cause which brings about rebirth (*punarbhava*) and suffering in the future has been eliminated, the appropriation which brings about rebirth in the future is abandoned. Because all the causes of defilements (*saṃkleśa*) in this life have been eliminated, all appropriation of the basis of the defilements in this life are eliminated. Free from all the spiritual corruption, only the mere conditions of physical life remain.
>
> (*Pravṛtti Portion* (5.b)C.3)[82]

This process of elimination (*prahāṇa*) of the ālaya-vijñāna, which will be treated in more detail in the final text we will be examining, the *Mahāyāna-saṃgraha*, throws interesting light upon the constitution of the ālaya-vijñāna itself and its ultimate role within the Yogācārin Buddhist world-view. Although the ālaya-vijñāna is identified in this text as the "cause of the continuance of the afflictions" (*kleśa-pravṛtti-hetu*), it also "possesses the seeds of skillful roots (*kuśala-mūla*) conducive to liberation and penetrating insight (*mokśa-*, *nirvedha-bhāgīya*)" ((5.b)B.1) – despite the fact that these are in contradiction (*virodhatva*) with the predominately samsaric character of the ālaya-vijñāna. This is only possible, of course, due to the heterogeneous nature of the mental processes and potentialities subsumed under the singular term, ālaya-vijñāna.

Liberation is realized by cultivating these karmically skillful dharmas, rather than succumbing to their opposite, a process which is expressed metaphorically in terms, as we might expect, of cultivating the skillful roots and seeds:

> If these [skillful roots] do occur, other mundane skillful roots will become very clear, and therefore they will have greater capacity (*sāmarthyavattara*) to uphold their own seeds and will have greater strength towards [their own future] realization through having nurtured [those very] seeds. Skillful dharmas from those seeds will in turn become clearer, and subsequently more desirable and more pleasant results (*vipāka*) will also be realized.
>
> (*Pravṛtti Portion* (5.b)B.1)[83]

It is not until far along this process, however, that one can begin to even recognize the existence of the ālaya-vijñāna and all of its maleficent influences. Specifically, it is only when practitioners attain entry into an understanding of the Four Noble Truths for the first time (and reach the stage of "guaranteed liberation," *samyaktvaniyāmam avakrānta*), that they are able to penetrate the ālaya-vijñāna and realize how bound they are, both cognitively by the "bonds of objective phenomena" (*nimitta-bandhana*) and affectively by the "bonds of spiritual corruption" (*dauṣṭhulya-bandhana*) ((5.b)B.2). This not only follows most Buddhist traditions, which also distinguish between obstacles due to mis-knowledge and those due to the afflictive tendencies (*kleśajñeyāvarāṇa*),[84] but these are reflected in the means of eliminating the ālaya-vijñāna as well:

> Because the ālaya-vijñāna is the constituent element (*dhātukatva*) of all the kinds of karmic formations (*saṃskārā*) comprised in proliferation (*prapañca*), [the practitioner] makes [them] into one collection, one heap, one hoard in the ālaya-vijñāna. Having collected [them all] into one, he revolves the basis (*āśrayaṃ parivartate*) [i.e. the ālaya-vijñāna] by the cause of assiduous cultivation of the wisdom (*jñāna*) which takes true reality (*tathatā*) as an objective support. As soon as the basis is revolved, the ālaya-vijñāna must be said to have been abandoned (*prahīṇa*); because it has been abandoned, it must be said that all the defilements also have been abandoned.
>
> (*Pravṛtti Portion* (5.b)C.1)[85]

What remains after the ālaya-vijñāna is abandoned is the "revolved basis" (*āśraya-parivṛtti*). That is, what was the basis of samsaric existence, the ālaya-vijñāna itself, has now been radically and irreversibly transformed so that one's life is no longer driven by the maleficent influences of ignorance, the cognitive and emotional afflictions (*kleśa*), and the activities they engender, but rather is infused with the wisdom and compassion emanating from awakened mind itself.

Conclusion

In sum, the *Pravṛtti* and *Nivṛtti Portions* of the *Yogācārabhūmi* represent the most systematic treatment of the ālaya-vijñāna as a cognitive form of awareness (*vijñāna*). The *Pravṛtti Portion* develops the earlier dichotomization of vijñāna – into the abiding ālaya-vijñāna and the forms of manifest cognitive awareness – by fully delineating their simultaneous and interactive relationship in systematic Abhidharmic terms. It also introduces *manas* as a distinct dimension of afflicted mentality, existing simultaneously with the ālaya-vijñāna and the other forms of cognitive awareness – a conception that will be more systematically developed in the *Mahāyāna-saṃgraha*, as we will see. And finally, the *Nivṛtti Portion* describes the ālaya-vijñāna as little more than the inertial mass of afflictions, hindrances, and attachments to samsaric existence, making it the veritable subject of samsara whose cessation is, in effect, the cessation of cyclic existence itself. In this process, the Yogācārin thinkers developed, within their own religious and metaphysical framework, a full-fledged depth psychology in all of its descriptive and systematic detail.

In doing so, the ālaya-vijñāna reached its most *systematic* development, fully integrating the two basic levels of Abhidharmic discourse – diachronic and synchronic, santāna and dharma – which themselves correspond closely to the two "aspects" of viññāṇa found the early Pāli texts. In this respect, the ālaya-vijñāna represents not so much a departure *from*, as an explication *of* earlier notions of mind. Although the Yogācārins have redrawn the Buddhist map of mind, along Abhidharmic lines, the territory remains much the same. What remains to be seen, however, is how they attempted to reconcile this innovative model of mind with the more traditional categories of their own inherited traditions, specifically, with the processes first articulated in the series of dependent arising. This new model of mind also raised further "Abhidharmic" questions of its own. These two, essentially retrospective, concerns will be broached in our next chapter on the great text of Asanga, the *Mahāyāna-saṃgraha*, to be followed by a treatment of its more prospective, explicitly Mahāyāna concerns in our concluding chapter.

4

THE ĀLAYA-VIJÑĀNA IN THE *MAHĀYĀNA-SAṂGRAHA*

1. Bringing it all back home

> Think of self as operating like cinematic film, composed of discrete, discontinuous pictures that, when run together, create something very much continuous and integral. Of course, with both film and selfhood, in a literal sense the experience of "motion" and continuity is an illusion. Yet this is an extremely dull and misleading literalness. The "illusion" creates an experience that has a powerful subjective richness of its own, creating a larger, "moving" picture, very different from (and much more than) the simple sum of the discrete pictures. Each frame is both a discrete, discontinuous image and a subunit of a larger, continuous process that takes on a life of its own. The most interesting feature of contemporary psychoanalytic perspectives on self is precisely the creative tension between the portrayal of self as multiple and discontinuous and of self as integral and continuous.
>
> (Stephen A. Mitchell, 1993)

We now come to the final text we will be examining, the *Mahāyāna-saṃgraha* by Asanga. The *Mahāyāna-saṃgraha* (MSg) presents the most extended formal treatment of the ālaya-vijñāna of any of the early Yogācāra texts.[1] Indeed, its entire first chapter (MSg I) is devoted to describing the multiple characteristics of the ālaya-vijñāna and presenting various exegetical and doctrinal arguments in support of this distinctive genre of mental process. Much of this has already appeared in one formulation or another in the texts we have examined above, making this chapter considerably more accessible than would otherwise be the case, and giving it the appearance, appropriate to its name, of a "Summary of the Great Vehicle." We will therefore focus primarily on those aspects of the ālaya-vijñāna complex that more explicitly contextualize it within its larger historical or metaphysical framework, that touch upon heretofore unexamined implications of this model, or that are more systematically developed within MSg I.

Throughout most of its first chapter, the MSg is concerned to authenticate and establish the concept of the ālaya-vijñāna in terms of its earlier canonical background and its contemporaneous Abhidharma context. It emphasizes the dichotomy between the two aspects of vijñāna, and then interprets the series of dependent arising in these terms, much as we have done in Chapter 1. The MSg further argues that in order for the six modes of manifest cognitive awareness to be able to infuse (*paribhāvita*) or reinforce the seeds and impressions (*vāsāna*) in the ālaya-vijñāna, these two forms of vijñāna must not only be distinct from, but must also arise simultaneously with, each other. This can only occur, the text argues, between distinct types of processes that arise simultaneously. MSg I also more systematically develops the notion of unconscious afflictive mentation (*kliṣṭa-manas*) as a distinct genre of mental processes. The implications of these developments extend, in the latter part of MSg I, into the influences that language and conceptualization have in effecting all our moment-to-moment experiences and, even more profoundly, in shaping the development of our peculiarly human form of life. We leave these more far-reaching considerations to our final chapter.

In its full conception of the ālaya-vijñāna model, the MSg has systematically reformulated the traditional categories of kleśa, karma, and their results in terms of the dynamic interaction between distinct processes within a singular, multi-tiered model of mind. The Yogācārins utilize these "new bottles" to reformulate the "old wine" of traditional themes, such as the formula of dependent arising and the parameters of samsaric existence, and to *explicitly* address the major conundrums of the Abhidharma Problematic, that is, the continuities of karma and kleśa, and the gradual nature of the path toward liberation. Hence, the main thrust of MSg I is apologetic – seeking to connect its innovative theories with the authoritative discourses of the Buddha or to reach out to its contemporaries with Abhidharmic arguments. As with the *Ālaya Treatise*, we will closely follow the basic outline of MSg I, directly citing and commenting on the most pertinent passages.

Appropriating the traditional Buddhist framework

At the beginning of the text, the MSg acknowledges the innovative character of the ālaya-vijñāna and the interpretive challenges it represents, and sketches out the major themes of the chapter: the scriptural justification for the apparent novelty of the ālaya-vijñāna, its larger soteriological significance, and its complex interrelations with the seeds, the forms of manifest cognitive awareness, and the affliction of self-grasping:

> I.1. Where did the Lord teach the ālaya-vijñāna using the name *ālaya-vijñāna*?
>
> In the *Mahāyāna-Abhidharma-Sūtra* the Lord spoke these verses:
>
> "The element since beginningless time is the common support of all dharmas;
> As this exists, so do all the destinies as well as the realization of Nirvana."[2]

I.2. And it is taught in the same [*sūtra*]:

> The consciousness (*vijñāna*) containing all the seeds is the receptacle (*ālaya*) of all dharmas.[3] Therefore it is called the *ālaya* vijñāna. I teach [it only] to the Superior Ones.
>
> Such is the scriptural [evidence].

I.3. Why is this consciousness (*vijñāna*) called the *ālaya-vijñāna?*
It is called *ālaya-vijñāna* because all afflicted dharmas which have an origin dwell (*ālīyante*) in this [vijñāna] as a fruit (*phalabhāva*), and because this [vijñāna] also dwells in them as cause (*hetubhāva*). Or it is called *ālaya* vijñāna because sentient beings adhere (*ālīyante*) to this consciousness (*vijñāna*) as [their] self.[4]

(MSg I.1–3)

Asanga is first concerned with citing the "scriptural proof" (*āgama*) from the *Mahāyāna-Abhidharma-Sūtra* to show that the ālaya-vijñāna had indeed been taught by the Buddha, though only to "the Superior Ones." Although the first verse does not mention the ālaya-vijñāna by name, it does place the succeeding discussion within its larger soteriological context: that of the continuity of samsaric existence and its possible cessation, Nirvana. These passages also obliquely refer to the central theme of this view: the possibility of becoming trapped in a vicious cycle between the potential effects of past actions persisting in the form of seeds in the ālaya-vijñāna, and the powerful influence they have in generating new actions – actions instigated, above all, by attachment to the ālaya-vijñāna as a self. This cycle only ceases when those karma-inducing activities come to a halt, and the afflictive motives instigating them are purified or abolished. This epitomizes the concepts of karma, kleśa, and the gradual path of purification, the three crucial components of the Abhidharma Problematic that had troubled thinkers from the time of the *Kathāvatthu*. It is the Yogācārins' core contention that only a multi-tiered model of mind, with mutually conditioning influences between their multifarious processes, can adequately account for both the dynamics of samsaric continuity and the possibility of its cessation.

Synonyms of the ālaya-vijñāna in the disciple's vehicle

To buttress his claim that the ālaya-vijñāna had indeed been taught by the Buddha, Asanga adduces a number of similar concepts, couched in different terms, which were taught by contemporaneous, non-Mahāyāna schools (called here the Disciple's Vehicle). After explaining the absence of the term *ālaya-vijñāna* in these schools, Asanga interprets their "synonymous" concepts as like-minded attempts to address the same conundrums of consciousness, karma, and kleśa, and concludes that what they all refer to is in fact nothing but the ālaya-vijñāna itself. (See Appendix II for further parallels with non-Mahāyāna Indian schools.) These sections are worth citing in full:

I.10. Why is this mind (*citta*) not called the ālaya-vijñāna or the appropriating consciousness (*ādāna-vijñāna*) in the Disciple's Vehicle (*śrāvakayāna*)?

Because it belongs (*saṃgṛhīta*) to the very subtle objects of knowledge (*sūkṣmajñeya*) and the Disciples do not aim (*adhikāra*) toward omniscience (*sarvajñeyajñāna*). Therefore, since they attain liberation (*vimukti*) by accomplishing knowledge (*jñāna*) even without the [ālaya-vijñāna] being taught, it is not taught [to them].

The Bodhisattvas do aim (*adhikāra*) toward omniscience. Therefore it is taught to them. Without that knowledge it is not easy to arrive at the knowledge of the Omniscient One (*sarvajñajñāna*).

I.11 a. Moreover, the ālaya-vijñāna is also taught in the Disciple's Vehicle through different figures of speech (*paryāya*)....

b. In the scriptures (*āgama*) of the Mahāsāṃghikas, too, the expression "root-consciousness" (*mūla-vijñāna*) occurs. By this synonym also this [ālaya-vijñāna] is taught. It is like a tree which depends upon its root.

c. In the scriptures of the Mahīśāsakas also the expression "the aggregate which lasts as long as samsara" (*āsaṃsārika-skandha*) occurs. By this synonym also this [ālaya-vijñāna] is taught, because although at certain places and at certain times it is seen that the bodily form (*rūpa*) and the mind (*citta*) are interrupted, their seeds in the ālaya-vijñāna are not interrupted.

d. In the scriptures of the Āriya Sthaviras, also, the following [stages of the perceptual process] occur: life-continuum, seeing, knowing, adverting, exerting, examining, and the seventh, engaging (*bhavānga, darśana, jñāna, āvarjana, iñjita, prekṣā, pravartana*).

I.12. Therefore, the support of the knowable (*jñeyāśraya*), which is taught as the ālaya-vijñāna, the appropriating-consciousness, *citta*, the ālaya,[5] the root-consciousness, the aggregate which lasts as long as samsara, and the life-continuum, are [all] the ālaya-vijñāna. [By these synonyms] the ālaya-vijñāna is established as the royal path.

(MSg I.10–12)

We have examined some of these "synonyms" of the ālaya-vijñāna in previous chapters, along with other concepts addressing related issues. With the exception of the *bhavaṅga-citta*, however, we have scant knowledge about the terms mentioned here and what little we do know is largely based upon later, mostly sectarian, sources. The MSg, alas, sheds little additional light on them. It does demonstrate, however, the extent to which the Abhidharma Problematic was recognized and other formulations were devised in order to account for the apparent exegetical and logical gaps that opened up between the earlier teachings and the newer Abhidharmic developments.

The two vijñānas and the two dependent arisings

The MSg now calls upon the series of dependent arising to justify the necessity for a multi-layered model of mind, specifically the need to distinguish the persisting aspect of vijñāna in the first part of this series from the cognitive aspect of vijñāna described later in the series. This explains, as we have done in Chapter 1, how the presence of the afflictions in the middle part of the series, craving and grasping, accompanies most cognitive processes and thus motivates karmic actions which result in the perpetuation of samsaric vijñāna – hence the feedback cycle from vijñāna, to kleśa, karma, and back to vijñāna again.

Moreover, the MSg interprets the reciprocal relationship between these two aspects of vijñāna in two ways, first as a sequential relation, as in the standard series of dependent arising, and then as a simultaneous relation between the distinct components of the multi-tiered model of mind itself, that is, between the ālaya-vijñāna and the six forms of manifest cognitive awareness (and the afflictive mentation). Consonant with other contemporaneous texts, MSg I.19[6] regards these as two distinct kinds of dependent arising, corresponding closely to what we have called diachronic and synchronic, respectively. Although the MSg discusses the synchronic type of dependent arising first, for expository reasons we will begin with the second, the *diachronic* dimension of the reciprocal causality between the two kinds of vijñāna. This largely recapitulates our earlier analysis in Chapter 1.

Since commentarial times, the twelve-limbed formula of dependent arising was often interpreted in terms of three distinct lifetimes. As we recall, the constructed karmic formations (*saṃskārā*) persisting from past lives directly condition the arising of vijñāna in the present life, beginning at the time of conception. (We will examine this important juncture at greater length below, while discussing the processes of rebirth.) When vijñāna "descends" into the womb of the mother, the basic constituents of sentient existence (name-and-form, *nāma-rūpa*) grow and develop into the six-sense spheres (*ṣaḍāyatana*) of a human being. These mental and physical bases subsequently facilitate contact (*sparśa*) with objects in their appropriate sense-fields – all of which together comprise the standard components of "cognitive" vijñāna – which then give rise to sensation and feeling. These typically elicit the afflictive processes of craving (*tṛṣṇā*) and grasping (*upādāna*), which in turn condition the arising of becoming (*bhava*), initiating the beginning of another round of birth and death.

But there is an apparent redundancy here which, the MSg contends, argues for another kind of vijñāna, the ālaya-vijñāna. That is, name-and-form is thought to consist of the five aggregates, with "bodily form" corresponding to the material aggregate (*rūpa-skandha*) and "name" to the remaining four, *including* vijñāna. Thus, when the formula states that name-and-form arises conditioned by the first vijñāna (which is conditioned by the saṃskārā), then this could be taken to imply that the vijñāna aggregate (*vijñāna-skandha*) arises conditioned by vijñāna, that is, conditioned by itself. This redundancy is exacerbated by several canonical passages which explicitly expound the *mutual* dependence between vijñāna and name-and-form, such as an early Pāli text called the *Sheaves of Reeds*, in which the Buddha declared:

> Just as two sheaves of reeds might stand leaning one against each other, so too, with name-and-form as condition, consciousness [comes to be];

> with consciousness as condition, name-and-form [come to be]. With name-and-form as condition, the six sense bases [come to be]; with the six sense bases as condition, contact ... Such is the origin of this whole mass of suffering.
>
> (S II 114)

Asanga in MSg takes this passage as grounds for a distinctive form of vijñāna, that is, an ālaya-vijñāna (or, more precisely, its synonym, the *vipāka-vijñāna*):

> I.36. Consciousness (*vijñāna*) and name-and-form function through mutually supporting each other (*anyonyaniśrayayogena*) like a sheaf of reeds (*naḍakalāpa*), which would also not be possible without the consciousness [which is a] result of maturation (*vipāka-vijñāna*).
>
> (MSg I.36)

The commentaries on the MSg elaborate on this. They explain that the first vijñāna in the series is the ālaya-vijñāna, while the second one, the vijñāna-aggregate included within name-and-form, refers to the forms of manifest cognitive awareness (*pravṛtti-vijñāna*).[7] It is this kind of vijñāna, then, that is involved in the succeeding parts of the formula (the six-sense spheres, contact, feeling, craving, and appropriation), and whose associated activities perpetuate the resultant ālaya-vijñāna, which will eventually be reborn again conditioned by karmic formations (*saṃskārā*) at the beginning of the formula. Thus, drawing upon the same textual sources we examined in Chapter 1, the Yogācārins explicitly state what we saw was implicitly the case: that the formula of dependent arising depicts a diachronically reciprocal relationship between two distinct forms of vijñāna.

But the MSg also delineates a *synchronically* reciprocal relationship between the ālaya-vijñāna and the forms of manifest cognitive awareness, much as we have seen in the *Pravṛtti Portion*. This is effectively introduced when MSg I.17 rhetorically asks:

> How shall we understand that the ālaya-vijñāna and the defiled dharmas are simultaneously (*samakāle*) and reciprocally causes (*anyonya-hetu*) of each other?
>
> (MSg I.17)

It responds with two similes we have seen before: the interdependent arising of the flame and wick (as in the *Pravṛtti Portion* (1.b)A.3) and the bundle of reeds which, "simultaneously resting upon one another, do not fall." MSg I. 17 expresses this more technically, stating that "just as the ālaya-vijñāna is the cause of the defiled dharmas, so the defiled dharmas also are established as the causal-condition (*hetu-pratyaya*) of the ālaya-vijñāna."

This synchronic reciprocity, which is called the "first dependent arising" (MSg I.28), is more fully explained in the following two sections:

> I.26. The other, manifest [forms of] cognitive awareness (*pravṛtti-vijñāna*) are considered that which experiences (*aupabhogika*) in all the existences (*ātmabhāva*) and destinies (*gati*). As it is taught in the *Madhyāntavibhāga* [I.9]:
>
> > The first is consciousness (*vijñāna*) as a condition [i.e. the ālaya-vijñāna]; the second is related to experience.
> > In the latter are the mental factors of enjoying, discerning, and stimulating.[8]
>
> I.27. These two vijñānas are mutually conditions of each other. In the *Mahāyāna-Abhidharma-Sūtra* a verse states:
>
> > All dharmas dwell in vijñāna; likewise it [dwells] in them.
> > [They are] always mutually effect and cause of each other.
>
> (MSg I.26–7)

This "first dependent arising" designates what the *Ālaya Treatise* had earlier formalized as the simultaneous and reciprocal conditionality (*sahabhāva-*, *anyonya-pratyayatā-pravṛtti*) between the ālaya-vijñāna and the forms of manifest cognitive awareness. As MSg I.14 puts it, the ālaya-vijñāna is the *result* of past karmic activity, because it is "arisen based upon the impressions since beginningless time of those very defiled dharmas" (i.e. the processes associated with the *pravṛtti-vijñānas*), and it is the *cause* (*hetu*) for manifest cognitive awareness to arise, "because the ālaya-vijñāna which has all the seeds (*sarvabījaka*) is present at all times as the cause of just those defiled dharmas." Similarly and reciprocally, the forms of manifest cognitive awareness, which *result* from the seeds of the ālaya-vijñāna, are in turn conjoined with the very mental factors, enjoying, discerning, stimulating, and so on, that are essential for *causing* new karmic activities – which in turn perpetuate the future arising of the ālaya-vijñāna. In this way, the ālaya-vijñāna is considered as both the result and the cause of the forms of manifest cognitive awareness, as they are of it.

In sum, the MSg claims that a concept of mind such as the ālaya-vijñāna is necessary to fully explain the dynamic, circular causality depicted in the series of dependent arising *both diachronically and synchronically*. Diachronically, the temporal feedback processes in which karmically generative processes of mind give rise to results that enable more such processes to occur, are best explained by regarding the vijñāna in the series as two distinct kinds, as "samsaric" and "cognitive" vijñāna. And synchronically, the simultaneous processes of mind are best conceived, much as Freud once put it, by "dividing them between two separate but interrelated component parts or systems" (Freud, 1984: 430–3; see n. 18) – that is, into the ālaya-vijñāna and manifest cognitive awarenesses – and then describing the synchronic, reciprocal relations between them. Thus, according to the MSg, even such traditional doctrines as the formula of dependent arising require a notion such as the ālaya-vijñāna.

This much we have seen before. Indeed, it only makes explicit what was either implicit or incipient in earlier formulations. But the MSg also elaborates upon issues that have not yet been fully explored. It is still unclear, for example, exactly *how* the arising vijñānas could instill or infuse (*paribhāvana*) their impressions (*vāsāna*) or seeds (*bīja*) into the ālaya-vijñāna. And what exactly is the process of seeding, after all? In clarifying these processes, the MSg more precisely establishes the disjunctive distinction, and simultaneous relation, between these two aspects of vijñāna.

Seeding the ālaya-vijñāna: the karmic process as simultaneous intrapsychic causality

The arguments presented here in favor of the ālaya-vijñāna, and of the entire model of mind centered around it, depend, first of all, upon the strictly dichotomous nature of these two aspects of vijñāna – a dichotomy ultimately derived from the presuppositions of dharmic analysis – and, second, upon their inseparable simultaneity. We can hardly understand the concepts of the ālaya-vijñāna and the afflictive mentation, and certainly not the specific arguments in their defense, without taking these two assumptions into account. Although simultaneous conditionality is implicit in the very formula of dependent arising – when X *is*, Y *arises* – few Buddhist texts, we venture, drive this point home as repeatedly and as relentlessly as the MSg.

The MSg critiques the standard model in which the forms of manifest cognitive awareness arise sequentially and argues instead that the various forms of vijñāna must arise simultaneously in order for the seeds and impressions to be able to be infused (*paribhāvita*) into the ālaya-vijñāna, and thus, by extension, for karma to be able to operate. (The seeds are, after all, a way of discussing the karmic relationship between cause and effect.[9]) Moreover, and as we have seen before, it argues that without the ālaya-vijñāna and the simultaneity it affords there would be no sufficiently continuous and homogenous medium through which the seeds and impressions could be transmitted in an unbroken succession of momentary processes of mind, and without this the very continuities the Buddhist world-view requires – of the afflictions, of karma, and of gradual progress along the path – would also be inexplicable. Hence, the MSg proceeds to establish the simultaneous relationship between the two kinds of vijñāna, first to demonstrate why this relationship is necessary for karmic theory to work, and then to extrapolate these ideas, *mutatis mutandis*, to the other conundrums that had plagued systematic Buddhist thinking since the time of the *Kathāvatthu*.

Once again, the core question is:

> How shall we understand that the ālaya-vijñāna and the defiled dharmas are simultaneously (*samakāle*) and reciprocally causes (*anyonyahetu*) of each other?[10]
>
> (MSg I.17)

Since causes (*hetu*) are represented here by the concept of seeds, and to a lesser extent the predispositions or impressions (*vāsanā*), discussion about causes and causal conditions is couched in terms of planting seeds and infusing impressions, and of their finally coming into fruition. In other words, the discussion about how the ālaya-vijñāna and the forms of manifest cognitive awareness, the "defiled dharmas," are able to impress and seed each other is a way of discussing karmic theory: how cause and effect might operate within and between various kinds of mental processes. The reciprocal relationship between the two vijñānas has been sufficiently discussed above, but the import of their *simultaneity* had not been fully emphasized before the MSg.[11]

In order for the impressions to be infused (or, put differently, the predispositions to be reinforced) and the seeds to be sown, and for both of these to eventually spring forth, it is necessary, according to the MSg, for the various forms of cognitive awareness to be simultaneous with each other. Thus, a *vāsanā* (literally "perfumation" but translated here as an impression or predisposition) is defined in the text as "that which, based upon *arising and ceasing simultaneously* with a dharma, is the cause of its arising (*utpāda-nimitta*) [in the future]" (MSg I.15).[12] Playing off the etymology of the term *vāsanā* as "perfume," the text illustrates this first by the example of a sesame seed, which in traditional India was thought of as the repository of its odor, and then – extrapolating this to mind – by the processes whereby occurrences of sensual desire reinforce their own dispositions, or, as the text puts it, "infuse impressions" into the mind (*citta*, i.e. ālaya-vijñāna), from which subsequent instances of desire subsequently arise:

> I.15. For example, when a sesame seed is perfumed by a flower (*puṣpab-hāvanā*), while the flower arises and ceases simultaneously with the sesame seed, the sesame seed [later] arises as the cause of the arising of another odor of that flower. Also, while the predisposition of sensual desire, etc. (*rāgādivāsanā*) of those who are engaged in sensual desire, etc. (*rāgādicarita*) arise and cease simultaneously with sensual desire, etc., mind (*citta*) [later] arises as the cause (*nimitta*) of that [desire]... The ālaya-vijñāna should be understood in the same way.
>
> (MSg I.15)

The text stresses that this process of infusion or impression occurs simultaneously, not sequentially. This is a crucial distinction which points to a notion of causality, that is, the causality of synchronic dependent arising, that differs considerably from more sequential linear models. This refers more to the simultaneous interaction between components of an interrelated system than to the isolated actions on the part of independent entities. That is, perfumation and infusion are processes wherein their respective components – the flower and seed, the desire and mind – arise simultaneously and inseparably with each other. This might best be illustrated by the imagery of waves in a stream, used in the *Saṃdhinirmocana Sūtra* V.5 (Ch. 3, p. 97, above). The stream is not independent of the arising of the wave, in the sense that they arise separately. The stream rises at the same time a wave rises, since the wave is part and parcel of the stream itself. Hence, whatever affects the waves affects the stream at the same time; it is not a separate process. Similarly, the stream of mind at that moment is not independent from the arising of sensual desire, in the sense that these are separate things. Rather, the stream of mind is affected at the same time a sensual desire arises, since that desire is part of the stream of mind itself. One cannot occur without the other being simultaneously affected, since these are ultimately not separate entities, nor are their arisings ultimately separate processes.[13] This, in our understanding, is what the text means by the simultaneous causality of the "first," synchronic dependent arising – when X *is*, Y arises – as applied to the processes of seeding and infusing mind, whether *citta* or ālaya-vijñāna.

Although this discussion of the simultaneous arising of impressions or predispositions along with the defiled dharmas of sensual desire and so on is reminiscent of the *Abhidharma-kośa*'s discussion of seeds which immediately produce a fruit,[14] that formulation did not get to the heart of the problem, since it lacked a simultaneous medium for those seeds that was distinct from the six modes of cognitive awareness themselves. In the light of this understanding of simultaneity, MSg restates the problem as follows: how can there be any infusing of seeds at all *unless* there is simultaneity between distinct forms of vijñāna, between what "infuses" and what is "infused"? Thus, any theory that holds that the six forms of cognitive awareness arise sequentially one at a time, like beads without a string,[15] would have trouble explaining not only how these seeds could continue from one moment to the next, but *how they could ever be infused into another form of vijñāna in the first place*. This reasoning was perhaps implicit in the *Proof Portion*, Proof 4, "The impossibility of mutual seeding," but it is now made fully explicit.

MSg I.22 thus describes the characteristics of seeds as follows:

> All seeds are considered to have six characteristics: [they are] momentary, simultaneous, they continue in an uninterrupted stream, are [karmically] determinate, require conditions, and are completed by their own fruit.
>
> (MSg I.22)

For the causal efficacy represented by the seeds to be imparted, the text argues, they must occur simultaneously with a karmically indeterminate form of mind, a form of mind that, as the next section stipulates, is "infusable" because it has the following characteristics:

> I.23. There is infusing (*bhāvanā*) in what is stable, indeterminate, infusable, and connected with infusing, not in another.
>
> (MSg I.23)

"Not in another" means that the six forms of cognitive awareness cannot infuse each other because they are intermittent, karmically determinate (i.e. associated with karmically determinate mental factors, such as enjoying, etc. – MSg I.26), and, in doctrinal systems without the ālaya-vijñāna, they are *not simultaneous*. They are incapable of being infused, MSg I.23 argues, echoing the *Proof Portion*, Proof 1, because:

> The six [forms of arising cognitive awareness] are not connected [to one another] and there is dissimilarity between their three distinctive aspects [physical bases, objects, and attention; and] because two [succeeding] moments [of cognitive awareness] are not simultaneous.[16]
>
> (MSg I.23)

In contrast to the forms of manifest cognitive awareness, however, the ālaya-vijñāna is stable, it does occur in a continuous, unbroken stream, it is indeterminate (*avyākṛta*), and always arises *simultaneously* with forms of manifest cognitive awareness. Therefore, the commentary explains, only the ālaya-vijñāna has the necessary properties that make it suitable for and capable of being infused.[17]

In short, the criteria of simultaneity – prominently included in the definitions of both the seeds and impressions themselves – requires an underlying stream of mind which co-occurs with each and every moment of supraliminal cognitive awareness. This is necessary not only in order to maintain karmic continuity, which the earlier texts had already argued for, but, even more importantly, in order for some form of mind to even be able to receive the seeds and impressions from the "defiled dharmas" in the first place. As we have seen, it is the ālaya-vijñāna that is considered this distinctive stream of mind upon whose upper layers the differentiated waves arise,[18] but which also simultaneously supports and inseparably co-arises with each and every wave, without, as *Saṃdhinirmocana Sūtra* (V. 5) puts it, being "either interrupted or exhausted in its current."

All of these arguments rely upon the dichotomization of the two vijñānas articulated in our earlier Yogācāra texts as well as in the MSg itself. We have seen the argument that their lack of homogeneity makes the six forms of manifest cognitive awareness incapable of seeding each other, and that their lack of continuity makes them incapable of conveying the karmic influences, which, by the logic of dharmic analysis, requires uninterrupted support from moment to moment. Now, however, the MSg contends that it is their sequential arising itself that makes them incapable of even receiving the seeds or the impressions. In one sense, what these analyses have done is gradually draw out the implications of the relatively narrow conception of vijñāna in synchronic, dharmic discourse – of vijñāna as *only* an immediate form of supraliminal cognitive awareness. To accept *both* the presuppositions of momentariness *and* the unifocal view of mind – in which only a single kind of cognitive awareness arises at one time in conjunction with a single object – is to effectively preclude the six forms of cognitive awareness from being able to absorb, preserve, or transmit causal influences from one moment to the next. This effectively prevents any systematic theory of karma from being formulated in relation to those forms of mind. And this is to virtually insure that some notion fulfilling those functions would soon be forthcoming – a consequence amply evidenced by the appearance as well as the content of the innovative conceptions of other contemporary Abhidharma schools.[19] And all these notions, even in (especially in) their efforts to resolve it, are still unavoidably couched in terms of the Abhidharma Problematic, a fact which is no less true of the ālaya-vijñāna.

To the extent that it represents a form of mind that can both receive and transmit the accumulated karmic potential in the form of seeds, the ālaya-vijñāna resolves the first major conundrum of that Problematic. On this basis, the MSg then proceeds to address the last two components of the Abhidharma Problematic: the persistence of the afflictions and the gradual nature of the path to liberation.

Resolving the Abhidharmic Problematic

The MSg directly addresses the three conundrums of the Abhidharma Problematic in the third major division of the text (MSg I.29–57), entitled "establishing (*vyavasthāna*) the ālaya-vijñāna." The first section of this division clearly states its purpose and its plan:

> I.29. The [above] establishes (*vyavasthāna*) the ālaya-vijñāna by its synonyms (*paryāya*) [I.1–13] and its characteristics (*lakṣaṇa*) [I.14–28]. How is it known that it is just the ālaya-vijñāna which is taught by the synonyms and similarly taught by the characteristics, and not the [forms of] arising cognitive awareness (*pravṛtti-vijñāna*)?[20]
>
> Because without the ālaya-vijñāna established in that way, then defilement (*saṃkleśa*) and purification (*vyavadāna*) are impossible. That is to say, the affliction defilements (*kleśa-saṃkleśa*), the action defilements (*karma-saṃkleśa*), and the birth defilements (*janma-saṃkleśa*) also are all impossible.[21] Mundane (*laukika*) and supramundane purification (*lokottara vyavadāna*) are also impossible.
>
> (MSg I.29)

This programmatic statement on defilement and purification echoes the last two portions of the *Ālaya Treatise*, the perpetuation (*pravṛtti*) and cessation (*nivṛtti*) of samsaric existence, respectively. That is, the afflictions (*kleśa*), karma, and their results (here, the "birth defilements"), belong to the category of defilement (*saṃkleśa*) insofar as our samsaric condition is defiled, stained, and unsatisfactory. And this condition is only countered by the gradual processes of purification (*vyavadāna*) leading to their cessation (*nivṛtti*). The text is claiming, in other words, that neither samsara nor Nirvana are explicable without the continuity of mind the ālaya-vijñāna epitomizes – explicating, in effect, the opening verse in MSg I.1: "As this [ālaya-vijñāna] exists, so do all the destinies as well as the realization of Nirvana." For expository reasons we will briefly discuss the action (*karma*) and birth defilements together in relation to the processes of rebirth, before examining the affliction defilements in relation to afflictive mentation (*kliṣṭa-manas*). This will serve to introduce the MSg's discussion of the gradual process of purification on the path toward liberation, taking up the remainder of this chapter.

Karma, rebirth, and the ālaya-vijñāna

The sections called the action defilements (*karma-saṃkleśa*) (MSg I.33) and the birth defilements (*janma-saṃkleśa*) (MSg I.34–42) largely focus upon the processes of rebirth. These were conceptually problematic because the series of material dharmas is completely severed during these periods of transition from one lifetime to the next. The text addresses both such junctures within the traditional three-lifetime interpretation of the formula of dependent arising: those which occur between the karmic formations (*saṃskārā*) and vijñāna, and between appropriation (*upādāna*) and existence (*bhava*). Since vijñāna was the only factor explicitly stated, in both the early Pāli and Abhidharma traditions, to continue from one lifetime to the next, the continuities of all the factors that must "last as long as samsara" would have to persist in some kind of relationship with this ongoing stream of vijñāna – at least at these crucial disjunctions. This much was shared by the various Abhidharma schools, though their explanations of the exact processes involved varied considerably.

MSg I.33, for its part, argues that this form of vijñāna must be the ālaya-vijñāna:

> I.33. For what reason would the defilements consisting of action (*karma-saṃkleśa*) be impossible [if there were no ālaya-vijñāna]? Because there would be no consciousness conditioned by the saṃskārās (*saṃskārā-pratyayam vijñānam*). Without that [ālaya-vijñāna], existence (*bhava*) conditioned by appropriation (*upādāna*) would also be impossible.
>
> (MSg I.33)

We have seen this basic argument in *Proof Portion*, Proof 1. Without the ālaya-vijñāna, which is conditioned by the persisting effects of past saṃskārās, the forms of manifest cognitive awareness could not by themselves provide the necessary continuity for the seeds and impressions to be transmitted over these disjunctive transitions, since they are strictly momentary and dependent upon present conditions.[22]

The question of which exact form of mind arises during the process of rebirth, however, involves further complications for which the dichotomous nature of the two forms of vijñāna is again deemed determinative. The next section, MSg I.34, initiates a series of statements on the process of rebirth, the most important process within the "birth-defilements" (and one which itself results from the other two: the defilements of actions and of the afflictions):[23]

> I.34. For what reason would the defilements consisting of birth (*janmasaṃkleśa*) be impossible [if there were no ālaya-vijñāna]? Because the rebirth connection (*pratisandhibandha*) would be impossible.
>
> When the mind (*manas*) which has deceased from an unconcentrated stage (*asamāhitābhūmi*, i.e. the Desire Realm) dwells in the intermediate life (*antarābhava*) it connects at rebirth by a defiled mental vijñāna (*kliṣṭa-manovijñāna*). This defiled mental vijñāna ceases in the intermediate life and [another] vijñāna coagulates (*saṃmūrcchati*) again as an embryo in the mother's womb. . . .
>
> That vijñāna which has coagulated cannot logically be a mental vijñāna because [mental vijñāna] always has an afflicted support (*kliṣṭāśraya*) [unlike a neutral, resultant vijñāna] and because the object of [this] mental vijñāna is not found. . . .
>
> Therefore, it is proven (*siddha*) that the coagulated vijñāna is not a mental vijñāna but that it is the resultant vijñāna which possesses all the seeds (*sarvabījaka vipākavijñāna*).[24]
>
> (MSg I.34)

This is the basic Yogācārin analysis of the rebirth process.[25] The text (MSg I.34c) here is critiquing the positions held by the Sarvāstivādins, and possibly the Sautrāntikas, that it is an afflicted mental cognitive awareness (*mano-vijñāna*) which arises at the moment of rebirth.[26] These arguments are predicated on the Yogācārin view examined above that the seeds and predispositions representing the continuity of karma and the afflictions can only be transmitted through a form of mind capable of receiving, maintaining, and transmitting them (MSg I.23). Thus, the type of mind that enters into the mother's womb after an intermediate existence (better known by its Tibetan name, *bardo*) cannot be a mental cognitive awareness (*mano-vijñāna*) because it does not enjoy the qualities of a resultant vijñāna (*vipāka-vijñāna*) that are necessary in order to carry all the seeds, that is, being karmically neutral, stable, and so on. Rather, the form of mind that coagulates with the embryonic materials upon reconnection at rebirth (*pratisandhi-citta*) must be a neutral, resultant mind fully capable of possessing all the seeds (*sarvabījaka vipākavijñāna*)[27] – regardless of what name it is called by.[28] These qualities, the MSg argues, only pertain to the neutral and subliminal level of mind called ālaya-vijñāna. Hence, the defilements due to action (*karma-saṃkleśa*) as well as those due to birth (*janma-saṃkleśa*) are only possible when supported by the continuous processes of mind constituting the ālaya-vijñāna.

The continuity of the afflictions (kleśa)

The text also addresses the second major component of the Abhidharma Problematic: the continuity of the afflictions. The problem of the persistence of the afflictions, even in a latent condition, until far along the path to liberation had been recognized and discussed in systematic Buddhist thinking since at least the time of the *Kathāvatthu*. Indeed, the basic elements of the debate can be traced back to various discourses of the Buddha. This actually entails two interrelated problems: most afflictions not only persist for many lifetimes, but are also only gradually eliminated. The gradual purification of the afflictions would be impossible if their continued presence until liberation prevented one from having any moments of karmically skillful states of mind. Hence, the simultaneous presence in the mental stream of karmically contradictory influences – the latent afflictions on the one hand and the karmically skillful states of purification on the other – raised problems of both exegesis and explanation. The problem of continuity of the afflictions and of their gradual purification are, in effect, mirror images of each other.

MSg I.30 uses the same basic reasoning involved in the processes of seeding to show why the problem of infusing the impressions (i.e. reinforcing the predispositions) is also unresolvable without the concept of the ālaya-vijñāna. The text rejects the possibility that any of the six modes of manifest cognitive awareness could either transmit the seeds of the impressions of the afflictions – since these forms of mind arise only momentarily and intermittently – or even receive them in the first place – since the impressions are only infused into a simultaneous form of mind *distinct from the one with which they are associated.* Only the ālaya-vijñāna, then, can receive the seeds of the impressions of the afflictions and preserve them throughout all the different realms of existence and types of consciousness without being in conflict with the supraliminal states of varying karmic natures. We cite this section in full, since it so well illustrates the form and content of the arguments involved:

> I.30. Why is defilement consisting of affliction impossible [without the ālaya-vijñāna]?
>
> Because the seed (*bījabhāva*) made by the impression (*vāsanā*) of the afflictions and the secondary afflictions (*kleśa-upakleśa*) cannot be in the six groups of cognitive awareness (*ṣaḍvijñānakāya*).
>
> (1) If, for instance, the seeds of those [afflictions] were [thought to be] infused into that same visual cognitive awareness which arose and ceased simultaneously with whatever afflictions and secondary afflictions, sensual desire (*rāga*), etc., but not into another [kind of a cognitive awareness], then, when another cognitive awareness has intervened (*antarāyita*), no impression would exist, nor is the support of an impression found, in that [previous] visual cognitive awareness which has already ceased. Since the visual cognitive awareness which has previously ceased is currently non-existent, having been replaced (*antarāyita*)

by another [kind of] cognitive awareness, it is not possible for [a new visual cognitive awareness] possessing sensual desire, etc. to arise from the past [visual cognitive awareness] which is currently non-existent. Similarly, the fruit of maturation (*vipāka-phala*) arising from a past action which is currently non-existent is impossible [if only the visual cognitive awareness and not the ālaya-vijñāna is infused].[29]

Nor is [infusion of the] impression possible [even] within a visual cognitive awareness which arises simultaneously with sensual desire (*rāga*), etc. [for the following additional reasons:] In the first place, (2) [the impression] is not in the sensual desire [itself] because the sensual desire depends upon (*āśrita*) that [form of cognitive awareness] and is not [itself] stable.[30] (3) Nor is there [infusing] into the other [types of] cognitive awareness because the bases (*āśraya*) of the [forms of] cognitive awareness are distinct and do not arise and cease simultaneously.[31] (4) Nor is [there infusing] into [another visual cognitive awareness] itself because [two moments of visual cognitive awareness] themselves do not arise and cease simultaneously.[32]

Thus, it is not possible that the visual cognitive awareness is infused by the impression of the afflictions or the secondary afflictions, sensual desire (*rāga*), etc. Nor is it possible for that cognitive awareness to be infused by [another kind of] cognitive awareness. It should be known that just as it is with visual cognitive awareness, so it is also, *mutatis mutandis* (*yathāyogam*), with the remaining [forms of] arising cognitive awareness (*pravṛtti-vijñāna*).

(MSg I.30)

The passages in this section successively argue against the possibility that any form of vijñāna other than the ālaya-vijñāna could receive and transmit the seeds of the impressions of an afflicted moment of cognitive experience. This can occur neither between similar nor different kinds of manifest cognitive awareness, nor within the same cognitive awareness itself. MSg I.30 (1) argues first that – given that all forms of manifest cognitive awareness and their accompanying mental factors are strictly momentary – a single moment of visual cognitive awareness which arises and ceases with an affliction will soon be replaced by another moment of cognitive awareness. The impression from the first moment of visual cognitive awareness cannot be infused into a subsequent moment of visual cognitive awareness since the first one no longer exists. "Nor," reason (3) asserts, "is there [infusing] in other [types of] cognitive awareness, because the bases of the [forms of] cognitive awareness are distinct and do not arise and cease simultaneously." In short, the transmission of the seeds and impressions cannot take place between two different moments of a similar kind of cognitive awareness – since their continuity is broken; nor can infusion take place between cognitive awarenesses of different types – since their bases, etc. are distinct and they are not, in fact, simultaneous.

Two possibilities of self-infusing are also ruled out, those of sensual desire and of cognitive awareness. The sensual desire (or other afflictions) that accompanies that moment of cognitive awareness cannot infuse itself since it is a mental factor (*caitta*) and mental factors themselves are supported (*āśrita*) by some form of mind (i.e. *citta/vijñāna*) and are therefore not stable. (2) Nor could that visual cognitive awareness infuse itself: first, according to the commentaries, because it is the support (*āśraya*) of the very mental factor – sensual desire – that infuses it, which would conflate the support with the supported, confusing that which is infused (the supporting moment of mind) with that which infuses (the supported afflictive mental factor);[33] and second, because two moments of visual cognitive awareness do not occur simultaneously (4). In short, since "the seed made by the impressions of the afflictions and the secondary afflictions cannot be in the six groups of cognitive awareness" (MSg I.30), there must be some other, distinct kind of mind that can receive and transmit the seeds, that is, the ālaya-vijñāna.

The dichotomy between the ālaya-vijñāna and the manifest vijñānas, dependent as the latter are upon their momentary and discrete cognitive objects, is also applied to the arguments concerning the persistence and reappearance of the latent afflictions during and after periods in which their continuity has been broken. The MSg cites three such conditions: the two meditative attainments of non-apperception and of cessation; lifetimes in their corresponding "realms of existence," which lack mental processes and hence manifest afflictions altogether; and when one's mind is engaged in the antidote to the afflictions.

MSg I.31 discusses the middle problem, the relation between our world of embodied and afflicted existence and life in realms without such bodies or obvious afflictions. This refers to the common idea in Indian religion that meditative states cultivated during intense yogic practice correspond to spiritual "realms" into which adepts may enter, either directly through meditation or indirectly through rebirth, as one of the fruits of that meditation. Beings in the realm of non-apperception, for example, were considered "mind-less" (*acittaka*), lacking all mental activities such as the forms of manifest cognitive awareness, the afflicting mental factors, and so on. They were, nevertheless, thought to possess at least the latent forms of the afflictions of ignorance, grasping to self, the conceit "I am," and so on, since they remain within samsaric existence. But the persistence of these afflictions in a latent state would seem to contradict the definition of these states as devoid of mental processes altogether. We have discussed this before. The problem the MSg addresses, however, concerns the antecedent conditions for the reoccurrence of these afflictions once their continuity has been cut during life in the non-apperceptual realm:

> I.31. Moreover, when those who are born here [in the Desire Realm] having descended from [a lifetime in] a higher stage (*bhūmi*), the realm of non-apperception, etc., the cognitive awareness which first arises, which is afflicted by the afflictions and the secondary afflictions, would arise without seeds [if there were no ālaya-vijñāna] because the impression

> [of the afflictions] along with its support are [already] past and [currently] non-existent (*atītābhāva*).
>
> (MSg I.31)

This line of argumentation should be straightforward by now, since parallel arguments concerning the continuity of vijñāna and its seeds subsequent to the attainment of cessation have been discussed in Chapter 2, as well as in earlier Yogācāra texts: without an immediate, yet neutral, support for the seeds and impressions, how would these afflictions ever reoccur? The MSg devotes several sections (I.38–41) to questions about the continuity of seeds and impressions in realms lacking the mental or physical faculties similar to our own mode of existence. Neither during the lifetimes within nor the transitions between these realms do there exist supports for, or antecedent and homogeneous conditions to, either the material bodies or the afflictive dispositions. These could never reoccur within this realm, the MSg argues, without a resultant cognitive awareness which possesses all the seeds (*sarvabījaka-vipākavijñāna*) for their reoccurrence. Whatever we may think of the "reality" of these realms, their circumstances were important, and peculiar, enough for Buddhist thinkers to address them in a systematically consistent fashion.

The last topic these sections take up is the difficulties of accounting for the continuity of the afflictions in the presence of their antidote (*pratipakṣa*). These arguments call upon the by-now familiar reasoning that without the ālaya-vijñāna to support them it would be impossible for the seeds of the afflictions to either persist during, or to arise after, even a single moment of the antidote:

> I.32. When the cognitive awareness which counteracts the afflictions (*kleśa-pratipakṣa-vijñāna*) has arisen, all the other [forms of] mundane cognitive awareness (*laukika-vijñāna*) have ceased. It is not possible that, without the ālaya-vijñāna, that counteracting mind [itself] could possess the seeds of the afflictions and the secondary afflictions, because it is liberated by nature (*svabhāva-vimukta*) and does not arise and cease simultaneously with the afflictions.
>
> If there were no ālaya-vijñāna, then afterward, when a mundane cognitive awareness arises, it would arise from what is without seeds, since the impression together with its support (*sāśrayam*) is [currently] non-existent, having long since passed away.
>
> Therefore, if there were no ālaya-vijñāna, the defilements consisting of affliction (*kleśa-saṃkleśa*) would be impossible.[34]
>
> (MSg I.32)

That is, if there were no separate stream of mind such as the ālaya-vijñāna persisting independently of the karmic nature of the momentarily manifest cognitive awarenesses, then even a single instance of the antidote to the afflictions (a supramundane moment of mind that inhibits afflicted mental factors) ought to entirely cut off the continuity of the afflictions and thus prevent them from ever arising again. In that case, as the commentary to MSg I.40 points out, if there were no ālaya-vijñāna, "then, when the antidote (*pratipakṣa*) is present, since all of the counteracted (*vipakṣa*) [dharmas] have ceased, *nirvāṇa* without remainder (*nirupadhiśeṣanirvāṇa*) would be attained naturally and without effort" (U 393c11–16; u 260b1–4). But this is not, in Indian traditions at least, what happens. Purification is typically a gradual and intermittent process. Therefore, the text argues, a distinct genre of mind such as the ālaya-vijñāna is required in order to account for the continuity of the afflictions in their latent state even during the powerful moments when the antidote or remedy to the afflictions is present.

Most of the arguments in this section – establishing that the defilements due to affliction would be impossible without the ālaya-vijñāna – affirm the continuity of the ālaya-vijñāna within both mindless and immaterial states, as well as its compatibility with karmically contradictory states. These arguments are all based on the few simple principles outlined at the beginning of this section: the dichotomy between the ālaya-vijñāna and the manifest vijñānas; the simultaneity of infusion between distinct yet simultaneous processes of mind; and, due to these first two, the inability of the forms of manifest cognitive awareness to either receive, preserve, or transmit any of the causal influences represented by the seeds or the impressions. So much for the first two conundrums of the Abhidharma Problematic, karma and kleśa.

The third conundrum is the gradual nature of the path of purification. Since the discussion of the processes of purification in the MSg proceeds into an extended discussion of the role of the ālaya-vijñāna within Mahāyāna Buddhist metaphysics, we shall raise these questions together. But first, we must briefly examine the most detailed discussion in Indian Yogācāra literature of that which one must be purified of: the cognitive and emotional afflictions insofar as they are associated with that underlying source of afflictive energies ever ready to instigate new karmic actions, that is, afflictive mentation (*kliṣṭa-manas*). The kleśa are indispensable to the perpetuation of samsaric existence as a whole, we remember, since, as the Yogācāra commentator Sthiramati stresses,

> the causes of samsara are karma and kleśa; of these two, the kleśa are foremost. … even the action (*karma*) which has projected rebirth (*punar-bhava*) will not produce rebirth if there is no *kleśa* … because they are foremost, the kleśas are the root of origination.[35]
>
> (*Pañcaskandha-prakaraṇa-vaibhāṣya*)

*Afflictive mentation (*kliṣṭa-manas*) in the* Mahāyāna-saṃgraha

It is in the MSg that the *kliṣṭa-manas* is finally developed into a fully distinct class of mental processes, which is systematically described and defended with the same kinds of argument we have seen for the ālaya-vijñāna – a mixture of exegetical, systemic, and logical reasons. The arguments rely upon common Abhidharma categories and revolve around three major points: the distinction between the latent afflictions being associated (*samprayukta*) as opposed to merely simultaneous (*sahabhū*) with *citta*; the need for mental cognitive awareness (*mano-vijñāna*) to have a simultaneous support similar to that of the sensory forms of manifest cognitive awareness; and the questions surrounding the gradual elimination of the afflictions along the path.

MSg I.6 first describes the two senses of the term *manas* used in the Yogācāra tradition. The first follows definitions of *manas* found throughout Indian Buddhist literature as the preceding moment of mind (*vijñāna*) insofar as it serves as the support (*āśraya*) for a succeeding mental cognitive awareness. The second sense is the innovation peculiar to Yogācāra:

> I.6 The second is the afflictive mentation (*kliṣṭa-manas*) which is always associated (*samprayukta*) with the four afflictions (*kleśa*): the view of self-existence (*satkāyadṛṣṭi*), the conceit "I am" (*asmimāna*), attachment to self (*ātmasneha*), and ignorance (*avidyā*). It is the support for the defilements (*saṃkleśāśraya*) of the [forms of] cognitive awareness (*vijñāna*). The cognitive awarenesses arise through the first [*manas*, as] support, but are made defiled by the second.
>
> (MSg I.6)

This differs little from the depiction of *manas* found in the *Pravṛtti Portion* ((I.4.b)B)4, where it already represented these four afflictions. It is, rather, the rationales adduced in support of the such afflictive mentation that are distinctive here. There must be afflictive mentation (*kliṣṭa-manas*), MSg I.7a.6. argues,

> because it is held (*upalabhyate*) that grasping to self (*ātmagrāha*) is present (*samudācāra*) at all times, even in skillful, unskillful, and indeterminate states of mind. Otherwise, since the affliction of the conceit "I am" (*asmimānakleśa*) is associated only with unskillful states of mind (*akuśala-citta*), it would be present [only in unskillful states] but not in skillful (*kuśala*) or indeterminate (*avyākṛta*) ones. Therefore, since [we consider] it to be present simultaneously (*sahabhū*) but not present associated (*samprayukta*) [with those forms of mind], this fault is avoided.[36]
>
> (MSg I.7a.6)

This argument rests upon the distinction we have seen in most Abhidharma systems between mental factors (*caitta*) that arise associated with *citta* (*citta-samprayukta*) and those that arise merely simultaneously or co-existent (*sahabhū*) with it.[37] An affliction that merely coexists with a moment of *citta* is not one that gives rise to intentions (*cetanā*) that accrue future karmic results. They are therefore karmically indeterminate or neutral. Coexisting afflictions simply "subsist along side of" (the literal meaning of *anuśaya*) the *citta*. On the other hand, when such afflictions arise "associated" or conjoined with that moment of *citta*, they influence the karmic quality of the intentional actions (*karma*) at that moment, making it accrue potential for future results, that is, karma.

Thus, if the four afflictions that are "present at all times, even in skillful, unskillful, and indeterminate states of mind" were always associated with the *citta*, then all those moments would be afflicted and it would be impossible for skillful moments of mind to ever occur. Since these particular afflictions persist until far along the path, how, Vasubandhu asks in his commentary on the MSg, "would wholesome states such as giving, etc., ever occur, since [they] are always associated with these" afflictions?[38] Therefore, they must continuously but unobtrusively coexist with all other processes of mind. Hence, the Yogācārins posit these as distinct, neutral processes of mind, that is, afflictive mentation.

Mental factors (*caitta*), however, can only arise in dependence upon mind (*citta*).[39] The MSg therefore further argues for the presence of such afflictive mentation on the grounds that these ubiquitous afflictions also require a simultaneous "support" or "basis" within the mental stream. Each type of sensory cognitive awareness has its own simultaneous support (*sahabhū-āśraya*), that is, the material sense-faculties (*rūpīṇyindriyāṇi*), upon which their proper functioning depends.[40] Mental cognitive awareness (*mano-vijñāna*), however, has no simultaneous support since traditionally its support is the previous moment of mind (though schools differ on this).[41] Thus, MSg I.7a.2 argues, without afflictive mentation (*kliṣṭa-manas*):

> There would also be the fault that [mental cognitive awareness] would be dissimilar to the five [other forms of sensory cognitive awareness], because the five groups of cognitive awareness necessarily have the eye, etc. as their simultaneous support (*sahabhū-āśraya*).
>
> (MSg I.7a.2)

There is more to this than a scholastic concern for formal symmetry. Even though these four afflictions are not associated with the main mental processes (*citta*), nonetheless they are mental factors and as such only arise in dependence upon the main processes of mind, upon *citta*. But even simultaneity (*sahabhū*) is karmically too close, it appears, as the commentary argues in the case of ignorance:

> Since ignorance [etc.] is also a mental factor (*caitta*), it does not occur without a support (*āśraya*). But [during a skillful *citta*] there is no other support except afflictive mentation (*kliṣṭa-manas*), [because] a skillful *citta* cannot be the support of ignorance [etc.].[42]
>
> (U 384c24–28; u 242b8–243a3)

Hence, there must be another stream of mental processes that can support the four afflictive dispositions during skillful states, that is, there must be afflictive mentation (*kliṣṭa-manas*). This notion of afflictive mentation is the simultaneous "support for the defilements (*saṃkleśa-āśraya*) of the cognitive awarenesses" by which, as MSg I.6 stated above, they are "made defiled."

As the continuous and simultaneous support of the four afflictive dispositions, afflictive mentation is now not only fully and systematically integrated into the model of the mind centered on the ālaya-vijñāna (and hereafter often designated the "seventh cognitive awareness"); but by couching these afflictions exclusively in synchronic, dharmic terms, it has also fundamentally addressed the problem of the persistence of the afflictions in the mental stream, the second major conundrum of the Abhidharma Problematic.

Once again, though, this solution is threatened by those meditative attainments during which the stream is broken, when all mental events come to a halt. Accordingly, just as the problem of these "mindless" (*acittaka*) attainments became one of the rationales leading to the postulation of the ālaya-vijñāna, so too, the absence of any manifest afflictions during these states became one of the rationales for postulating an underlying level of afflictive mentation. Considering these meditative attainments themselves, as well as the lifetimes within their corresponding realms, MSg I.7a5 argues that without afflictive mentation:

> There would also be the fault that if one who is in [the state of] non-apperception does not have grasping to self (*ātmagrāha*) or the conceit "I am" (*asmimāna*), then [s/he] would not be afflicted (*kliṣṭa*) for the duration of life in the state of non-apperception.
>
> (MSg I.7a5)

And if there were no grasping to self at all in the attainment of non-apperception, then, first, there would be no way to distinguish between the "absorption of non-apperception" and the "absorption of cessation," which, the text argues, are distinguished precisely by the presence or absence of afflictive mentation.[43] But perhaps even more significantly, if the afflictive mind were totally absent in these states, then as Vasubandhu argues in his commentary on the MSg:

> it properly follows that there would be no self-grasping (*ātmagrāha*) amongst beings belonging to [the realm of] non-apperception (*āsaṃjñika*); [they] would no [longer] be ordinary worldlings (*pṛthagjana*) [that is, they would be Aryans], and their mental stream (*santāna*) would be temporarily free of self-grasping.[44]
>
> (Bh 326b7–11)

And this would be tantamount to having entered the Path of Seeing and becoming a stream-enterer, one who has an assurance of final liberation – becoming, in short, an Aryan. But this contradicts the traditional definition of this absorption and those who attain it, for it, and they, are decidedly mundane. Hence, there must be a continuing locus of afflictive mentality whose presence or absence distinguishes these differing attainments and their respective realms.

The second commentary to the MSg (U 384c3; u 24164–7) adopts the distinction between these two types of meditative attainment to argue that it is the presence or absence of afflictive mentation within the mental stream as a whole that differentiates an ordinary worldling from an Aryan.[45] This is worth reiterating: it is the presence or absence of afflictive mentation (specifically, the four afflictions comprising the *kliṣṭa-manas*) within the mental stream (*santāna*) that distinguishes an Aryan from an ordinary person.

We recall that this was one of the problems generated by the strictures of Abhidharma dharmic discourse: how to find a criterion, within the strictly momentary analysis of mind and its concomitant mental factors alone, for distinguishing the relative presence of the afflictive dispositions within the mental stream, and hence the relative progress upon the path of purification. The concepts of possession (*prāpti*) or seeds (*bīja*) of the afflictions were two ways that the schools represented in the *Abhidharma-kośa* distinguished Aryans from ordinary beings. Now, we see the Yogācārins formulating the latent afflictions (*anuśaya*) into a distinctive class of mental processes in their own right – afflictive mentation – and using their presence or absence to distinguish these levels of attainment. This common search for indicators existing relatively independently of the transient contents of immediate cognitive awareness epitomizes the problem of the gradual elimination of the afflictions – the third and last major conundrum we have identified in the Abhidharma Problematic.

The path of purification: mundane and supramundane

In its introduction to the rationales for the existence of the ālaya-vijñāna, MSg I.29 claimed that the processes of purification would also be impossible without the continuity of mind afforded by this continuous, subliminal, and karmically neutral level of mentality. The remaining sections of this part of the text, "establishing (*vyavasthāna*) the ālaya-vijñāna" (MSg I.43–57), take up this question. The basic reasoning here is expressed in the same formulation found throughout the "proofs": without the possibility of multiple mental processes provided for in the ālaya-vijñāna model of mind, there can be no continuity, and indeed no progress, on the path of purification. This problem is exacerbated primarily by the qualitative gulf between the mundane states of mind (*citta*) that are preparatory to the supramundane attainments and the *cittas* within those supramundane attainments themselves, and secondarily by the progressive nature of the path wherein the more concentrated *cittas* (*samāhitacitta*) that initially attain these meditative states are followed by the less concentrated *cittas* that cultivate and perfect them. There could be no such relations, according to the MSg, without the mediating graces of a neutral yet simultaneous form of mind that could receive, preserve, and transmit the seeds of these attainments in spite of any intervening states of mind. This problem is in effect the mirror image of that of the seeds and impressions persisting and co-existing with *cittas* of differing karmic natures, and the arguments are accordingly much the same. What is at issue here, of course, is not the accumulation of karmic potential or the persisting latent dispositions, but the seeds for attainments upon the path. And these arguments primarily concern the lack of simultaneity between lower and higher levels of meditative concentration, mundane or supramundane, and the inability of these beneficent influences to pass between them without the mediation provided by the ālaya-vijñāna.

Specifically, MSg I.43 argues that those who are practicing *mundane* purification (*laukika-vyavadāna*) carry out their practices with a *citta* belonging to our level of embodied existence, the Desire Realm. The *citta* of practice within the Desire Realm, however, can never be the direct *cause* for a form of mind belonging to a higher, more concentrated level of the Form Realm because, MSg I.43 argues, "the mind of practice belonging to the Desire Realm does not *simultaneously* arise and cease with the *citta* belonging to the Form Realm." That is to say, that one and the same *citta* cannot simultaneously belong to both realms, nor can the causal influences of these attainments pass from one moment to the next since, as with the other types of seeds, they must be infused into a simultaneous yet distinct form of mind. Achieving progress along the path *without* the distinct medium provided by the ālaya-vijñāna, in other words, would be like trying to climb a ladder with just one leg: one cannot use the same leg to push up from a lower rung that one uses to step onto a higher one. One must have two legs, one which serves as a support on the lower rung while the other simultaneously reaches for a higher rung.

And if the lower leg cannot do it alone, neither can the upper leg. Accordingly, if there were no ālaya-vijñāna to preserve the seed of previous attainments, then even a *citta* of the Form Realm which has *already* been attained in the past could not "be the seed of a present concentrated *citta* (*samāhitacitta*) because the past *citta* belonging to the Form Realm which has been interrupted (*antarāyita*) by other *cittas* in many lifetimes no longer exists either" (MSg I.43). And since it is no longer present, the higher state of mind (*citta*) cannot directly infuse (*bhāvita*) a lower one. And without this infusion of seeds from a more concentrated realm, even the present purificatory practices in the Desire Realm cannot – in and of themselves – bring about these higher meditative attainments. Therefore, MSg I.43.3 concludes:

> It is established that the resultant consciousness which possesses all the seeds (*sarvabījaka vipākavijñāna*) [and] which continues successively (*paraṃparāgata*) is the present causal condition (*hetu-pratyaya*) of the concentrated mind (*samāhita-citta*) which belongs to the Form Realm, while the skillful *citta* of practice (*prāyogika-citta*) is the predominant condition (*adhipati-pratyaya*).
>
> (MSg I.43.3)

Note the crucial role of practice here. Vasubandhu's commentary (Bh 333b2–6; bh 162a2–4) states that even though such preparatory practice is not the *cause* of that concentrated mind (*samāhita-citta*) belonging to the Form Realm, the seed of that mind (*citta*) only bears fruit in this realm when the practice of eliminating the passions is its predominant condition. Paramārtha's Chinese translation of this commentary (T 31.172b1–4) adds that without the *citta* of practice one could not destroy the passions in the Desire Realm; and if the passions of the Desire Realm do not cease, then even the seeds from a previous concentrated mind (*samāhita-citta*) belonging to the Form Realm could not give rise to more such concentrated *cittas* (*samāhita-citta*). Though they are themselves lower states of mind, such practices are essential for enabling the seeds of concentrated *cittas* to bear fruit within this mode of existence.

Just as with the processes of mundane purification, the MSg similarly argues that the processes of *supramundane* purification (*lokottara-vyavadāna*) would be impossible without the ālaya-vijñāna. MSg I.44 first utilizes familiar arguments – the disjunctions and discontinuities of the forms of manifest cognitive awareness – to show why these forms of mind could not be infused with the supramundane impressions of "perfect view":

> I.44. The Lord has said, "Depending on the speech of others and depending on one's own (*adhyātmaṃ*) thorough reflection (*yoniśo-manasikāraḥ*) – from these causes perfect view (*samyag-dṛṣṭi*) arises."[46]
>
> [Some think that hearing] the speech of others [teaching the Dharma] and thorough reflection [upon that teaching] will infuse (**bhāvita*)[47] [the impressions of perfect view] into either an auditory cognitive awareness (*śrota-vijñāna*), a mental cognitive awareness (*mano-vijñāna*), or both of them.
>
> In that case [however], the auditory cognitive awareness does not arise during the time when [the mental cognitive awareness] is thoroughly reflecting upon that Dharma [teaching]. The mental cognitive awareness will also be interrupted (*antarāyita*) by other distracted [forms of] cognitive awareness (*vikṣepa-vijñāna*).
>
> (MSg I.44)

Both hearing and reflection (along with meditation, *śruta-cintā-bhāvanā*) are necessary for cultivating a perfect view of reality (*samyag-dṛṣṭi*), and hence for progressing along the path. But the impressions from *hearing* the teaching through the "speech of others" cannot co-exist, in the standard model, with reflection upon that teaching because the auditory and mental cognitive awarenesses upon which they depend cannot exist simultaneously – and that, the MSg reiterates, is the only way that infusing happens. The forms of arising cognitive awareness are, once again, insufficient by themselves to allow for such infusion and the purification that depends upon it.

And, as with mundane purification, what the lower leg cannot do alone, neither can the upper leg. MSg I.44 thus also argues that without the ālaya-vijñāna even a supramundane *citta* associated with perfect view which one has previously attained could never infuse its seeds into a mundane *citta*, since they do not occur simultaneously:

> I.44. The mundane *citta* which is associated with thorough reflection does not arise and cease simultaneously with the supramundane *citta* which is associated with perfect view. Therefore this [mundane] *citta* is not infused by that [the supramundane *citta*]. Because it is not infused, it cannot be the seed of that [supramundane *citta*].
>
> (MSg I.44)

Again, without the ālaya-vijñāna the seeds for these attainments cannot be transmitted between the forms of arising cognitive awareness alone. There must be, the MSg concludes, a resultant cognitive awareness which possesses all the seeds (*sarvabījaka-vipāka-vijñāna*), including the impressions of hearing the teaching (*śruta-vāsanā*), that can serve as the ever-present causal condition (*hetu-pratyaya*) for the supramundane *citta* to arise.

In "establishing the ālaya-vijñāna" in this way, the Yogācārins have now finally addressed the last of the major conundrums of the Abhidharma Problematic: How can one progress through higher and higher attainments despite both the momentary nature of each *citta* that initially attains them and the gradual, drawn-out process of completing the path of purification? Even such traditional notions as the gradual progress along the path, the MSg argues, would remain inexplicable without the simultaneous multi-dimensionality of mind provided by the ālaya-vijñāna model. We have, however, not reached our final goal.

Beyond Abhidharma: adventitious defilements, pure seeds, and luminous minds

This chapter, and indeed this book as a whole, is focused primarily upon the problematics toward which the ālaya-vijñāna was initially addressed rather than the purposes for which it was subsequently employed, reflecting the predominantly apologetic concerns of the first chapter of the *Mahāyāna-saṃgraha* itself. The idea of hearing the "speech of others," however, raises questions that extend well beyond the Abhidharma context of the ālaya-vijñāna as we have examined it so far and move into the broader reaches of Mahāyāna soteriology: what are the ultimate origins of these supramundane seeds? How do they co-exist with the other seeds within the ālaya-vijñāna? How are these related to the processes of purifying the ālaya-vijñāna itself? And what is the nature of the ālaya-vijñāna once it has been utterly eradicated? Answers to questions such as these constitute the ultimate "proof" of the ālaya-vijñāna. That is, most of the remaining sections (MSg I.45–9, 57)[48] address these deeper issues insofar as they "establish why supramundane purification would be impossible without the ālaya-vijñāna." We, too, will examine these fascinating questions only insofar as they are adduced to "establish" the ālaya-vijñāna. For if the content and context of these sections suggest a substantive departure from the Abhidharmic milieu in which we have heretofore been immersed, the basic approach, and even the specific arguments, decidedly do not.

MSg I.45 introduces this new set of concerns with several rhetorical questions, first raising the issue of compatibility between the mundane mind represented by the ālaya-vijñāna and the seeds of the supramundane *cittas* of the higher meditative attainments, and second, the question of the ultimate origins of these seeds of supramundane *cittas*:

> I.45. If the resultant consciousness which possesses all the seeds is the cause of defilement (*saṃkleśa-hetu*), how can it [also] be the seed[49] of a supramundane *citta*, which is its antidote (*pratipakṣa*)?
>
> Since the supramundane *citta* has not been experienced [before] (*anucita*),[50] its impression (*vāsanā*) definitely does not exist. If that impression does not exist, from which seed should we say it has arisen?
>
> (MSg I.45)

Offhand, this would suggest a vicious circle: no experience will ever occur without a previous seed, but no seed is ever created without a previous experience – creating an unorthodox, but certainly not inherently contradictory, condition in which "you can't get there from here." MSg I.44, however, had already intimated a way out, which MSg I.45 now flatly declares: "[The supramundane *citta*] arises from the seed of the impression of [the Dharma which has been] heard, which issues from the perfectly pure realm of dharma (*suviśuddha-dharmadhātu-niṣyanda-śruta-vāsanā-bīja*)."

The concept of originally pure elements within the defiled minds of ordinary beings has deep roots in the early Buddhist traditions, which only fully blossomed in Mahāyāna soteriology. A passage in one Pāli text, for example, states that "this mind (*citta*), O monk, is luminous (*pabhassaram*), but it is defiled by adventitious defilements (*āgantuka*)" (A I 10), a doctrine repeated nearly verbatim in Yogācāra sources which speak of "a *citta* which is pure and luminous in its original nature (*prakṛti-prabhāsvara-citta*)" and whose faults are always "adventitious" (*āgantuka*), extraneous, added on.[51] The commentary to the *Abhidharma-kośa* also cites a canonical passage which speaks of the "seeds of liberation" (*mokṣa-bīja*) which are so extremely subtle (*susūkṣma*) only the Buddha knows them for sure.[52] The co-existence of these pure dharmas, or their seeds, within the same mind-stream as the root afflictions was one of the issues raised by the Abhidharma Problematic, leading Vasubandhu in the *Abhidharma-kośa* (*ad* II 36c–d), for example, to distinguish between two types of skillful dharmas: those which come about through efforts (*prāyogikāḥ*), such as the practice of meditation, and those which are innate (*utpattipratilambhikāḥ*), the seeds of which are not destroyed even in those who have otherwise cut off all of their skillful roots (*samucchinna-kuśalamūlaḥ*).[53]

It is just these issues – the origins of these seeds, their co-existence with the defilements, and the progressive cultivation of supramundane *cittas* – that, it would seem, prompted the MSg to associate the issue of supramundane purification with the existence of the ālaya-vijñāna in the first place. For the MSg attempts to tie all these loose strands together into a tapestry woven around the ālaya-vijñāna, utilizing arguments already found throughout the text. In a few short sections (I.45–9) it states that in order for perfect view to arise, the Dharma must first be taught by an awakened Buddha, whereby the seeds of hearing the Dharma are infused into one's ālaya-vijñāna. These seeds are thereafter gradually nurtured through thorough reflection and constant cultivation so that, eventually, the impressions from the Dharma gradually increase and other mundane seeds gradually decrease until, finally, the ālaya-vijñāna and all of its mundane seeds are "diminished in all aspects." This is, on the whole and in spite of the specialized terminology of the Yogācāra school, a rather conventional picture commensurate with most Buddhist accounts of the path to liberation (i.e. the practices of *śruta-cintā-bhāvanā*).

What is distinctive is the concept of the ālaya-vijñāna combined with Mahāyāna soteriology. MSg I.45 stated that a supramundane *citta* "arises from the seed of the impression of [the Dharma which has been] heard, which is the outflow from the perfectly pure realm of Dharma."[54] That is, the *citta* that constitutes supramundane insight (perfect view, *samyag-dṛṣṭi*) into the true nature of reality arises within the mind-stream of the practitioner from the seeds of having heard the Dharma – which is itself an expression or outflow of the perfectly pure *dharma-dhātu*, the realm of reality which issues from the Buddha's complete and perfect awakening. It is thus the advent of a Buddha in the world, his teaching and transmission of the Dharma, and its eventual seeping into the minds of sentient beings, that constitutes the initial, necessary causal condition (*hetu-pratyaya*) for liberation.

These seeds are then maintained and supported by the ālaya-vijñāna itself, despite the basic incongruity between the ālaya-vijñāna as the cause of defilement (*saṃkleśa-hetu*) and the seeds of insight that directly counteract it. This is possible because, MSg I.46 declares:

> Until attaining the *bodhi* of the Buddhas,[55] when[ever] the impression of [the Dharma] which has been heard arises on some kind of support, it arises on the resultant consciousness (*vipāka-vijñāna*) by existing simultaneously with it (*sahasthānayoga*) like milk and water. But that [impression] is not the ālaya-vijñāna [itself] because it is the very seed of its antidote (*pratipakṣa*).
>
> (MSg I.46)

Being a result of maturation (*vipāka*), and hence karmically neutral, this form of mind is able to possess and support all types of seeds (*sarvabījakaṃ vipākavijñānaṃ*), even those of its own destruction. Since "the ālaya-vijñāna and what is not the ālaya-vijñāna abide simultaneously in the same place" (MSg I.49), like milk and water, the seeds of the antidotes can co-exist with afflicted dharmas in the same mental stream. Once again, it is the simultaneity and multidimensionality of mind that facilitates this, which would not be possible through the manifest cognitive awarenesses alone (MSg I.32).

But the seeds of a supramundane *citta* are nevertheless only seeds, only *potentials* for something to occur.[56] They must still be brought to fruition through assiduous efforts with a *citta* of practice (*prāyogika-citta*) as a predominant condition (*adhipati-pratyaya*) (MSg I.43) – a notion which parallels Vasubandhu's above-mentioned distinction (*ad* AKBh II 36c–d) between the skillful dharmas that are innate and indestructible and those that arise through spiritual efforts (*prāyogikāḥ*). Thus the gradual nature of the path:

> I.47. Because [the impression of having heard the Dharma] is accompanied by repeatedly practicing (*bahulīkṛta*) hearing, contemplation, and cultivation (*śruta-cintā-bhāvanā*), depending on the weak impression (*mṛduvāsanā*) [it] becomes a medium impression (*madhyavāsanā*); depending on the medium impression, it becomes an excessively strong impression (*adhimātravāsanā*).
>
> (MSg I.47)

The process of transforming the seeds and impressions, which are the causes of defilement (*saṃkleśa-hetu*) contained within the ālaya-vijñāna, into the seeds and impressions of supramundane *citta*s included (*samgṛhīta*) within the *Dharmakāya* of the first-stage Bodhisattva, is gradual and intermittent. Eventually, however, the cultivation of these impressions counteracts (*pratipakṣa*) the ālaya-vijñāna itself, gradually eliminating it "in all aspects"[57] until finally the ālaya-vijñāna becomes completely "seedless," that is, the "basis is revolved":

> I.48. Inasmuch as the weak, medium, and strong [impressions from having heard the Dharma] gradually increase (*vardhate*), so much does the resultant consciousness (*vipāka-vijñāna*) diminish, and the basis is revolved (*āśrayaparāvṛtti*). When the basis is revolved in all aspects, the resultant consciousness possessing all the seeds (*sarvabījakaṃ-vipākavijñānam*) also becomes without seeds and is eliminated in all aspects as well.[58]
>
> (MSg I.48)

This revolution of the basis (*āśraya-parāvṛtti*) constitutes the final formal "proof" establishing the ālaya-vijñāna, since, the text argues, this revolution is only possible by means of the two-tiered model of mind that not only supports the very processes that eliminate its contents, but also preserves the distinctions between the antidote as *cause* and the revolved basis as *result*, without which any prolonged process of purification would be impossible.[59] Thus, MSg I.57.2 argues:

> It is not possible that the antidote is [itself] the revolution [of the basis], because it is not the elimination (*prahāṇa*) [of those defilements]. If that [antidote] were [itself] the elimination [of the defilements] then there would be no distinction between cause and effect.
>
> (MSg I.57.2)

This argument is the converse of one we have already seen concerning the co-existence of the seeds of skillful dharmas within an overtly afflicted mind: if the contents of mind were singular and that moment of mind were wholly encompassed by the afflictions, then how could the seeds of skillful dharmas co-exist there? Here we have the opposite scenario: if that moment of mind were wholly encompassed by the antidote to the defilements, then how could the seeds of unskillful dharmas co-exist there? A single moment of the antidotal mind would eliminate all the seeds of defiled dharmas and there would no longer be any need, nor indeed the possibility, for gradual purification. For without the persistence of further seeds to be eradicated in the ālaya-vijñāna, the commentary points out, the mere generation of the antidote would, in and of itself, be tantamount to attaining Nirvana.[60] In other words, if the antidote were the same as the revolved basis, rather than a gradual means toward that goal, then once the antidote arose there would no longer be anything to counteract. The cause, the antidote, would be the same as the effect, the elimination of all the seeds and the revolution of the basis. Hence, the text argues, not only gradual progress along the path but complete liberation itself is only possible because there is a distinct dimension of mind, a resultant form of consciousness possessing all the seeds, that is capable of simultaneously supporting both the antidote and that to which the antidote is applied. In short, as the Buddha's verse cited at the very beginning of the first chapter stated:

> The element since beginningless time is the common support of all dharmas,
> As this exists, so do all the destinies as well as the realization of Nirvana.
>
> (MSg I.1)

5

THE ĀLAYA-VIJÑĀNA IN THE *MAHĀYĀNA-SAṂGRAHA*

2. Looking beyond

> The manner and sensory means by which living things construe their environment will be the same media through which the environment – "the world" – gives itself back to them. ... Language names what the world is, and the world complies, delivering itself back to us through our own namings. Languages are indeed like habitats.
>
> (William Paden, 1992)

> We live our lives in this shared virtual world. ... The doorway into this virtual world was opened to us alone by the evolution of language.
>
> (Terrence Deacon, 1997)

Our concluding chapter focuses upon the last sections of the first chapter of the *Mahāyāna-saṃgraha* (I.58–61) which return, after a fashion, to the conception of the ālaya-vijñāna as the fundamental constituent of samsaric existence – its origination, perpetuation, and individual cessation. This returns us to familiar waters, but in a rather different light. These terse passages formulate these traditional themes in terms of the interrelationships between language, perception, and action in the ongoing construction of our shared world of human experience. For to fully appreciate the dependent arising of our human world, the text suggests, we will have to reconsider how our minds, our mental processes, *and each one of us* continuously and simultaneously arise together. As before, we will initially approach our text and its commentaries in terms of the background and context of early, Abhidharma, and Yogācāra Buddhist traditions.

The first section, MSg I.58, merely names the types or divisions (*prabheda*) of the ālaya-vijñāna, leaving it to the commentaries to delineate their deeper implications. The ālaya-vijñāna is categorized here in terms of three kinds (*viśeṣa*) of impressions or predispositions (*vāsanā*): (1) those of speech (*abhilāpa-vāsanā*), (2) of self-view (*ātmadṛṣṭi-vāsanā*), and (3) of the factors of existence (*bhavāṅga-vāsanā*). These denote the cognitive, afflictive, and psycho-ontological dimensions of the ālaya-vijñāna, respectively. That is, (1) insofar as it comprises the seeds and predispositions (MSg I.45), the ālaya-vijñāna represents the continuing influences of past actions (*karma*) and experiences upon present processes of mind, expressed here in terms of the predispositions of speech, the influences of language upon all our forms of cognitive awareness; (2) as the object of an entrenched yet subliminal view of self-identity (*satkāyadṛṣṭi*), our subliminal mental processes – that is, ālaya-vijñāna – continuously evoke self-centered notions and afflictive complexes which color our every thought and deed; and (3) as the form of consciousness (*vijñāna*) that results from the first two, the ālaya-vijñāna epitomizes the continuation of samsaric existence itself, represented here in terms of the impressions of the twelve factors of existence (*bhavāṅga*) in the series of dependent arising. The commentaries, and in fact the remaining sections of MSg I, draw out the implications of these three dimensions of the ālaya-vijñāna, which correspond closely with the standard categories of karma, kleśa, and their results. Of these, language, and the concepts it both enables and evokes, impart particularly important and fatefully productive influences. We will first briefly review the text and commentaries of this short section before examining their unfolding implications.

The predispositions of speech, self-view, and the life-constituents

The commentaries on this section describe the influences of language upon perception and cognitive awareness, the apprehension of a self, and the activities these instigate. First, the commentary, the *Upanibandhana*, states that cognitive awareness (*vijñāna*) arises in regard to expressions of selves (*ātman*), dharmas, and actions (*krīya*) due to the "special power" (*śakti-viśeṣa*) of the "predispositions or impressions of speech" (*abhilāpa-vāsanā*). That is, the text continues, cognitive awareness arises due to the impressions of conventional expressions (*vyavahāra*) such as humans and gods, eyes and visible forms, and comings and goings, respectively. Vasubandhu's *Bhāsya* reinforces this point, stating that the impressions of speech in the resultant consciousness (*vipāka-vijñāna*) serve as the "manifesting cause" (*abhinirvṛtti-hetu*) for objects to arise. For example, the very act of uttering the name "eye" contributes to the arising of an eye (as an object of awareness), and similarly for all the other expressions of dharmas, ears, and so forth.[1] That is to say, the conventional expressions of everyday speech (*vyavahāra*), which delineate the world into innumerable discrete objects and categories, subtly condition the way in which awareness of those "objects" arises. The kinds of cognitive experience people have, the categories of "things" we see and touch, are indelibly influenced by the expressions and figures of speech to which we are habituated.

Often the least discernible, arguably the most consequential, and certainly the most stubbornly ineradicable categorization to which we are habituated is the distinction between self and other. The predisposition of self-view (*ātmadṛṣṭi-vāsanā*), according to the *Upanibandhana*, refers to the predisposition of grasping to *self* (ātmagrāha) due to the *view* of self-existence (*satkāya*-dṛṣṭi). It is this predisposition, Vasubandhu explains, that creates the very distinction between self and other,[2] one of the root causes of the repeated activities that accrue karma and perpetuate the cycle of samsaric existence.

And it is these actions – informed by the predispositions of conventional expressions and the ingrained view of self-existence – that perpetuate the cycle of existence, the impressions of which are also encompassed within the ālaya-vijñāna. The *Upanibandhana* glosses "the impression of the factors of existence" (*bhavāṅga-vāsanā*) as the special impressions of the twelve factors of dependent arising, from ignorance until old age and death within the diverse destinies (*gati*) of gods, and so on, all of which arise due to the predominant power (*ādhipatya*) of karmically determinate activities (*saṃskārā*). (See n. 1.)

Common experience, common embodiment: language, the ālaya-vijñāna, and "the arising of the world"

These three categories are consistent with the traditional Buddhist themes already identified with the ālaya-vijñāna complex, as outlined in the *Saṃdhinirmocana Sūtra* and the *Ālaya Treatise*: new karma is produced by actions informed by the afflictions, predominate amongst which is the view of self-identity, which are evoked by forms of cognitive awareness that are themselves supported by and based upon "the appropriation which consists of the predispositions toward profuse imaginings in terms of conventional usage of images, names, and concepts" (Saṃdhi V 2: *nimitta-nāma-vikalpa-vyavahāra-prapañca-vāsanā-upādāna*). The MSg and its commentaries develop upon these ideas by considering how language influences karmic activity, a topic which raises a variety of heretofore unsuspected issues. If language use is somehow causally efficacious, as the texts suggest (i.e. the "special power" of the predispositions of speech), then what is the significance of its inescapably intersubjective nature? Do we share intersubjective "causes"? And do we dwell within an intersubjective "reality" created by the actions of beings similarly influenced by shared language use? If we are not mistaken, this seems to be exactly what the remaining sections of MSg I suggest.

Whereas at the beginning of this section, MSg I.58 categorized the kinds (*prabheda*) of ālaya-vijñāna according to its types of impression (*vāsanā*), MSg I.59 distinguishes it according to its different functions or aspects, the last of which – our focus here – is its characteristics (*lakṣaṇa*). The text characterizes the ālaya-vijñāna first with one, and then, in succeeding sections, with a series of binary characteristics whose elaborations take up most of the rest of the chapter. The first pair is the springboard for the others:

> I.59. [The ālaya-vijñāna] distinguished by [its] characteristic is that very consciousness which has a common characteristic (*sādhāraṇa-lakṣaṇa*) [and] that which has an uncommon characteristic (*asādhāraṇa-lakṣaṇa*).[3]
> (MSg I.59)

The next section elaborates:

> I.60. The common [characteristic of the ālaya-vijñāna] is the seed of the receptacle world (*bhājana-loka*). The uncommon [characteristic of the ālaya-vijñāna] is the seed of the individual sense-spheres (*prātyātmikāyatana*).
>
> (MSg I.60)

We need to examine these statements closely. The distinction between the "receptacle world" and "individual sense-spheres" is often understood as a distinction between "objective" and "subjective" worlds, respectively. This interpretation is part of a much larger debate about whether or not Yogācāra Buddhism should be considered a form of idealism, a debate which is somewhat tangential to our more narrow focus on the development of the concept of the ālaya-vijñāna.[4] But since the distinction between the "common" and "uncommon" characteristics of the ālaya-vijñāna is adduced here as one of the arguments for the ālaya-vijñāna in the MSg, it requires careful consideration.[5] We will interpret these notions – particularly the relation between the "common" aspect of the ālaya-vijñāna and the "receptacle world," and the role that language plays in mediating between them – primarily according to the MSg and its commentaries. But first we wish to contextualize this discussion by revisiting some of our earlier and contemporaneous texts on the potent interdependencies between "the world," language and perception, and the results of actions informed by grasping to self-identity.

* * *

We begin by briefly reviewing some of the early Pāli materials. From the very beginning, it would seem, the doctrine and practice of early Buddhism focused upon the *experienced phenomenal world*,[6] since it is our responses to phenomena as we experience them that keep us trapped in the vicious circle of samsara. This is the basic message of the famous first verse of the *Dhammapada*:

> All states (*dhammā*) have mind (*mano*) as their forerunner, mind is their chief, and they are mind-made. If one speaks or acts with a defiled mind, then suffering follows one even as the wheel follows the hoof of the draught-ox.
>
> (*Dhammapada*, 1; Rahula, 1959: 125)

Analysis of phenomenal experience and the practical techniques to transform it were central features of nearly all Indian Buddhist traditions, which focused on understanding and eventually transforming our habitual dispositions and embedded cognitive structures, and thereby forestalling actions they may instigate. To this end, Buddhist thought both articulated *and* critiqued the processes whereby we construe reality. These "world-constructive" aspects of consciousness were part of the larger cultural context into which Gautama Siddhārtha was born and within which Indian Buddhist traditions also developed.[7] As the Buddha repeatedly[8] stated:

> I further proclaim, friend, that it is in this very fathom-long body with its perception and thoughts that there is the world (*loka*), the origin of the world, the cessation of the world, the path leading to the cessation of the world.[9]
>
> (A II 48)

The "world" (*loka*) then, in these contexts at least, was a way of speaking about "the experienced world." As we have argued above, this is neither a form of idealism, which denies the ultimate reality of anything independent of the shifting contents of mind, nor of realism, which assumes a close if not exact correspondence between knowledge and an "objective reality" it purportedly reflects.[10] Rather, this is the world of dependent arising: when X is, Y arises. In this case, cognitive awareness (*vijñāna*) arises depending upon the concomitance of sense faculties, their respective objects and attention. Since *what counts* as an "object of experience," of cognitive awareness, is dependent upon the structures of the particular sense organs and faculties involved, the possible objects of any kind of cognitive awareness are significantly circumscribed from the outset. As Bhikkhu Ñāṇananda notes:

> The world is what our senses present it [to] us to be. However, the world is not purely a projection of the mind in the sense of a thorough going idealism; only, it is a phenomenon which the empirical consciousness cannot get behind, as it is itself committed to it. One might, of course, transcend the empirical consciousness and see the world objectively in the light of *paññā* [wisdom] only to find that it is void (*suñña*) of the very characteristics which make it a "world" for oneself.
>
> (Ñāṇananda, 1976: 84)

The physiological organs and psychological faculties that condition this "world of experience" – that is, the karmic structures (*saṃskārā*) that enable us to have any cognitive experience (*vijñāna*) at all – are themselves largely results of past karma, results that are preserved and perpetuated by further karmic activities informed by these very cognitive structures and instigated by their deeply entrenched dispositions. This is the vicious cycle outlined in the formula of dependent arising.

One of the chief conditions giving rise to our human experience of the world is language, since most moments of awareness are *already* heavily mediated by linguistic categories. We can find the rudiments of this idea in early Buddhist thought, especially in the operation of mental cognitive awareness. Mental cognitive awareness, we remember, arises in conjunction with two kinds of *dharmas*, a previous moment of sensory awareness, as well as its own "mental" objects, which are closely connected with reflection and analysis (*vitakka-vicāra*). In one sense, however, conscious awareness of even sensory objects depends upon mental cognitive awareness, since it is this form of awareness that is reflexively aware "*that* such and such a sensory cognitive awareness" has occurred. And this reflexivity is possible only because mental cognitive awareness itself arises based upon the faculty of *manas*, a faculty with several noteworthy properties. First, unlike the five forms of sensory cognitive awareness, which are individually separate and distinct, *manas* alone "experiences [each of] their fields and domains" (M I 295),[11] allowing reflexive awareness of each of them to arise. Even more importantly, *manas* is the means whereby thought itself – considered in ancient India as a predominately linguistic process – is carried out.[12] It does this through its role as the faculty involved in reflection and analysis, both of which are karmic formations of speech (*vitakka-vicārā vacīsaṇkhārā*, M I 301). In short, for both kinds of object,[13] mental cognitive awareness arises – via the *manas* – conditioned by the categories and structures (*saṃskāra*) of speech, which enable, perhaps even constitute, thinking, reflection, and analysis.[14]

This "linguistification of human experience" introduces a new dimension to the interrelationship between sensory forms of cognitive awareness, mental awareness of non-sensory objects such as thoughts or ideas, and the ensnaring web of conceptual proliferation (S. *prapañca*; P. *papañca*) that is enabled and entailed by language use.[15] For this reflexive self-awareness, like the linguistic structures it depends upon, is endlessly open-ended, entailing a nearly inescapable recursivity. As one Pāli text states: "Apperceptions (*saññā*) result in conventional expressions (*vohāra*). As one comes to know a thing, so one expresses (*voharati*) oneself, 'Thus I have apperceived'" (A III 413). And what one has apperceived and cognized, another text observes, becomes a condition for further cogitation, conceptualization, and the deleterious consequences that follow:

> Dependent on the eye and forms, eye-consciousness arises. The meeting of the three is contact. With contact as condition there is feeling. What one feels, that one apperceives. What one apperceives, that one thinks about. What one thinks about, that one mentally proliferates. With what one has mentally proliferated as the source, apperceptions and notions tinged by mental proliferation [*papañca-saññā-sankhā*] beset a man with respect to past, future, and present forms cognizable through the eye. . . . [and] mind-objects cognizable through the mind.
>
> (M I 111 f.)[16]

That is, the arising of cognitive awareness and apperceptions (which occur in nearly every moment of mind)[17] trigger processes of mental proliferation which give rise to further apperceptions and notions regarding other objects of cognitive awareness, and so on. In this way (see p. 38f.), contact, apperception, and conceptual proliferation together engender successive series of self-perpetuating feedback cycles that are so characteristic of our world of experience that proliferation (S. *prapañca*) is often used as a synonym for cyclic existence itself.

The most consequential effect of these recursive and self-referential processes, which also generates its own recursive web, is no doubt our ingrained sense of self as an independent agent or enduring subject of experience, that is, the conceit that "I am" (*asmimāna*). As one text puts it, "'I am' is a proliferation; 'I am this' is a proliferation; 'I shall be' is a proliferation" (S IV 202 f.). And not only is "the label 'I,'" as Bhikkhu Ñāṅananda (1976: 11) observes, an "outcome of *papañca*," but, as the *Sutta-nipāta* (915–6) puts it, it is the root of proliferation as well – without whose eradication the recursive feedback cycle of apperceptions, conceptual proliferation, and further apperceptions, and so on, could never come to an end.

In short, this sense of self-identity, this conceit "I am" which is so karmically significant, appears not as some simple, albeit abstract, referent *of* language, but arises as a virtual by-product of the recursivity that *is* language. The "I" is not found in any of the five aggregates, as Buddhists texts continuously declare, because the "I" is not some "thing" that exists some "where" in the first place. This sense of self *is itself* a conceptual proliferation, an endlessly receding cipher arising out of the complex interrelations between the recursivity of linguistically informed reflexive consciousness, the interdependent web of linguistic reference, and the intersubjective nexus between language users – a cipher whose sole "reality" consists of its influences upon the hearts and minds, the thoughts and deeds, of symbol-sharing sentient beings such as ourselves.[18] And it is our compulsive attempts to grasp onto this insubstantial will o'the wisp that keeps us running in circles.

* * *

The Yogācāra texts we have examined above similarly address the complex interrelationships between the phenomenal world of experience, the influences of language upon our cognitive processes, and the conceptual proliferations these give rise to, especially the sense of self-identity surrounding the conceit "I am."

Consistent with this view of early Buddhism, both Abhidharma and Yogācāra teachings associate the "arising of the world" with the experiences and activities of sentient beings.[19] The *Abhidharma-kośa*, for example, states that both the sentient and insentient worlds (*sattva-bhājanaloka*) result from the accumulated actions of numberless beings.[20] Asanga associates these two with the actions that bring them about: the inanimate "receptacle" world (*bhājana-loka*) and the animate "sentient" world (*sattva-loka*) result from the common and the uncommon actions of sentient beings, respectively.[21] That is to say, on the one hand, it is the common or similar actions of beings that create the seeds for them to experience a similar inanimate world – the seeds which comprise what MSg I.60 above calls the "common characteristics of the ālaya-vijñāna" of similar beings. And, on the other hand, it is the uncommon or dissimilar actions of beings that create the seeds for them to experience their dissimilar, individual sense-spheres (*prātyātmikāyatana*) – the seeds which comprise what the text calls the "uncommon aspect of the ālaya-vijñāna" of each individual being. This is just another way of saying that similar actions cause similar seeds that lead to similar results, while the converse is true for individual actions, their seeds, and their results. The commentary to MSg I.60 elaborates upon this passage:

> 'The common [characteristic of the ālaya-vijñāna] is the seed of the receptacle-world' means that it is the cause (*kāraṇa-hetu*) of perceptions (*vijñapti*) which appear as the receptacle world. It is common because these perceptions appear similarly to all who experience them through the force of maturation (*vipāka*) that is in accordance with their own similar karma.[22]
>
> (U 397c12 f., u 267a8–268a1)

This is a profoundly significant passage. Put simply, our "world" appears to us in similar ways because we have similar karma to experience it similarly. But to what extent do our past actions make our "experienced world" similar? And how or why do we come to have similar karma? At first, this appears relatively straightforward.

Part of what karma entails in most Indian religion is that members of the same species have similar karma: since the structures of our mind and bodies (*saṃskārā*) are – by definition – brought about by past karma (S II 64), and members of the same species have similar kinds of bodies and minds, this means that they have similar karma, similar causal conditions that brought about their birth into similar kinds of bodies. This is why we live in a human world, for example, as opposed to that of cats, bats, or gnats: our common species-wide cognitive capacities facilitate and circumscribe the kinds of things we can normally see, feel, and think, so that we experience the world in distinctively human ways. The specific structures and corresponding receptivities of these capacities effectively define and delimit the possible "worlds" we normally inhabit.[23] As the Buddha said, "it is in this very fathom-long body with its perception and thoughts that there is the world, the origin of the world, the cessation of the world," etc. (A II 48). Thus, most Indian Buddhist traditions would argue, the world that we experience is similar because our capacities, our *saṃskārā*, are similar, and these capacities are similar because – by definition – our karma is similar. This is what the commentary just cited says: *the inanimate world is common because perceptions appear similarly to all who experience them in accordance with the results of their own similar karma.*

We may now more deeply appreciate the implications of the "predispositions of speech" (*abhilāpa-vāsanā*), the first of the "types of the ālaya-vijñāna" in MSg I.58 with which we opened this chapter, for it is language that provides the means through which the "common aspects" of the ālaya-vijñāna give rise to a "common" receptacle world (*bhājana-loka*).[24] As a medium for conceiving, expressing, and sharing awareness, language provides the means for similar kinds of cognitive experiences to arise,[25] experiences that tend to provoke similar responses[26] which, in turn, typically give rise to similar results. That is, actions that are informed by similar conditions and instigated by similar intentions give rise, over the long term, to similar kinds of "experienced worlds." Let us briefly elaborate.

The ālaya-vijñāna is characterized in *Saṃdhinirmocana Sūtra* V 2, for example, as a subliminal awareness of the world which arises based upon perceptual and conceptual structures that are informed by linguistic convention. In addition to arising in dependence upon the sense faculties, the *ādāna-*/ālaya-vijñāna also arises based upon the "appropriation which consists of the predispositions toward mental proliferation in terms of conventional expressions regarding objective phenomena, names, and concepts" (*nimitta-nāma-vikalpa-vyavahāra-prapañca-vāsanā-upādāna*). That is, the form of subliminal mind which underlies all other forms of cognitive awareness itself arises in conjunction with this "substratum," this appropriation (*upādāna*) of the predispositions (*vāsanā*) to conceptually proliferate (*prapañca*) the conventional expressions (*vyavahāra*) regarding phenomena (*nimitta*), names (*nāma*), and discriminations (*vikalpa*). And insofar as the ālaya-vijñāna – thus constituted – serves as the "simultaneous support" of *all* forms of manifest cognitive awareness (*pravṛtti-vijñāna*), these proliferating tendencies indelibly yet unconsciously influence every moment of waking consciousness. That is to say, all our sensory and mental modes of awareness are preconditioned by the expressions and discriminations of language because, in this Yogācāra model of mind, they arise based upon the ālaya-vijñāna which is *already* structured by the categories, conventions, and, above all, conceptual proliferations incumbent upon language use. Cognitive awareness is never *simply* seeing, tasting, or hearing, etc.,[27] because it is, at bottom, indelibly configured by linguistic categories.

And it is just because our cognitive structures are constituted by these linguistic predispositions (*abhilāpa-vāsanā*) from the bottom up, so to speak, that cognitive awareness itself is subject to language's endless recursivity. The "predispositions or impressions of speech" that have the "special power" (*śakti-viśeṣa*) to give rise to cognitive awareness in regard to expressions of selves, dharmas, and actions, etc. (as the commentary to MSg I.58 puts it), are never fully "used up" (*anupabhukta*), according to MSg I.61.2, because "the seeds of the impressions of language give rise to conceptual proliferation since beginningless time," without which, the text continues, "the new arising of the impressions of language would be impossible."[28]

This reformulates in Yogācāra terms what we have already seen in the Pāli texts: "Apperceptions (*saññā*) result in conventional usage (*vohāra*; S. *vyavahāra*)" (A III 413), and "what one apperceives, that one … mentally proliferates" resulting in yet further "apperceptions and notions tinged by mental proliferation [that] beset a man with respect to … forms cognizable through the eye … [and] mind-objects cognizable through the mind" (M I 111). Here, however, this entire process is conceived in terms of the imperceptible impressions (*vāsanā*) of linguistic and conceptual categories and their subconscious influences upon every moment of waking awareness.[29]

And, as with the Pāli materials before them, in the Yogācāra texts as well it is the conceit "I am" that serves as the focal point through which these proliferating proclivities become effectively engaged with the perceptions and experiences of the phenomenal world. It does this, once again, through the mediation of mental cognitive awareness insofar as such mental awareness arises based upon the subliminal processes of conceiving and thinking "I am" – in other words, insofar as it is informed by "mentation (*manas*) which has the mode of conceiving 'I-making' and the conceit 'I am'... [and] of conceiving and taking the ālaya-vijñāna as 'I am [this]' and '[this is] I'" (*Pravṛtti Portion* (4.b)A.1. (a)). It is this that keeps us caught up in the endlessly proliferating cycles of samsaric life because, "as long as [this] mentation (*manas*) has not ceased, [mental cognitive awareness] is not freed from the bondage of perception (*vijñapti*) in regard to phenomena (*nimitta*)" (ibid. (4.b)A.2.). That is, as long as mental cognitive awareness is colored by the afflictive disposition toward the conceit "I am" – which Vasubandhu says creates the very discrimination between "self" and "other"[30] – then so long will beings remain bound to phenomenal perceptions. But since the discrimination between self and other is itself inextricably involved with the recursivity of language, it too gives rise to boundless proliferation. As MSg II.16.1 points out:

> Mental cognitive awareness is conceptual discrimination (*parikalpita*).... It arises from its own seeds of the impressions of language, and from the seeds of the impressions of language of all perceptions (*vijñapti*). In this way, it arises through conceptual discrimination whose aspects are endless (*anantākāravikalpena*).[31]
>
> (MSg II.16.1)

In other words, we remain bound to phenomenal perception (and the vicious circle of action, result, and reaction, which this entails) as long as mental cognitive awareness arises on the one hand, in conjunction with the impressions of language whose discriminations are endless and, on the other hand, based upon the ingrained, subliminal sense of self-identity represented by afflictive mentation – a sense of self which is not only a product of linguistic proliferation, but which also arises in regard to a form of subliminal awareness (the ālaya-vijñāna) that is itself based upon tendencies toward linguistic recursivity (i.e. "the predispositions toward mental proliferation in terms of conventional expressions regarding objective phenomena, names, and concepts"). We are encircled, it appears, in circles within circles within circles.

The proliferating tendencies associated with language thus entail several overlapping feedback processes. First, *diachronically* – as spelled out in the Pāli materials – between our cognitive processes, the recursivity of conceptual proliferations (at the center of which is the sense "I am"), and the karmic activities these instigate.

Then, *synchronically* – as explicitly spelled out in the Yogācārin texts – between the ālaya-vijñāna, the subliminal sense of "I am" represented by afflictive mentation (*kliṣṭa-manas*), the manifest forms of cognitive awareness these first two bring about, and the actions that they collectively instigate, actions which in turn reinforce the seeds in the ālaya-vijñāna, and so on. This picture of *intrapsychic cyclic causality* applies equally appropriately to the simultaneous processes arising from moment to moment in the course of a single lifetime as well as, in traditional Buddhist metaphysics, throughout the multiple lifetimes of one's samsaric destiny.

The Yogācāra texts, however, developed two further dimensions which had remained relatively rudimentary in the early Pāli texts. First, this linguistic recursivity, which colors so much of our perceptual experience including our innate (*sahaja*) forms of self-grasping, now operates unconsciously, imperceptible "even for the wise;" and second, these processes are karmically productive at a collective as well as individual level – that is, they create a common "world." The fact that we are "linguistified" creatures[32] constitutes a distinctive third, unconscious yet thoroughly *intersubjective* feedback system which, like the other major "engines" of samsara, karma and kleśa, continuously proliferates and perpetuates samsaric existence, but which, unlike them, *bridges our individual and collective experience of the "world,"* connecting our similar karmic activities with the similar "worlds" these activities bring about.

Since language is a shared medium of interaction, the impressions of conventional usage (*vyavahāra*) impart similar influences upon our perceptual and conceptual processes, conveyed through the most fundamental levels of unconscious mind. These influences in the form of the "impressions of language" comprise the common aspect (*sādhāraṇa-lakṣaṇa*) of the ālaya-vijñāna, our common "psychic inheritance" if you will, which allows us to experience the world through similar perceptions and, all too often, provokes us to respond to these perceptions in similarly afflicted ways. The impressions of conventional usage thus both *reflect* the common discriminative concepts (*vikalpa*), names, and phenomena that comprise our social and cultural lives, as well as *facilitate* further common experiences and activities which, over time and in the aggregate, bring about and perpetuate this common "receptacle world" which "appears similarly to all who experience it in accordance with their own similar karma."

Our shared, consensual world, facilitated and sustained through our common linguistic conventions (*vyavahāra*), is thus brought about by the common causes, the common karma, of multiple beings. These mostly indiscernible processes give rise to the cultural, social, and cognitive "worlds" we inhabit, not simply as individuals but even more essentially as social beings, since "language," as our epigraph observes, "is a primary medium through which humans inhabit their world" (Paden, 1992: 7). "Languages are indeed like habitats," he continues, because they give rise to the inexhaustibly proliferating processes (*prapañca*) of classification and conceptualization (*vikalpa*) through which we habitually, nearly unavoidably, and mostly unknowingly engage, construct, and sustain the "world" around us, one which reciprocally and simultaneously sustains and ensnares us all. And this, we suggest, is the central *Mahāyāna* sense of the ālaya-vijñāna: *it is the unconscious habits of body, speech, and mind to which we are habituated that give rise, in the long term and in the aggregate, to the habitats we inhabit, the "common receptacle world" we experience all around us.*[33]

And these "worlds" persist, in the aggregate, regardless of the fate of particular individuals. According to MSg I.60, at the tail-end of the first chapter, even though the individual characteristic of the ālaya-vijñāna – that is, of our own subliminal and afflicted cognitive and emotional dispositions – may have been personally eliminated on the path toward Buddhist liberation, nevertheless "the vision of the common [world] which is apprehended by the discrimination of others (*paravikalpa-parigṛhīta*)" still persists. This common world does not come to an end, the commentary explains, "because it [continues to be] grasped by the discriminative concepts (*vikalpa*) of others."[34]

This suggests, we venture, that we all have a larger responsibility in the construction of our "world" than we commonly acknowledge. For if we are not trapped exclusively inside our heads, but are causally as well as cognitively intersubjective, from the groundless ground on up, then the issue of which particular concepts, categories, and classifications we produce, proclaim, and protect – unconsciously or otherwise – is of vital importance. We can and must strive to collectively unravel our "common bonds" (*sādhāraṇa-bandhana*), "difficult to cut (*duṣheya*) and difficult to fully comprehend (*dusparijñeya*)" though they may be (MSg I.60). How we can do that, however, is another story.

Part III

APPENDICES

APPENDIX I

The series of dependent arising: affliction, action, and their results

As is illustrated in the following chart, the chain of affliction, action, and their results occurs *twice* within the standard series of dependent arising, illustrating the cyclic nature of samsaric existence. In this chart, the 12 members are categorized into karma-generating activities, the results they lead to, and the afflictive responses these elicit. This, and the three lifetime schema, stem from the commentarial period somewhat later than the early discourses.

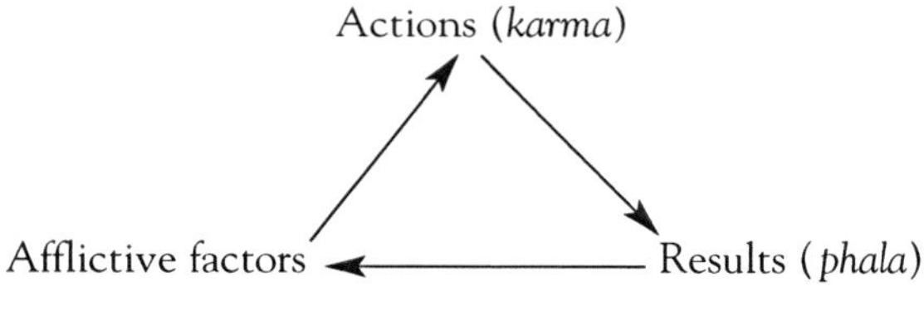

The round of afflictions (*kleśa*) is:	(1) ignorance, (8) craving, and (9) grasping.
The round of *karma* or cause is:	(2) karmic formations and (10) becoming.
The round of result is:	(3) vijñāna, (4) name-and-form, (5) the six sense-spheres, (6) sensation or contact, (7) feeling, (11) birth and, (12) old age, etc.

Source: Visuddhimagga, XVII 298. (AKBh III 26a–b has the same schema.)

1. Ignorance (P. *avijjā*; S. *avidyā*)	Afflictive (*kleśa*)
2. *Sankhārā* (karmic formation or complex)	Karmic action – Causal
3. Consciousness, or cognitive awareness (*viññāṇa*)	Resultant
4. Name and form (*nāmarūpa*)	Resultant

5. Six sense-spheres (*saḷāyatana*)	Resultant
6. Sensation, contact, or sense-impression (*phassa*)	Resultant
7. Feeling (*vedanā*)	Resultant
8. Craving (P. *taṇhā*; S. *tṛṣṅā*)	Afflictive (*kleśa*)
9. Grasping or appropriation (*upādāna*)	Afflictive (*kleśa*)
10. Becoming (*bhava*)	Karmic action – Causal
11. Birth (*jāti*)	Resultant
12. Old age and death, etc. (*jarāmaraṇaṃ soka-parideva-dukkha-domanassupāyāsā*)	Resultant

APPENDIX II

Index of related controversies

The Abhidharma tradition laid ultimate validity upon the momentary factors (*dharma*) constitutive of each individual's experience, whose (mostly) unbroken succession is conventionally designated the mental stream (*citta-santāna*). The discernment of dharmas as they inform, indeed constitute, one's thoughts and actions provided a powerful analytic in service of the higher religious aims of purification of mind and the cessation of karmic accumulation, facilitating gradual progress toward these goals. This newer Abhidharmic analytic, however, became increasingly problematic when contextualized within the larger soteriological framework in which it was ultimately meaningful and coherent. For when it came time to describe the traditional understandings of karma and the afflictions (*kleśa*) and their gradual eradication in terms of the analysis of momentary processes of mind and their concomitant mental factors (*citta-caitta*), the exegetical, systemic, and empirical problems became glaring indeed. The inability of the *dharmic analytic* to adequately account for these indispensable phenomena undermined the very purposes for which it was conceived in the first place: discerning the influences of karma and *kleśa* on the momentary processes of mind and thereby overcoming their pernicious consequences.

The totality of the problems created by the Abhidharmic analytic suggests they were of a systemic nature, elicited by the disjunction between two distinct sets of discourses, represented (roughly) by the synchronic, dharmic analysis and the diachronic analysis of the mental stream (*santāna*), championed by the Sarvāstivādins and Sautrāntikas, respectively. These two discourses also corresponded with exceptional felicity to the two temporal dimensions of *vijñāna* discernable within the early Pāli materials. These problems all lie along a similar fault-line, skirting the margins between these two distinct discourses. The common thread connecting them is that they all refer to, rely upon, or require aspects of mind that persist in some fashion beyond, outside, or separately from momentary, conscious cognitive processes. And while these continuing elements or energies must be passively present, their direct karmic influences must also be strictly *neutral*. Otherwise, their continuing presence until far along the path to liberation (which all schools accepted) would preclude any karmically skillful states from arising whatsoever.[1]

We present here a short outline of these issues, most of which are discussed in the body of the text, along with a brief note on the various positions of contemporary schools. The sheer number of related issues not only confirms their systemic nature (which we will discuss further below), but reflects as well the widespread recognition of the what we have called the Abhidharmic Problematic.[2]

Karma

1 Is there a distinct factor of karmic accumulation (*karma-upacaya*)?[3]
2 Is karmic accumulation (*karma-upacaya*) related to cognitive awareness (*vijñāna*)?[4]

Distinction between latent and manifest afflictions (*anuśaya/kleśa*)

3 Are the manifest outbursts (*paryavasthāna*) of the afflictions (*kleśa*) distinct from their latent dispositions (*anuśaya*)?[5]
4 Are the latent dispositions (*anuśaya*) dissociated from mind (*citta-viprayukta*), and thus karmically neutral?[6]
5 Are the latent dispositions (*anuśaya*) simultaneous or compatible with wholesome states (*kuśala-citta*)?[7]
6 Are there innate, but karmically neutral afflictions (*kleśa*)?[8]
7 Are there seeds (*bīja*) that represent the latent dispositions, their impressions (*vāsanā*), the potential for *karmic* result, and/or subtle forms of vijñāna?[9]

Stages upon the path

8 Do Aryans harbor afflictions or latent dispositions (*anuśaya*)?[10]
9 Is there a distinct attainment which distinguishes those who are or will be Aryans from the non-liberated?[11]

Continuity of consciousness

10 Is a subtle form of consciousness (*vijñāna*) present during the attainment of cessation or unconscious states?[12]
11 Are there subtle (*sūkṣma*) and enduring forms of mind at other times?[13]
12 Is there a distinct type of consciousness (*vijñāna*) that transits at rebirth?[14]

Simultaneity of different mental processes

13 Can ordinary consciousness (*citta* or *vijñāna*) retain or receive the seeds (*bīja*) or impressions (*vāsanā*)?[15]
14 Is there a distinct type of consciousness (*citta* or *vijñāna*) underlying the cognitive modes as their basis (*āśraya*) or root (*mūla*)?[16]
15 Do the different cognitive modes (*vijñāna*) function simultaneously?[17]

* * *

When a whole series of related problems arises like this, it suggests that their origins lie within the presuppositions they rest upon, which piecemeal solutions alone cannot fully address. The various concepts proffered by different Abhidharma schools were, in the end, simply ad hoc solutions that singly addressed one or another of these issues without, however, either challenging their underlying presuppositions nor fully contextualizing them within a larger, more encompassing conceptual framework. It is our thesis that this latter, meta-critical approach was taken only when the Yogācārins fundamentally restructured the theory of mind with the ālaya-vijñāna at its center. They did this by systematically transposing those diachronic aspects of *vijñāna* that had become marginalized within Abhidharma analysis of mind into the terms of synchronic, *dharmic* discourse, thereby reuniting those manifold functions that were originally undifferentiated in the early notion of *vijñāna*.

These developments suggest a correspondence with Kuhn's (1970) analysis of the dynamics of a "paradigm shift." The shift is instigated by a "crisis" in the previous paradigm due to the number of "recognized anomalies whose characteristic feature is their stubborn refusal to be assimilated to existing paradigms" (1970: 97). The "proliferation of versions of a theory," Kuhn observes, is therefore "a usual symptom of crisis" (p. 71). The Abhidharmists' initial response to the anomalies mentioned above was to devise "numerous articulations and ad hoc modifications of their theory in order to eliminate any apparent conflict" (p. 78). Each modification expresses "some minor or not so minor articulation of the paradigm, no two of them quite alike, each partially successful, but none sufficiently so to be accepted as paradigm[atic]" (p. 83). And finally, the new paradigm represents a transformation of "some of the field's most elementary theoretical generalizations" through a "reconstruction ... from new fundamentals" (pp. 84 f.).

The various "demonstrations" or "proofs" for the ālaya-vijñāna typically describe and defend the ālaya-vijñāna while demonstrating the inadequacy of alternative theories. These too are suggestive of such a paradigm shift: since "paradigms gain their status because they are more successful than their competitors in solving a few problems that the group of practitioners has come to recognize as acute" (ibid.: 23), Kuhn says, "the decision to reject one paradigm is always simultaneously the decision to accept another, and the judgment leading to that decision involves the comparison of both paradigms with nature *and* with each other" (p. 77). Hence the formal "proofs" of the existence of the ālaya-vijñāna, with their insistent critique of the traditional six-*vijñāna* theory and its presupposition of unifocal and serial functioning.

APPENDIX III

Translation: the *Pravṛtti* and *Nivṛtti Portions* of the *Viniścayasaṃgrahaṇī* of the *Yogācārabhūmi*

Unlike the *Proof Portion*, which immediately precedes them in the *Yogācārabhūmi*, the *Pravṛtti/Nivṛtti Portions* are not available in their original Sanskrit. We must rely upon their Tibetan and Chinese translations. Fortunately, we have two Chinese versions, by Hsüan Tsang (T. 1579.579c23–582a28) and Paramārtha (T. 1584.1019a25–1020c22), and Tibetan versions in both the Peking and Derge collections which are nearly identical (P. edn, 5539, Zi, 4a5–11 a8; D. edn, 4038, Shi, 3b4–9 b3). Textual references bracketed within the translation refer to the Derge (D.), Hsüan Tsang (H.), and Paramārtha (P.) translations, respectively. This text has also been edited, analyzed, and translated into Japanese by Hakamaya Noriaki (1979), and it is upon this edited text that our translation is based. We have also followed the outline from Hakamaya's study, with some minor modifications, for ease of reference to both Hakamaya's and Schmithausen's work (1987). Since *all* the Sanskrit terms here are reconstructions from Tibetan and Chinese, primarily based upon Hakamaya's and Schmithausen's works, we have also dispensed with the usual asterisk. Notes have been largely limited to textual or terminological matters.

The *Pravṛtti Portion:*[1] the arising of *ālaya-vijñāna*

I. (O.a) Summary (*uddāna*)

[The continuous arising of *ālaya-vijñāna* is explained by five aspects, according to its:]

(1) Objective support (*ālambana*),
(2) Association (*saṃprayukta*),
(3) Reciprocal conditionality (*anyonya-pratyayatā*),
(4) Concurrent arising (*sahabhava pravṛtti*), and
(5) The cessation (*nivṛtti*) of all defilements (*saṃkleśa*).

(O.b) Briefly, the continuous arising (*pravṛtti*) of the *ālaya-vijñāna* is established by [the first] four aspects, while [its] cessation (*nivṛtti*) is established by [the remaining] one aspect. That is to say, [its] continuous arising (*pravṛtti*) is established by means of these four aspects: (1) by [its] objective support, (2) by association, (3) by reciprocal conditionality, and (4) by concurrent arising, while [its] cessation is proved (5) by the cessation (*nivṛtti*) of the defilements.

[D. 3b4–7; H. 579c23–580a2; P. 1019a25–8]

1. [Establishing that *ālaya-vijñāna* arises by means of an objective support (*ālambana-pravṛtti-vyavasthāna*)].

(1.a) Of these, how is it established that [*ālaya-vijñāna*] arises by means of an objective support?

(1.b) Briefly, *ālaya-vijñāna* arises by means of a twofold objective support: (1) By the perception of the inner appropriation (*upādāna-vijñapti*); and (2) By the outward perception of the receptacle world whose aspects are not clearly delineated (*bahirdhā aparicinnākāra-bhājana-vijñapti*).[2]

(1.b)A.1. Of these, the "inner appropriation" (*adhyātmam upādāna*) means (1) the impressions which are attached to the falsely discriminated (*parikalpita-svabhāvābhiniveśa-vāsanā*) and (2) the material forms of the sense faculties along with [their] bases (*sādhiṣṭhānam indriya-rūpam*).[3] Moreover, [they both occur] in the realms with material form [i.e. *kāma-* and *rūpa-dhātu*]. Only the appropriation of impressions (*vāsanā-upādāna*) [occurs] in the Formless [Realm] (*ārupya-*[*dhātu*]).

(1.b)A.2. The "outward perception of the receptacle world, whose aspects are undiscerned" means the continuous, uninterrupted perception of the continuity of the receptacle world based upon that very *ālaya-vijñāna* which has inner appropriation as an objective support.[4]

(1.b)A.3. Thus, one should know that the way *ālaya-vijñāna* [arises] in regard to the objective support of inner appropriation and the objective support of the receptacle [world] is similar to a burning flame which arises inwardly while it emits light outwardly on the basis of the wick and oil, respectively.

[D. 3b7–4a3; H. 580a2–12; P. 1019a29–b7]

(1.b)B.1. The objective support [of *ālaya-vijñāna*] is subtle (*sūkṣma*) because it is difficult to discern (*duṣpariccheda*) even by worldly sages.

(1.b)B.2. The objective support [of *ālaya-vijñāna*] is always there, it is not sometimes this and sometimes that (*anyathātva*). However, from the first moment of appropriation [of the body at conception] until as long as life lasts (*yāvaj jīvam*) [its] perception (*vijñapti*; T. *rigs pa*) arises with a single flavor (*ekarasatvena*)[5] [i.e. homogeneously].

(1.b)B.3. It should be understood that *ālaya-vijñāna* is momentary regarding [its] objective support, and though it continuously arises in a stream of instants,[6] it is neither singular (*ekatva*) (Ch. adds: "nor eternal").[7]

[D. 4a3–5; H. 580a12–18; P. 1019b7–10]

(1.b)C.1. One should say that *ālaya-vijñāna* has a small appropriation (**upādāna*)[8] as [its] objective support in the Desire Realm (*kāma-dhātu*).

(1.b)C.2. [It] has large appropriation as [its] objective support in the Form Realm (*rūpa-dhātu*).

(1.b)C.3. [It] has a measureless appropriation as [its] objective support in the sphere of infinite-space (*ākāśānantyāyatana*) and in the sphere of infinite consciousness (*vijñānānantyāyatana*) in the Formless Realm (*ārūpya-dhātu*).

(1.b)C.4. [It] has a subtle appropriation as [its] objective support in the sphere of nothing-whatsoever (*ākiṃcanyāyatana*).

(1.b)C.5. One should know that [it] has very subtle appropriation as [its] objective support in the sphere of neither-apperception nor non-apperception (*naivasaṃjñā-nāsaṃjñāyatana*).

(1.c) [Summary] In this way one should understand that the arising of *ālaya-vijñāna* by means of an objective support is established through the perception (*vijñapti*) of two kinds of objective supports [A.1,2,3.], through the perception of a subtle [objective support] [B.1.], through the [continual] perception of a similar [objective support] [B.2.], through the perception of a momentary [objective support] [B.3.], through the perception of an objective support of small appropriation [C.1.], through the perception of an objective support of large appropriation [C.2.], through the perception of an objective support of measureless appropriation [C.3.], through the perception of an objective support of subtle appropriation [C.4.], and through the perception of an objective support of very subtle appropriation [C.5.].[9]

[D. 4a5–b2; H. 580a18–28; P. 1019b10–16]

2. [Establishing that *ālaya-vijñāna* arises by means of association (*saṃprayoga-pravṛtti-vyavasthāna*)].

(2.a) How is it established that [*ālaya-vijñāna*] arises by means of association?

(2.b) A. *Ālaya-vijñāna* is associated through association (*saṃprayoga*) with the five omnipresent factors associated with mind (*cittasaṃprayukta-sarvatraga*): attention (*manaskāra*), sense-impression (*sparśa*), feeling (*vedanā*), apperception (*saṃjñā*), and volitional impulse (*cetanā*).

(2.b)B. These dharmas, then,

(1) are included (*saṃgṛhīta*) in [the category of] resultant states (*vipāka*);
(2) are subtle (*sūkṣma*) because they are hard to perceive (*durvijñānatva*) even for wise ones of the world;
(3) always arise in the same manner regarding a single objective support (*ekālambana*).

Moreover, among these mental factors (*caitta*), the feeling (*vedanā*) which is associated with *ālaya-vijñāna* is:

(4) neither exclusively (*ekāntika*) pain nor pleasure (*aduḥkhāsukha*);
(5) and it is [karmically] indeterminate (*avyākṛta*).

The other mental factors (*caitta-dharma*) are also explained in the same way.

(2.c) [Summary] In this way, one should understand that the arising of *ālaya-vijñāna* by association is established: by [its] being associated with the omnipresent mental factors (*sarvatraga-caitasika-saṃprayukta*) [A.], by [its] being associated with [mental factors of the] same class, that is, resultant states (*vipāka-sāmānya-jāti-saṃprayukta*) [B.1.], by [its] being associated with the subtle arising (*sūkṣma-pravṛtti-saṃprayukta*) [of the mental factors], [B.2.], by [its] being associated with [the mental factors] arising in the same manner in regard to a single objective support [B.3.], by [its] being associated with [mental factors that are] neither pain nor pleasure [B.4.], and by [its] being associated with [mental factors that are karmically] indeterminate [B.5.].

[D. 4b2–7; H. 580a29–b8; P. 1019616–22]

3. [Establishing the arising of *ālaya-vijñāna* by means of reciprocal conditionality (*anyonya-pratyayatā-pravṛtti-vyavasthāna*)].

(3.a) How is it established that [*ālaya-vijñāna*] arises by reciprocal conditionality?

(3.b) A. *Ālaya-vijñāna* functions (*kāritra*) as the condition of [the forms of] arising cognitive awareness (*pravṛtti-vijñāna*) in two ways: by being their seed (*bīja-bhāva*), and by providing their support (*āśraya-kara*).

(3.b)A.1. Of these, "being a seed" means that whichever wholesome, unwholesome or indeterminate [forms of] arising cognitive awareness occur, they all have *ālaya-vijñāna* as [their] seed.

(3.b)A.2. "Providing a support" means that the five groups of cognitive awareness will arise based upon the material sense faculties (*rūpīṇy-indriyāṇi*) that are appropriated (*upātta*) by *ālaya-vijñāna*, but not from those that are not appropriated [by *ālaya-vijñāna*].

Like the [material sense faculties, such as] the eye, etc., which are the support of the five groups of cognitive awareness, *ālaya-vijñāna* is the support of the mind (*manas*) and mental-cognitive awareness (*mano-vijñāna*). When there is [*ālaya-vijñāna*], mind and mental consciousness will also arise, but not when there is not.[10]

(3.b)B. Then, the [forms of] arising cognitive awareness function as the condition of *ālaya-vijñāna* in two ways: by nurturing (*paripuṣṭi*) the seeds in this life and by causing [it] to grasp to the seeds of its own reproduction (*abhinirvṛtti*) in the next life.[11]

(3.b)B.1. Of these, "nurturing seeds in this life" means that insofar as [karmically] skillful, unskillful, and indeterminate [moments of] arising cognitive awareness arise based on *ālaya-vijñāna*, their simultaneous arising and ceasing, supported by their own supports, infuses (*bhāvayati*) the impressions (*vāsanā*) (Ch. adds: "into *ālaya-vijñāna*"). By that cause (*hetu*) and that condition (*pratyaya*), through being skillful, etc., the [forms of] arising cognitive awareness will also arise successively more well-nurtured, well-tempered, and quite distinct.

(3.b)B.2. [Summary] The other type of impressions (*vāsanā*) will cause [*ālaya-vijñāna*] to grasp to the result (*vipāka*) which is that very *ālaya-vijñāna* in the future.[12]

(3.c) [Summary] In this way one should understand that the arising [of *ālaya-vijñāna*] is established by means of *ālaya-vijñāna* and the [forms of] arising cognitive awareness being reciprocal conditions of each other: by means of [*ālaya-vijñāna*] being the seed [for] [A.1.], and creating the base [of, the forms of arising cognitive awareness] [A.2.], and by [the forms of arising cognitive awareness] nurturing the seeds [in *ālaya-vijñāna*] [B.1.], and by [causing *ālaya-vijñāna*] to grasp the seeds [of its own persistence in the future] [B.2.].

[D4b7–5a7; H. 580b9–29; P. 1019b22–c6]

4. [Establishing the arising of *ālaya-vijñāna* by means of concurrence (*sahabhāva-pravṛtti-vyavasthāna*)][13].

(4.a) How is it established that [*ālaya-vijñāna*] arises by concurrence?

(4.b)A.1. (a) Sometimes *ālaya-vijñāna* arises concurrently (*saha pravartate*) with just one of the [forms of] arising cognitive awareness, for example, with mind (*manas*). In this way, the mind (*manas*) whose mode (*ākāra*) is conceiving (*manyanā*) "I-making" (*ahaṃkāra*), the conceit "I am" (*asmimāna*), always arises and functions simultaneously with *ālaya-vijñāna* in states with mental activity (*sacittaka*) and even in states lacking mental activity (*acittaka*). That [mind (*manas*)] has the mode of taking *ālaya-vijñāna* as [its] object and conceiving [it] as "I am [this]" (*asmīti*) and "[this is] I" (*aham iti*).[14]

(b) Sometimes [*ālaya-vijñāna*] arises and functions concurrently with two [other mental processes, i.e.] mind (*manas*) and mental-cognitive awareness (*mano-vijñāna*);
(c) sometimes with three [mind and mental-cognitive awareness] and any [additional] one of the five groups of cognitive awareness;
(d) sometimes with four, with any [additional] two of the five groups of cognitive awareness arising simultaneously;
(e) [And so on up to]: sometimes [*ālaya-vijñāna*] arises and functions concurrently with up to seven, with [all] the five groups of cognitive awareness arising simultaneously.[15]

(4.b)A.2. Mental-cognitive awareness is said to be based on mind (*manas*), because as long as mind (*manas*) has not ceased [mental-cognitive awareness] is not freed from the bondage of perception (*vijñapti*) in regard to phenomena (*nimitta*);[16] but if [*manas*] has ceased, [it] will be freed. Mental-cognitive awareness (*mano-vijñāna*) has the sense objects (*viṣaya*) of other [forms of cognitive awareness] as its objective support (*paraviṣayālambana*) and its own object (*svaviṣayālambana*) as its objective support.

Here, "[having] the sense objects of others as an objective support" means its objective support is any of the sense objects of the five groups of cognitive awareness [which arises] either simultaneously (*yugapad*) or not simultaneously.

"[Having] its own sense object as an objective support" means the [mental-cognitive awareness] which arises having a [purely mental] *dharma* as its objective support, without the objective supports of the five groups of cognitive awareness.

[D. 5a7–b6; H. 580b29–c13; P. 1019c6–17]

(4.b)A.3. *Ālaya-vijñāna* also sometimes arises intermingled with the feelings of pain (*duḥkha*), pleasure (*sukha*), and neither pain nor pleasure (*aduḥkhāsukha*), because [it] arises depending upon the [forms of] arising cognitive awareness, depending upon whatever feeling they are (Ch. adds: "associated with" (*saṃprayukta*) H. 580c15 f.; P. 1019c17).

Of these, amongst human beings, the gods of the Desire Realm (*kāmāvacarā*), animals, and some of the hungry ghosts, the stream of feelings (*vedanā-santāna*) of the [forms of] arising cognitive awareness, whether pain (*duḥkha*), pleasure (*sukha*), or neither pain nor pleasure (*aduḥkhāsukha*), simultaneously arises and functions intermingled with the innate (*sahaja*) feeling [of *ālaya-vijñāna*], which is neither pain nor pleasure (*aduḥkhāsukha*).[17]

In the sentient hells, the feeling [of *ālaya-vijñāna*], which is neither pain nor pleasure (*aduḥkhāsukha*), is overwhelmed; [it] occurs and functions simultaneously only with that unalloyed stream of pain (*duḥkha*). Moreover, because it is overwhelmed [the neutral feeling of *ālaya-vijñāna*] is difficult to perceive.

[The feeling of *ālaya-vijñāna* arises concurrently] with pleasure (*sukha*) for the gods in the Stage of the Three Blissful Concentrations in the same way [that it arises] with pain (*duḥkha*) in the sentient hell realms. For beings from the Fourth meditative stage (*dhyāna*) up to the Peak of Existence (*bhavāgra*) [it arises] with neither pain nor pleasure (*aduḥkhāsukha*).

[D. 5b6–6a4; H. 580c13–25; P. 1019c17–24]

(4.b)A.4. Sometimes *ālaya-vijñāna* arises concurrently with skillful, unskillful, and indeterminate mental factors (*caitasika-dharma*) belonging to the [forms of] arising cognitive awareness.

(4.b)B.1. In this way, *ālaya-vijñāna* arises and functions concurrently with the [forms of] arising cognitive awareness. It also arises and functions concurrently with adventitious (*āgantuka*) feelings as well as with adventitious skillful, unskillful, and indeterminate (mental-) factors ((*caitasika-*)*dharma*).[18] But it is not said to be conjoined (*saṃprayukta*) with them. Why is that? Because it arises with a different objective support (*asamālambana*).[19]

This should also be understood according to the proper kind of similarity (*sādharmya*),[20] just as, for example, the visual-cognitive awareness arises concurrently (*sahabhū*) with the eye but is not conjoined (*saṃprayukta*) with it.

[D. 6a4–6; H. 580c26–581a2; P. 1019c24–8]

(4.b)B.2. Thus, for example, just as there is no impediment (*avirodha*)[21] to the simultaneous arising of the mental factors (*caitasika-dharma*) because [they] have diverse characteristics, [since they] are undifferentiated [insofar] as [they are] mental accompaniments (*caitasika*), so, too, should one understand that there is no impediment to the [forms of] arising cognitive awareness arising simultaneously with *ālaya-vijñāna*.

Just as, for example, there is no impediment to a wave arising concurrently with the river stream, and there is no impediment to a reflected image occurring simultaneously with the bright surface of the mirror, so, too, should one understand that there is no impediment to the [forms of] arising cognitive awareness arising concurrently with the *ālaya-vijñāna* as well.[22]

[D. 6a6–6b2; H. 581a2–9; P. 1019c28–1020a4]

(4.b)B.3. For example, a visual-cognitive awareness sometimes apprehends in a single thing (*vastu*) a visual form (*rūpa*) with one kind of unvariegated aspect, and sometimes apprehends [one with] many diverse aspects simultaneously.

Just as the visual-cognitive awareness [apprehends] visual forms, so too [*mutatis mutandis*] the auditory-cognitive awareness [apprehends] sounds, the olfactory-cognitive awareness smells, and the gustatory-cognitive awareness tastes.

So, for example, just as the tactile-cognitive awareness sometimes apprehends[23] in regards to a single tangible thing a tangible [objective support] with one kind of unvariegated aspect, and sometimes apprehends [one with] many diverse aspects simultaneously, so too should one understand that there is no impediment to the perception (*vijñapti*) of mental-cognitive awareness (*mano-vijñāna*) apprehending (a sense object with) either one or many diverse (aspects simultaneously).[24]

[D. 6b2–5; H. 581a9–17; P. 1020a4–7]

(4.b)B.4. The mind (*manas*) which was explained above always arises and functions concurrently with *ālaya-vijñāna*. One should know that until that [mind] is completely destroyed [it] is always associated with the four afflictions (*kleśa*)[25] which by nature arise innately (*sahaja*) and concurrently: a view of self-existence (*satkāya-dṛṣṭi*), the conceit "I am" (*asmimāna*), self-love (*ātmasneha*), and ignorance (*avidyā*).

One should see that these afflictions arise without impeding (*avirodha*) the [karmic quality of] skillfulness (*kuśala*), etc., in states of collectedness (*samāhita*) or non-collectedness, and are obscured-indeterminate (*nivṛtāvyākṛta*).[26]

(4.c) [Summary] In this way, one should understand that the arising of *ālaya-vijñāna* is established by being concurrent: by being concurrent with the [forms of] arising cognitive awareness [A.1.], being concurrent with [diverse] feelings [A.3.], and being concurrent with [karmic] skillfulness, etc. [A.4.].

[D. 6b5–7a1; H. 581a17–24; P. 1020a7–13]

The *Nivṛtti* Portion

5. [Establishing the cessation of the root of the defilements (*saṃkleśamūla-nivṛtti-vyavasthāna*)].

(5.a) What is establishing the cessation[27] of defilements?

(5.b)A. Briefly, *ālaya-vijñāna* is the root of all defiled [*dharmas*]. Accordingly:

(5.b)A.1. It is the root of the coming-about (*nirvṛtti*) of the animate world (*sattva-loka*) because [it] is what brings forth (*utpādaka*) the sense-faculties with their material bases (*sādhiṣṭhānam indriyam*) and the [forms of] arising cognitive awareness.

(5.b)A.2. [It] also is the root of the coming-about of the receptacle (i.e. inanimate) world (*bhājana-loka*)[28], because [it] is what brings forth the receptacle world.[29]

(5.b)A.3. Moreover, because all sentient beings mutually condition (*anyonya-adhipatyāt*) each other, [it] is also the root of sentient beings acting upon each other.[30] This is because there are no sentient beings at all who would not experience (*nānubhavet*) pleasure (*sukha*) and pain (*duḥkha*), etc., by seeing, [hearing, tasting], etc. other sentient beings (*sattva-dṛṣṭādi*). In this way, one should understand that the world of sentient beings (*sattva-dhātu*) is mutually conditioned.

[D. 7a1–5; H. 581a24–b4; P. 1020a13–18]

(5.b)A.4. Thus, because this very *ālaya-vijñāna* is what has all the seeds (*sarvabījaka*) it:

(a) is the nature (*svabhāva*) of the Truth of Suffering (*duḥkha-satya*) in the present;
(b) is that which brings about (*utpādaka*) the Truth of Suffering in the future;
(c) and [it] is also that which brings about the Truth of Origin (*samudaya-satya*) in the present.[31]

(5.b)A.5. In this way one should understand that *ālaya-vijñāna* is the root of all that is defiled, by being that which creates (*nirvataka*) the animate world [1.3.], that which creates the receptacle world [2.], the nature of the Truth of Suffering [4(a)], that which creates the Truth of Suffering in the future [4(b)], and that which creates the Truth of Origin in the present [4.(c)].

[D. 7a5–7; H. 581b4–9; P. 1020a18–20]

(5.b)B.1. The *ālaya-vijñāna*, which holds the seeds of the skillful roots (*kuśala-mūla*) conducive to liberation (*mokṣa-bhāgīya*) and conducive to penetrating insight (*nirvedha-bhāgīya*), is [however] not the cause (*hetu*) of the Truth of Origin, because those skillful roots conducive to liberation, etc., are indeed impediments (*virodhatva*) to the arising [of defilements].

If these [skillful roots] do occur, other mundane skillful roots will become very clear, and therefore they will have greater capacity (*sāmarthyavattara*) to uphold their own seeds and will have greater strength towards [their own future] realization through having nurtured [those very] seeds. Skillful dharmas from those seeds will in turn become clearer, and subsequently more desirable and more pleasant results (*vipāka*) will also be realized.

[D. 7a7–b3; H. 581b10–17; P. 1020a20–5]

Intending this *ālaya-vijñāna* which has all the seeds (*sarvabījakam ālaya-vijñānam*), the Buddha taught the eye-element (*cakṣur-dhātu*), the form-element (*rūpa-dhātu*), and the visual-cognitive awareness-element (*cakṣur-vijñāna-dhātu*), up to the mind-element (*mano-dhātu*), the *dharma*-element (*dharma-dhātu*), and the mental-cognitive awareness-element (*mano-vijñāna-dhātu*), because various elements (*dhātu*) exist within *ālaya-vijñāna*. Also, because it [says] in the *sūtra* that there are many elements (*dhātu*) within *ālaya-vijñāna*. It is as in the *akṣa-rāśi* parable.[32]

(5.b)B.2. Thus[33] one should understand that *ālaya-vijñāna*, which is the root of the defilements, ceases (*vinivṛtta*) through the cultivation of skillful *dharmas* (*kuśala-dharma-bhāvanā*) in this way.

[D. 7b3–5; H. 581b17–23; P. 1020a25–9]

In cultivating skillful *dharmas*, ordinary people (*pṛthagjana*) fix [their] minds (*manaskāra*) to the [forms of] arising cognitive awareness as an objective support in order to stabilize their minds, cultivating [these *dharmas*] in order to attain (*praveśana*) complete understanding of the [Four] Truths (*satyābhisamaya*) for the first time. [This is] because those who have not yet seen the Truths, who have not obtained vision into the [Four] Truths (*adṛṣṭa-satya*), cannot penetrate (**pra-tividh-*) the *ālaya-vijñāna* which has all the seeds, either.

Having attained that, one has attained either the Fully Determined Stage (*samyaktvaniyāma*) of the Disciple (*śravaka*) or the Fully Determined Stage of the Bodhisattva.[34] Then [he or she] penetrates the *dharma-dhātu* of all the *dharmas* and penetrates the *ālaya-vijñāna* as well. Thereupon, [he or she] fully comprehends the defiled [*dharmas*] and personally realizes [the fact] that [he] himself is bound by the external bonds of objective phenomena (*nimitta-bandhana*) and by the internal bonds of spiritual corruption (*dauṣṭhulya*).[35]

[D. 7b5–8a2; H. 581b23–581c2; P. 1020a29–b8]

(5.b)C.1. Because *ālaya-vijñāna* is the constituent element (*dhātukatva*) of all the kinds of karmic formations (*saṃskārā*) comprised in proliferation (*prapañca*), [the practitioner] makes [them] into one collection, one heap, one hoard in the *ālaya-vijñāna*.[36] Having collected [them all] into one, he revolves the basis (*āśrayaṃ parivartate*) [i.e. *ālaya-vijñāna*] by the cause of assiduous cultivation of the wisdom (*jñāna*) which takes true reality (*tathatā*) as an objective support. As the basis is revolved, *ālaya-vijñāna* must be said to have been abandoned (*prahīṇa*); because it has been abandoned, it must be said that all the defilements also have been abandoned.

[D. 8a2–4; H. 581c3–8; P. 1020b8–11]

(5.b)C.2. One should know that the revolution of the basis impedes (*virodha*) and so counteracts (*pratipakṣa*) *ālaya-vijñāna*.[37]

(a) *Ālaya-vijñāna* is impermanent and accompanied by appropriation (*sopādāna*)[38], while the revolved basis is permanent and without appropriation, because it is transformed by the path which has true reality for its objective support.

(b) *Ālaya-vijñāna* is accompanied by spiritual corruption (*dauṣṭhulya*), while the revolved basis is forever removed from all spiritual corruption.[39]

(c) *Ālaya-vijñāna* is the cause of the continuance of the afflictions (*kleśa-pravṛtti-hetu*) but not the cause of the continuance of the path, while the revolved basis is not the cause of the continuance of the afflictions but is the cause of the continuance of the path, because it is the supportive cause (*pratiṣṭhā-hetutva*) [of the latter] but is not the generative cause (*janma-hetutva*) [of the former].

(d) *Ālaya-vijñāna* does not control (*avibhutva*) skillful and indeterminate *dharmas*, while the revolved basis does control skillful and indeterminate dharmas.

[D. 8a4–7; H. 581c8–17; P. 1020b11–19]

(5.b)C.3. The distinguishing characteristic of *ālaya-vijñāna* being eliminated (*prahāṅa*) [is that] as soon as it is eliminated the two aspects of appropriation are abandoned and the body remains like an apparition (*nirmāṇa*). [Why is that?] Because the cause which brings about renewed existence (*punarbhava*) of suffering in the future has been eliminated, the appropriation which brings about rebirth in the future is abandoned. Because all the causes of defiled (*saṃkleśa*) [*dharmas*] in this life have been eliminated, the entire appropriation of the basis of the defiled [*dharmas*]in this life is eliminated.[40] Free from all the spiritual corruptions (*dauṣṭhulya*), only the mere conditions of physical life remain.[41] If so, one experiences the feeling (*vedanā*) of the end of the body and the end of life. Therefore, as it is taught extensively in the *sūtras* "to that extent all those feelings come to an end in this life."[42]

[D. 8a7–b3; H. 581c17–24; P. 1020b19–26]

(5.c) [Summary] In this way, one should understand that the cessation of the defiled [*dharmas*] of *ālaya-vijñāna* is established by establishing [*ālaya-vijñāna* as] the root of the defiled [*dharmas*] [A.], by establishing the attainment (*praveśana*) of [complete understanding of the Truths, which enables one to] penetrate (*pratividh-*) [*ālaya-vijñāna*, having] cultivated (*bhāvanā*)[43] [skillful *dharmas* by] fixing one's mind (*manaskāra*)[B.], and [finally] by establishing the revolved basis [C.].

6. Therefore, this is the correct way (*samyak-nyāya*) of establishing thought (*citta*), mind (*manas*), and consciousness (*vijñāna*). All the ways of [explaining] purity and defilement should follow the same way in which all thought, mind, and consciousness of the three realms have been explained. Any other way of explaining thought, mind, and consciousness is for the level of the trainee (*vineya*), that is, in order to facilitate attainment [of the Path] by easy means (*upāya*) according to the understanding of common trainees.

[D. 8b3–7; H. 581c24–582a3; P. 1020b26–c3]

II. 1. Do those who have *ālaya-vijñāna* also have the [six forms of] arising cognitive awareness, and do those who have the [six forms of] arising cognitive awareness also have *ālaya-vijñāna*?

2. There are four possiblities:

(a) those who have *ālaya-vijñāna* without the [six forms of] arising cognitive awareness are those who are in unconscious sleep (*acittaṃ middham*), mind-less unconsciousness (*acittakā-mūrcchā*), who have attained the attainment without apperception (*asaṃjñī-samāpatti*) and the attainment of cessation (*nirodha-samāpatti*), and those who are born in [the realm of] sentient beings without apperception.[44]

(b) those who have the [six forms of] arising cognitive awareness but do not have *ālaya-vijñāna* are Arhats, Pratyekabuddhas, irreversible (*avinivartanīya*) Bodhisattvas, or a Tathāgata in conscious states (*sacittakāvasthā*).

(c) those who have both [the six forms of cognitive awareness and *ālaya-vijñāna*] are those in conscious states other than those [mentioned above].

(d) those who have neither are Arhats, Pratyekabuddhas, irreversible Bodhisattvas, or a Tathāgata in the attainment of cessation, or those in the realm of *nirvāṇa* without remainder (*nirupadhiśeṣa-nirvāṇadhātu*).

[D8b6–9a3; H. 582a4–12; P. 1020c3–13]

NOTES

THEMATIC INTRODUCTION

1 The term "Buddhist" is being used as a generic term for a large number of diverse traditions and perspectives.

2 See Ch. 5, n. 15, for a more detailed sense of how the term "symbolic" is being used here.

3 We appreciate the objections to using the masculine noun and pronoun to refer to humanity in general and resort to this usage here for stylistic purposes and below in accordance with our sources.

4 Brain scientist Michael Gazzaniga (1998: 151) puts it this way: The sense of self "creates the illusion that we are in control of all our actions and reasoning . . . Is it truly a human instinct, an adaptation that supplies a competitive edge in enhancing reproductive success? I think it is and my guess is that the very device which helped us conquer the vicissitudes of the environment enabled us to become psychologically interesting to ourselves as a species." And even more colorfully: " 'Goddamn it, I am me and I am in control.' Whatever it is that brain and mind scientists are finding out, there is no way they can take that feeling away from each and every one of us. Sure, life is a fiction, but it's our fiction and it feels good and we are in charge of it" (ibid.: 172).

5 We have been unable to find a single English term to satisfactorily translate the range of meanings of *ālaya*, with its multiple senses of "home, store, and clinging." "Store-house consciousness" seems too awkward, "container consciousness" too mechanistic. Even "consciousness" seems to subtly substantialize a term which in our texts is unequivocally another dharma, another form of momentarily arising cognitive awareness. We regrettably leave it untranslated, allowing its semantic nuances to make their own impressions upon the reader.

1 THE EARLY BUDDHIST BACKGROUND

1 Since nearly all of the textual sources in this first chapter are found in the early Pāli texts, we will cite the Pāli forms (P.) of Indic words first, followed, where relevant, by their Sanskrit equivalents (S.).

2 S IV 259 describes the traditional classification of suffering (*dukkha*) into suffering itself, the suffering of compounded phenomena due to their impermanence, and the suffering inherent in change (*dukkha-dukkhatā, sankhāra-dukkhatā, vipariṇāma-dukkhatā*) (Nyanatiloka, 1980: 46).

3 Modern perspectives would question the notion of a single purpose to Buddhist teachings and practices, on the grounds that religious traditions always serve multiple and overlapping religious, psychological, and sociological functions. Most Buddhist traditions, however, claim that their ultimate aim is liberation from cyclic existence, and it is these normative perspectives that we are primarily investigating. This acknowledgment of normative perspectives accounts for the awkward vacillation

between a historical past, "the Buddha said...," and a philosophical present, "the causes of suffering are..."

4 These represent the first and third, and second and fourth Noble Truths, respectively.

5 S III 22. "What is impermanent is suffering. What is suffering is nonself. What is nonself should be seen as it really is with correct wisdom thus: 'This is not mine, this I am not, this is not my self.'"

The citations of Pāli texts in this chapter are primarily from recent translations published by Wisdom Publications (see abbreviations in Bibliography, A, D, S, and M) unless noted otherwise, where we have usually utilized the translations of the Pāli Text Society (PTS). In most cases, though not always, we have modified the specific terms for consistency, particularly the following: *viññāṇa*, from consciousness to cognitive awareness; *saññā*, from perception to apperception; *sankhāra*, from volitional formations to karmic formations; *saḷāyatana*, from the six sense bases to the six sense spheres; *upādāna*, from clinging to grasping; and *bhava*, from existence to becoming. Also, "Bhikkhus" has been translated into "Monks."

6 Following tradition, we will provisionally ascribe these early teachings to the Buddha himself. Many of the historical facts of the early Buddhist movement, of the earliest texts, and of the Buddha's life itself admittedly remain far from certain.

7 M I 8. (*Yo me ayaṃ attā vado vedeyyo tatra tatra kalyāṇapāpakānaṃ kammānaṃ vipākaṃ paṭisamvedeti, so kho pana me ayaṃ attā nicco dhuvo sassato avipariṇāmadhammo sassatisamaṃ tath' eva ṭhassatīti*).

8 S III 23. Indeed, the Buddha asks: "Form [and feeling, apperception, the volitional formations, and consciousness] is impermanent. The cause and condition for the arising of form [etc.] is also impermanent. As form has originated from what is impermanent, how could it be permanent?... Form [etc.] is suffering. The cause and condition for the arising of form [etc.] is also suffering. As form has origination from suffering, how could it be happiness? Form [etc.] is nonself. The cause and condition for the arising of form [etc.] is also nonself. As form has origination from nonself, how could it be self?"

9 M II 32. (*Imasmiṃ sati idaṃ hoti; imass' uppādā idaṃ uppajjati. imasmiṃ asati idaṃ na hoti; imassa nirodhā idaṃ nirujjhati*).

10 For the translations and the discussion that follows we have consulted, among other texts, Nyanatiloka (1980: 157–67); Sopa (1986: 105–19); D. W. Williams (1974: 35–63).

11 Philosopher A. W. Sparkes describes what he calls "'process–product ambiguity', that is, it is used to refer both to the *process* (or, more accurately, *activity*)... and to the *product* of that activity" (Sparkes, 1991: 76). Participial words such as painting or building often exhibit this ambiguity.

12 Cognitive awareness (*viññāṇa*) is listed in this short *sutta* (S II 3–4) as the cognitive awarenesses of the eye, ear, nose, tongue, body, and mind (*mano*). We shall return to this issue on pages 19–22.

13 Form (*rūpa*) specifically refers to materiality comprised of "the four great physical elements" and the forms derived from them (*cattāro ca mahābhūtā catunnañca mahābhūtānaṃ upādāya rūpaṃ*). Name (*nāma*) is specified here as "feeling, apperception, intention, contact and attention" (S II 3 f. *vedanā, saññā, cetanā, phassa, manasikāro*).

14 "Object" here is *dhamma*, which, as Nyanatiloka explains, "as an object of mind may be anything past, present or future, corporeal or mental, conditioned of not, real or imaginary" (Nyanatiloka, 1980: 56).

15 The Desire Realm, the Form Realm and the Formless Realm, are the different realms of existence into which, according to traditional Buddhist cosmology, sentient beings may be born.

16 There are variations in which key members are missing (name-and-form, the six sense-spheres, and birth and becoming), in which certain factors condition

completely different ones, or in which the same principles are applied to different terms altogether. The chain starts and ends at different place in some versions, and the cessation of different links brings about the cessation of the entire chain. Conze thus suggests that, "it is therefore not impossible that originally the formula had nothing to do with the problem of rebirth, and that its distribution among three lives is a scholastic addition. The remaining eight factors (1–3, 6–10) could be interpreted as giving the basic mental conditions which, operating at any given time, account for the origin of suffering and of erroneous apperceptions. The formula may perhaps originally have explained nothing but the origination and cessation of ill, without any direct reference to a series of successive lives" (Conze, 1973: 157).

17 *Kamma* in Pāli. We use the Anglicized form "karma," derived from the Sanskrit *karman*, which literally means "action," or "deed."

18 A III 415. PTS. (*Cetanāhaṃ bhikkhave kammaṃ vadāmi; cetayitvā kammaṃ karoti kāyena vācāya manasā*). This reflects a traditional threefold division of karma into body, speech, and mind: breathing is bodily sankhāra, thought and deliberation (*vitakka-vicāra*) are sankhārā of speech, and apperception and feeling (*saññā ca vedanā*) are sankhārā of mind (*citta*). (M I 301).

19 Piatigorsky asserts that "the only thing it [karma] really does is that it *connects* cause with effect" (1984: 50, emphasis in original).

20 A III 110 in Nyanaponika (1999: 315, n. 70), corresponds to A I 249 of PTS edition. See also Johansson (1979: 146).

21 M III 204, *Cūḷakammavibhanga Sutta, The Shorter Exposition of Action*: "Beings are owners of their actions, heirs of their actions; they originate from their actions, are bound to their actions, have their actions as their refuge." (Ñāṇamoli, 1995: 1053). A V 57: "I am the owner of my actions, heir of my actions, actions are the womb (from which I have sprung), actions are my relations, actions are my protection. Whatever actions I do, good or bad, of these I shall become the heir" (Nyanaponika, 1999: 135). There are numerous such passages in the Pāli Canon.

22 S II 64. (*Nāyam … kāyo tuṃhākaṃ na 'pi aññesaṃ. purāṇam idam kammam abhisankhatam abhisañcetayitam vediniyaṃ daṭṭhabbaṃ*) (Johansson, 1979: 148). Translation modified.

23 This is easy enough to express in a few words, but the implications of this simple idea are hard to overestimate. As Kaisa Puhakka puts it: "according to the Doctrine of Dependent Origination, phenomena arise and pass away in mutual dependence, and such a mutual dependence constitutes the very essence of phenomena.… [But] actually there are no essences at all, if by 'essence' is meant a discrete, independently existing entity. By contrast, in the West dependence is commonly thought to affect the spatial and temporal relations among phenomena but not their distinct identities…"

"In sharp contrast with the western concept of causation as an abstract and extraneous principle, the karmic principle may be characterized as concrete and intrinsic to the phenomena it governs. It is intrinsic because it is *constitutive* of the phenomena rather than being an extraneous force acting upon phenomena that are already there. It is concrete because it refers to the phenomena themselves rather than to abstract relations among them. Put differently, karma does not work upon phenomena but rather phenomena *are* the very workings of karma" (Puhakka, 1987: 424, emphasis in original).

24 O. H. de A. Wijesekera discusses the relationship between these two aspects of *viññāṇa*: "From what has been said above regarding the nature of the Buddhist concept of Viññāṇa it will not be difficult to understand why most writers have come to the conclusion that the term Viññāṇa in Buddhist literature has *several senses*.… [I]t has the sense of cognitive or perceptive consciousness in most of the passages. In addition, however, Viññāṇa also means the surviving factor in the individual, denoted by the special term *saṃvattanika viññāṇa* in Pali.… [I]t is clear that the

so-called 'separate meanings' of Viññāṇa do not refer to so many different entities but to *aspects* of the same phenomenon ... Thus, the conclusion forces itself upon one that in the early Buddhist view as reflected in the Pali Canon Viññāṇa was the basis for all conscious and unconscious psychological manifestations pertaining to individuality as it continued in Saṃsāra or empirical existence" (Wijesekera, 1964: 259, emphasis in original).

25 It is worth citing the entry in the *Pali–English Dictionary* in full since it so tellingly attests to the extreme multivalence of the term viññāṇa: "(as a special term in Buddhist metaphysics) a mental quality as a constituent of individuality, the bearer of (individual) life, life-force (as extending also over rebirths), principle of conscious life, general consciousness (as function of mind *and* matter), regenerative force, animation, mind as transmigrant, as transforming (according to individual kamma) one individual life (after death) into the next. In this (fundamental) application it may be characterized as the sensory and perceptive activity commonly expressed by 'mind.' It is difficult to give any one word for v[iññāṇa], because there is much difference between the old Buddhist and our modern points of view, and there is a varying use of the term in the Canon itself ... Ecclesiastical scholastic dogmatic considers v[iññāṇa] under the categories of (a) khandha; (b) dhātu; (c) paṭicca-samuppāda; (d) āhāra; (e) kāya" (PED 618).

26 S II 13. "The viññāṇa sustenance (*viññāṇāhāro*) is a condition of renewed existence of rebirth in the future" (*viññāṇāhāro āyatiṃ punabbhavābhinibbattiyā paccayo*). The ālaya-vijñāna is also called the vijñāna sustenance is such texts as MSg I.37.

27 S II 101. (*Kabaliṃkāre ... phasse ... manosañcetanāya ... viññāṇe ce ... āhāre atthi rāgo atthi nandī atthi taṇhā patiṭṭhitaṃ tattha viññāṇaṃ virūḷhaṃ. yattha patiṭṭhitaṃ viññāṇaṃ virūḷhaṃ atthi tattha nāmarūpassa avakkanti*). Note the discrepancy with D II 62, cited above, where it is viññāṇa, rather than name-and-form, that descends into the mother's womb.

28 S III 143 PTS. "When, then, the three factors of life, heat, and consciousness abandon this body, it lies cast away and forsaken like an inanimate stick of wood." Cf. M I 296 and *AKBh* II 45a–b (Schmithausen, 1987: 285, n. 165).

29 S II 65 (PTS). (*Tasmiṃ patiṭṭhite viññāṇe virūḷhe āyatiṃ punabbhavābhinibbati hoti*). D II 68, S III 54 also describes the persistence of viññāṇa from life to life; viññāṇa passes over into another body in S I 122 and S III 124 (PED 618).

30 Wijesekera refers to a number of terms denoting a rebirth viññāṇa in the canonical and commentarial literature. It is "technically called '*saṃvattanika-viññāṇa*' or 'the Viññāṇa that evolves (into the next life),'" for which "in the later scholastic period the term '*paṭisandhi-viññāṇa*' was substituted. ... Now, this saṃsāric Viññāṇa cannot be different from the *stream of Viññāṇa (viññāṇa-sota)* referred to as extending into both the worlds in the Dīgha Nikāya (iii 105; cf. SN 1055, etc.), called also the 'stream of becoming' (*bhava-sota*) in the Saṃyutta Nikāya (iv. 291)" (Wijesekera, 1964: 255).

31 S III 61. (*viññāṇassa nibbidā virāgā nirodhā anupādā vimuttā te suvimuttā*) (Trans. Johansson, 1965: 200).

32 S III 61. "The Noble Eightfold Path is the way leading to the cessation of consciousness" (ibid.).

33 M II 265. (*anupādāno ... bhikkhu parinibbāyati*). Johansson, 1979: 71.

34 S III 53. (*tad apatiṭṭhitaṃ viññāṇaṃ avirūḷhaṃ anabhisankhārañca vimuttaṃ*). Dutt comments on this sutta: "The sense of *apatiṭṭhita-viññāṇa* is given elsewhere in the *Saṃyutta Nikāya*, where it is explained as consciousness which arises only when attachment (*rāga*) to material elements of the body (*rūpa*), and the other four constituents is removed. It is unconstituted, devoid of growth and independent of any cause and condition and hence free. Being free it is steady; being steady it is happy; being happy it is without any fear of change for the worse; being fearless it attains *parinibbāna*" (Dutt, 1960: 285 f.).

35 This is a common epithet of the Buddha or an Arhat. D III 105; S I 122; S II 66, 103; S III 54.

36 As is often the case with the study of the early Pāli texts, this statement needs some qualification. There are other passages that suggest that viññāṇa continues in some form beyond samsaric existence. SN 734–5 describes both the cessation and calming of viññāṇa in the same breath: "If viññāṇa is destroyed, there will be no origin of suffering; through the calming of viññāṇa the monk becomes free from craving and completely free;" M I 329 reads: "*Viññāṇa* becomes free from attributes, endless and radiating all round" (Johansson, 1979: 62 f.). As we just saw, the viññāṇa of a Buddha or Arhat is said to be without a resting place or support (*appatiṭṭhita-viññāṇa*); but it is not said to be utterly extinct.

It is surely no coincidence that the expression, *apratiṣṭhita-nirvāṇa*, is used in connection with the Yogācāra conception of liberation, in the *Mahāyāna-saṃgraha*, IX.1. Here, the impure or defiled portions of the ālaya-vijñāna, which is the support or basis (*āśraya*) of samsaric life, are removed and that basis is utterly transformed leaving the Bodhisattva with no fixed abode (*apratiṣṭhita*). For Yogācāra treatments of this concept, see Griffiths *et al.* (1989: 244 f.) for commentaries on MSg X.34; Nagao (1991: 23–34); and Sponberg (1979). Cp. MVBh II.1, IV.12cd.

These conflicting conceptions of a post-samsaric *viññāṇa* adumbrate many of the later controversies concerning nirvana and Buddhahood. The complex and often contradictory passages preserved in these early texts serve to remind us not only of the antecedents of many of the contested issues later raised within Indian Buddhist thought, but also of the continuing relevance of these early texts for the study of virtually every phase of Indian Buddhism.

37 As Collins puts it in a slightly different context, the sankhārā are "both the activity which constructs temporal reality, and the temporal reality thus constructed" (1982: 202). This twofold nature as both "constructed" and "constructive" is predicated of many key Buddhist terms, such as the *saṃskārā*, and *upādāna* (appropriation), and is expressed in terms of an active/passive or causal/resultant bivalence based on participial forms. It corresponds to what Sparkes (1991: 76; n. 11, above) calls "the 'process–product ambiguity.'" Bivalence is perhaps more appropriate here than "ambiguity."

38 "Feedback is a central feature of life: All organisms share this ability to sense how they're doing and to make changes in 'mid-flight' when necessary. The process of feedback governs how we grow, respond to stress and challenge, and regulate factors such as body temperature, blood pressure, and cholesterol level. This apparent purposefulness, largely unconscious, operates at every level – from the interaction of proteins in cells to the interaction of organisms in complex ecologies" (Hoagland and Dodson, 1995: 125).

39 S III 60 defines *sankhāra* as the "group of intentions," *cetanākāya*, that is, intentions in regard to form, sounds, etc., the five objects of the senses and of mind (*rūpasañcetanā, saddasañcetanā* ...) (also A III 60). Sankhārā and intention are at times virtually interchangeable: the various fruits of karma, pleasure or suffering, arise due to the *intentions* motivating those actions of body, speech and mind. (A II 157, IV 171, #84 in Nyanaponika, 1999. *Kāye va* ... *kāya*sañcetanā*hetu uppajjati ajjhattaṃ sukkhadukkhaṃ*). In the very next paragraph of this text "intention" is substituted by "sankhāra": pleasure or suffering arise for one by performing a *sankhāra* of body, etc. (*Kāyasankhāraṃ* abhisankharoti *yaṃ paccayā 'ssa taṃ uppajjati ajjhattaṃ sukhadukkhaṃ*). Karmic actions are analyzed according the result they will bring: meritorious, non-meritorious, and neutral (D III 217).

40 S II 101. (*Kabaliṃkāre* ... *phasse* ... *manosañcetanāya* ... *viññāṇe ce* ... *āhāre atthi rāgo atthi nandī atthi taṇhā patiṭṭhitaṃ tattha viññāṇaṃ virūḷhaṃ. yattha patiṭṭhitaṃ viññāṇaṃ virūḷhaṃ atthi tattha nāmrūpassa avakkanti. yattha atthi nāmarūpassa avakkanti atthi*

tattha sankhārānaṃ vuddhi. yattha atthi sankhārānaṃ vuddhi atthi tattha āyatiṃ punabbhavābhinibatti). We may point out that most of the remaining limbs of the twelve-member series are replaced here by sankhārā. We are indebted to Aramaki (1985: 94) for pointing out the significance of this passage in this context.

41 The *Sangīti Sutta* (D III 228), although probably from a later strata of the Pāli Canon, lists four stations of consciousness (*viññāṇa-ṭṭhitiyo*), that is, the other four aggregates: "consciousness gains a footing either (a) in relation to materiality, with materiality as object and basis, as a place of enjoyment, or similarly in regard to (b) feelings, (c) perception or (d) mental formations, and there it grows, increases and flourishes" (Walshe, 1987: 491).

42 S III 54. (This phrase "come to come to growth, increase, and expansion" (*pañcabījajātāni vuddhiṃ virūḷhiṃ vepullam āpajjeyyunti*) will later be used in reference to the *ālaya/ādāna-vijñāna* in the *Saṃdhinirmocana Sūtra* (see p. 94, above). The five kinds of seeds refers to plants that are propagated through their roots, stems, joints, cuttings, and seeds proper. (Walshe, 1987: 69; D I 5, III 44, 47). Cf. A III 404–9 for passages concerning *akusala-citta* and *bīja*.

43 S II 82. (*avijjāgato yaṃ ... purisapuggalo puññaṃ ce saṅkhāraṃ abhisaṅkharoti, puññūpagaṃ hoti viññāṇaṃ. apuññaṃ ce saṅkhāraṃ abhisaṅkharoti, apuññūpagaṃ hoti viññāṇaṃ.*) (Johansson, 1979: 61; 1965: 195f.). The key terms are "*puñña/apuñña*".

44 This is not to say that viññāṇa continues unchangingly from life to life. In a famous passage the Buddha specifically denies this "thesis of Sāti": "As I understand the Dhamma taught by the Blessed One, it is this same consciousness that runs and wanders through the round of rebirths, not another ... it is that which speaks and feels and experiences here and there the result of good and bad actions." To which the Buddha responds: "apart from conditions there is no origination of consciousness" (M I 258. *aññatra paccayā natthi viññāṇassa sambhavo ti*). (A similar formulation regarding a subject of experience was denied by the Buddha in M I 8.)

Rather, it is that the continuity or stream of viññāṇa that continues unbroken (see S III 58). Though the term "stream of consciousness" (*viññāṇasotaṃ*) belongs more properly to the later literature, it does appear once in the earlier literature, in D III 105: "He understands a man's stream of *viññāṇa* which is uninterrupted at both ends is established in both this world and the next" (*purisassa ca viññāṇasotaṃ pajānāti ubhayato abbocchinnaṃ idhaloke patṭhitañ ca paraloke paṭṭhitañ ca.*) See Johansson (1965: 192) and Jayatillike (1949: 216) for differing interpretations of this obscure passage.

45 Compare two typical formulations: Depending on karmic formations (*sankhārā*) viññāṇa arises (S II 2); Depending on eye and forms visual viññāṇa arises (S II 73).

46 This more elaborate formula is found, for example, in M I 190: "When internally the eye is intact and external forms come into its range and there is the corresponding conscious engagement, then there is the manifestation of the corresponding class of consciousness" (Ñāṇamoli, 1995: 284). See Jayatilleke (1963: 433f.) and Johansson (1979: 84).

47 M I 295. "Friend, these five faculties each have a separate field, a separate domain, and do not experience each other's field and domain, that is, the eye faculty, the ear faculty, the nose faculty, the tongue faculty, and the body faculty. Now these five faculties, each having a separate field, a separate domain, not experiencing each other's field and domain, have mind as their resort, and mind experiences their fields and domains" (Ñāṇamoli, 1995: 391). Johansson (1965: 183).

48 SN 834 speaks of thinking on the views in the *manas* (*manasā diṭṭhigatāni cintayanto*) and S I 207 of the "reflective thoughts of *mano* (*manovitakkā*)" (Johansson, 1965: 183, 186).

49 Varela *et al.*, in *The Embodied Mind*, compare the Buddhist approach to cognition and contact with the more recent concept of emergence within cognitive

science: "Contact [*sparśa*] ... is a relational property involving three terms: one of the six senses, a material or mental object, and the consciousness based upon these two. There is evidence to suggest that this sensitivity was conceived as a dynamic process giving rise to emergence: the evidence is that contact, as a process, is described as being both a cause and an effect. As a cause contact is the coming together of three distinct items – a sense, an object, and the potential for awareness. As an effect, contact is that which results from this process of coming together – a condition of harmony or rapport among the three items. This rapport is not the property of either a sense, an object, or an awareness per se. It is a property of the processes by which they interact, in other words, an emergent property.... Early Buddhism developed the idea of an emergent both at the (relatively) global level of codependent origination and the (relatively) local level of contact; this development was of central importance to the analysis of the arising of experience without a self" (Varela *et al.*, 1991: 119).

50 An analysis of experience focused on cognitive awareness therefore represents neither pure subjectivity nor total objectivity. Describing cognitive awareness as a phenomenon which arises in dependence upon its originating conditions precludes either of these positions and points to a different notion altogether. Like a transaction that takes place between individuals, cognitive awareness occurs at the interface or concomitance of a sense-organ and its correlative sense object. Since cognitive awareness is an interactional phenomenon, and neither an action nor a faculty, an epistemology based upon the dependent arising of cognitive awareness steers a middle path between the Charybdis of correspondence or realist theories of truth and the Scylla of strong constructivist or idealist theories. That is, cognitive awareness reflects neither an exact "mirror of nature" supposing representing things "as they are" – since what constitutes a cognitive "object" is necessarily defined by the cognitive capacities of particular sense organs and faculties; nor is it a unilateral projection of a priori categories upon the world – since the cognitive capabilities of sense organs are always correlatively defined by the kinds of "objects" that may impinge upon them. That is, the so-called "subjective" sense-organs (or faculties) and "objective" sense-objects necessarily function in relation to, and are ultimately only intelligible in terms of, each other in interaction. On the one hand, this is simply common sense, and nearly tautological: we can only perceive what we can discern, and what we can discern depends upon our means of perception. On the other hand, the implications of this relational view of cognition are often overlooked, even in later Buddhist traditions.

51 Though composed much later than the materials in this chapter, the *Abhidharmakośa* of Vasubandhu makes exactly this point: "The Sūtra teaches: 'By reason of the organ of sight and of visible matter there arises the visual consciousness': there is not there either an organ that sees, or visible matter that is seen; there is not there any action of seeing, nor any agent that sees; this is only a play of cause and effect. In the light of [common] practice, one speaks, metaphorically, of this process: 'The eye sees, and the consciousness discerns.' But one should not cling to these metaphors" (Pruden, 1990: 118). This is frequently lost sight in discussions of Buddhist psychology, where more "conventional" expressions such as "cognition cognizes" and "a person has six types of consciousness" are the rule rather than the exception.

52 M I 111 (*cakkhuñ ... paṭicca rūpe ca uppajjati cakkhuviññāṇaṃ, tiṇṇaṃ saṇgati phasso, phassapaccayā vedanā*).

53 M I 293. In another text the close relations between feeling, apperception and the karmic formations (*sankhārā*) are demonstrated in the similar conditions for their arising: "with the arising of a contact (*phassa*) there is the arising of feeling ... with the arising of contact there is the arising of apperception ... with the arising of contact there is the arising of karmic formations" (S III 60).

54 In another text, viññāṇa is simply inserted into the formula, leaving all the other factors intact: "Dependent on the eye and forms, eye-cognition arises; the meeting of the three is contact; with contact as condition there is feeling; with feeling as condition there is craving" (M III 282). This can be most clearly seen in a table:

Standard series of dependent arising:
six sense-spheres > contact > feeling > craving
saḷāyatana > phassa > vedanā > taṇhā

Process of cognition (M III 282):
six sense-spheres, objects > cognitive awareness > contact > feeling > craving
saḷāyatana, rūpa > viññāṇa > phassa > vedanā > taṇhā

55 See Appendix I for a schematization of this analysis, albeit from a somewhat later period. For purposes of exposition we are being slightly anachronistic here.
56 Etymologically, *upādāna* is composed of the prefix *upa*, "towards, near, together with," plus the noun *ādāna*, "receiving, taking for oneself" (SED 136), or even "the material out of which anything is made," thus, derivatively, "grasping, attachment, drawing upon, finding one's support by, nourished by, taking up" (Apte, 1986: 471; PED 149). See also Schmithausen (1987: 72).
57 M III 16. "These five aggregates affected by grasping are rooted in desire … It is the desire and lust in regard to the five aggregates affected by grasping (*pañc' upādānakkhandhā*) that is the grasping [or appropriation, fuel, *upādāna*] there." See also M II 265.
58 S IV 399. See Johansson (1979: 65) and Matthews (1983: 33).
59 Although relatively undeveloped in the early Pāli texts, the *anuśaya* merited an entire chapter in Vasubandhu's *Abhidharma-kośa*, the classic fifth-century CE text we will discuss in the next chapters. Pertinent scholarship on *anusaya* in the Pāli materials includes Johansson (1979), de Silva (1972; 1979), and Matthews (1983). Collet Cox (1995: 68f.) has discussed the *anuśaya* in her superb study on Sarvāstivāda Abhidharma.
60 The Sanskrit term *anuśaya*, cognate with the Pāli, is composed of the prefix *anu-*, "along, follow behind," and the root *śī*, meaning "to lie down, to sleep, to dwell." The verbal form *anuśeti* (Pāli: *anuseti*), thus means "to lie down with, to dwell on;" when referring to ideas, however, the PED defines it as "to fill the mind persistently, to lie dormant and be continually cropping up" (PED 44). This last is closer to the nominal form most used in Buddhist texts, *anusaya*, for which the Dictionary gives: "Bent, bias, proclivity, the persistence of a dormant or latent disposition, predisposition, tendency. Always in bad sense" (ibid.).
61 M I 303. (*sukhāya … vedanāya rāgānusayo anuseti, dukkhāya … vedanāya paṭighānusayo anuseti, adukkhamasukhāya … vedanāya avijjānusayo anusetīti*). Ñāṇamoli, translator of the *Majjhima Nikāya*, cites the commentary on this passage: "The three defilements are called *anusaya*, underlying tendencies, in the sense that they have not been abandoned in the mental continuum to which they belong and because they are capable of arising when a suitable cause presents itself" (1995: 1241, n. 473). This concept of mental continuum, belonging to a later period in Buddhist thought, will raise problems of its own, as we shall see on pages 76–80.

There are several other classifications of the underlying tendencies. One into seven types: the three "unhealthy roots" (*akusala-mūla*) – corresponding to the three mentioned above – of greed (*lobha*), hatred (*dosa*), and delusion (*moha*); plus the underlying tendencies toward speculative views (*diṭṭhi*), skeptical doubt (*vicikicchā*), pride (*māna*), and craving for existence (*bhavarāga*) (S V 60; A IV 9). D III 254 provides a slightly different list: "sensuous greed (*kāma-rāga*), resentment (*paṭigha*), views, doubt, conceit, craving for becoming (*bhava-rāga*), ignorance" (Walshe, 1987: 503). There is yet another list to which we shall return shortly: "dispositions to a view of personal existence" (*sakkāyadiṭṭhānusaya*), "attachment to rules and observances" (*sīlabbataparāmāsānusaya*), "desire for sensual pleasure" (*kāmarāgānusaya*), the "disposition toward the pride that creates 'I' and 'mine'" (*ahankāra-mamankāra-māna-anusaya*). The PED warns, however, that "these lists govern the connotation of the word; but it would be wrong to put that connotation back into the earlier passages" (PED 44).

62 M I 47. "When a noble disciple thus understood the unwholesome and the root of the unwholesome, the wholesome and the root of the wholesome, he entirely abandons the underlying tendency to lust, he abolishes the underlying tendency to aversion, he extirpates the underlying tendency to the view and conceit 'I am,' and by abandoning ignorance and arousing true knowledge he here and now makes an end to suffering. In that way too a noble disciple is one of right view, whose view is straight, who has perfect confidence in the Dhamma, and has arrived at this true Dhamma."

63 See Gazzaniga (1998), cited in "Thematic Introduction" n. 4.

64 S III 131. The last paragraph reads: *evam eva kho āvuso kiñcāpi ariyasāvakassa pañcorambhāgiyāni saññojanāni* pahīnāni bhavanti. atha khvassa hoti yeva pañcasu upādānakkhandhesu anusahagato asmīti māno asmīti chando asmīti anusayo asamuhato.* Schmithausen (1987: 437f., n. 918) reads "*samyojanani*" in a parallel passage, S III 130. S I 23 also has a similar passage regarding Non-Returners.

65 Derived from the Sanskrit root *man*, "to think, believe, imagine, suppose, conjecture," *manas* (P. *mano*) is related to the Latin *mens*, "mind, reason, intellect," and ultimately to the English "mind, mentate," and "to mean." (PED 515, 520; SED 783).

66 "Language was thought of as a discovery of the inherent conceptual relationships among things, so that from a very early period in Indian thought, conceptualization was regarded as primarily a verbal phenomenon" (Reat, 1990: 305).

67 See Ñāṇananda's *Concept and Reality* for a book-length treatment of this important concept in the early Pāli sources. Ñāṇananda defines *papañca* "in the realm of ideation – the individuating, generalizing, particularising and dichotomising tendencies which provide the scaffolding for theoretical superstructures" (1976: 17). He says that "*papañca* is used to denote verbosity… [C]onceptual activity presupposes language, so much so that thought itself may be regarded as a form of sub-vocal speech" (ibid.: 5).

68 (Ñāṇamoli, 1995: 203). Translation altered for terminological consistency.

69 Apperception is not commonly used in English; it is neither "perception" nor "conception," but rather something in between. According to the *Concise Oxford English Dictionary* (1976), "apperception" means: "perception with recognition or identification by association with previous ideas," with the verb "to apperceive" meaning "unite and assimilate (a perception) to ideas already possessed, and so comprehend and interpret". This is precisely the term "*saññā*."

Usually translated as "perception," the Sanskrit form *saṃjñā* is composed of the prefix *saṃ*, "together," plus the root verb *jña*, "to know, perceive, understand," that is, a "knowing-together." *Saṃjñā* (P. *saññā*) thus means "conception, idea, impression, perception" (BHSD 551–2). Interestingly, it is etymologically parallel with "conscious": *com*, "together, with," plus *scire* "to know." *Saṃjñā* is formally the opposite of *vijñāna* (P. *viññāṇa*), which is composed of *vi-*, "dis-," plus the same root, *jña*. While *vijñāna* stresses disjunctive discernment, *saṃjñā* emphasizes a conjunctive construction of an image or idea that brings disparate sensations together into a whole, often connected with a name or concept. This is why *saṃjñā* is a *saṃskārā* (P. *sankhārā*) of mind, a construction or complex (S IV 293: *saññā ca vedanā ca cittasankhāre ti*).

Saññā is often described as the apperceptions of forms, sounds, smells, tastes, tangibles, and mental phenomena (*dhamma*) (D II 309). The example of *saññā* most typically given is color perception (M I 293: "And what does [one] apperceive (*sañjānāti*)? [One] apperceives what is green, yellow, red, white" (Johansson, 1979: 92).

70 A III 413. (*vohāravepakkaṃ bhikkhave saññāṃ vadāmi; yathā yathā naṃsañjānāti, tathā tathā voharati 'evam saññī ahosin 'ti*). *Vōhara* is the Pāli equivalent of *vyavahāra*. We have slightly adapted the Pāli Text Society's translation of this passage.

71 A II 161. "Whatever is the range of the six spheres of contact, that itself is the range of prolific conceptualization [*papañca*]. And whatever is the range of the prolific conceptualization, that itself is the range of the six spheres of contact" (Ñāṇananda, 1976: 21).

72 SN 874 states that "the series of prolific ideation is caused by apperception"; S IV 71 states that "All men who have prolific ideation go on proliferating when apperceiving" (Johansson, 1979: 192f. translation altered).

73 Ñāṇananda describes the feedback relationship between thought (*vitakka*) and the series of proliferation-apperception, "*papañca-saññā-saṅkhā*" (a compound which he glosses as "concepts, reckonings, designations or linguistic conventions characterised by the prolific conceptualizing tendency of the mind" 1976: 5) as follows: "the word or concept grasped as an object for ratiocination, is itself a product of '*papañca*.' This, in its turn breeds more of its kind when one proceeds to indulge in conceptual proliferation (*papañca*). Concepts characterised by the proliferating tendency (*papañca-saññā-saṅkhā*) constitute the raw-material for the process and the end product is much the same in kind… Thus there is a curious reciprocity between '*vitakka*' [thought] and '*papañca-saññā-saṅkhā*' – a kind of vicious circle, as it were. Given '*papañca-saññā-saṅkhā*,' there comes to be '*vitakka*' and given '*vitakka*' there arise more '*papañca-saññā-saṅkhā*'" (1976: 25).

74 See Schmithausen (1987: 509ff., n. 1405; 522ff., n. 1425) for lengthy discussions of this topic.

75 (Ñāṇananda, 1976: 34f.). Translation modified. (SN 915–16. *kathaṃ disvā nibbāti bhikkhu anupādiyāno lokasmiṃ kiñci. Mūlaṃ papañcasaṅkhāyāti Bhagavā mantā asmīti sabbaṃ uparundhe*). Ñāṇananda takes *mantā* as "thinker" rather than "thought" (1976: 35, n. 1).

76 A I 132 states: "When, Sāriputta, a monk has no more I-making, mine-making and underlying tendency to conceit [*ahaṃkāra-mamaṅkāra-mānānusayā*] either in regard to this conscious body or in regard to external objects [*saviññāṇake kāye… bahiddhā ca sabbanimittesu*] and when he thus enters and dwells in the liberation of mind, liberation by wisdom, he is then called a monk who has cut off craving and removed the fetters, one who, by fully breaking through conceit, has made an end of suffering" (Nyanaponika, 1999: 49).

77 Although the text itself is somewhat ambiguous, a commentary explains that the Buddha was criticizing the view of Malunkyaputta because he "held the view that a person is fettered by the defilements only at times when they assail him, while at other times he is not fettered by them. The Buddha spoke as he did to show the error in this view" (Ñāṇmoli, 1995: 1265, n. 650).

78 According to the early Buddhist view, our animate world is largely created by the compelling energies of past afflicted activities, and powerful dispositions continuously predispose us to act in certain karmically harmful (and some not so harmful) ways. These afflicting dispositions, however, while "innate" in the sense of that we are "born with" them at each rebirth, are neither "essential" nor "inherent" to us as a species or an individuals. They are conditioned phenomena that result from the aggregate of past actions and can be controlled or eradicated through rigorous religious practice.

Comparatively speaking, the Buddhists thus stake out a middle ground between the extremes of those (like biological determinists) who maintain, on the one hand, that human nature is innate and ineradicable, and those (like strong social constructivists) who deny, on the other hand, that there are any innate dispositions whatsoever, who consider human beings as primarily products of our immediate environment, blank slates upon which "society" can do its dirty work. In the Buddhist view, however, this "nature versus nurture" debate is based upon a false dichotomy: "nature," in the sense of a fixed species essence, is nothing but conditioned phenomena, however remote those conditioning causes may be from their present results, while "nurture," that is, the social conditioning due to one's environment, could not even begin to occur without the innate ability to grow and to learn, which is itself conditioned by past actions. Pure "nurture" then is as incoherent as unconditioned "nature" is unexampled. We have explored these issues further in Waldron (2000), "Beyond Nature/Nurture: Buddhism and Biology on Interdependence."

79 M I 434. (*na sakkāyadiṭṭhipariyuṭṭhitena cetasā viharati na sakkāyadiṭṭhiparetena, uppannāya ca sakkāyadiṭṭhiyā nissaraṇaṃ yathābhūtaṃ pajānāti; tassa sā sakkāyadiṭṭhi sānusaya pahīyati*). The Sautrāntika school will call upon this last phrase, "eliminated along with the underlying tendency" (*sānusaya pahīyati*), to support their distinction between the latent tendencies (*anuśaya*) and their patent counterparts, the manifest outbursts (*paryavasthāna*). We shall examine this issue at greater length in Chapter 2.

80 The editors of the English translation of the *Majjhima-nikāya*, Ñāṇmoli and Bodhi, relate that: "In the commentaries the defilements are distinguished as occurring at three levels: the *anusaya* level, where they remain as mere latent dispositions in the mind; the *pariyuṭṭhāna* level, where they rise up to obsess and enslave the mind; and the *vītikkama* level, where they motivate unwholesome bodily and verbal action. The point of the Buddha's criticism is that the fetters, even when they do not come to active manifestation, continue to exist at the *anusaya* level so long as they have not been eradicated by the supramundane path." (Ñāṇamoli, 1997: 1265, n. 651).

81 A II 157 (n. 39): the various fruits of karma, *pleasure or suffering*, arise due to the diverse intentions behind those actions of body, speech, and mind.

82 Although composed later than the Pāli texts we have been discussing, *Milinda's Questions* makes this point explicitly: "Even so, sire, are those cycles that are spoken of by the Lord: 'Visual consciousness arises because of eye and material shapes, the meeting of the three is sensory impingement; conditioned by sensory impingement is feeling; conditioned by feeling is craving; conditioned by craving is kamma; vision [*cakkhuṃ*, lit.: eye] is born again from kamma – is there an end of this series?' 'There is not, revered sir'" (1963–4: 51).

83 This is not to say that this distinction can be or need be discerned in all occurrences of the term. The point is that these two divergent contexts of meaning form part of a complex, with all its inherent tensions, whose unity as well as differentiation calls for some sort of explication.

84 Ñāṇamoli (1995: 1110), with the relevant Pāli terms reinstated.

85 M III 260. (*Na viññāṇaṃ upādiyissāmi, na ca me viññāṇanissitaṃ viññāṇaṃ bhavissati*).

86 Later Abhidharma doctrine will assert that a preceding moment of viññāṇa (in one modality or another) conditions the arising of the next moment of cognitive awareness.

87 To bring out this nuance of the term, Johansson frequently translates *sankhārā* as "creative act, creativity, creative activity." Varela *et al.* make a similar point: "The visual system is never simply presented with pregiven objects. On the contrary, the determination of what and where an object is, as well as its surface boundaries, texture, and relative orientation (and hence the overall context of color as a perceived attribute), is a complex process that the visual system must continually achieve" (Varela *et al.*, 1991: 167).

88 Wijesekera concurs: "[T]he conclusion forces itself upon one that in the early Buddhist view as reflected in the Pali Canon Viññāṇa was the basis for all conscious and unconscious psychological manifestations pertaining to individuality as it continued in Saṃsāra or empirical existence" (1964: 259).

2 THE ABHIDHARMA CONTEXT

1 According to the *Abhidharma-kośa*: "Karma, craving and ignorance are the cause of *saṃskāras* in the future" (AKBh *ad* VI 3, Shastri 887: "*karma ca tṛṣṇā ca atho avidyā saṃskārāṇāṃ hetur abhisaṃparāye" iti*), quoting a *sūtra* that Poussin (1971, 137; *ad* AKBh VI 3) identifies as *Samyukta* 13, 6.

2 Frauwallner's description of the early Sarvāstivādin Abhidharma text, the *Dharmaskandha*, could well apply to Abhidharma as a whole: it concentrated on "the basic concepts used in the earliest attempts at the creation of a system, the doctrinal concepts that were of especial importance for the practice of liberation, together with a group of mental elements considered especially significant with regard to entanglement in the cycle of existence" (1995: 17).

3 There are some extant Sanskrit versions of early *sūtras*, several in Central Asian languages, as well as extensive collections preserved in Chinese and Tibetan translations. The texts in Pāli are, regrettably, the only extensive collection in an Indic language.

4 The specific books in the *Abhidharma-piṭaka* vary from school to school. In the first part of this chapter we will present a composite picture of the psychological notions of Abhidharma in general, unavoidably painting in broad strokes, before discussing the specific positions of particular schools on pertinent doctrines.

5 According to an old-standing etymology, *sūtra* is, like the Latin "textus," derived from a root word meaning "to sew or weave," and hence conveys the sense of "that which like a thread runs through or holds together everything, rule, direction" (SED 1241). Interestingly, the Chinese term for a classic, *ching*, which is used to translate *sūtra*, is also composed of the semantic radical used to signify silk (*ssu*) or cloth manufacture.

6 Frauwallner divides the Abhidharma literature into older, core layers, which underlie both the Sarvāstivādin and Pāli Abhidharma texts, and the newer parts which diverge significantly. He dates them as follows: "200 BC would seem probable for the origin of the oldest layer. All the Abhidharma works that were written later come after this point... Pāli Abhidharma – apart from the oldest core of texts – were written in the period between 200 BC and AD 200 in the mother country and were brought to Ceylon from there" (1995: 41 f.).

7 What Frauwallner said twenty-odd years ago could be said today as well: "A wide gulf separates the comprehensive and finely developed system of the Abhidharmakośa from the ancient and simple teachings of the Buddha. The distance in time between them is also immense since the Buddha died in *c*.480 BC and the Abhidharmakośa was written in AD *c*.450, almost a thousand years later. It thus became the task of future research to bridge this gap, a task which still remains largely incomplete even today" (1995: 120).

8 The Theravāda school descends from and preserves the textual traditions of the Sthaviravāda school of classical India. Due to its present position and greater renown, we will, anachronistically, use the term "Theravāda" to refer the Sthaviravāda school of antiquity.

9 This is unfortunate because the antecedents of many aspects of the ālaya-vijñāna may be found in the doctrines of these lesser-known schools. In his valuable reference work, Bareau (1955) has collated the doctrinal positions of the early schools based upon a variety of sources, both contemporaneous and subsequent. See Appendix II for a tabulation of some of these topics. See also the *I Pu Tsung Lun Lun* (1975),

a Chinese translation of the **Samaya-bhedoparacana-cakra*, an early doxographical writing.

10 The full title is the *Abhidharmakośa-bhāṣya* (abbrev.: AKBh., and sometimes *Kośa*), the *Commentary on the Treasury of Abhidharma*. Pradhan's Sanskrit edition (1967), though standard in its day, has not been available for some time. To facilitate reference to any edition or translation of the work, we will refer to the chapter and verse of the *Abhidharmakośa-bhāṣya* itself, and then to the page number of the Sanskrit edition of S. D. Shastri (1981; abbrev: Shastri). This latter edition also includes the Sanskrit text of the commentary of Yaśomitra, the *Abhidharmakośa-vyākhyā* (abbrev.: Vyākhyā). We have also referred extensively to the French translation by La Vallèe Poussin (1971; abbrev.: Poussin) of Hsüan Tsang's seventh-century CE Chinese translation (T 1558), by the page number of the appropriate volume (which does not, however, completely correlate with the chapter numbers of the *Kośa* itself). We have relied upon all of these editions in our renditions of these passages. Poussin's French edition has been translated into English in Pruden (1988), whose English version is also cited on occasion.

11 Frauwallner says of Asanga, "one of his most important achievements was to develop the system of the Yogācāra by appropriating and integrating the dogmatics of the Hīnayāna so that it could in every respect be considered the equal of the great Hīnayāna schools of that time" (1995: 144).

12 The aim of this essay, understanding the ālaya-vijñāna in the context of Indian Buddhist history, precludes even a general presentation of Abhidharma as a whole. This has, in any case, been ably done elsewhere. For more comprehensive treatments on Abhidharma, from which much of the following is also drawn, see Stcherbatsky (1956), La Vallèe Poussin (1937a), Conze (1973: 138 f.), Jaini (1959); also Collins (1982), Chaudhuri (1983), Griffiths (1986), and Cox (1995).

13 AKBh I 3; Shastri: 15; Poussin: 5; Pruden, 1988: 57: "Apart from the discernment of the *dharmas*, there is no means to extinguish the defilements, and it is by reason of the defilements that the world wanders in the ocean of existence. So it is with a view to this discernment that the Abhidharma has been, they say, spoken [by the Master.] ... without the teaching of the Abhidharma, a disciple would be incapable of discerning the *dharmas*" (*yato vinā dharmapravicayena nāsti kleśopaśamābhyupāyaḥ, kleśāś ca lokaṃ bhramayanti saṃsāramahārṇave 'smin, atas tad hetos tasya dharmapravicayasyārthe śāstrā kila buddhenābhidharma uktaḥ; na hi vinā abhidharmopadeśena śiṣyaḥ śakto dharmān pravicetum iti*).

14 The term *dharma* is exceptionally multivalent in Indian religions. One of its important senses is "doctrine, teaching, way." "Buddhism," a modern coining, refers to the "buddha-dharma," the doctrine or way of or toward Buddhas and Buddhahood. Its verbal root is *dhṛ*, "to hold, bear, carry, maintain, preserve, keep, possess, use, place, fix, etc." Derived meanings of *dharma* include "that which is established or firm, steadfast, law, statute, prescribed conduct, duty, right, justice, virtue, morality, religion, etc." (SED 510, 519). Dharma also has a special, more technical meaning in Abhidharma discourse which we shall examine forthwith.

15 AKBh *ad* I 2b. Shastri: 12; Poussin: 4 (*tadayaṃ paramārthadharmaṃ vā nirvāṇaṃ dharmalakṣaṇaṃ vā pratyabhimukho dharma ityabhidharmaḥ*). The *Aṭṭhasālinī* (III 488), of the Theravādins, concurs: *abhidhammo nāmo paramatthadesanā* (as cited in Guenther, 1959: 2).

The distinction between ultimate and conventional truths or teachings has a long and important history in Buddhist thought. Jayatilleke (1963: 361–8) discusses the earliest meanings of ultimate (*paramattha*) and conventional (*sammuti*) discourse and their relation to definitive teachings (*nītattha*) and interpretive, indirect teachings (*neyyattha*). Although instances of the terms "ultimate" and "conventional" are found in the early texts (S I 135: "just as much as the word 'chariot' is used when the parts are put together, there is the use (*sammuti*) of the term 'being' (*satto*) when the (psycho-physical) constituents are present"), they are, he claims, "nowhere contrasted in the Canon" (p. 366), and are used only to refer to a "distinction of subject matter and not a distinction of two kinds of truth" (p. 368). See also *Kathāvatthu*, V 6; *Visuddhimagga*, XVIII 25; *Compendium* 6, 11, 81, n. 1, 200, n. 1.

16 *Yogācārabhūmi* (Tib. 189b4 f.) has a similar definition: "Vijñāna has the distinguishing characteristic of making known (*vijñapti*) each separate sense object" (*rnam par shes pa ni yul so sor rnam par rig pa'i mtshan nyid gang yin pa'o*). Schmithausen (1987: 426, n. 824) tentatively reconstructs this as: *vijñānaṃ yad viṣayaprativijñaptilakṣaṇam.*

17 Hence, Bateson continues: "and all perception of difference is limited by threshold. Differences that are too slight or too slowly presented are not perceivable. They are not food for perception" (1979: 31 f.).

18 AKBh IV *ad* 2b–3b (Shastri: 568; Poussin: 4) defines as momentary (*kṣaṇikaḥ*) that which ceases immediately after it attains its existence (*ko 'yaṃ kṣaṇo nāma? ātmalābho 'nantara vināśī, so 'syāstīti kṣaṇikaḥ*), while Yaśomitra (ibid.; in Shastri) glosses *kṣaṇa* simply as the limit or boundary of time (*kālaparyantaḥ kṣaṇaḥ*).

This, of course, needs some qualification. The Theravādins and the Sarvāstivādins held that each moment lasted for only an instant, but divided this instant into three and four parts of arising, abiding and passing away, and impermanence, respectively (Nyanatiloka, 1980: 34; *Compendium*, 25). Later Theravādin Abhidhamma, moreover, holds that each moment of matter lasts for seventeen mind-moments. (*Kathāvatthu* XXII 8, denies that *all* phenomena last merely a single mind-moment; *eka-citta-kkhaṇikā sabbe dhamma.*)

Though this division of a single instant was elsewhere criticized as not strictly instantaneous (AKBh *ad* II 46a–b; Shastri: 259; Poussin: 228), this did not prevent the term "instantaneous" (*kṣaṇika*) from being widely used, nor was this objection raised in the arguments surrounding the ālaya-vijñāna. Since these are not "differences that make a difference" to the issues at hand, we will use "momentary" and "momentariness" without further qualification.

19 We depart here from orthodox Abhidharma presentations, particularly that of the Sarvāstivādins.

20 A *dharma* is defined as "that which can carry it own characteristic" (AKBh *ad* I 2b; Shastri: 12; Poussin: 4: *svalakṣaṇadhāraṇād dharmaḥ*).

21 The concept of *dharma* thus retained the ambiguity, suggesting a tenuous unity, between its sheer existence (*svabhāva*) and its distinguishing characteristic (*svalakṣaṇa*). Guenther: "All texts agree that the term dharma is derived from the verbal root *dhṛ* 'to hold, to carry, to possess.' However, it seems that in the notion of what a dharma holds or possesses, there was a wavering between what in Western scholastic usage was referred to as *existentia*, a designation of thatness (*quid est*), on the one hand, and, on the other hand, *essentia*, a designation of whatness (*quod est*) by virtue of which existing entities are marked off from each other" (Guenther, 1989: 11). This general statement must be modified for each particular school. The relative emphasis of one side or the other of these two aspects of *dharma* are represented in divergent tendencies in Abhidharma Buddhist thought, tending toward the ontological substantialism of the Sarvāstivādins on the one end and the nominalism of the Sautrāntikas on the other.

22 As Piatigorsky puts it: "From the point of view of consciousness, it can be said that, *when consciousness is conscious of one's mind, thought, or consciousness* [manas, citta, viññāṇa] *directed to their objects, then it is 'being conscious of' that may be named 'a state of consciousness' or a dharma*" (1984: 182, emphasis in original).

23 This is also why the Abhidharma context is indispensable for understanding the explicit "defenses" of the ālaya-vijñāna examined below. The Yogācārins argue for its conceptual superiority over other models of mind on the basis of these underlying assumptions and in terms of the same technical vocabulary.

24 This reflects notions such as the following from the *Paramārtha-śūnyatā-sūtra* (*Samyukta*, 13, 22): "The eye, Oh Bhikṣus, arising, does not come from any place; perishing, it does not remain in any place. In this way, Oh Bhikṣus, the eye exists after having been non-existent and, after having existed, disappears" (cited in AKBh *ad* V 27b; Poussin: 59; trans. Pruden: 814).

25 See n. 13.

26 These do not correspond exactly to Buddhist categories of analysis. We are using them as heuristic categories, to clarify the problems under discussion. Their presentation in these terms, however, entails a certain amount of unavoidable overlap.

27 The commentary to the *Anguttaranikāya* (AA I 94, cited in Jayatilleke, 1963: 363), for example, states that "person" and "being" are conventional teachings, while such topics as "the impermanent," "the suffering," "selfless," and "the aggregates" are ultimate teachings.

28 Wittgenstein's similar attempts to forge a subjectless language entailed similar consequences: "It is because a language designed for the sole function of expressing everything that a subject might experience has no need for a term designating that subject that one cannot refer to the subject of experience from within the phenomenological language ... From within, one cannot individuate a subject at all. The metaphysical subject is not an object of experience, but a way of indicating the overall structure of experience ... The grammar of the phenomenological language ensures that all statements about experience are expressed in the same – ownerless – way" (Stern, 1995: 84).

29 And skirts the boundaries of incoherence as well. Thomas Luckmann has pointed out the inconceivability of purely momentary experience devoid of a larger interpretive framework: "Subjective experience considered in isolation is restricted to mere actuality and is void of meaning. Meaning is not an inherent quality of subjective processes but is bestowed on it in interpretive acts. In such acts a subjective process is grasped retrospectively and located in an interpretive scheme ... The meaning of experience is derived from the relation of ongoing processes to the scheme of interpretation [which] ... rests upon a certain degree of detachment. Such detachment cannot originate in a simple succession of isolated subjective processes ... a genuinely isolated subjective process is inconceivable" (Luckmann, 1967: 45).

30 The PED entry suggests that *citta* is also characterized by the "process–product" bivalence found in other Buddhist terms. *Citta* is "the centre and focus of man's emotional nature as well as that intellectual element which inheres in and accompanies its manifestations: thought. In this wise *citta* denotes both the agent and that which is enacted" (PED 266 f.). Guenther (1989: 1 f.) makes similar observations.

31 *Citta* is frequently equated with cognitive awareness (*vijñāna*) and mentation (*manas*) in both the early discourses (i.e. S II 95) and in Abhidharma literature (AKBh II 34a–b; Shastri: 208; Poussin: 176 f.: *cittaṃ mano 'tha vijñānam ekārthaṃ*). These terms are distinguished, however, by their characteristic functions and nuances: *citta*, in Vasubandhu's usual folk etymology (ibid.), accumulates (*cinoti*), and refers to a variety (*citram*) of pure and impure elements; *manas* mentates and refers to the previous state of mind inasmuch as it supports the succeeding one; while vijñāna discerns objects and arises supported by two conditions, that is, sense organ and object.

The Yogācārins, however, will systematically distinguish these three, significantly designating the ālaya-vijñāna as *citta*, while the *manas* will be equated with "afflictive mentation" (*kliṣṭa-manas*), and vijñāna with manifest cognitive awareness (*pravṛtti-vijñāna*).

32 D II 81: "*Citta*, when thoroughly infused with wisdom (*paññā-paribhāvitaṃ cittaṃ*) is set quite free from the maleficent influences (*āsava*), namely the maleficent influences of sensual pleasure, existence, views and ignorance" (Johansson, 1965: 176;

1970: 23). The verb *paribhāvita*, "to be infused" is used in the AKBh and in Yogācāra texts in connection with the notion of seeds (*bīja*) and impressions (*vāsanā*), and will have important implications for ālaya-vijñāna theory.

33 Each moment of mind (*citta*) is by definition already momentary, lasting but one instant (*kṣaṇa*). Though redundant, the expression "mind-moment" or "moment of mind (*citta*)," is used to emphasize the momentary nature of dharmas and mind.

34 Since mind (*citta*) and its concomitant functions (*caitta*) are the mutual effect of one another they are also simultaneous causes (AKBh *ad* II 53; Poussin: 268; Shastri: 307: *anyonyaphalārthena sahabhūhetuḥ*; Vyākhyā, ibid.: *cittaṃ caittasya phalam, caitto 'pi cittasya ity anyonyaphalam iti tena arthena sahabhūhetuḥ*). The Sautrāntika school rejected this category of cause, which the Sarvāstivādins accepted, on the grounds that it contradicts the accepted principle that cause and effect necessarily follow one another. This misses the point, however, as Tanaka (1985) points out, since this cause refers to the conditions that simultaneously support a phenomena, just as, for example, each leg of a tripod must be simultaneously present for the others to function. The commentator of the *Abhidharma-kośa*, Yaśomitra, defends it, citing the scriptural formula that sensation is the concomitance of feeling, apperception and intention born together (AKBh *ad* II 49; Shastri: 279; Poussin: 245: *taiḥ saha jātā vedanā saṃjñā cetanā ca iti sahabhūhetuḥ*).

This corresponds closely to the co-nascent condition (*sahajāta-paccaya*), the sixth condition of the *Paṭṭhāna* of the Pāli Abhidhamma. Later Theravādin Abhidhamma commentaries hold a similar concept in MA II 77 (*tam phassaṃ paṭicca sahajātādivasena phassapaccayā vedanā uppajjati*; cited in Jayatillike, 1963: 435 f.).

Although this causal factor is not emphasized within the *Abhidharma-kośa*, Yogācārins will thoroughly exploit it in the ālaya-vijñāna model.

35 This is part of a larger scheme of concomitances between the *citta* and its accompanying mental factors (*caitta*). Mental functions are said to be associated (*saṃprayukta*) with *citta* when they share five specific commonalities (*samatā*): (1) the same physical basis (*āśraya*), that is, the five sense-faculties and the mental-faculty (*mano-indriya*); (2) the same object (*ālambana*), that is, the same respective sense object (*viṣaya*); (3) the same aspect (*ākāra*), that is, they both conform to the character of the object; (4) the same time of occurrence (*kāla*); and (5) the same number of *dharmas* at a time, that is, one (AKBh II 34b–d; Shastri: 208 f. Poussin: 177 f.).

This schema began at an early date in Abhidharma thought, for the same basic formula is found in the *Kathāvatthu*, VII.2, where "conjoined" (*sampayutta*) appears to be defined as having the same physical basis (*ekavatthuka*) and the same object (*ekārammaṇa*), arising and ceasing together (*ekuppāda, ekanirodha*), and being concomitant, co-existent and compounded (*sahagata, sahajāta, saṃsaṭṭha*). The *Paṭṭhāna* gives the same three commonalities for the *sampayuttha-paccaya*, the nineteenth condition, though the whole system of causes and conditions found in this work is more complex and formal than that found in either the Sarvāstivādin or Yogācāra literature. See also the much later *Abhidhammatha-sangaha* (*Compendium*, II 1, 94) where *citta* and *caitta* are also *saṃpayuttha* due to the simultaneity of the objects and basis or support. See also Nyanatiloka (1983: 125).

36 AKBh IV 1b (Shastri: 567; Poussin: 1) quoting a *sūtra*, defines *karma* as intention and action having intended (*kiṃ punastat karma? ityāha cetanā tatkṛtaṃ ca tat. sūtra uktam "dve karmaṇī cetanā karma cetayitvā ca" iti*).

37 AKBh IV 45; Shastri: 652; Poussin: 106 (*kṣemaṃ karma kuśalam, yadiṣṭavipākaṃ ... akṣemamakuśalam ... yasyāniṣṭo vipākaḥ ... punaḥ trīṇi-sukhavedanīyaṃ karma, duḥkhavedanīyam, aduḥkhāsukhavedanīyaṃ ca*). This last set of terms, "karma leading to happiness or suffering," etc. (*sukhavedanīyaṃ karma, duḥkhavedanīyam*) is similarly found in A IV 382, S V 211.

38 The Sarvāstivādins, for example, also make an interesting distinction, which will have larger ramifications, between those moments that are only "conjoined" or associated with ignorance (*avidyā*) or false view (*dṛṣṭi*), and those that are also conjoined with more active afflictions (*kleśa*). This distinction highlights a difference in kind between moments of mind accompanied solely by cognitive errors from those whose *actions* are instigated by the afflictions. More specifically, while moments of mind that are conjoined with the views of self-existence (*satkāyadṛṣṭi*) and grasping to extremes (*antagrāhadṛṣṭi*) (AKBh *ad* II 30a–b; Poussin: 168; Chaudhuri, 1983: 108), and which are accompanied by deliberation (*vikalpitā*), are karmically unskillful (*akuśala*), those which are accompanied only by their innate counterparts, such as presumably exist in birds and animals, are karmically neutral (*avyākṛta*) (AKBh *ad* V 19; Poussin: 41; Shastri: 794: *sahajā satkāyadṛṣṭiravyākṛta ... vikalpitā tvakuśaleti*). This particular point – the presence of ignorance which is karmically neutral – will be revisited on pages 117–18, 146–50; in the context of the "proofs" of a new level of subliminal mind, "afflicted mentation" (*kliṣṭa-manas*).

39 This analysis of the types of mind and accompanying mental processes specifically applies to human beings in this realm of existence. It becomes much more complex when meditators take rebirth within higher realms of existence, or as they progress along the path eliminating their afflictions one by one. The problems entailed by the continued presence of the afflictions even in these higher states will be touched on pages 61, 73, 78f., 144f., 149f., 150–3.

40 AKBh II *ad* 35–46; Poussin: 178–244; Chaudhuri, 1983: 108–9. See Jaini (1959a) and, more recently, Cox's (1995) superb study of this topic and its associated disputes as found in Sanghabhadra's *Nyāyānusāra*.

41 Which also implies that they were developed sufficiently enough for such disputes to arise.

42 AKBh *ad* IV 120; Shastri: 746; Poussin: 242 f.: "What is done and what is accumulated (*upacita*) is called karma" (*kṛtaṃ ca, upacitaṃ ca karmocyate*).

43 AKBh *ad* IV 120; Shastri: 746f. Poussin: 242 f. (*sañcetanā ... vipākācca karmopacitam ucyate ... kathaṃ sañcetanataḥ? sañcintya kṛtaṃ bhavati ... kathaṃ vipākataḥ? vipākadāne niyataṃ bhavati*).

44 Suggestively, this is translated as "conservation" (*Kathāvatthu*, 300f.), though in later Abhidhamma "*upacaya*" typically, and tellingly, also means "growth, development" (*Compendium*, 252f.). Interestingly, *kamma* is translated in the PTS version as "karma as conscious process," and *kammūpacayo* as "continuation of karmic accumulation as product." The commentary to the *Kathāvatthu*, a later source, attributes these specific views to the Andhakas and the Sammatīyas.

45 Being directed toward a common object, we remember, is one of the five criteria of being associated with *citta*. See n. 35.

46 *Kathāvatthu-Aṭṭhakathā*, 156 (cited in Dube, 1980: 336), summarizing the positions of the heterodox interlocutors (*Kathāvatthu*, IX.4; XI.1).

47 As with many issues presented in the *Kathāvatthu*, however, later Theravāda positions are considerably more nuanced. In his commentary, variously called the *Paramatthamañjūsā* or the *Visuddhimagga-mahāṭīkā*, Theravāda commentator Dhammapāla discusses a passage from the *Visuddhimagga* ("it is only when it is past that kamma is a condition for kamma-originated materiality"): "If the fruit were to arise from present kamma, the fruit would have arisen in the same moment in which the kamma was being accumulated; and that is not seen. ... kamma has never been shown to give fruit while it is actually being effected; nor is there any text to that effect – But is it not also the fact that no fruit has ever been shown to come from a vanished cause either? ... when the fruit arises from kamma that is actually past it does so because of kamma having been performed and because of storage" (Pm. 768, as cited in *Visuddhimagga*, 695).

48 *Kathāvatthu*, XI.1 (*tisso pi anusayakathā*). The Sammatīyas and the Mahāsaṅghikas assert that the latent dispositions are karmically neutral (*anusayā abyākatā*), and can thus co-exist with skillful or neutral types of *citta*. In the text, Theravādin orthodoxy presses the point, implying that since the dispositions are indistinct from the manifest afflictions, the manifest afflictions must also be dissociated from mind, which of course is unacceptable to either party. The two sides do not seem to be defining their terms in the same way. The Theravādins seem to be understanding the term *sārāgo*, "possessed of or having passion," as referring to the manifest passion itself – in which case, of course, it must be associated with mind. But their opponents seem to be taking *sārāgo* to refer to one who still has the underlying disposition toward passion – which of course applies to everyone who is not yet liberated. A debate over the interpretation of such terms will appear in the *Abhidharma-kośa* as well.

49 *Kathāvatthu*, XIV.5 (Of Latent Bias as Something Apart, *añño anusayo ti kathā*). The opponent here, the Andhakas according to the commentary, maintain that the two must be distinguished on the grounds that an ordinary person whose mind is skillful or neutral must still possess the affliction in its latent form. The Theravādins dissent, again, on the grounds that the dispositions should be treated no differently than other active afflictions, such as sensual desire (*rāga*). This seems to be at odds with their own later commentarial traditions, as cited in Ch. 1, n. 80, which distinguish between three levels of the afflictions, the *anusaya*, the *pariyuṭṭhāna*, and the *vītikkama*.

50 In a discussion on the possibility of an Arahat, a liberated being, falling away (I.2.61, *parihānikathā*), the Sammatīyas, Vajjiputtiyas, Sabbatthivādins, and some of the Mahāsamghikas, according to the commentary, claim that this occurs due to an outburst of passion (*rāgaparyuṭṭhito*) which arises conditioned by its underlying disposition (*anusayaṃ paṭicca uppajjatīti*). Arahats, however, are not said to have these dispositions. Even more pertinent is the discussion in III.5 (*aṭṭhamakakathā*) concerning whether or not eradicating the outbursts on the first stage of entering the path also entails eradicating their latent dispositions. According to the commentary, the Andhakas and the Sammatīyas maintain that it does not; the Theravādins, consistent with their equation of the outbursts with the underlying dispositions, disagree.

The *Visuddhimagga* of Buddhaghosa, a Theravāda work contemporary with the *Abhidharma-kośa*, seems to contradict the *Kathāvatthu* on this. XXII.45 (1976: 797) correlates the successive eradication of afflictions and their latent tendencies with gradual progress upon the path: the Once-returner eliminates gross fetters, the gross inherent tendencies of greed for sense desires and resentment; the Non-returner, the residual fetters and the residual inherent tendencies of the same; the Arahat, greed for existence, conceit, agitation and ignorance, and the inherent tendencies toward conceit, greed for becoming and ignorance. Also, its definition of the term *anusaya* seems more consistent with the heterodox position: "For it is owing to their inveteracy that they are called inherent tendencies (*anusaya*) since they inhere (*anusenti*) as cause for the arising of greed for sense desires, etc., again and again," XXII.60 (p. 800).

51 As Piatigorsky claims, "the only thing it [karma] really does is that it *connects* cause with effect" (1984: 50, emphasis in original).

52 We stress "potential" here because not all karmically significant actions actually do result in some fruition. The causal chain they set into motion can be interrupted for a variety of reasons, foremost amongst which is the cultivation of repentance and other countervailing religious practices.

53 Though the schemas are similar, the specifics vary considerably from school to school. The Yogācārins discuss these in ASBh 35–43. The *Abhidharma-kośa* presents the Sarvāstivāda system of causes, conditions, and results. This includes the main or efficient cause (*kāraṇa-hetu*), the simultaneous cause (*sahabhū-hetu*), the cause by

association (*saṃprayukta-hetu*), the homogeneous cause (*sabhāga-hetu*), the omnipresent cause (*sarvatraga-hetu*), and the cause of karmic maturation (*vipāka-hetu*) (AKBh *ad* II 49–73; Poussin: 244–331; Verdu, 1985: 66–128; and Chaudhuri, 1983: 108–15).

We will not examine the first cause, the *kāraṇa-hetu*, the "efficient cause," which is the most general sense of cause such as when an eye-cognition arises due to a visual form and the unimpaired eye-organ (AKBh *ad* II 50). Two other causes which seldom arise in the debates under consideration here are the "homogeneous cause" (*sabhāga-hetu*), from which resultant *dharmas* follow uniformly and automatically (*niṣyanda-phala*) (which also means they have the same karmic nature as their cause, that is, as skillful, unskillful or neutral; AKBh II 54c–d); and the "all-pervading cause" (*sarvatraga-hetu*), which usually refers to ignorance (*avidyā*) insofar as it has not been fully eradicated and therefore colors all actions (AKBh II 57c).

For Vasubandhu, two of the conditions – the *adhipati-pratyaya*, the "predominant condition," and the *hetu-pratyaya*, the "root condition" – comprise the *kāraṇa-hetu* and the remaining *hetus*, respectfully, while the "object condition" (*ālambana-pratyaya*) refers to the objective support of cognition (AKBh *ad* II 61–4c). Theravādin doctrine differs here from the *Abhidharma-kośa*, for the system preserved in the *Paṭṭhāna* of the Pāli *Abhidhamma-piṭaka* lists a series of twenty-four conditions (*paccaya*) (Nyanatiloka, 1983: 117–27), which, however, have been reduced in the *Abhidhammattha-sangaha* (*Compendium*, VIII.12: 197) to four main conditions: the object condition (*ārammaṇa-paccaya*), the sufficing condition (*upanissaya-paccaya*), the action condition (*kamma-paccaya*), and the presence condition (*atthi-paccaya*).

This system of causes, conditions, and fruits is well illustrated by Stcherbatsky using the example of the process of visual cognition: "The *Sarvāstivādins* establish several kinds of causal relations between the elements. If, for example, a moment of the sense of vision produces in the next moment a visual sensation, it is termed *kāraṇa-hetu* and its result *adhipati-phala* [predominant result]. … When the next moment is just the same as the foregoing one, thus evoking in the observer the idea of duration, this relation is termed *sabhāga-hetu* [homogeneous cause] as to a *niṣyanda-phala* [uniform fruit]. If this moment appears in a stream (*santāna*) which is defiled by the presence of passions (*kleśa*), this defiling character is inherited by the next moments, if no stopping of it is produced. Such a relation is called *sarvatraga-hetu* as to *niṣyanda-phala*. Finally every moment in a stream is under the influence of former deeds (*karma*) and many, in its turn, have an influence on future events. This relation is termed *vipāka-hetu* as to *vipāka-phala*" (Stcherbatsky, 1956: 67).

54 And karmic theory, it need hardly be stressed, is at the heart of the Buddhist worldview. As we have seen: "This body does not belong to you, nor to anyone else. It should be regarded as [the results of] former action that has been constructed and intended and is now to be experienced" (S II 64). Even more strongly, AKBh IV 1a states that the world in its variety comes into being due to the actions of sentient beings. See discussion on pages 67–70 as well as Ch. 5, n. 20.

55 *Vipāka* is derived from the verbal root, *pac*, "to mature or ripen," or "to come to perfection," while the prefix *vi-* conveys the sense of "dis-", here approximate to "difference."

56 AKBh *ad* II 57a–b; Shastri: 330; Poussin: 289 (*vipāko 'vyākṛto dharmaḥ anivṛtāvyākṛto hi dharmaḥ vipākaḥ … ya uttarakālaṃ bhavati na yugapad na api antaraṃ sa vipākaḥ*). This contrasts with the "homogeneous cause" (*sabhāga-hetu*) and "all-pervading cause" (*sarvatraga-hetu*) and their uniform fruit (*niṣyanda-phala*).

57 AKBh II 62a–b; Shastri: 342; Poussin: 300 (*cittacaittā acaramā utpannāḥ samanantaraḥ … samaś ca ayam anantaraś ca pratyaya iti samanantarapratyayaḥ*).

58 The "formations dissociated from mind" (*citta-viprayukta-saṃskārā*) are therefore not subject to this condition (AKBh *ad* II 62a–b; Shastri: 344; Poussin: 303). This category, we have noted, allows for the unobtrusive presence of certain factors within the

synchronic analysis of mind, a point we shall revisit on page 71f. It also allows for the continuity of their succession over time relatively independent of overt karmic activities.

59 AKBh *ad* V 25b; Shastri: 805; Poussin: 51: "If the past would not exist, how would there be the future fruit of pure and impure karma, since at the time the fruit arises the cause of karmic maturation (*vipākahetu*) is not present?" See also Poussin (1937a: 77) and the *Visuddhimagga-mahāṭikā* (Ch. 2, n. 47, above).

60 Conze has succinctly summarized this issue: "Saints are credited with a number of possessions and achievements which are lasting in the sense that they are not lost as soon as the present moment has passed. A Streamwinner need never again be reborn in a state of woe, and thus has won a quality which he will always have. The Arhat, according to some, can never fall away... Even while he does not actually realize it, a saint has the power to realize at his will this or that attainment, and thus possesses it potentially. The fact that a mental state is definitely abandoned or definitely established lies outside the momentary series of states, and so does permanent ownership or potential ownership of a spiritual skill. One speaks of a person being 'destined' (*niyata*) for some future condition, and asserts that he will certainly obtain it. For instance people are said to be 'destined for Nirvana,' or 'to be destined' either for salvation (*samyaktva*) or perdition (*mithyātva*). There are spiritual attainments the future realization of which becomes fixed at a certain point in one's religious practice" (1973: 137f.).

The *Abhidharma-kośa* (AKBh *ad* VI 26a; Poussin: 180f.; Shastri 923) discusses "*niyāma*" as follows: "It is called 'entering into assurance' because it is entering into the assurity of perfection (*samyaktva-niyāma*). In the *sūtra* it is called 'the perfection which is *nirvāṇa*', obtaining which is 'entering,' and from whose production one is called an Āryan person. The state of being a worldling is destroyed by the future state" (*saiva ca niyāmāvakrāntir ity ucyate; samyaktvaniyāmāvakramaṇāt. "samyaktvaṃ nirvāṇam" ity uktaṃ sūtre... tasyābhigamanam avakramaṇam. tasyāṃ côtpannāyām āryapudgala ucyate. anāgatayā pṛthagjanatvaṃ vyāvartyate*).

See also *Kathāvatthu*, V,4; VI,1; XII,5; XIII,4; on *sammatta-niyāma* (Skt. *samyaktva-niyāma*) see S I 96; S III 225; A I 121f. SN 55, 371. The Appendix of the English translation of the *Kathāvatthu* (*ad* XXI, 7, 8: 383) discusses *niyāma* at some length.

61 A typical example of this occurs in the *Abhidharma-kośa* (AKBh *ad* VI 3; Shastri: 887; Pruden: 909). It first cites a passage: "The Blessed One said, 'Karma, craving and ignorance are the cause of *saṃskāras* in the future.'" (Poussin traces this to *Samyuktāgama*, T 2.88b9). Then, after citing another discourse equating vijñāna with seeds (S III 54), the *Abhidharma-kośa* states: "The teaching in the *sūtra* is the sense (*abhiprāyika*), whereas [the teaching] in the Abhidharma is the defining characteristic (*lākṣaṇika*)." This is then followed by a commentary on yet another *sūtra* which elaborates upon the first: action is the cause of different births, craving of further existence, etc.

62 The root verses of the *Abhidharma-kośa* were traditionally taken to represent the Sarvāstivādin view while the prose commentary, the *Abhidharmakośa-bhāṣya*, also by Vasubandhu, was thought to include many Sautrāntika positions.

63 AKBh III 19a–d; Shastri: 433f.; Poussin: 57–9 (*yathā ākṣepaṃ kramād vṛddhaḥ santānaḥ kleśakarmabhiḥ. paralokaṃ punar yāti... iti anādibhavacakrakam*). The text elaborates on the reciprocity implicit in this latter statement, stating both that the afflictions and karma are due to birth and that birth is due to the afflictions and karma. (AKBh III *ad* 19a–d; Shastri: 435f.; Poussin: 57–9: *etena prakāreṇa kleśakarmahetukaṃ janma tad hetukāni punaḥ kleśakarmāṇi tebhyaḥ punar janma iti anādibhavacakrakaṃ veditavyam.*)

64 AKBh *ad* V 34; Shastri: 829f.; Poussin: 72f. (*aprahīṇād anuśayād viṣayāt pratyupasthitāt ayoniśo manaskārāt kleśaḥ... sampūrṇākāraṇaḥ*).

65 Frauwallner suggests that the growing importance of the underlying dispositions (*anuśaya*) in Abhidharma thought was because the concept of the maleficent influences (*āsava*) was already so clearly defined, while *anusaya* was "a younger, more flexible term which [the author] then reformulated for his own purposes" (1995: 155). It seems more likely to us that the *anuśaya* became prominent because they were already so intimately involved in the cognitive and affective processes central to the perpetuation of samsara, and could, for etymological reasons, be so easily interpreted in a latent or underlying sense.

66 AKBh *ad* V 1a; Shastri: 759; Poussin: 106 (*karmajaṃ lokavaicitrayam iti uktam. tāni ca karmāṇi anuśayavaśād upacayaṃ gacchanti, antareṇa ca anuśayān bhavābhinirvartane na samarthāni bhavanti. ato veditavyāḥ mūlaṃ bhavasya anuśayāḥ*). See Ch. 4, p. 146, for the Yogācāra commentator, Sthiramati's, similar comments regarding the afflictions.

67 AKBh *ad* IV 55c–d; Shastri: 664; Poussin: 124 (*vipākaḥ punar vedanāpradhānaḥ*). See n. 37, on the categorization of karmic fruit according to feeling. Feeling as a result of karma is mentioned in A II 157 (Ch. 1, n. 81).

68 AKBh V 45; *ad* II 3; Shastri: 843; Poussin: 88. (Quoting *sūtra*: *sukhāyāṃ vedanāyāṃ rāgo 'nuśete, duḥkhāyāṃ pratighaḥ, *aduḥkhāsukhāyām avidyā iti uktaṃ sūtre.* *Emended from "*aduḥkhādukhāyāṃ*"). This is consonant with the early texts (M I 303, etc.) cited in Ch. 1 (n. 61) above, and as quoted in the *Kathāvatthu*, XIII.8.

69 In this case, the disposition (*anuśaya*) is considered the cause (*hetu*), the *dharma* the object, and the lack of thorough attention or comprehension (*ayoniśo manaskāra*) the preparatory condition (*prayoga*). These are all called "forces" (*bala*) (AKBh *ad* V 34; Shastri: 829; Poussin: 72 f.: *tat yathā rāgānuśayo 'prahīṇo bhavati aparijñātaḥ kāmarāgaparyavasthānīyāś ca dharmā ābhāsagatā bhavanti. tatra ca ayoniśo manaskāra evaṃ kāmarāga utpadyate. tānyetāni yathākramaṃ hetuviṣayaprayogabalāni. evam anyo 'pi kleśa utpadyata iti veditavyaḥ*). And, AKBh *ad* V 36c–d asserts, ignorance is the root of them all (Shastri: 831; Poussin: 74: *sarveṣāṃ teṣāṃ mūlam avidyā*).

70 AKBh *ad* V 22; Shastri: 801; Poussin: 48 (*yasya pudgalasya yo 'nuśayo yasmin ālambane 'nuśete sa tena tasmin saṃprayuktaḥ*). Though this last term, *saṃprayukta*, technically means "associated," Yaośmitra (Vyākhyā, 801), however, glosses it here simply as *baddha*, "bound."

71 AKBh *ad* V 18c–d; Shastri: 793; Poussin: 39 (*yena yaḥ saṃprayuktastu sa tasmin saṃprayogataḥ ... te cānuśayāḥ saṃprayogato 'nuśayīrannālambanataḥ*).

72 AKBh V 61c–d; Shastri: 856; Poussin: 104; trans. Pruden: 856: "The *kleśa* is supposed to become abandoned through separation from its object." The text explains that while the afflictions (*kleśa*) cannot be separated from the bonds themselves, it can be separated from the object to which it is attached, so that it no longer arises in relation to that object (*na hi samprayogāt kleśo vivecayituṃ śakyate. ālambanāc ca śakyate; yasmān na punas tad ālambyo 'tpadyate.*)

73 This conception is strikingly similar to that of the depth psychologists: the latent afflictions are attached to a certain kind of phenomena, such as a pleasurable feeling; when certain situations, images, or thoughts arise which are related to the *kind* of phenomena the afflictions are attached to, those latent afflictions will burst out with all their emotion-laden and karma-generating energies. In Freudian terms, we would say that the unconscious energies are "invested" (*besetzen*) in types of objects and these energies are evoked or brought to consciousness whenever similar conditions are found. And in both traditions, we are bound up in this complex for as long as such emotionally entangling energies bind the underlying dispositions and their associated objects together, as long, that is, as this bond is "neither abandoned nor correctly understood." "Neurosis," Freud once remarked, is "the result of a kind of ignorance, a not-knowing of mental processes which should be known" (1965: 291, Lecture 18).

74 Guenther calls *vipāka* an "energetic process" intimately related to *karma*, such that "in its potential state energy is 'heaped up' (*upacita*), while in its kinetic state it develops (*vipacyate*) toward a certain effect" (1959: 19–20).

75 M I 434, as cited in Ch. 1 (p. 40): "together with the underlying tendency to it is abandoned in him" (*sānusaya pahīyati*).

76 Vyākhyā, 15 *ad* AKBh I 3, (*ye sūtraprāmāṇikāḥ, na tu śāstraprāmāṇikās te sautrāntikāḥ*). Jaini sides with the Sautrāntikas, "it is clear from these discussions that the Theravādin as well as the Vaibhāṣika [Sarvāstivādin] interpretation of the term *sānuśaya*, and the subsequent identification of the *anuśayas* with *paryavasthāna*, are contrary to the sūtra quoted above [the *Mahā-Māluṅkya-sutta*, M I 433]. They show a determined effort to uphold the Abhidharma in preference to the sūtra" (Jaini, 1959b: 242).

77 AKBh *ad* V 1d–2a; Shastri: 761; Poussin: 3–4 (*katham idaṃ jñātavyam – kāmarāga eva anuśayaḥ kāmarāgānuśayaḥ, ahosvit kāmarāgasya anuśayaḥ kāmarāgānuśayaḥ? kiṃ cātaḥ? kāmarāga eva anuśayaś cet sūtravirodhaḥ... "tatkāmarāgaparyavasthānaṃ... sānuśayaṃ prahīyate." iti/kāmarāgasya anuśayaś ced viprayuktānuśayaprasaṅgād abhidharmavirodhaḥ – "kāmarāgānuśayas tribhir indriyaiḥ samprayuktaḥ" iti*). The Vyākhyā (762) glosses *indriya* as: *sukha-saumanasya-upekṣendriyaiḥ samprayuktā iti*, upon which our interpretation of *indriya* as "feeling" is based.

78 They argue that Abhidharma understands the word literally, that is, that an *anuśaya* *is* the affliction, because it is that which makes the mind afflicted, it obstructs wholesome states from occurring and it eliminates them once they have occurred; thus the *anuśaya* cannot be dissociated (AKBh V *ad* 1d–2a; Shastri: 762; Poussin: 5).

79 Although the *Abhidharma-kośa* often presents the Sarvāstivādin or Vaibhāṣika positions from a slightly polemical perspective, the *Abhidharma-dīpa* (edited by Jaini (1977), and still extant in its original Sanskrit) preserves orthodox Vaibhāṣika responses to Vasubandhu's criticisms. Poussin (1937a), *Documents d'Abhidharma*, translates important Sarvāstivādin texts from their Chinese translations. See Cox (1995) for a succinct discussion of the Vaibhāṣika treatment of many of these same issues, and Williams (1981) and Bareau (1955: 131–52) on Vaibhāṣika ontology.

80 AKBh *ad* V 25b; Shastri: 805; Poussin: 50 f. (*yadi ca atītaṃ na syāt śubhāśubhasya karmaṇaḥ phalam āyatyāṃ kathaṃ syāt. na hi phalôtpattikāle varttamānāṃ vipākahetur asti iti. tasmād asti eva atītānāgatam iti vaibhāṣikāḥ*). See Poussin (1937a: 77f.) on a passage from the *Abhidharma-nyāyānusāra* of Sanghabadra (T.29.1562.629a28f).

81 AKBh II 36c–d; Shastri: 211; Poussin: 179: "Possession and non-possession fall into their own stream" (*prāptyaprāptī svasantānapatitānāṃ*). It does not fall into another's stream (*parasantāna*), the text says, since no one possesses (*samanvāgataḥ*) what belongs to another, nor does it fall into what is not a stream, since no non-living being possesses anything. Note that even this putatively dharmic explanation depends upon a non-dharmic metaphor, *santāna*, to contextualize its function.

82 AKBh *ad* II 36c–d; Shastri: 214; Poussin: 182 (*utpattihetur dharmāṇāṃ prāptir... sahajaprāptihetukā*). As Jaini points out, the concept of possession also addresses the thorny problem of heterogeneous succession, since it is a present "possession" which allows for the contiguous arising of heterogeneous dharmas. See Jaini (1959b: 245).

83 AKBh II 35a–b; Shastri: 209; Poussin: 178 (*viprayuktās tu saṃskārāḥ prāptyaprāpti*). Jaini (1959b: 240, 245).

84 AKBh V *ad* 1d–2a; Shastri: 762; Poussin: 5 (*aupacāriko vā sūtre 'nuśayaśabdaḥ prāptau*).

85 AKBh *ad* II 36c–d; Shastri: 214f.; Poussin: 183 (*vyavasthāhetuḥ prāptiḥ. asatyāṃ hi prāptau lokikamānasānām āryapṛthagjanānām "āryā ime", "pṛthagjanā ime" iti na syād vyavasthānam. prahīṇāprahīṇakleśatā viśeṣād etad bhavitum arhati*). See Conze (1973: 138).

86 At the end of a long exchange, Vasubandhu rhetorically asks why possession is in fact a real entity (*dravyadharma*) rather than merely a conventional one (*prajñaptidharma*), as the Sautrāntikas charge, to which Vasubandhu, the author of the *Kośa*, has the Sarvāstivādins respond, "because that's our doctrine" (*eva hi naḥ siddhānta iti*)

(AKBh *ad* II 36c–d; Shastri: 218; Poussin: 186). The concept of possession was also open to the criticism of infinite regress: what, after all, determines the possession of the possession, but another possession?

87 Conze observes a further problem of using *prāpti* to reconcile synchronic with diachronic discourses: "The term *prāpti* obviously sails very near the concept of a 'person' or 'self.' 'Possession' is a relation which keeps together the elements of one stream of thought, or which binds a dharma to one 'stream of consciousness,' which is just an evasive term for an underlying 'person'... 'Possession' implies a support which is more than the momentary state from moment to moment, and in fact a kind of lasting personality, i.e., the stream as identical with itself, in a personal identity, which is here interpreted as 'continuity'" (Conze, 1973: 141).

88 AKBh *ad* V 1d–2a; Shastri: 763 f.; Poussin: 6 f. (*kathaṃ ca sautrāntikānām? ... prasupto hi kleśo 'nuśaya ucyate, prabuddhaḥ paryavasthānam. kā ca tasya prasuptiḥ? asammukhībhūtasya bījabhāvānubandhaḥ. kaḥ prabodhaḥ? sammukhībhāvaḥ. ko 'yaṃ bījabhāvo nāma? ātmabhāvasya kleśajā kleśotpādanaśaktiḥ. yathā anubhavajñānajā smṛtyutpādanaśaktiḥ, yathā ca ankurādīnāṃ śāliphalajā śāliphalotpādanaśaktir iti*).

89 The etymological parallelism of these two terms is telling. *Anu-bandha* is "being bound along with or along side of," while *anu-śaya* is "lying or sleeping along side of."

90 AKBh *ad* II 36d; Shastri: 217; Poussin: 185 (*kiṃ punar idaṃ bījaṃ nāma? yan nāmarūpaṃ phalotpattau samarthaṃ sākṣāt pāramparyeṇa vā; santatipariṇāmaviśeṣāt. ko 'yaṃ pariṇāmo nāma? santater anyathātvam. ka ce iyaṃ santatiḥ? hetuphalabhūtās traiyadhvikāḥ saṃskārāḥ*). Note the tautological nature of this definition: a seed is what produces a result (causes an effect) through the mental stream, which is just the *saṃskārās* existing as cause and effect.

91 AKBh, Ch. 9, Shastri: 1230; Poussin: 295; Stcherbatsky, 1976: 72 (*yaḥ karmapūrva uttarottara cittaprasavaḥ sā santatiḥ ... sa punaryo 'nantaraṃ phalotpādanasamarthaḥ so 'ntyapariṇāmaviśiṣṭatvāt pariṇāmaviśeṣaḥ*). In addition, the last moment of the specific modification (*pariṇāma-viśeṣaḥ*) is characterized here as the "capacity to immediately produce a result."

92 A I 135. "It is monks, as with seeds that are undamaged, not rotten, unspoiled by wind and sun, capable of sprouting and well embedded: if a man were to burn them in fire and reduce them to ashes, then winnow the ashes in a strong wind or let them be carried away by a swiftly flowing stream, then those seeds would have been radically destroyed, fully eliminated, made unable to sprout and would not be liable to arise in the future. Similarly, it is, monks, with actions done in non-greed, non-hatred and non-delusion. Once greed, hatred and delusion have vanished, these actions are thus abandoned, cut off at the root, made barren like palm-tree stumps, obliterated so that they are no more subject to arise in the future." (A I 135; Nyanoponika, 1999: 50).

93 AKBh *ad* II 36c–d; Shastri: 215 f.; Poussin: 183 (*āśrayo hi sa āryāṇaṃ darśanabhāvanāmārgasāmarthyāt tathā parāvṛtto bhavati yathā na punas tat praheyāṇāṃ kleśānāṃ prarohasamartho bhavati. ato 'gnidagdhavrīhivadabījībhūta āśrayaḥ kleśānāṃ prahīṇakleśa iti ucyate. upahatabījabhāve vā laukikena mārgeṇa*).

94 Jaini has observed the similarity between them: "the theory of bīja was employed primarily ... to replace prāpti in explaining the phenomena of immediate succession between two cittas of heterogeneous nature, and secondarily to reconcile the abiding nature of santati with the momentary flashes of dharma" (Jaini, 1959: 244–5).

95 Vyākhya *ad* AKBh II 36; Shastri: 219: "Power, seed and impression have the same sense. The seed is a specific power ... It doesn't really exist at all, because it is nominally existent" (*śakti bījaṃ vāsanā iti eka ayam arthaḥ ... śaktiviśeṣa eva bījam. na bījaṃ nāma kiñcit asti, prajñaptisattvāt*).

96 Accordingly, the Sautrāntikas claim that the dispositions are neither associated nor dissociated from mind, since they too are not real entities (AKBh *ad* V 1d–2a;

Shastri: 763 f.; Poussin: 6 f.: *na ca anuśayaḥ samprayukto na viprayuktaḥ, tasya adravyāntaratvāt*).

97 Which was itself, at least once in the *Kośa*, explicitly equated with the mental stream. The ninth chapter of the Abhidharma states that *vijñāna* itself is a conventional name for the mental stream with nothing but its own series as cause, one after the other (AKBh IX; Shastri: 1219 f.; Poussin: 281; Pradhan, 473; Stcherbatsky, 1976: 57: *vijñānasantānasya vijñāne kāraṇabhāvāt vijñānaṃ vijānāti iti vacanān nirdoṣam... evaṃ vijñānam api cittānāṃ santāna upacaryate*).

98 On "heat" and "vitality" see AKBh II 45a–b (Shastri: 248; Poussin: 215); Poussin cites parallels in S III 143 and M I 296. For vijñāna as the basis (*āśraya*) which lasts throughout life, see AKBh I 28c–d (Shastri: 78; Poussin: 50). Poussin (49, n. 2) identifies the *sūtra* cited in the *Abhidharma-kośa* as *Dhātuvibhaṅgasutta*, M III 239.

99 AKBh *ad* I 34; Shastri: 91; Poussin: 63: "What is the meaning of 'appropriating?' That which the mind and mental factors grasp as the foundation, because they mutually benefit and harm each other" (*upāttam iti ko 'rthaḥ? yac cittacaittair adhiṣṭhānabhāveno upagṛhītam; anugraho 'paghātābhyām anyonyānuvidhānāt*). The sense faculties are also called the support (*āśraya*) of *citta* and are therefore the root constituents of sentient existence. As such they are the very basis of the continuation of samsaric life (AKBh *ad* II 5–6; Shastri: 142 f.; Poussin: 110 f.).

100 There are, however, two occasions in which cognitive awareness appears to come to a halt: deep sleep and certain meditative attainments, as we shall discuss shortly.

101 AKBh III 41c–d; Shastri: 496; Poussin: 125 f. (*anyostāvadihotpannasya bhavasya poṣaṇe prādhānyam. manaḥsañcetanayā punarbhavasyā ākṣepaḥ. ākṣiptasya punaḥ karmaparibhāvitād vijñānabījād abhinirvṛttir iti anayor anutpannasya bhavasya ākaraṇe prādhānyam*).

102 AKBh IV 1c; Shastri: 568 (*cetanā mānasaṃ karma*).

103 In both Pāli and Sanskrit *bhāvanā* (cultivation) is a nominal form derived from the causative form of the verb *bhū*, "to be," meaning "causing to be, effecting, producing." From this derives its typical yogic meaning of "cultivation, meditation" in the sense of "forming in the mind" (SED 755; PED 503). Secondary meanings in the SED include "steeping, infusing," while its past participle, *bhāvita*, in addition to "produced, fostered, cultivated," is also glossed as "soaked in, steeped, infused, perfumed with, scented." *Paribhāvita*, with the intensifying prefix *pari-* expressing fulness or "all around, completely, altogether," has the sense of "penetrated, supplied, filled with, pervaded, soaked, saturated." All the forms of *bhāvanā* are commonly used as adjectives of *citta*. We find in D II 81, for example (n. 32), the expression *paññā paribhāvitaṃ cittaṃ*, "the citta infused, pervaded with wisdom."

In the *Abhidharma-kośa* (*ad* IV 123c–d), *bhāvanā* is closely related to *vāsanā*, "perfumations, impressions": "For what reason is that [wholesome collected state] called *bhāvanā* (cultivation)? Because it perfumes/impresses the mind." (AKBh IV 123c–d; Shastri: 751; Poussin: 249: *samāhitaṃ tu kuśalaṃ bhāvanā ... kim artham etat bhāvane iti ucyate? cittavāsanāt*).

104 AKBh III 28a–b; Shastri: 460 (*tasyāvidyā pratyayāḥ saṃskārāḥ karmākṣepavaśāc ca vijñānasantatis tāṃ tām gatiṃ gacchati. ... tadanya saṃskārāpratyayaṃ vijñānam*).

105 Vasubandhu's *Karmasiddhiprakaraṇa* most succinctly presents this debate and the positions taken by various schools (Lamotte, 1935–6: 234–47; Pruden, 1988: 58–65; Anacker, 1972; 1984). AKBh treats it in II *ad* 42–4; Poussin: 200–14. See Griffiths's (1986) monograph devoted to the topic of the absorptions and their problematics within Abhidharma doctrine, particularly pp. 122–8, Appendix B. As we shall see, Schmithausen (1987: 18 ff.) considers the absorption of cessation (*nirodha-samāpatti*) the originating context for the concept of ālaya-vijñāna.

106 A single moment of mind or cognitive awareness (*vijñāna*) has (at least in the human realm) two types of support: the simultaneous support (*sahaja āśraya*) of its respective

sense organ (*indriya*) and the "mind support" (*mana āśrayaḥ*) of its immediately antecedent mental cognition (AKBh I 44c–d; Shastri: 125 f.; Poussin: 95 f.).

107 *Karmasiddhiprakaraṇa*: "But the mind of entry into the absorption has been destroyed (*vinaṣṭa*) for a long time. How could it constitute an equal and immediate antecedent?" (Lamotte, 1935–6: 235; Pruden, 1980: 58).

108 *Karmasiddhiprakaraṇa*: "If the fruit arises afterwards from the mental stream (*citta-santāna*) which has been infused by the power of karma, then how can the fruit of an earlier action arise afterwards from the interrupted mental stream of those in the two mindless attainments and unconscious existence?" (Lamotte, 1935–6: 233; Pruden, 1988: 57, para. 21; slightly paraphrased from the Tibetan, P mDo #58 sems-tsam Si, 161b3 f.; D. 4062,139a5 f.).

109 For a closer examination of these passages, their related textual materials and some the philosophical issues involved see Griffiths (1986: 122–8, App. B).

110 AKBh II *ad* II 44d; Shastri: 245; Poussin: 211; Griffiths, 1986: 123 (*katham idānīṃ bahukālaṃ niruddhāc cittāt punar api cittaṃ jāyate? atītasya api astitvād iṣyate vaibhāṣikaiḥ samanantarapratyayatvam*).

111 AKBh *ad* II 44d; Shastri: 246; Poussin: 212; Griffiths, 1986: 124 (*cittam api asmād eva sendriyāt kāyāt jāyate, na cittāt. anyonyabījakaṃ hi etad ubhyaṃ yad uta cittaṃ ca sendriyaś ca kāya iti pūrvācaryāḥ*). See also *Karmasiddhiprakaraṇa*, para. 23.

112 Sthiramati strongly criticized this notion, however, as abrogating the principle that the effect be similar to the cause, that is, that a mental-dharma must give rise to a mental-dharma, and a bodily dharma to a bodily dharma, that is, "a specific effect arises from a specific cause" (Vyākhyā, Shastri: 218; Jaini: 1959: 243; *tataḥ kāraṇaviśe-ṣāt kāryaviśeṣa iti viśiṣṭam*). See Griffiths (1986: 125).

113 *Karmasiddhiprakaraṇa* (para. 24). Griffiths (1986: 125 f.) discusses a nearly identical passage (Muroji, 1985: 27) in AKBh ad VIII 33b (Poussin: 207 f.); see also AKBh ad II 44d (Shastri: 245 ff.; Poussin: 211, 212, n. 2). This "subtle mind" is considered an "unmanifesting mental-cognition" (*aparisphuṭa-manovijñāna*) by the Vyākhyā on this passage.

Bareau (1955) cites a number of schools regarding this point (see Appendix II, points 10, 11) He also states (p. 240) that the Theravādins (thesis 217) agree with this, citing the Siddhi (pp. 142, 202–3, 207) as his source. Collins, however, argues the opposite, citing the Theravādin texts, the *Visuddhimagga* (XXIII. 43,47), which reads "without mind" (*acittako*), and the later *Abhidhammattha-sangaha* (Compendium, IX.9), which states that "mental continuity is suspended" (*cittasan-tati vocchijjati*). He concludes that "personal continuity spanning a period of cessation, then, is guaranteed by the continued existence of the body, or rather the material life-faculty, and not by the continued occurrence of *bhavaṅga*-moments" (Collins, 1982: 245 f., 304). This accords closely with the Sautrāntika position. Schmithausen (1987: 19 f.; nn. 149–67) discusses all the passages pertinent to a subtle form of mind.

114 Vyākhyā *ad* AKBh II 44c; Shastri: 245; Muroji, 1985: 27.

115 This flies in the face of most South Asian Buddhist traditions, which hold to some form of mind–body dualism. Roger Jackson has succinctly delineated these basic issues: "Buddhist views of the mind–body relation tend to be interactionist, maintaining that the mental and physical are alike in being causally conditioned types of phenomena, but heterogeneous enough in nature that the one cannot be the 'direct special basis' (i.e. substantial cause or indispensable cooperative condition) of the other – rather, they interact indirectly. ... *some* sort of dualism is fundamental to the establishment of past and future lives (after all, the body dies, while the mind, in some sense, continues), and few Buddhists will want to disavow it entirely" (1993: 232, n. 34, emphasis in original).

116 The role of the *bhavaṅga-citta* within the Theravādin Abhidhamma, especially in its complex theory of perception, is discussed in Collins (1982: 225–61, esp. 240–6),

Mizuno (1978: 853 f.), and Cousins (1981: 35–7), the latter including some interesting comparisons with the ālaya-vijñāna.

117 Collins characterizes this double role in a way that is strikingly similar to our analysis of vijñāna in the early texts: "It is a condition of existence in two senses: first, in the sense of its mere occurrence as a phenomenon of the saṃsāric, temporally extended sphere, as a necessary part of any individual name-and-form. ... it is both a causal, 'construct-ive' and a resultant, 'construct-ed' factor. ... Secondly, it is itself a conditioning factor of existence, in the particular sense of being a necessary condition for any *conscious* experience of life. It is only on the basis of *bhavaṅga* that any mental processes can arise. Thus it is said that while *karma* is the general condition of any 'resultant mind,' it is *bhavaṅga* which is the condition for 'active mind'" (1982: 239). In his *Théorie des Douze Causes*, Poussin identifies this concept with *viññāṇa*, which "on account of its permeating [all the other parts] and its persistence, receives *par excellence* the name of *bhavaṅga*, chief of existence" (Poussin, 1913: 40, as cited in Collins, ibid.).

118 The early Pāli doctrines (D II 63, etc.), as we observed above, held that vijñāna descends and coagulates in the mother's womb enabling *nāma-rūpa* to develop. But the question is now raised as to as exactly *which type* of vijñāna this is. Early Theravādin doctrine agrees with most schools that it is *manovijñāna* (*Vibhanga*, 414: *manoviññāṇa-dhātu* is the only viññāṇa at the time of rebirth (*upapatti*)). See also *Miln.*, 299; *Visuddhimagga*, XIV 111–14, 124. *Visuddhimagga*, XIV 98 adds that the *bhavaṅga-citta*, is classified along with this rebirth-mind as a "resultant mind-consciousness element without root cause" (*vipākāhetuka-manoviññāṇadhātu*). See also the *Aṭṭhasālinī* III 581–3 (as cited in Guenther, 1959: 25 f.).

The Sarvāstivādin position (AKBh III 42b–c; Shastri: 501; Poussin: 131: "Death and birth are considered to be [moments of] mental cognitive awareness," *cyutyupapattayaḥ manovijñāna eveṣṭāḥ*) is that it is a mental cognitive awareness which transits at rebirth and coagulates in the womb, a position with which the Sautrāntikas are in substantial agreement (Schmithausen 1987: 301, n. 232, citing VGPVy 416b1–4; *Pratītyasamutpādā vyākhyā* 20b7: *mdo sde pas smras pa – yid kyi rnam par shes pa ma'i mngal du mtshams sbyor ba*).

119 *Visuddhimagga*, XIV 114. "When the rebirth-linking consciousness has ceased, then, following on whatever kind of rebirth-linking it may be, the same kinds, being the result of that same kamma whatever it may be, occur a *life-continuum* consciousness with that same object; and again those same kinds. And as long as there is no other kind of arising of consciousness to interrupt the continuity they also go on occurring endlessly in periods of dreamless sleep, etc., like the current of a river." See *Abhidhammatthaa-sangaha* (*Compendium*, 1979: 266–7).

120 *Visuddhimagga*, XV 39: *bhavaṅgamana-dhamma-manasikāre paṭicca uppajjati manoviññāṇaṃ* (cited in Collins, 1982: 241).

121 The translator, Shwe Zan Aung, of the *Compendium* explains: "The passage from a state of anger to one of joy would be too abrupt without the mediation of a *hedonically indifferent* element, which acts as a sort of buffer between two opposing natures" (*Compendium*, 268).

122 *Visuddhimagga*, XIV 115 "With the life-continuum continuously occurring thus, when living beings' faculties have become capable of apprehending an object, then when a visible datum has come into the eye's focus, there is impinging upon the eye-sensitivity due to the visible datum. Thereupon, owing to the impact's influence, there comes to be a disturbance in [the continuity of] the life-continuum. Then, when the life-continuum has ceased, the functional mind-element arises making that same visible datum its object, as it were, cutting off the life-continuum, and accomplishing the function of *adverting*. So too in the case of the ear door and so on."

123 This is in sharp contrast, as we shall see, with the concept of the ālaya-vijñāna which always arises simultaneously with the forms of cognitive awareness.

124 See n. 113. This is similar to the Sautrāntikas' idea that it is the mental stream (*citta-santāna*) as the stream of *citta* or vijñāna per se that insures the continuity of karmic potential, except during the absorption of cessation.

125 AKBh *ad* V 1d–2a (p. 74, above); AKBh and Vyākhyā *ad* II 36d (Shastri: 219; see n. 95); AKBh IX (*phalotpādana-samarthaḥ*). The elusive concept of "force, power" is to be met with throughout Vasubandhu's Yogācāra works, including his commentary on the *Mahāyāna-saṃgraha*.

126 In fact, the definition of *santati-pariṇāma-viśeṣa* examined above follows immediately upon an explanation of the karmic process in terms of seeds, flowers, and fruits. Also, AKBh III 19a–d; Shastri: 433–4; Poussin: 57–9: "The stream (*santāna*) grows and increases by *kleśa* and karma" (*vṛddaḥ santānaḥ kleśakarmabhiḥ*).

127 The category that "possession" (*prāpti*) belongs to, *saṃskārā* dissociated from mind (*citta-viprayukta-saṃskāra*), is an obvious exception to this. The issue here is not so much the difficulty these systems have in accounting for mental continuities that do not overtly affect the ongoing processes of mind, but rather what is the most parsimonious model for describing these continuities which is at the same time fully consistent with the insights and innovations of dharmic discourse.

128 Terms which Conze sardonically characterizes as "pseudo-permanencies" and "pseudo-selves" (1973: 132, 138).

129 Defined earlier in the same work by Nyanaponika Thera himself as "the systematisation of the ... Sutta doctrines in strictly philosophical (*paramattha*) or truly realistic (*yathā-bhūta*) language that as far as possible employs terms of a function or process without any of the conventional (*vohāra*) and unrealistic concepts assuming a personality, an agent (as different from the act), a soul or a substance. ... In the Abhidhamma, this Sutta terminology is turned into correct functional forms of thought, which accord with the true 'impersonal' and everchanging nature of actuality; and in that strict, or highest, sense (*paramattha*) the main tenets of the Dhamma are explained" (Nyanaponika, 1976: 3, 5).

130 As Piatigorsky cautions: "the Abhidharma does not deal with what is non-conscious, because the Abhidhamma is a 'theory of consciousness,' and the rest simply does not exist in the sense of the Abhidhamma" (1984: 202, n. 17).

131 Vijñāna is just a conventional name for the mental stream in AKBh IX (n. 97).

3 THE ĀLAYA-VIJÑĀNA IN THE EARLY TRADITION

1 Painting in such broad strokes, we forgo a more detailed investigation into the exact origins of both the term "*ālaya-vijñāna*" itself and each of its discrete attributes and synonyms. These questions have already been addressed with prodigious rigor and acumen by Lambert Schmithausen (1987) in his *Ālayavijñāna. On the Origin and the Early Development of a Central Concept of Yogācāra Philosophy*. Any study focusing on the specifics of its long, drawn-out development will have to contend with Schmithausen's reconstruction of this complex history and the imposing textual research supporting it. Our aims – to provide a general introduction to this development and the logic underlying it – complement rather than compete with these, and we have benefited immensely from his chronology, his philological reconstructions, and from other aspects of his monumental work.

2 Nor was this spirit limited to Buddhist thought, for many of the same concerns, even the same terms, are found in the roughly contemporaneous *Yogasūtras*. They were all

products of the classic, Gupta-era of Indian civilization. See for example, Eliade (1973)

3 Lamotte (Saṃdhi, 1935: 25) dates this *sūtra* from the second to third century CE.

4 We have drawn upon his reconstruction of the history and development of the ālaya-vijñāna for the basic chronological framework of our presentation. Our general account does not begin to suggest the difficulties involved in this: the multilingual textual exegesis (of texts that are often, if not usually, corrupt), the intertwined complexity of even the most basic terms, or the murky histories masking their interrelated development.

5 The account of the ālaya-vijñāna that follows is drawn from numerous texts, developed over a number of centuries. In order to avoid the redundancy found in the original materials, we will generally discuss the characteristics of the ālaya-vijñāna in connection with the text in which they first play a prominent role, relegating later developments and other sundry matters to the endnotes.

6 Our modern understanding of the processes of historical development, not inconsistent with the principles of dependent arising, recognizes that most texts underwent extensive periods of gestation, evolution, and compilation before reaching their present state, which is itself often just one of several versions. Schmithausen, amongst other scholars, has therefore attempted to stratify this text based primarily upon its doctrinal content. He finds (1987: 12–14) that there are pre-ālaya-vijñāna sections, such as the *Bodhisattvabhūmi* and parts of the Basic Section (the *Saptadaśabhūmika*), sections that only sporadically refer to the ālaya-vijñāna, and others, such as the *Viniścaya-saṃgrahaṇī*, that describe the ālaya-vijñāna in considerable detail, quoting, for example, from the *Saṃdhinirmocana Sūtra*.

7 Schmithausen: "When [a person] has entered [Absorption into] Cessation (*nirodha(samāpatti)*), his mind and mental [factors] have ceased; how, then, it is that [his] mind (*vijñāna*) has not withdrawn from [his] body? – [Answer: No problem;] for [in] his [case] *ālaya-vijñāna* has *not* ceased [to be present] in the material sense-faculties, which are unimpaired: [ālaya-vijñāna] which comprises (/possesses/has received) the Seeds of the forthcoming [forms of] mind (*pravṛttivijñāna*), so that they are bound to re-arise in future (i.e. after emerging from absorption)" (1987: 12, 18, n. 146). *Yogācārabhūmi* manuscript 78b5 (Y-T dzi 172a6–8; Y-C 340c27 ff.): *nirodhaṃ samāpannasya cittacaitasikā niruddhā bhavanti/kathaṃ vijñānaṃ kāyād anapakrāntaṃ bhavati/tasya hi rūpiṣv indriye* < *ṣv a* > *pariṇateṣu pravṛttivijñāna-bījaparigṛhītam ālaya-vijñānam anuparataṃ bhavati āyatyāṃ tadutpattidharmatāyai.*

8 *Ālaya* is a nominal form composed of the prefix *ā*, "near to, towards" with the verbal root *lī*, "to cling or press closely, stick or adhere to, to lie, recline, alight or settle upon, hide or cower down in, disappear, vanish" (SED 903; PED 109). See also Schmithausen (1987: 24; 275, n. 137; 294, nn. 202–3). See Saṃdhi V 3; *Karmasiddhiprakaraṇa*, para. 33; ASBh 11, 9; MSg I.3, I.11a.; TrBh 18, 24–6; Siddhi 92.

9 Pāli texts: S III 143, M I 296 (see Ch. 1, n. 28). This also parallels doctrines in the *Kośa*, as we saw above (Ch. 2, n. 98). See also Schmithausen (1987: 20 f., n. 165).

10 The Sautrāntika position, we remember (Ch. 2, n. 111), was that of reciprocal causality: "Two dharmas are the seed of one another *(anyonyabījaka)*: these two *dharmas* are the *citta* and the body together with it material organs" (AKBh *ad* II 44d; Shastri: 246; Poussin: 212).

11 This is a exceedingly abbreviated and oversimplified account of the complex issues, and even more complex textual evidence, involved. For more detail, see Schmithausen (1987: 18–33).

12 For historical and textual information concerning this *Sūtra*, see Lamotte's comments accompanying his translation (Saṃdhi, 1935: 7–29). There are, in addition to Lamotte's French, two English translations of the *Sūtra*: Keenan (2000) and Powers (1995).

13 Saṃdhi, V.2 (*sa bon thams cad pa'i sems rnam par smin cing 'jug la rgyas shing 'phel ba dang yangs par 'gyur ro*). Sanskrit reconstruction by Schmithausen (1987: 356, n. 508): *(*sarvabījakaṃ cittaṃ*) *vipacyate saṃmūrcchati vṛddhiṃ virūḍhiṃ vipulatām āpadyate*. This closely parallels passages found in Pāli texts examined above (p. 26), S III 54, D III 228: *viññāṇaṃ ... vuddhiṃ virūḷhiṃ vepullam āpajjeyya*. Also noted above, this expression is used in an analogy between seeds and vijñāna in S III 54. The term *sarvabījakaṃ cittam* is used in one of the "etymological" explanations for the ālaya-vijñāna in MSg I.2: "The consciousness (*vijñāna*) containing all the seeds is the receptacle (*ālaya*) of all dharmas. Therefore it is called the ālaya-vijñāna." See also ASBh: 11.

14 Saṃdhi, V.2 (*'gro ba drug gi 'khor ba 'di na sems can gang dang gang dag sems can gyi ris gang dang gang du '... mngal nas skye ba ... 'i skye gnas su lus mngon par 'grub cing 'byung bar 'gyur ba der dang por 'di ltar len pa rnam pa gnyis po rten dang bcas pa'i dbang po gzugs can len pa dang/mtshan ma dang ming dang rnam par rtog pa la tha snyad 'dogs pa'i spros pa'i bag chags len pa la rten nas/sa bon thams cad pa'i sems rnam par smin cing 'jug la rgyas shing 'phel ba dang yangs par 'gyur ro//de la gzugs can gyi khams na ni len pa gnyi ga yod la/gzugs can ma yin pa'i khams na ni len pa gnyis su med do*).

The first appropriation, that of the material sense-faculties, is not present in the Formless Realm because no material forms exist in this realm. Schmithausen points out that "accepting the presence of *ālaya-vijñāna* in *ārūpyadhātu* ... inevitably implies that *ālaya-vijñāna* has to transcend its original character of mind sticking or hiding in corporeal matter, which is also the rationale of its name" (1987: 48).

This paragraph is paralleled in the *Pravṛtti Portion* ((I.b)A.1) of the *Yogācārabhūmi* and the TrBh 19.7f., 18f., where it is styled the "inner appropriation" (*adhyātman upādānam*).

15 *Vāsanā*, "perfumations, traces," or as I have translated it more technically, "impression," has a long history in Indian and Buddhist literature. The PED defines *vāsanā* as "that which remains in the mind, tendencies of the past, impression, usually as pubba-vāsanā former impression" (PED 610), raising questions, however, about its etymology. The PED connects the term to the verb *vāsa*, derived from the root *vas*, "to stay, abide, dwell, remain" (PED 604). Rhys-Davids, following the Pāli commentaries, derives it from a homophonous verb meaning "to perfume." Thus the past participle *vāsita*, derivable from either verb, conveys the sense of both "scented" and "made to be or live," and when used in the compound *vāsita-vāsanā* or *vāsanā-vāsita* means "one who is impressed with (or has retained) a former impression" (610). Such expressions as *vāsanāya vāsita-citta*, "a *citta* perfumed by the impressions" (which SnA 583 equates with *pubba-vāsanā*), are then somewhat ambiguous; the PED states, "if taken as *vāseti* [to perfume], then to be translated as 'scented, filled, permeated,' but preferably as *vaseti* [to dwell, remain]."

In Monier-Williams's SED, *vāsanā* is not categorized under the root *vās*, "to perfume or make fragrant, scent, incense, steep," with its participle *vāsita*, "infused, steeped, perfumed, scented," but rather under the verb *vāsa*, "staying, dwelling, remaining." As a psychological factor he defines it as "the impression of anything remaining unconsciously in the mind, the present consciousness of past perceptions, knowledge derived from memory," the participle *vāsita* then meaning "knowledge (especially derived from memory)" as well as "caused to dwell" (SED 947).

This term was used in the *Abhidharma-kośa* as nearly synonymous to seed; the Vyākhyā in fact equates them (*ad* AKBh II 36. *śakti bījaṃ vāsanā iti eka ayam arthaḥ*) (see Ch. 2, n. 95). The Vyākhyā elsewhere defines *vāsanā*: "And what is that called the impressions of the Disciple (*śrāvaka*)? That particular deed of previous afflicted action which is a special power in the mind (*citta*) to be the unaltered cause of [future] activities of body and speech is called 'impression' (*vāsanā*). The Bhadanta Anantavarma says that 'a special indeterminate *citta* is *vāsanā*'" (*ad* AKBh VII 32d;

Shastri: 1093; Poussin: 77: *kā punariyaṃ vāsanā nāma śrāvakāṇām? yo hi yatkleśacaritaḥ pūrvam tasya tatkṛtaḥ kāyavākceṣṭāvikāra-hetu-sāmarthyaviśeṣaś-citte vāsaneti ucyate/avyākṛtaś cittaviśeṣo vāsanā iti bhadantānantavarmā*). We will discuss its definition in the MSg.

The term is also used in Hindu Yoga literature in much the same sense. See Eliade (1973: esp. 36–46).

16 Based upon the Chinese renderings, Schmithausen (1987: 289f., n. 181, 183) suggests these verbs are derivatives of *lī* or *ālī*, either "*ālayana-pralayanatām*" or "*ālīyana-pralīyanatām*," "to dwell in and stick to, or be attached to," meaning that the ālaya-vijñāna "dwells in," and "sticks to" the body. He therefore interprets this passage as an "etymological" explanation along with the other two, focused on *ādāna-vijñāna* and *citta*. It is interesting that the important sense of *ālaya* as "receptacle" or "store" is absent here.

17 Saṃdhi, V.3 (*rnam par shes pa de ni len pa'i rnam par shes pa zhes kyang bya ste/'di ltar des lus 'di bzung zhing blangs pa'i phyir ro//kun gzhi rnam par shes pa zhes kyang bya ste/ 'di ltar de lus 'di la grub pa dang bde ba gcig pa'i don gyis kun tu sbyor ba dang rab tu sbyor bar byed pa'i phyir ro//sems zhes kyang bya ste/'di ltar de ni gzugs dang sgra dang dri dang ro dang reg bya dang chos [rnams kyis] kun tu bsags pa dang nye bar bsags yin pa'i phyir ro*) (Emendation by Lamotte).

The "folk etymology" of the last verse is based upon the similarity between the term *citta*, "thought, mind," derived from the verbal root, *cit*, "to observe, understand, think," (with possible derivatives such as *citra*, "variegated, different, distinguished"), and the terms *ācita* and *cita*, derived from the verbal roots *ci* and *āci*, "to accumulate, to heap up." This explanation of *citta* has older models, for example, A V 107: *sañña* (S. *saṃjñā*) is accumulated, *paricita* in *citta*. It is also found in the *Abhidharma-kośa* (AKBh *ad* II 34a): "It is *citta* because it accumulates ... because it is heaped up with pure and impure elements" (*cinoti iti cittam ... citaṃ śubhāśubhair dhātubhir iti cittam*). Yaśomitra adds that the Sautrāntikas or the Yogācāras consider it *citta* because it is imbued with the impressions (*vāsanā*) (Vyākhyā 208: *vāsanāsanniveśayogena sautrāntikamatena, yogācāramatena vā*). Also AKBh I 16a; MSg I.6, 9; TrBh 3.2. Pāli passages touching on *citta, mano* and *vijñāna* include: D I 21; S II 95; *Visuddhimagga*, 452.

18 Schmithausen gives an excellent and succinct definition of *nimitta* here in relation to the rest of this formidable formulation: "In this context: objective phenomena as they are experienced or imagined, admitting of being associated with names, and being (co-)conditioned by subjective conceptual activity (*vikalpa*), which has become habitual so that it permeates all (ordinary) perceptions and cognitions" (1987: 357, n. 511).

19 Saṃdhi, VIII.37.1.1. Sanskrit reconstruction by Schmithausen (1987: 385, n. 629) based upon the Chinese (Hsüan Tsang, T.676.702b25, and Bodhiruci, T.675.679a26), and Tibetan versions (including the term *mi rig pa*), and consistent with TrBh 19.9, 3a (*asaṃviditaka-upādhi-sthāna-vijñaptikaṃ ca tat*).

20 Bareau (1955: 72) states that the Mahāsāṃghikas (Thesis #78) also posited a root-consciousness (*mūla-vijñāna*) said to be the support (*āśraya*) of the *pravṛtti-vijñānas* with which it occurs simultaneously.

21 A Sanskrit equivalent for much of this passage appears in a quote from this *sūtra* in TrBh 33.25–34.4.

22 According to some ancient traditions "animal or vegetable energy on this earth is after all little else than bottled sunshine" (Hocart, 1927, repr. 1969: 45), as quoted in Becker (1975: 54).

23 This view is understandable in terms of the evolutionary development of our own species-specific forms of mind. That is, the human race necessarily builds upon the species from which it descended, as well as upon its own gradual historical, cultural, and social developments. What is most distinctive about the Buddhist notion of the

evolution of mind is that individual mind-streams are seen to course from one lifetime to the next, whose changes or alternations accrued over time are transmitted by karmic potential, a seemingly Lamarkian notion.

24 Saṃdhi, V.7 (*ādānavijñāna gabhīrasūkṣmo ogho yathā vartati sarvabījo/bālāna eṣo mayi na prakāśi mā haiva ātmā parikalpayeyuḥ*). Also found in MSg I.4; *Karmasiddhiprakarana*, para. 32; TrBh 34; Siddhi, 173.

25 In the *Yogācārabhūmi*, the *Proof Portion* immediately precedes the *Pravṛtti* and *Nivṛtti Portions*. Although these latter portions are extant only in Tibetan and Chinese translation, a Sanskrit equivalent of the *Proof Portion* is still extant. For the specific textual details, see bibliography under *Ālaya Treatise*. The *Proof Portion* has been rather well studied. See Hakamaya (1978) for a Japanese translation, and Griffiths (1986: 129–38) for an English one. Sparham (1993) has recently translated a commentary on this portion of the text by Tsong-khapa. A critical edition and Japanese translation of the *Pravṛtti* and *Nivṛtti Portions* are found in Hakamaya (1979).

26 Consistent with the aims and methods of his major work, Schmithausen (1987: 194–6) has analyzed the eight arguments or "proofs" into four distinct strata based upon the conceptual development of the ālaya-vijñāna relative to other texts, specifically the *Basic Section* of the *Yogācārabhūmi*, the *Saṃdhinirmocana Sūtra*, and the latter portions of the *Ālaya Treatise*. The first strata comprises the "somatic functions" in Proofs #1 (appropriation of the basis), #6 (the multiplicity of bodily experience), #7 (the mindless, *ācittaka*, absorptions), and #8 (the gradual exiting of vijñāna from the body at death). These substantially agree with the conception of the ālaya-vijñāna found in the *Basic Section*, prior to the *Saṃdhinirmocana Sūtra*. Likewise for the second strata, consisting of Proof #4, the possibility of mutual seeding. In these sections, the continuity of the ālaya-vijñāna is "not expressly stated, but it is unequivocally presupposed" (1987: 45). The third layer, Proof #2 on simultaneous functioning of the forms of *pravṛtti-vijñāna*, and Proof #3 on clear functioning of *mano-vijñāna*, presupposes the *Saṃdhinirmocana Sūtra* and is "decisively advanced over the situation met with in *Basic Section*" (p. 196). The fourth layer consists of the fifth proof (#5), the various functions (*karma*) of cognition, where "the concept of the ālaya-vijñāna as an *actual perception* goes not only beyond the *Basic Section* of the Yogācārabhūmi but even beyond Saṃdhinirmocana Sūtra V and, as regards perception of one's corporeal basis, even beyond the Saṃdhinirmocana Sūtra as a whole. Hence, and also in view of the fact that it obviously presupposes the new *manas* … proof v represents rather a stage of development quite close to the *Pravṛtti Portion*" (1987: 196).

27 The later Theravādins articulate this relationship between *sankhārā* (*saṃskārā*) and viññāṇa with a concept remarkably similar in some ways to the ālaya-vijñāna: the *abhisankhāra-viññāṇa*. The PED (70) glosses *abhisankhāra* as "store, accumulation (of karma, merit or demerit), substratum," etc. and refers to C. Rhys-Davids's translation of *abhisankhāra-viññāṇa* as a "constructing, storing intellect" in *Dhammasangaṇi* (1974: 262). The notion of *abhisankhāra-viññāva* is also regularly used to gloss *bīja* in the Abhidhamma commentaries.

Collins (1982) describes the components and characteristics of this intriguing concept as follows: "The term *abhisaṃkhāra* denotes a karmically forceful, 'constructive' act, which determines a specific length of *saṃsāric* continuity … The idea of such constructions, such acts, as being conditions for the future occurrence of an appropriate form of consciousness, which is itself the 'dependently originated' condition for psycho-physical individuality … and so on, is expressed also by the use of the term 'construction-consciousness' (*abhisaṃkhāra-viññāṇa*) [p. 205] … The concept of *abhisaṃkhāra-viññāṇa*, then, refers to that consciousness which continues throughout *saṃsāra*, both constructing future temporal existence, and itself constituting the medium for the temporal reality thus constructed" (p. 208). Moreover, and further resembling the ālaya-vijñāna, the concept of the *abhisaṃkhāra-viññāṇa* is also used to explain why the destruction and non-persistence of viññāṇa constitutes the "reversal and cessation of *saṃsāra*" (p. 207).

28 Or more precisely, according to Abhidharma doctrine, it is the mental factors with which these forms of cognitive awareness are associated that make them karmically qualified.

29 *Proof Portion*, 1a. (ASBh: 12. 2f.): "The ālaya-vijñāna has past saṃskāras as its cause, while the [forms of] arising cognitive awareness, visual, etc., have present conditions as their cause. As it is taught in detail: 'the [forms of] arising cognitive awareness come about due to the sense-faculties, the sense-objects and attention.' This is the first reason. (b) Moreover, the six groups of cognitive awareness are experienced as skillful or unskillful. This is the second reason. (c) Also, none of the kinds of the six groups of cognitive awareness are considered to be included in indeterminate resultant states. This is the third reason. (d) Also, the six groups of cognitive awareness occur each possessing a specific basis. Of these, it is not right to say that whatever [form of] cognitive awareness occurs with such and such a basis would appropriate only that [basis] while the remaining ones are unappropriated; nor is it right [that they are] appropriated, being without an [appropriating form of] cognitive awareness. This is the fourth reason. And there follows the fault of appropriating the basis again and again. For instance, sometimes a visual cognitive awareness occurs and sometimes it does not occur; similarly for the remaining [forms of cognitive awareness]. This is the fifth reason" (*kena kāraṇenāśrayopādānaṃ na yujyate/āha – pañcabhiḥ kāraṇaiḥ/tathāhi (a) ālayavijñānaṃ pūrvasaṃskārahetukam/cakṣurādipravṛttivijñānaṃ punar-vartamānapratyayahetukam/yathoktam-indriyaviṣayamanaskāravaśādvijñānānāṃ pravṛttirbhavatīti vistareṇa/idaṃ prathamaṃ kāraṇam/api ca (b) kuśalākuśalāḥ ṣaḍvijñānakāyā upalabhyante/idaṃ dvitīyaṃ kāraṇam/api ca (c) ṣaṇṇāṃ vijñānakāyānāṃ sā jātirnopalabhyate, yā 'vyākṛtavipākasaṃgṛhītā syāt/idaṃ tṛtīyaṃ kāraṇam/api ca (d) pratiniyatāśrayāḥ ṣaḍvijñānakāyāḥ pravartante, tatra yena yenāśrayeṇa yadvijñānaṃ pravartate tadeva tenopāttaṃ syādavaśiṣṭasyānupāttateti na yujyate, upāttatāpi na yujyate vijñānavirahitatayā/idaṃ caturthaṃ kāraṇam/api ca (e) punaḥ punarāśrayasyopādānadoṣaḥ prasajyate/tathāhi cakṣurvijñānamekadā pravartate ekadā na pravartate evamavaśiṣṭāni/ idaṃ pañcamaṃ kāraṇam*).

30 Though the text does not state this directly, the arguments assume the preeminence of dharmic discourse, in contrast with the "living" metaphor of seeds used in Theravādin Abhidhamma. (Collins, 1982: 224; Ch. 2, p. 84f., above).

31 MSg I.23 discusses this point in more detail (see p. 137f.).

32 *Proof Portion*, 4 (*kena kāraṇena bījatvaṃ na saṃbhavati ṣaṇṇāṃ vijñāna-kāyānām anyonyam/tathāhi kuśalānantaramakuśalam utpadyate, akuśalānantaraṃ kuśalam, tadubhayānantaramavyākṛtam, hīnadhātukānantaraṃ madhyadhātukam, madhyadhātukānantaraṃ praṇītadhātukam, evaṃ praṇītadhātukānantaraṃ yāvad dhīnadhātukam, sāsravānantaram anāsravam, anāsravānantaraṃ sāsravam, laukikānantaraṃ lokottaram, lokottarānantaraṃ laukikam/na ca teṣām tathā bījatvaṃ yujyate/dīrghakālasamucchinnāpi ca saṃtatiściren̄a kālena pravartate, tasmādapi na yujyate*).

33 See p. 29, above. As defined in *Abhidharma-kośa*, "the visual cognitive awareness is cognitively aware of blue, but not 'that it is blue;' the mental cognitive awareness is cognitively aware of blue, and cognitively aware 'that it is blue'" (AKBh *ad* III 30c–d: *cakṣurvijñānena nīlaṃ vijānāti, no tu nīlam; manovijñānena nīlaṃ vijānāti, nīlam iti ca vijānāti*).

34 *Proof Portion*, 3 (*kena kāraṇenāsatyāṃ yugapadvijñānapravṛttau manovijñānasya cakṣurādivijñāna sahānucarasya spaṣṭatvaṃ na saṃbhavati/tathāhi yasmin samaye 'tītamanubhūtaṃ viṣayaṃ samanusmarati tasmin samaye 'vispaṣṭo manovijñānapracāro bhavati na tu tathā vartamānaviṣayo manaḥpracāro 'vispaṣṭo bhavati/ato 'pi yugapatpravṛttirvā yujyate 'vispaṣṭatvaṃ vā manovijñānasya*).

35 *Proof Portion*, 2. [Initial functioning of the sense-faculties is impossible] "For what reason is initial functioning not possible? If anyone were to say 'If the ālaya-vijñāna exists, then there will be the simultaneous functioning of two [forms of] cognitive awareness,' one should reply, 'You imagine what is without error to be erroneous,' because actually (*eva*) two [forms of] cognitive awareness do function simultaneously. Why is that? Because it is incorrect that the cognitive awarenesses of one who simultaneously desires to see [etc.], up to desires to discern, occur one after the other from the beginning. Because in that case, the attention, the sense-faculties, and the sense-objects [of each respective form of cognitive awareness] would be indistinct" (*kena kāraṇenā 'dipravṛttisaṃbhavo na yujyate/sa cet kaścid vaded yady-ālayavijñānam asti tena dvayoḥ vijñānayoḥ yugapatpravṛttir bhaviṣyati/sa idaṃ syād vacanīyah – adoṣa eva bhavāndoṣasaṃjñī/tathāhi bhavatyeva dvayorvijñānayor yugapatpravṛttiḥ/tatkasya hetoḥ/ tathāhyekatyasya yugapaddraṣṭukāmasya yāvad vijñātukāmasyādita itaretaravijñānapravṛttir na yujyate/tathāhi tatra manaskāro 'pi nirviśiṣṭa indriyamapi viṣayo 'pi*).

6. [The impossibility of bodily experience] "For what reason is bodily experience not tenable if there were no ālaya-vijñāna? Because, for a certain person who is either thinking or deliberating, correctly or incorrectly, or whose mind is collected or uncollected, the bodily experience that arises in the body could not be manifold, of many kinds. But [they] are experienced [as manifold]. Because of this, too, there is an ālaya-vijñāna" (*kena kāraṇenāsatyālayavijñāne kāyiko 'nubhavo na yujyate/ tathāhyekatyasya yoniśo vā'yoniśo vā cintayato vā'nuvitarkayato vā samāhitacetaso vā 'samāhitacetaso vā ye kāye kāyānubhavā utpadyante 'nekavidhā bahunānāprakārāste na bhaveyur upalabhyante ca/tasmād apyastyālayavijñānam*).

36 See the latter part of n. 26, for Schmithausen's comments on this particular proof.

37 *Proof Portion*, 5 (*kena kāraṇenāsatyāṃ yugapadvijñānapravṛttau karma na saṃbhavati/ tathāhi samāsataś caturvidhaṃ karma – bhājanavijñaptir āśrayavijñaptir ahamitivijñaptir viṣayavijñaptiś ceti/etā vijñaptayaḥ kṣaṇe kṣaṇe yugapatpravartamānā upalabhyante/na caikasya vijñānasyaikasmin kṣaṇe idam evaṃrūpaṃ vyatibhinnaṃ karma yujyate*).

38 As in *pravṛtti-vijñāna*, the term *pravṛtti* is a multivalent term meaning "to come forth, manifest, issue, originate, occur, commence, arise, continue" (SED 693). No single English term seems to cover this same range of meaning. In this text *pravṛtti* has both the sense in which the ālaya-vijñāna arises in conjunction with certain objects, associated with certain mental factors, and so forth, as well as the sense that the ālaya-vijñāna continues throughout samsaric existence. This contrasts with the *Nivṛtti Portion* of the text, which describes its cessation, its disappearance.

39 *Pravṛtti Portion* (1.b)A.1. (refers to outline of the *Pravṛtti* and *Nivṛtti Portions* in appended translation). This expression bears comparison with the *Saṃdhinirmocana Sūtra*, V2: "predispositions towards profuse imaginings in terms of conventional usage of images, names and concepts" (*nimitta-nāma-vikalpa-vyavahāra-prapañca-vāsanā*). See also ASBh. 92.5 f. (*sarvadharma-nāma-abhiniveśa-vāsanā ālayavijñāne saṃniviṣṭā 'nādikālānusṛtā, ya 'sāv ucyate prapañca-vāsaneti*) (Schmithausen, 1987: 360, n. 532).

40 We are using "informed" in the sense of the process of something coming into form, as in "to give shape to, fashion, impart quality to."

41 *Pravṛtti Portion* (1.b) (2). There is a parallel Sanskrit passage referring to the two objective supports for the arising of the ālaya-vijñāna in the TrBh., 19.5 f. (*ālayavijñānaṃ dvidhā pravartate/adhyātmam upādānavijñaptito bahirdhā 'paricchinnākāra-bhājana-vijñaptitas' ca*).

42 *Pravṛtti Portion* (1.b)A.2. (*de la phyi rol gyi snod rnam pa yongs su ma bcad pa rnam par rig pa ni kun gzhi rnam par shes pa nang gi len pa'i dmigs pa gang yin pa de nyid la brten nas/rtag tu rgyun mi 'chad par 'jig rten dang snod kyi rgyun rnam par rig pa ste*).

43 *Pravṛtti Portion* (1.b)B.2. (*dmigs pa de ni rtag tu yod pa yin te/lan 'ga' gzhan du 'gyur la/lan 'ga' gzhan du 'gyur ba ma yin no* ... (1.b)B.3. *kun gzhi rnam par shes pa de ni dmigs pa*

la skad cig pa yin par blta bar bya ste/skad cig pa'i rgyun gyi rgyud kyis 'jug pa yin gyi/gcig pa nyid ni ma yin no). Hsüan Tsang reads "neither unitary nor eternal" (*fei i fei chang*) for *skad cig pa'i rgyun gyi rgyud kyis 'jug pa yin*. Hakamaya (1979: 55) has reconstructed this last phrase: *kṣaṇika-srotaḥ-santāna-vartin*.

This telling statement should dispel, at least for the classical Yogācāra treatises our study focuses upon, all temptation to interpret the ālaya-vijñāna as a reified entity or surrogate "self" smuggled in from non-Buddhist quarters. Such an interpretation ignores the larger framework of dependent arising within which most Indian Buddhist thinking about mind and mental processes takes place – the very framework that ought to most inform our interpretation of its basic terms. This is why we have emphasized the early Buddhist background and contemporaneous Abhidharma context of the ālaya-vijñāna so strongly. There are distinctive and innovative features of the ālaya-vijñāna, to be sure, but, in these texts at least, it overwhelmingly falls within widely accepted understandings and definitions of vijñāna. Such an interpretation, moreover, is overtly contradicted by passages, such as these, which explicitly state that the ālaya-vijñāna "is not unitary" (*ekatva*) and only arises in dependence upon a variety of objective supports (i.e. *saṃskārā* and *ālambana*). This is why we find it more edifying to interpret the ālaya-vijñāna as a conceptual rubric for those dimensions of mental processes – most of which are also associated with the category of vijñāna in other schools of Indian Buddhism – which were not readily expressible in the Abhidharmic terms of analysis of overt cognitive processes.

44 *Pravṛtti Portion* (1.b)A.3 (*'di lta ste/dper na mar me 'bar ba ni snying po dang snum gyi rgyus ni nang du 'jug par 'gyur la/phyi rol du ni 'od 'byung bar byed pa bzhin du nang gi len pa'i dmigs pa dang/phyi rol gyi dmigs pa 'di la yang kun gzhi rnam par shes pa'i tshul de dang 'dra bar lta bar bya'o*).

45 We remember that *upādāna* also means "fuel, supply, substratum by means of which an active process is kept alive or going" (PED 149). See p. 32.

46 *Pravṛtti Portion* (1.b)A.2. Another passage in a key Yogācāra text states that the object is "unperceived" (*asaṃvidita*) because it is not perceived like knowing "it is that, it is here" (TrBh 19.14–15: *so 'sminn idaṃ taditi pratisaṃvedanākāreṇāsaṃvidita ityatas tad asaṃviditakopādi iti ucyate*). Also ASBh 21.9f. (*asaṃviditavijñaptiḥ bhājanavijñaptiḥ, sarvakālamaparicchinnākāratvāt*).

Schmithausen (1987: 391, nn. 634, 637) suggests translating the expression *aparicchinnākāra* as "in an uninterrupted (and/or indistinct, not clearly delimited) form", in order to reconcile both nuances of this ambiguous and variously interpreted term. See his extensive note on *aparicchinna* (1987: 389f.). Also Hakamaya (1979: 71, nn. 6, 7.), and Saṃdhi, VIII.37.1.

47 *Pravṛtti Portion* (1.b)B.1 (*dmigs pa de ni 'jig rten gyi mkhas pa rnams kyis kyang yongs su gcad par dga' ba'i phyir phra ba yin no*). Moreover, those who have not attained the path of seeing cannot understand the ālaya-vijñāna. (5.b)B.2: (*bden pa ma mthong ba bden pa rnams la mig ma thob pas ni kun gzhi rnam par shes pa sa bon thams cad pa yang rtogs par mi nus pa'i phyir ro*).

48 For example, while the Yogācārins held that these five "omnipresent" (*sarvatraga*) processes operated at every moment of mind, the Theravādins reckoned there were two additional ones, individuality of object (*ekaggatā*) and life faculty (*jīvitindriya*), while the Sarvāstivādins included an additional five – desire, discernment, discriminatory awareness, recollection or mindfulness, determination, and concentration (*chanda, mati, prajñā, smṛti, adhimokṣa, samādhi*) – resulting in ten processes operating in each mind-moment.

Furthermore, the Sarvāstivādins posited ten skillful mental factors in every skillful mind-moment, the Yogācārins eleven, and the Theravādins nineteen. In unskillful mind-moments, the Sarvāstivādins figure that mind (*citta*), when conjoined with ignorance (*avidyā*) and false views (*dṛṣṭi*), is also conjoined with six factors that universally occur with the afflictions (*kleśa-mahābhūmikā*), two universal unskillful dharmas (*akuśala-mahābhūmikā*), and reflection and investigation (*vitarka, vicara*). A further category of unskillful states is made when *citta* is conjoined with one of the four afflictions (*kleśa*) or ten secondary afflictions. The Theravādins simply list fourteen dharmas that accompany unskillful states, while the Yogācārins list the primary and secondary afflictions (*kleśa, upakleśa*) in place of the Sarvāstivādin category of the factors that universally occur with the afflictions (*kleśa-mahābhūmikā*). AKBh *ad* II 24–9; Shastri: 186–98; Poussin: 149–68; Hirakawa, 1973: Vol. I. pp. xii–xxiv; *Compendium*, 94–110; Chaudhuri, 1983: 105–8.

49 Functioning in regard to a similar object, we remember, is one of the criteria of being "associated" (*saṃprayukta*) in the *Abhidharma-kośa*, which contrasts with merely arising simultaneously (*sahabhāva*). See Ch. 2, n. 35.

50 *Pravṛtti Portion* (4.b)B.1 (*de ltar na kun gzhi rnam par shes pa ni 'jug pa'i rnam par shes pa rnam dang yang lhan cig 'byung zhing 'jug go//glo bur gyi tshor ba rnams dang/glo bur gyi chos dge ba dang/mi dge ba dang/lung du ma bstan pa rnams dang yang lhan cig 'byung zhing 'jug ste/de ni de dag dang mtshungs par ldan pa yin par ni mi brjod do//de ci'i phyir zhe na/dmigs pa mi mtshungs pa la 'jug pa'i phyir te*).

51 See *Proof Portion*, 2 (n. 35). Also, the *Karmasiddhiprakaraṇa* (paras. 38–9) explicitly defends the idea of two distinct types of mental stream within a single individual on the grounds that the two occur inseparably as cause and effect and because the stream of the resultant consciousness (*vipāka-vijñāna*) is infused (*paribhāvita*) by the forms of manifest cognitive awareness (*'o na de lta na ni rnam par shes pa'i rgyun rnam par smin pa'i rnam par shes pa dang/gzhan dang gnyis cig car 'byung bar 'gyur ro zhe na/de lta yin na ci nyes / . . . de gnyis ni rgyu dang 'bras bu'i dngos po dang tha dad pa ma yin par 'jug pa nyid kyi phyir dang/rnam par smin pa'i rnam par shes pa'i rgyud la cig shos kyis kyang yongs su sgo bar byed pa'i phyir ro*).

52 AKBh *ad* II 53 (*anyonyaphalārthena sahabhūhetuḥ*). See Ch. 2, n. 34. ASBh (37.6f.) states that the simultaneous or concomitant cause is the necessary concomitance of anything, specifically of *citta* and *caitta*, which cannot exist separately (*sahāyanaiyam yena sahabhūhetur vyavasthāpitaḥ/bhūtāni bhautikaṃ ca ity udāharaṇamātram etad veditavyam, cittacaitasikānām anyonyam avinābhāva niyamāt*).

53 What has been said about psychoanalytic divisions of mind applies equally well here: "The reader should bear in mind that there are no sharp boundaries between the three systems. Just because they have different names does not mean that they are separate entities. The names, id, ego, and superego, actually signify nothing in themselves. They are merely a shorthand way of designating different processes, functions, mechanisms, and dynamisms within the total personality" (Hall, 1954: 34f.).

54 This merely makes explicit what had long been implicit: that in order for the modes of manifest cognitive awareness to occur at all, their material sense faculties have to be continuously "appropriated," a function, the *Proof Portion*, 1d (n. 29) argued, that could only be accomplished by a form of mind that both pervades the entire body, and hence subserves all the sense-faculties, and that arises continuously and without interruption from the moment of conception until the time of death.

55 *Pravṛtti Portion* (3.b)B.1 (*de la tshe 'di la sa bon yongs su brtas par byed pa ni/ji lta ji ltar kun gzhi rnam par shes pa la brten pa 'jug pa'i rnam par shes pa dge ba dang/mi dge ba dang/lung du ma bstan pa 'byung bar 'gyur ba de lta de ltar rang gi rten la rten de dang lhan cig skye ba dang 'gag pas bag chags sgo bar byed do//rgyu de dang rkyen des na 'jug pa'i rnam par shes pa rnams kyang phyir zhing phyir zhing dge ba la sogs pa'i dngos pos shin tu brtas pa dang/shin tu sbyangs pa dang/shin tu 'od gsal ba dag tu 'byung bar 'gyur ro*). Following Hakamaya's edited text (1979).

56 ASBh 11.9: "Increasing [or 'fattening'] their seeds when the aggregates, etc. are present is called 'impression'" (*skandhādīnāṃ samudācāre tadbījaparipuṣṭir vāsānā iti ucyate.*)

57 Except for the explicit idea of rebirth, there is nothing unusual, mysterious, or even necessarily profound, about this process. Character traits, dispositions, memory, mental and physical skills, etc. (not to mention the stages of normal growth and development) are all processes of learning that develop over extended periods of time, and in which one builds up a repertoire of subroutines which form the basis upon which further skills and habits are practiced and acquired. And all of these subsist, moreover, relatively independently of, though continuously conditioned by, the moment to moment processes of conscious perception.

58 *Pravṛtti Portion* (4.b)B.2. (*'di lta ste/dper na chu'i rgyun dang chu rlabs rnams lhan cig gi dngos pos 'jug par 'gal ba med pa dang/me long gi dkyil 'khor gsal ba dang/gzugs brnyan rnams lhan cig gi dngos pos 'jug par 'gal ba med pa de bzhin du kun gzhi rnam par shes pa la yang 'jug pa'i rnam par shes pa rnams lhan cig gi dngos pos 'jug par 'gal ba med par blta bar bya'o*).

59 S III 131 speaks of the "subtle remnant of the conceit 'I am,' of the desire 'I am,' of the disposition toward 'I am,' still not removed [from the Ariyan disciple]." A III 32 and M I 47 describe the final eradication of these tendencies in those who are liberated and have acquired perfect view. See pp. 36–9.

60 Hence, these latent afflictions (*anuśaya*) must be karmically indeterminate: "In the Desire Realm (*kāmadhātu*) the view of self-existence (*satkāyadṛṣṭi*) and holding to extreme views are, along with the ignorance that is associated with them, indeterminate. Why is that? Because [they] are not in contradiction with giving, etc.: Thinking 'I will be happy in the next life' one gives gifts and guards morality" (AKBh *ad* V 19; Shastri: 794; Poussin: 40: *kāmadhātau satkāyāntagrāhadṛṣṭī tatsamprayuktā cāvidyā avyākṛtāḥ/kiṃ kāraṇam ? dānādibhiraviruddhatvāt/'ahaṃ pretya sukhī bhaviṣyāmi' iti dānaṃ dadāti śīlaṃ rakṣati.... sahajā satkāyadṛṣṭiravyākṛtā*). The *Abhidharma-kośa* suggests that this is a doctrine of *pūrvācāryāḥ*, "former masters," a term which Yaśomitra explains is Vasubandhu's usual reference to doctrines associated with the Yogācārins (Poussin, Intro, LIX; Vyākhyā *ad* III 53, IV 162, VI 141).

61 See Ch. 2, n. 38, above.

62 Similarly, the *Yogācārabhūmi* states: "the innate (*sahaja*) view of self-existence in the Desire Realm is indeterminate, because it always arises again and again and because it is not a support for harm to self or others. That which is attachment through deliberation is unwholesome" (Derge #4038, Y Shi 110b3–4: *'dod pa na sbyod pa'i 'jig tshogs la lta ba lhan cig skyes pa gang yin pa de ni lung du ma bstan pa yin te/yang dang yang kun tu 'byung ba'i phyir dang/bdag dang gzhan la shin tu gnod pa'i gnas ma yin pa'i phyir ro/rtog pas mngon par zhen pa gang yin pa de ni mi dge ba yin no*). Y-C (621b9) also echoes the *Abhidharma-kośa*, cross-referenced in the previous note, to the effect that birds and beasts have an innate, as opposed to a deliberative, self-view.

The *Abhidharma-samuccaya*, just before quoting from a *Sūtra* (parallel to the Pāli text, S III 131), also mentions that the conceit "I am" is present even in those Arhats who have reached the Path of Seeing (ASBh 62.3 ff.: *yām adhiṣṭhāyotpannadarśanamārgasyāpy āryaśrāvakasyāsmimānaḥ samudācarati*; Schmithausen, 1987: 440, n. 931). See ibid.: 146 for further discussion of the relevant materials and issues surrounding the development of this new level of subliminal mind.

63 AKBh *ad* IV 55c–d (*vipākaḥ punar vedanāpradhānaḥ*). See Ch. 2, n. 67, above, and Pāli texts, A II 157 (Ch. 1, n. 39).

64 Feelings are resultant states in every Abhidharmic system. For example, the *Yogācārabhūmi* declares: "[All] other sensations[, especially those which are] pleasant (*sukha*) or painful (*duḥkha*), are to be regarded as [sprung from results] *vipākaja*" (Schmithausen, 1987: 335, n. 402; Y zi 225a1 f.; Y-C 665a3f).

Feeling states are one of the dharmas that accompany every moment of mind (*citta*) (n. 48, above), so they occur nearly continuously. This means that these results of maturation, represented by the seeds, are also coming to fruition in nearly every moment. We also saw in an early Pāli text (M I 293, p. 31, above) that feeling, apperception, and viññāṇa are virtually inseparable.

65 See MSg I.3, TrBh 18.24–6 for similar passages.

66 This set of explanations and synonyms of the ālaya-vijñāna appears immediately prior to the *Proof Portion* within the ASBh as well, which preserves the original Sanskrit text: "[What is the definition of the aggregate of vijñāna?] Increasing their seeds when the aggregates, etc. are present is called '*impression*' (*vāsanā*). [It] '*has all the seeds*' (*sarvabījakaṃ*) because it has the seeds for the arising of just those aggregates, etc. Because dharmas dwell (*ālīyante*) there as seeds, or because beings grasp [it] as a self, [it is] the '*ālaya*'*-vijñāna*. Because it is formed by past action (karma) [it is] the *vijñāna as a result of maturation* (*vipākavijñānam*). Because it takes up (or appropriates, *upādana*) personal existence (*ātmabhāva*) again and again in the reconnection at re-birth [it is] the *appropriating-vijñāna* (*ādana-vijñāna*). Furthermore, it is called *citta* because it has accumulated (*citta*) the impressions of all *dharmas*." (ASBh 11. 9–14; T 31.701a.23–b3; D. 4053. 9b4–6: *skandhādīnāṃ samudācāre tadbījaparipuṣṭir vāsanā iti ucyate/sarvabījakaṃ teṣām eva skandhādīnām utpattibījair yuktatvāt/ālīyante tasmin dharmā bījataḥ, sattvā vātmagrāheṇa iti ālaya-vijñānam/ pūrvakarmanirmitatvāt vipākavijñānam/punaḥ punaḥ pratisaṇdhibandhe ātmabhāvôpādānād ādānavijñānam/tatpunar etac cittam iti ucyate/sarvadharma vāsanācittatvāt*). The last phrase here, *vāsanā-citta*, is ambiguous. The verse passage in the *Abhidharmasamuccaya* upon which this text comments, reads *vāsanācitatam*. Based upon this and the readings of both Chinese (*chi chi*, T 31.701b2 f.) and Tibetan (*bsags pa*, D. 9b6.) we have translated this as "accumulated." See n. 17, for further discussion of the etymology of *citta*.

67 The Sanskrit term *manas* (Pāli *mano*) always implies somewhat of an intellectual process. Derived from the Sanskrit root *man*, "to think, believe, imagine, suppose, conjecture", *manas* is related to the Latin *mens*, "mind, reason, intellect", and ultimately to the English "mind, mentate," and "to mean" (PED 515, 520; SED 783). See Harvey (1995: 40) for a discussion of the strong relation between *manas* and the conceit (*māno*) "I am."

In early Pāli and Abhidharma Buddhist texts, *citta*, *vijñāna*, and *manas* were said to be synonymous, but different contexts of usage evinced difference ranges of meaning. For example, the *Kośa* states that: "*citta*, *mano* and *vijnana* have the same referent. Because it accumulates it is *citta*; because it thinks it is *manas*; because it distinguishes [objects] it is *vijñāna*. Because it is a mass of pure and impure elements it is *citta*; because it is a support (*āśraya*), it is *manas*; because it is supported it is *vijñāna*, [it is] nothing more. Thus *citta*, *manas*, and *vijñāna* have one referent" (AKBh II 34a; Poussin: 177; Shastri: 208: *cittaṃ mano 'tha vijñānamekārthaṃ cinotīti cittam/manuta iti manaḥ/vijānātīti vijñānam/citam* śubhāśubhairdhātubhiriti cittam/tadevāśrayabhūtaṃ manaḥ/āśritabhūtaṃ vijñānamityapare/yathā cittaṃ mano vijñānamityeko 'rthaḥ*). (Shastri's text reads *citaṃ* in both the root text and the Vyākhyā, supported by the Tibetan (*bsags pa*) and Paramātha's Chinese (*sho tseng ch'ang*). Poussin, however, quotes *citram* from the Vyākhyā, which also agrees with Hsüan Tsang's usual translation of *citra*: *chung chung* (T 29.21c21) (Schmithausen, 1987: 536, n. 1433).

Cf. also from the Pāli texts, D I 21, S II 95; the contemporaneous Theravādin work *Visuddhimagga*, 452; AKBh I 16a. For the Yogācārins, however, these three terms refer to three distinct dharmas: *citta* refers to the ālaya-vijñāna, which of course accumulates pure and impure dharmas in the form of seeds; *manas*, from the MSg on, refers to the *kliṣṭa-manas* (as well as an antecedent vijñāna as the support of a succeeding one, *ṣaṇṇāmapi vijñānakāyānāmanantaraniruddhaṃ*), while vijñāna itself refers to the traditional classification of six forms of sensory and mental cognitive awareness (*yadālambanavijñaptau pratyupasthitaṃ*) (Y 11.4–8). See also TrBh 3.2; MSg I.6 f. (Lamotte, 1973: 4; Nagao, 1982: 92).

68 AKBh *ad* I 39a–b (*ahaṃkāra sanniśrayatvāc cittam 'ātmā' ity upacaryate*) (Schmithausen, 1987: 55, n. 386).

69 *Pravṛtti Portion* (1.b)B.2 (*'on kyang dang po pa'i len pa'i skad cig la brten nas/ji srid 'tsho'i bar du rnam par rig pa ro gcig pas 'jug par 'gyur ro*). See Ch. 2, n. 119, above, on the *bhavaṅga-citta* in the *Visuddhimagga* (XIV 115), which is said to preserve throughout a single lifetime the character it takes on at birth.

70 *Pravṛtti Portion* (4.b)A.1.(a) (*ngar 'dzin pa dang/nga'o snyam pa'i nga rgyal dang/rlom pa'i rnam pa can gyi yid gang yin pa de ni sems yod pa dang/sems med pa'i gnas skabs dag na yang dus rtag tu kun gzhi rnam par shes pa dang lhan cig 'byung zhing 'jug ste/de ni kun gzhi rnam par shes pa la nga'o snyam pa dang/bdag go snyam du dmigs shing rlom pa'i rnam pa can yin no*). We follow Schmithausen (1987: 444) in taking **manyanā* as a verb related to *ahaṃkāra* and *asmimāna*, as is quite clear in Hsüan Tsang's text (T 30.580c3).

71 *Pravṛtti Portion* (4.b)B.4 (*gang sngar bstan pa'i yid gang yin pa de ni dus rtag tu kun gzhi rnam par shes pa dang lhan cig 'byung zhing 'jug ste/de ni yang dag par ma bcom gyi bar du dus rtag pa kho nar lhan cig skyes pa'i rang bzhin 'dra ba'i kun nas nyon mongs pa rnam pa bzhi po 'jig tshogs la lta ba'i kun nas nyon mongs pa dang/nga'o snyam pa'i nga rgyal gyi kun nas nyon mongs pa dang/bdag la chags pa'i kun nas nyon mongs pa dang/ma rig pa'i kun nas nyon mongs pa dang mtshungs par ldan pa yin par blta bar bya'o//kun nas nyon mongs pa rnam pa bzhi po de dag kyang mnyam par bzhag pa dang/mnyam par ma bzhag pa'i sa la dge ba la sogs pa dag la 'gal ba med par 'jug pa dang/bsgribs la lung du ma bstan pa yin par blta bar bya'o*).

72 S IV 69, "Mental-cognitive awareness arises conditioned by *mano* and *dhamma*" (*manañca paṭicca dhamme ca uppajjati manoviññāṇaṃ*). This traditional assignment (AKBh I 17a–b; Poussin: 31–2: "whichever of the six vijñānas that has immediately passed is the manas" *ṣaṇṇāṃ anantarātītaṃ vijñānaṃ yad dhi tan manaḥ*) is reiterated in Yogācārin texts relevant to the ālaya-vijñāna, as for instance Y 4.10–11 ("what is *manas?* It is any [form of] cognitive awareness which has passed away immediately [before, as for example] the visual cognitive awareness" *manaḥ katamat/ yaccakṣurvijñānasyānantarātītaṃ vijñānaṃ*) as well as, more exactly but in a slightly different context, in Y 58.14–15 ("the mano-vijñāna necessarily arises immediately after the five groups of cognitive awareness that have arisen within a single moment" *ekakṣaṇotpannānāṃ pañcānāṃ kāyavijñānānāmanantaraṃ manovijñāna-mavaśyamutpadyate*). Manas is also stated to be the immediately antecedent and homogeneous support (*manaḥ samanantarāśrayaḥ*) in Y 4.6.

73 In more technical terms, each of the sensory vijñānas has a specific sense-organ as its simultaneous support, which is also considered its predominant condition (*adhipati-pratyaya*). The traditional support of *mano-vijñāna* is *manas*, which here refers to the immediately antecedent support (*anantara-āśraya* or *anantara-pratyaya*). But many Abhidharma schools, including the Yogācārins, thought that the *mano-vijñāna* needs to have a simultaneous or co-existent support for itself as well. This led them to a variety of positions. The *Upanibandhana* mentions two theories, that either matter or a material substance located in the heart (*hṛdayastharūpavastu*, Lamotte, 1973: 19) serves as the support of the *mano-vijñāna*, positions identified with the Sautrāntikas and the Theravādins, respectively. For the Sarvāstivādins, however, there is no *manas* other than the antecedent moment of cognitive awareness (AKBh *ad* I 16 c–d; Poussin: 30–3). Lamotte (1973) gives copious references to theories of other schools. See also Bareau (1955: Ther, #220).

74 *Pravṛtti Portion* (4.b)A.2 (*yid kyi rnam par shes pa de ni yid la brten pa zhes bya ste/rgyu mtshan gi yid ma 'gags na rnam par rig pa'i 'ching ba mi 'grol la/'gags na ni de 'grol ba'i phyir ro*). We have drawn heavily here upon Schmithausen's (1987: nn. 1293–8)

lengthy discussion of this passage. A similar statement occurs in Y-T zi 190a2 (and Y-C 651c3 f.): "the manas is called the support (*āśraya) of mano-vijñāna because *discrimination (vikalpa) occurs in that way with that support*" [Emphasis added] (*gzhi des de ltar rnam par rtog pa 'jug pa nyid kyi phyir yid de ni yid kyi rnam par shes pa'i gnas zhes bya'o*). Text cited in Schmithausen (1987: 487).

75 For the so-called "identities" (*samatā*) linking mind (*citta*) and the mental factors, see Ch. 2, n. 35, above.

76 A few schools at least, according to Bareau (1955: 137 f., 188, 197), held that dharmas are entirely knowable (*jñeya*), perceptible (*vijñeya*) and comprehensible (*abhijñeya*) (Sarvāstivāda thesis #3, the later Mahīśāsaka thesis #3, and *Śāriputrābhidharmaśāstra* thesis #31).

77 This development from a basal consciousness in the *Saṃdhinirmocana Sūtra* to a full-fledged cognitive vijñāna in the *Pravṛtti Portion*, and then back to a more passive possessor of the seeds in the *Mahāyāna-saṃgraha* evinces interesting parallels with developments in Freud's conceptions of the unconscious. The unconscious was gradually distinguished from consciousness, which was equated more or less with the functions of ego; this became a "systematic" distinction. But then the ego was recognized to have unconscious aspects to it (or, to put it the other way around, unconscious had ego functions in it), at which point, the distinction between the "systems" of unconscious, preconscious, conscious were replaced by the concepts ego, id, and superego, all of which also had unconscious aspects to them. See Archard (1984: 18–36, particularly 33–6).

78 AKBh I.3; Pruden, 1988: 57: "Apart from the discernment of the dharmas, there is no means to extinguish the defilements . . . without the teaching of the Abhidharma, a disciple would be incapable of discerning the dharmas." See Ch. 2, n. 13, above.

79 *Pravṛtti Portion* (5.b)A.1 (*kun gzhi rnam par shes pa . . . sems can gyi 'jig rten 'grub pa'i rtsa ba yin te/dbang po rten dang bcas pa rnams dang/'jug pa'i rnam par shes pa rnam skyed par byed pa yin pa'i phyir ro*).

80 *Pravṛtti Portion* (5.b)A.4 (a) (*kun gzhi rnam par shes pa de nyid ni sa bon thams cad pa yin pa'i phyir . . .* (b) *ma 'ongs pa'i dus na sdug bsngal gyi bden pa skyed par byed pa dang/* (c) *da ltar gyi dus nyid na kun 'byung ba'i bden pa skyed par byed pa'ang yin no*).

81 *Pravṛtti Portion* (5.b)A (*kun gzhi rnam par shes pa ni/mdor na kun nas nyon mongs pa thams cad kyi rtsa ba yin no*); (5.b) C.2. (c) (*kun gzhi rnam par shes pa ni nyon mongs pa rnams kyi 'jug pa'i rgyu*).

82 *Pravṛtti Portion* (5.b) C.3 (*kun gzhi rnam par shes pa de'i spangs pa'i mtshan nyid ni de spangs ma thag tu len pa rnam pa gnyis spong ba dang/sprul pa lta bu'i lus kun tu gnas pa ste/phyi ma la sdug bsngal yang 'byung bar byed pa'i rgyu spangs pa'i phyir/phyi ma la yang 'byung bar byed pa'i len pa spong ba dang/tshe 'di la kun nas nyon mongs pa'i rgyu thams cad spangs pa'i phyir/tshe 'di kun nas nyon mongs pa'i gnas ngan len* thams cad spong ba dang/gnas ngan len thams cad dang bral zhing srog gi rkyen du gyur pa tsam kun tu gnas so*). *Schmithausen (1987: 366) emends *gnas ngan len* to *gnas len pa* following Chinese.

83 *Pravṛtti Portion* (5.b) B.1 (*de byung na de las gzhan pa 'jig rten pa'i dge ba'i rtsa ba rnams ni ches 'od gsal bar 'gyur zhing/des na de dag rang gi sa bon yons su bzung ba la ches mthu dang ldan pa dang sa bon yongs su brtas pas bsgrub pa la ches stobs dang ldan par 'gyur ro//sa bon de las dge ba'i chos de dag kyang ches 'od gsal bar 'grub pa dang/phyi ma la yang rnam par smin pa ches sdug pa dang/ches 'dod pa 'grub par 'gyur ro*).

84 These two types of bondage, the *nimitta-bandhana* and the *dauṣṭhulya-bandhana*, are said to be removed by calming (*śamatha*) and insight meditation (*vipaśyanā*) in Saṃdhi, VIII 32.

85 *Pravṛtti Portion* (5.b) C.1 (*kun gzhi rnam par shes pa ni 'du byed kyi rnam par spros par bsdus pa de dag thams cad kyi khams pa yin pa'i phyir/kun gzhi rnam par shes pa la gcig tu sdud pa dang/gcig tu spungs pa dang/gcig tu sogs par byed de/gcig tu bsags nas de bzhin nyid*

*la dmigs pa'i shes pas kun tu brten** *cing goms par byas pa'i rgyus gnas 'gyur bar byed do//gnas 'gyur ma thag tu kun gzhi rnam par shes pa spangs par brjod par bya ste/de spangs pa'i phyir kun nas nyon mongs pa thams cad kyang spangs par brjod par bya'o*). * Schmithausen (1987: 199) emends to *bsten* following Ch. *hsiu hsi*.

4 THE ĀLAYA-VIJÑĀNA IN THE *MAHĀYĀNA-SAṂGRAHA* 1. BRINGING IT ALL BACK HOME

1 The *Mahāyāna-saṃgraha* (MSg) is no longer extant in its original Sanskrit, but is preserved in Tibetan and Chinese translations. The Peking and Derge editions of the Tibetan texts are nearly identical. There are four Chinese translations, produced by Hsüan-tsang, Paramārtha, Buddhaśānta, and Dharmagupta over the course of several hundred years; discrepancies between these translations abound. For our English translations herein, we have depended primarily upon the Tibetan texts and Hsüan Tsang's Chinese. We have also relied heavily upon the two major commentaries, the *Mahāyāna-saṃgraha-bhāṣya* by Vasubandhu (Bh and bh, Chinese and Tibetan texts, respectively) and the *Upanibandhana* by Asvabhāva (U and u). A more obscure commentary, called the **Vivṛtagūḍhārtha-piṇḍavyākhyā* (VGPVy), available only in Tibetan and commenting upon only part of the first chapter, has also been referred to where relevant.

Our translations have also benefited throughout from Lamotte's (1973) and Nagao's (1982) translations into French and Japanese, as well as Schmithausen's indispensable opus. We have made explicit reference to these works, however, only when directly citing their commentary or notes. The Sanskrit terms in parentheses in the MSg are *all* reconstructions, so we have dispensed with the usual asterisk. In most cases I have utilized those of Lamotte, Nagao, or Schmithausen. See Bibliography for textual details concerning the MSg and its various commentaries and translations.

2 MSg I.1 (*anādikāliko dhātuḥ sarvadharmasamāśrayaḥ/tasmin sati gatiḥ sarvā nirvāṇādhigamo 'pi ca*). Sanskrit original in TrBh 37, except that the final *ca* is *vā*. This verse is also commented on in Siddhi, 169–72. See also MSg I.21.

3 Following Schmithausen (1987: 273, n. 136). Commented on in Siddhi, 172–3. Sanskrit reconstruction discussed in Hakamaya (1978a: 223 f.).

4 See Ch. 3, n. 8, above, for etymology and multiple senses of *ālaya*.

5 We have skipped over two subsections here (MSg I.11a, 13b), in which the text argues that the term *ālaya* which appears in many early Pāli texts should be interpreted as the *ālaya-vijñāna*. This discussion chiefly concerns what it is that is grasped as a "self," a topic which will be discussed further in connection with the *kliṣṭa-manas*, afflicted mentation.

6 This twofold interpretation of the series of dependent arising is found in many Abhidharma-era texts. For example, AKBh *ad* III 24d discusses dependent origination as both momentary (*kṣaṇikaḥ*), and diachronic, that is, referring to distinct temporal states (*āvasthikaḥ*). The *Madhyāntavibhāgaṭīkā* (ad MV I.9–11; D. #4032. 205a2 f.) by Sthiramati calls these the *pravṛtti-lakṣaṇa* and the *saṃkleśa-lakṣaṇa*, respectively, namely the momentary, simultaneous causality as found between the *ālaya-vijñāna* and the *pravṛtti-vijñānas*, and the temporal, sequential causality as depicted in the twelve-member series (Nagao, 1982: 149 f.).

7 The commentaries also refer to another *sūtra*, which corresponds to part of the *Mahānidāna-sutta*, the Great Discourse on Causation (D II 63), wherein the Buddha also describes the reciprocal interdependence between name-and-form and consciousness: "'I have said that *name-and-form is conditioned by consciousness* ... Were consciousness not to descend into the mother's womb, would name-and-form

coagulate therein?' 'It would not, Lord.' 'Were consciousness after having descended into the mother's womb, to become extinct, would name-and-form come to birth in this state of being?' 'It would not, Lord.' 'Were consciousness to be cut off in one still young, a youth or maiden, would name-and-form attain to growth, development, expansion?' 'It would not, Lord.' 'Therefore, Ananda, just this is the cause, the ground, the arising, the condition of name-and-form, namely, consciousness ... I have said that *consciousness is conditioned by name-and-form* ... Were consciousness to gain no support in name-and-form, would there then be manifested ... birth, old age, death and the arising of suffering?' 'There would not, Lord.' 'Therefore, Ananda, just this is the cause, the ground, the arising, the condition of consciousness, namely, name-and-form.'" (PTS, translation altered.)

The *Upanibandhana* (U 393a29–b9; u 259b2–7) comments on these points as follows: "Regarding [the text:] 'vijñāna and name-and-form (*nāma-rūpa*) which function through mutually supporting each other (*anyonyaniśrayayogena*) like a sheaf of reeds (*naḍakalāpa*) would also not be possible without the resultant consciousness (*vipāka-vijñāna*),' the Buddha has said that 'name-and-form are conditioned by vijñāna' (*vijñānapratyayaṃ nāmarūpa*). Of these 'name' (*nāma*) is the four non-material aggregates (*skandha*). 'Form' is the embryo (*kalala*). The consciousness which is the condition (*pratyaya*) of these two, which succeeds one instant after the other and which is that very support (*āśraya*), is none other than the ālaya-vijñāna. If you maintain that 'name' refers to the [forms of] manifest cognitive awareness (*pravṛtti-vijñāna*), then what would be meant by 'vijñāna?' ... And the teaching (in D II 63) 'Were cognition to be cut off in one still young, a youth or maiden, would name-and-form attain to growth, development, expansion?' 'It would not, Lord,' would also not be reasonable if there were no ālaya-vijñāna."

8 The commentary on this verse in the *Madhyāntavibhāga-bhāṣya*, attributed to Vasubandhu, states: "Because the ālaya-vijñāna is the condition of the other [forms of] vijñāna it is the vijñāna-as-condition. The [forms of] arising cognitive awareness (*pravṛtti-vijñāna*) conditioned by it experience [phenomena]. Enjoying [refers to the mental factor of] feeling, discerning to apperception, stimulating to the karmic formations (*saṃskārā*) of vijñāna: intention, attention, etc." (MVBh *ad* I.9: *ālaya-vijñānam anyeṣāṃ vijñānānāṃ pratyayatvāt pratyaya-vijñānam/tat pratyayaṃ pravṛtti-vijñānam aupabhogikam/upabhogo vedanā/paricchedaḥ saṃjñā/prerakāḥ saṃskārā vijñānasya cetanā-manaskārādayaḥ*). MVBh (Nagao, 1964: 21); Stcherbatsky, 1977: 54; Anacker, 1984: 215.

9 MSg I.16: "the ālaya-vijñāna which is arisen in such a way that it has the special capacity for the [defiled dharmas] to arise (*utpādaśaktiviśeṣaka*) is called 'having all the seeds' (*sarvabījaka*)."

10 The commentary by Aśvabhāva, the *Upanibandhana*, states not only that the simultaneous relationship (*sahabhū-hetu*) pertains between the ālaya-vijñāna and the *pravṛtti-vijñānas* (388b5 f.), but also that the five causes (*hetu*) subsumed within the category of *hetu-pratyaya* are synonyms (*paryāya*) of the ālaya-vijñāna (U 250a1f.; u 388b3f.: *gang dag gis rgyu lnga ni rgyu'i rkyen to zhes smra ba de dag kyang rnam grangs kyis kun gzhi rnam par shes pa nyid du smra'o*). See Ch. 3, n. 52, for ASBh's definition of *sahabhū-hetu*, and Ch. 2, n. 34 for its sense in the *Abhidharma-kośa*.

11 Schmithausen refers to this requirement for simultaneity as the "central argument of the Mahāyāna-saṃgraha" (1987: 418, n. 784).

12 See Ch. 3, n. 15, for a discussion of the etymology and usage of *vāsanā*. It is often accompanied by the terms *bhāvanā* or *paribhāvita*, which we have translated in this context as "infusion" or "infusing," and "infused," respectively. See Ch. 2, n. 103, for its etymology and usage.

13 This is similar to Hall's remarks about the concepts used in Freudian analysis, the ego, id, and superego: "Just because they have different names does not mean that

they are separate entities ... They are merely a shorthand way of designating different processes, functions, mechanisms, and dynamisms within the total personality" (1961: 34f.).

14 AKBh *ad* II 36d: "What is called a 'seed?' Any psycho-physical organism (*nāma-rūpa*) that is capable of producing a fruit, either mediately or immediately, through a specific modification of the mental stream (*santati-pariṇāma-viśeṣāt*)." See Ch. 2, p. 73f., above for further discussion.

15 *Pace* the Theravāda position that karmic continuity "is simply a string of beads ... which have no underlying connecting thread, save the overall force of *karma* which creates them" (Collins, 1982: 248).

16 "Three distinctive aspects" refers to their respective supports (*āśraya*), objects (*ālambana*) and attention (*manaskāra*) directed thereto (Bh 330a7–9; bh 156b1–2).

17 Lamotte, 1935: 241; U 389b24; u 252a8–b3.

18 On the distinctiveness of the ālaya-vijñāna from the forms of *pravṛtti-vijñāna*, see *Proof Portion*, Proof 2; *Pravṛtti Portion* (4.b)B. 1; *Karmasiddhiprakaraṇa*, paras. 38–9.

This point is effectively made by Freud (1984: 430–3) in a discussion referring to a "Mystic Writing Pad," modern versions of which may still be found in toy shops. It typically consists of a cardboard base covered with an impressionable wax coating, over which lays a plastic sheet only attached at the top of the cardboard base. When one writes down on the plastic sheet with a stylus, an impression is dug into the underlying wax coating, making the plastic sheet adhere to it, which appears as marks or letters. These marks immediately disappear from the sheet when it is pulled away from the wax base, while the base still retains the impressions. Freud remarks: "Our mental apparatus ... has an unlimited receptive capacity for new perceptions and nevertheless lays down permanent – even though not unalterable – memory-traces of them ... Thus the Pad provides not only a receptive surface that can be used over and over again, like a slate, but also permanent traces of what has been written, like an ordinary paper pad: it solves the problem of combining the two functions *by dividing them between two separate but interrelated component parts or systems*." [Emphasis in original]. Having cited this, Harland comments: "The base can be compared to the unconscious mind, which retains what it does not perceive, and the paper (and celluloid) can be compared to the perception-consciousness system, which transmits what it does not retain" (1987: 142).

19 See L. L. Whyte, *The Unconscious before Freud* (1978), for similar conclusions about the relationship between a Cartesian "ego" and the various conceptions of unconscious mind which soon followed in European thought.

20 This question inaugurates the next section, MSg I.29–56, nearly the remainder of the first chapter, which present arguments for the existence of the ālaya-vijñāna, primarily by pointing out the inability of the model of six modes of cognitive awareness to account for this or that traditionally accepted function of vijñāna. As formal "proofs" this section bears comparison with the Proof Portion.

21 The defilements are threefold, according to the *Upanibandhana*, since they are made by the afflictions, by action, and by birth (i.e. result) (U 391a17f.; u 255a5: *kun nas nyon mongs pa rnam pa gsum ni nyon mongs pas byas pa dang/ las kyis byas pa dang skye bas byas pa'o*). See also TrBh *ad* v.11 (28.25); MVBh *ad* V.23–6 (71.4).

This threefold division of defilements is a common division in Buddhist schools, and is commonly correlated with the twelve members of the series of dependent arising, as in our Appendix I. See *Visuddhimagga*, 581 (672, para. 298); AKBh *ad* III 26a–b; Shastri: 442; Poussin: 68; MVBh 21.

22 U 392a12–16; u 257a2–5. The *Bhāṣya* adds that existence conditioned by appropriation (*upādānapratyayo bhava*) would also be impossible, since existence arises because the impressions within the vijñāna that is infused by the *saṃskārās* increase through the power of appropriation (*upādāna-bala*) (Bh 331b24–7; bh 159a4f.: *len*

pa'i rkyen gyis srid pa yang mi rung ste/gang gi phyir 'du byed kyis yongs su bsgos pa'i rnam par shes pa len pa'i dbang gyis bag chags rgyas pas srid pa 'byung bas so).

23 As the partial commentary, VGPVy, reminds us (P. 416a4: *skye ba'i kun nas nyon mongs pa ni rnam par smin pa'i mtshan nyid do*) (Nagao, 1982: 192, 196f.).

24 The Chinese translations, H and P, include a third reason here: "and because it would never be interrupted."

All these arguments rest upon systemic considerations: The *mano-vijñāna* must have both an object (*ālambana*) and support or basis (*āśraya*) for its defilements, the latter of which, in MSg I.6 as in *Pravṛtti Portion* ((4.b)A.2), is afflictive mentation (*kliṣṭa-manas*). In his commentary, Vasubandhu thus explains that this mental cognitive awareness is supported by the *manas* that is afflicted by the afflictions of desire (*rāga*), etc., since it arises with the process of birth as its object. As a resultant state, by contrast, the reconnecting mind (*pratisandhi-citta*) must always be indeterminate and thus cannot have an afflicted support (Bh 332a6f.; bh 159b4f.). See also Lamotte (1973: 57). Moreover, according to the other major commentary, a mental cognitive awareness always has a discernible object while this reconnecting vijñāna does not, and so it cannot be a moment of mental cognitive awareness (U 393a2f.; u 258b6f.).

25 This does not, however, tell us how the Yogācārins did conceive of the process of rebirth. A more detailed description is found in the *Yogācārabhūmi* (Y 24.1–10). This long passage, translated here by Schmithausen (1987: 127f.), graphically illustrates the Yogācāra understanding of the process of rebirth: "When in the parents who [have become more and more] impassioned [while making love] sexual passion reaches the [most] vehement state, finally viscid semen is discharged, and in the end [of this process] inevitably [a drop of fluid] comes forth in both of them, [viz.] a drop of semen [in the father] and [a drop of] blood [in the mother]. These two drops of both of them, [viz. the drop] of semen and [the drop] of blood, get mixed in the mother's womb and form a film, having become one single lump, just like boiled milk when cooling down [forms a film]. Into this [congealing mixture of blood and semen] merges that *ālaya-vijñāna* containing all Seeds, comprised in [the category of 'Result-of-]Maturation' and appropriating the basis [of personal existence]."

"How does it merge? Together with that lump of semen and blood which has formed a film, the [being of the] intermediate state, which has that [blood-and-semen] for its object [though] in a wrong way, ceases to exist. Simultaneously with its cessation, there arises, by virtue of that same mind containing all Seeds another lump of semen and blood, which is similar to the [preceding one but] is mixed with the gross elements of the subtle sense-faculties – which are different from the [gross elements that constitute blood-and-semen as such] – and is [already] furnished with [one] sense-faculty (and is thus a living body). At this stage one speaks of mind being [re-]established [in a new basis-of-existence], and of Linking up having taken place. This is the state of *kalala*."

In this connection, there is an interesting passage in the *Abhidharma-kośa* that is revealing of the Indian Buddhists' understanding of human psychology. They not only recognized that beings about to be born are attracted to the parent of the opposite sex, but that they also experience antipathy towards those of the same sex: "[The being of the intermediate existence] through a divine eye possessed by virtue of its karma looks on the place of its own birth seeing its parents in union. Regarding its father and mother contrarily, for a male being a masculine desire arises towards the mother; for a female being a feminine desire arises towards the father; they have antipathy for their opposites." (AKBh *ad* III 15a–b; Shastri: 426f.; Poussin: 50) (paraphrased from French).

26 See Ch. 2, n. 118, above, for the positions of the Sarvāstivādins, Sautrāntikas, and Theravādins, on the exact type of mind that reconnects at rebirth.

27 The *Upanibandhana* states that it is the resultant consciousness (*vipāka-vijñāna*) that unites in the mother's womb with the semen and blood to form the initial stage of an embryo, uniting with it in a common destiny (*ekayogakṣema*) (U 392c1 f.; u 257b7). The ASBh agrees with the MSg here, stating that the last moment of the intermediate state (*antarābhava*) is always afflicted (*kliṣṭa*) while the first moment of the rebirth is a resultant (*vipāka*) state (ASBh 39.19–40.3). The Yogācārin position is complex due in large part to the many contradictory passages reflecting the developmental history of these systems (see Schmithausen, 1987: 307f., nn. 256, 259, 266).

28 MSg I.34.3: "If you assert that the coagulated consciousness is a mental-cognitive awareness, then either that coagulated mental-cognitive awareness is what possesses all the seeds (*sarvabījaka*), or it is another mental-cognitive awareness which arises supported by that [first cognitive awareness] that possesses all the seeds. If it is the coagulated consciousness which possesses all the seeds, then the so-called 'mental-cognitive awareness' is just the ālaya-vijñāna established as a synonymous term."

29 According to the *Upanibandhana* (U 391b14 f.; u 255b3 f.) this last point reproduces the debates between the Sarvāstivādins and Sautrāntikas over the way in which the maturation of karma works. See Ch. 2, p. 73f., for further discussion.

30 The *Upanibandhana* (U 391b23 f.; u 255b7 f.) explains that since desire (*rāga*) is a *caitta*, a mental factor, it rests upon the corresponding form of cognitive awareness. Although that which is supported (*āśrita*) can infuse that which supports it (*āśraya*), the opposite is not possible. See n. 39, below, for the inseparability of *citta* and *caitta*.

Nagao (1982: 181) reads this argument somewhat differently: "Nor is it possible, when a visual consciousness arises simultaneously with desire, etc., for (that visual consciousness) to [do the] infusing. (And as long as the visual consciousness is not infusing, it is all the more impossible that a defiled visual consciousness could arise from it later.) In the first place, (2) (the visual consciousness) does not (infuse the seeds) into the desire (*rāga*), (since it is consciousness itself that is infused, not the other way around,) because it is desire which depends upon (*āśritatva*) that (consciousness), and because (desire) is not stable (*adhruvatva*)."

31 This reflects arguments in *Proof Portion*, #1.d., as well as MSg I.23.

32 We follow the *Bhāṣya* here, which states that two forms of visual cognitive awareness do not arise simultaneously (Bh 331a16 f.; bh 158a8: *rang gi dngos po la yang ma yin te zhes bya ba ni/mig gi rnam par shes pa la mig gi rnam par shes pa'i bag chags kyang ma yin te/mig gi rnam par shes pa gnyis 'byung ba ni med de/gnyis kyi ngo bo med pas na lhan cig 'byung ba dang 'gag pa med pa'i phyir ro*).

33 The *Upanibandhana* comments on the argument, stating that self-infusion would entail the fault of confusing (*saṃkara*) the object (*karma*), that is, the infused, and the act (*kāraka*), infusing (U 391b29 f.; u 256a5: *bsgo bar bya ba dang sgo bar byed pa las dang byed pa dag 'tshol ba'i skyon du 'gyur ba'i phyir ro*).

34 According to the *Upanibandhana*, the antidotal mind that counteracts the manifest afflictions (*kleśa-pratipakṣa-vijñāna*) occurs when the Aryan has gained the fruit of a stream-winner, which is the first moment in the Path of Seeing (*darśana-mārga*). However, the latent dispositions (*anuśaya*) remain even into the next stage on the path, the Path of Cultivation (*bhāvanā-mārga*). Where, the text asks, would the latent afflictions which are eliminated by the Path of Cultivation reside if there were no ālaya-vijñāna, especially considering that the antidotal mind cannot be connected with seeds of contradictory natures? (U 391c26–9; u 256b3–5). ASBh 62 also states that the view of self-existence is present even in Aryans and Disciples who have reached the Path of Seeing. See Ch. 3, n. 62, above.

35 *Pañcaskandha-prakaraṇa-vaibhāṣya*. (Tib. Peking #5567, Hi 52b3–6: *'khor ba'i rgyu ni las dang nyon mongs pa rnams so//de gnyis las kyang nyon mongs pa ni gtso bo ste/ … yang srid ba 'phangs pa'i las kyang nyon mongs pa med na yang srid pa 'byung bar mi*

'gyur te/ ... de ltar na gtso bo yin pa'i phyir nyon mongs nyid mngon par 'jug pa'i rtsa ba ste/). See AKBh *ad* V 1a (Ch. 2, p. 68; n. 66) for a similar view.

36 We follow Hsüan Tsang's Chinese text (T 31.1594.133c22) for the negative *fei*, "not present associated," in this last sentence, which makes more sense from the point of view of standard Abhidharma doctrine. In the Tibetan, however, both relationships are expressed in the positive: "it is present simultaneously *and* present associated" (D.4a5: *de'i phyir lhan cig 'byung bar kun tu 'byung ba dang/mtshungs par ldan par kun tu 'byung bas skyon 'di dag tu mi 'gyur ro*).

37 See Ch. 2, n. 35, the definition of *samprayukta* in Abhidharma traditions.

38 Bh 326a2–3; bh: 151b1 *ad* MSg I.7a. (*ji ltar sbyin ba la sogs pa dge ba'i sems 'byung bar 'gyur/de dang mtshungs par ldan pa las te*). This passage actually comments on ignorance unaccompanied by other afflictions (*avidyā-āveṇekī*), but the point applies equally here since they all arise in every moment.

39 The inseparability of *citta* and *caitta* (mental factors) is a common theme in Abhidharma-style literature. Vyākhyā *ad* AKBh II 23a; Shastri: 185: *cittacaittāḥ sahāvaśyaṃ iti/na cittaṃ caittair vinā utpadyate, nāpi caittā vinā cittenetyavadhāryate*; ASBh 37,6f.: *cittacaitasikānām anyonyam avinābhāva niyamāt*. And Vasubandhu's Bhāṣya on MSg *ad* I.53.1 (Bh 335b11–13; bh 165b3–5): "'Because it is not possible to separate the supported from the support.' The support (*āśraya*) is the *citta*. The supported (*āśrita*) are the *caitta*. The support and the supported, that is, the *citta* and the *caitta*, have since beginningless samsara been mutually inseparable, since they mutually attract each other."

40 As well as, in the Yogācāra tradition (*Pravṛtti Portion* (I.3.b)A.2.a), the ālaya-vijñāna, which indirectly provides the support (*āśraya-kara*) for the sensory cognitive awarenesses by appropriating (*upādāna*) their direct supports, the material sense-faculties.

41 See Bareau (1955 Ther, #220); AKBh *ad* I 16; and Lamotte (1973: 5*) for further references to various non-Mahāyāna viewpoints.

42 U 384c24–8; u 242b8–243a3. This is preceded by the comment: "Even skillful states giving, etc. are endowed with self-grasping, because one thinks 'I am practicing giving.' Self-grasping does not occur without ignorance. Since ignorance is a mental factor (*caitta*) too ..."

43 MSg I.7a.4–5. This question well illustrates the evolving nature of the concept of the ālaya-vijñāna. The *Pravṛtti Portion* (I.4.b) A.1.(a), mentioned *manas* in connection with the absorption of cessation, stating that the *manas* "always arises and functions simultaneously with ālaya-vijñāna in states with mental activity (*sacittaka*) and even in states lacking mental activity (*acittaka*)," which includes the attainment of cessation. A later part of the *Nivṛtti Portion* (II.2.a), however, describes those who still have the ālaya-vijñāna but lack the six *pravṛtti-vijñānas*, mentioning these two attainments as examples. As Schmithausen notes, (1987: 481, n.1232) this new *manas* seems not to have been fully incorporated into the Yogācāra system at this point, only reaching its full development in the MSg.

44 There is no Tibetan corresponding to this. Lamotte (1935: 194).

45 The differences between these two types of meditative states are explained in the AKBh *ad* II 44d. The attainment of non-apperception and of cessation occur at different levels of existence; the intentions (*prayoga*) prior to attaining them differ; the *santāna*, in this case the type of person, attaining them differ – an ordinary worldling attains the former, while only an Arhat attains the latter; the results from the meditation differ; and the possible locales for producing these states for the first time differ. What is common between them is the cessation of *citta* and *caitta* (AKBh II *ad* 44cd; Poussin: 210–12: *cittacaittanirodhasvabhāva*). See Griffiths (1986).

46 This closely corresponds to the Pāli text A I 87: *dve 'me bhikkhave paccayā sammādiṭṭhiyā uppādāya. katame dve? parato ca ghosa yoniso ca manasikāro. ime kho bhikkhave dve paccayā sammādiṭṭhiyā uppādāyā ti*. See also M I 294. A corresponding Sanskrit

sūtra is quoted in the Vyākhyā *ad* II 49 (Shastri: 278; Poussin: 245: *tathā hyuktaṃ bhagavatā – "dvau hetū dvau pratyayau samyagdṛṣṭerutpādāya/ katamau dvau? parataśca ghoṣo 'dhyātmaṃ ca yoniśoma[na]skāraḥ" iti*). See Nagao (1982: 218f.).

47 The Tibetan (D. 10a5) reads *bag chags su bsgos bar 'gyur*, an expression not found in any of the standard indexes; it is something like **vāsanā bhāvita*. Hsüan Tsang's Chinese (136b18) reads *wei hsün*, no doubt a verbal form of *bhāvita*.

48 We will not discuss sections I.50–5 concerning the attainment of cessation (*nirodha-samāpatti*), as this has already been discussed in relation to both the *Abhidharma-kośa* and the *Proof Portion*. Schmithausen (1987: 402, n. 710) points out that sections I.50–5 are not an "organic" part of the systematic organization which started at I.29 and actually ended at I.44, but is only formally concluded in I.56 without even mentioning *nirodha-samāpatti* (with sections I.45–9 being, in his analysis, a supplement from the point of view of supramundane purification).

49 As Schmithausen points out, the ālaya-vijñāna in this section is characterized as both "possessing" or "containing" the seeds, and "being" the seed, demonstrating that these two characterizations are "by no means felt to be contradictory" (1985: 156, n. 29).

50 *Anucita* literally means "unusual, unaccustomed, strange." We have translated it more freely here based upon both commentaries (Bh 333c12c; bh 162b5: "since it has not previously arisen;" *'jig rten las 'das pa'i sems ni ma 'dris pa ste zhes bya ba dang*/de ni sngar ma skyes pas; U 394b26f.: "the pure *citta* has not been previously attained").

51 A I 10. (*pabhassaram idaṃ* ... *cittaṃ taṃ ca kho āgantukehi upakkilesehi upakkiliṭṭhaṃ*). Nyanaponika, 1999: 36. See also Jaini, 1959: 249; Johansson, 1979: 102.

The term *āgantuka* is used in Yogācāra texts, particularly the *Mahāyāna-sūtrālaṅkāra* and the *Madhyānta-vibhāga*, in expressions such as *prakṛti-prabhāsvara-citta*, "a *citta* which is pure and luminous in its original nature." (MSA XIII, 19: *mataṃ ca cittaṃ prakṛti-prabhāsvaraṃ sadā tad āgantuka-doṣa-dūṣitaṃ/na dharmatā-cittam ṛte 'nya-cetasaḥ prabhāsvaratvaṃ prakṛtau vidhīyate*; MVBh. I.22.c–d: *prabhāsvaratvāc cittasya/kleśasyāgantukatvataḥ*).

Interestingly, the *Ālaya Treatise* ((I.4.b)B.1) also calls both the feelings and the various dharmas that arise simultaneously with the ālaya-vijñāna *āgantuka*, "adventitious." See Keenan (1982) for a lengthy discussion of this question in early Yogācāra.

52 Vyākhyā *ad* AKBh VII 30; Poussin: 72: "I see his extremely subtle seed of salvation like a seam of gold hidden in metal-bearing rock" (*mokṣa-bījam ahaṃ hy asya susūkṣmam upalakṣaye/dhātu-pāṣāṇa-vivare nilīnam iva kāñcanam*). Translation from Jaini (1959: 248).

53 *ad* Akbh II 36c–d; Shastri: 216; Poussin: 184. Jaini, 1959: 248. Although the *Kośa* does not indicate exactly how such seeds relate to the mental stream as a whole, Jaini (1959: 249) notes that "the theory of an innate, indestructible, and pure (*anāsrava*) element existing in the midst of destructible, phenomenal, and impure elements shows an affinity with the Mahāyāna doctrine of *prakṛti-prabhāsvara-citta*, according to which mind is essentially and originally pure but becomes impure by only adventitious afflictions."

54 The term *śruta*, literally "heard," has an unusually evocative meaning in Indian traditions where oral transmission of knowledge from teacher to pupil was, and is to this day, the usual method of transmitting "texts." Thus, *śruta* has the primary meaning of "heard, taught, mentioned, orally transmitted, famous, etc." and derived meanings such as "that which has been heard, oral tradition or revelation, sacred knowledge, learning or teaching, instruction, etc." (SED 1101). One who has heard much, *bahuśruta*, is "well learned, well versed."

The Bhāṣya (Bh 333c14–23; bh 162b6–163a2) gives a classic commentarial gloss of the expression "the seed of the impression of [the dharma] which has been heard, which is the outflow of the perfectly pure realm of dharma" (*suviśuddha-dharma-dhātu-niṣyanda-śruta-vāsanā-bīja*). The expression "completely pure" (*suviśuddha*), indicates the difference with the other two vehicles, that of the Disciple, etc, because it eliminates the two obstructions, the obstructions due to the afflictions (*kleśāvaraṇa*) and the obstructions to knowledge (*jñeyāvaraṇa*). The outflow of the completely pure *dharmadhātu* is the *dharma* which has been taught (*deśanādharma*), the *sūtras*, etc. Hearing the *sūtras*, etc., is "the outflow of the *dharmadhātu* which has been heard." The impression (*vāsanā*) of that is "the impression of what has been heard, the outflow of the *dharmadhātu*." The supramundane *citta* will arise from the cause which is the impression which remains within the ālaya-vijñāna. (The Chinese uses the expression "impression-series," *vāsanā-santāna*, in this last phrase.)

55 An alternative reading, based on the Tibetan, is: "when the impression of [the dharma] which has been heard arises depending on the *bodhi* of the Buddhas." This passage is problematic since the Chinese and the Tibetan translations, in both the root texts and the commentaries, diverge. The Tibetan texts read *brten nas*, usually "depending on." The Chinese versions read "until attaining" (*nai chih cheng te*, or *nai chih te*) (D. 10b5; H 30.136a8).

Nagao (1982: 224, n. 2) wonders if there may have been two different original texts. He also notes that both Paramārtha's translation of the Bhāṣya (T 31.173b21 ff.: "From what does the efficacy (**samartha*) of this hearing arise? It continues until reaching what stage?") and the VGPVy (432a3 f.) are asking what are, in effect, two different questions: from where or what does the impression of hearing arise, and what is its basis, its support?

Paramārtha's Bhāṣya replies: The teaching, which is the outflow of the completely pure *dharmadhātu*, is the origin of the impression from the dharma which has been heard. The basis, or support, of the *śruta-vāsanā* is the *santāna*, the mental-stream (T 31.173b21 ff.; Bh 334a8 f.; U 394c15f., u 262a2 f.: *gnas gang la zhes bya ba smos te/rgyud gang la 'jugs pa de*; VGPVy 432a4: *gnas gang la zhes bya ba ni sems can gyi rgyud gang la'o*).

56 And are thus themselves mundane (MSg I.48): "Although mundane (*laukika*) [it] is the seed of the supramundane *citta* (*lokottaracitta*) because [it] is the outflow of the supramundane and perfectly pure realm of dharma (*lokottara-suviśuddha-dharma-dhātu-niṣyanda*)."

57 After describing the various stages of attainment and the *aspects* of the ālaya-vijñāna that each has eliminated, MSg I.61 argues that: "Without this [characteristic of the ālaya-vijñāna being partially eliminated] the gradual cessation (*kramanivṛtti*) of the defilements (*saṃkleśa*) would be impossible." This also supports our interpretation of the ālaya-vijñāna as an aggregated class of functions or process rather than a singular entity.

58 Becoming without seeds means, according to the commentary, that all aspects of the seeds of the defilements (*saṃkleśa-bīja*) have been eliminated (U 395b10–12; u 263a3 f.: *sa bon thams cad pa yang sa bon med par 'gyur zhes bya ba la sogs pa ni sa bon gyi rnam pa thams cad spangs pa'i phyir te/kun nas nyon mongs pa'i sa bon thams cad med pa nyid 'di'i spangs par rig par bya'o*).

59 This argument occurs in Msg I.57b, the verse section supplementing sections I.29–56 which present the "proofs" of the ālaya-vijñāna due to defilement and purification, which are summarized in I.56.

60 U 397a10 f.; u 266a8 f. We have already seen a variation of this argument involving the persistence of the afflictions (MSg I.40): without the ālaya-vijñāna "when the antidote (*pratipakṣa*) is present, then since all of the counteracted (*vipakṣa*) [dharmas] have ceased, *nirvāṇa* without remainder (*nirupadhiśeṣanirvāṇa*) would be attained naturally and without effort."

5 THE ĀLAYA-VIJÑĀNA IN THE MAHĀYĀNA-SAṂGRAHA 2. LOOKING BEYOND

1 Ad MSg I.58 (U 397a24–b4; u 266b4–267a1: *mngon par brjod pa'i bag chags kyi bye brag ces bya ba ni bdag dang chos dang/bya bar mngon par brjod pa tha snyad btags pa rnams te/lha dang/mi* (D. 217b6) *dang/mig dang/gzugs dang/'gro'o zhes bya ba la sogs pa'i bag chags sna tshogs yin te/nus pa'i khyad par gang las bdag dang/chos dang/bya ba'i mngon par brjod par 'byung ba'o/bdag tu lta ba'i bag chags kyi bye brag ces bya ba ni nyon mongs pa bzhis nyon mongs par gyur pa'i yid 'jig tshogs la lta ba'i dbang gis kun bzhi rnam par shes pa la bdag go snyam pa'i bag chags kyi bye brag go/srid pa'i yan lag gi bag chags kyi bye brag ches bya ba ni bsod nams dang bsod nams ma yin pa dang/mi gyo ba'i 'du byed kyi dbang gyis lha* (D. 218a1) *la sogs pa'i 'gro ba rnams su ma rig pa nas rga shi la thug pa rnams gyi bag chags kyi bye brag go*). (Bh 336c5 f.; bh 168b7 f.: *ngon bar brjod pa'i bag chags kyi bye brag ni 'di lta ste/mig ces rjod par byed pa'i rnam par smin pa'i rnam par shes pa'i bag chags de ni mig mngon par 'grub pa'i rgyur 'gyur te/mig gang grub cing rnam par smin pa las skyes par brjod par bya ba de mig ces brjod pa'i rgyu las gyur pa'o/de bzhin du rna ba la sogs pa brjod par bya ba thams cad la zhes bya ba ni 'di' bye brag go.*)

2 For text of U, see previous note. Bh 336c9 f.; bh 169a2 (*gang gis bdag zhes bya ba dang/bzhan zhes bya ba'i bye brag 'dir 'gyur par byed do*).

3 *Sādhāraṇa* here means "having or resting on the same support or basis" (SED 1202).

4 A few comments, however, are not out of place. We have largely contextualized the ālaya-vijñāna within its Abhidharmic milieu broadly conceived, that is, as the basic intellectual and metaphysical framework of Buddhist thinking in the few centuries preceding and succeeding the beginning of the Common Era. Nearly every argument adduced in MSg I for a new and distinct level of vijñāna, and most of the terms used to describe it, depends upon such Abhidharmic systematics and is incomprehensible without reference to its general doctrines and aims, as well as their attendant problematics. This is the overarching context within which the "defense" of the ālaya-vijñāna occurs in these texts and these are the underlying assumptions upon which they are made. And in none these arguments are the notions of "mind-only" (*vijñapti-mātra*) or the unreality of "external objects" ever directly adduced; they seem, in fact, to be irrelevant in making the case for the ālaya-vijñāna. Since our investigation is largely limited to ālaya-vijñāna as described in the parts of early Yogācāra texts which most systematically discuss and defend it, we have omitted any in-depth discussion of this topic.

5 MSg I.60. "Without [these characteristics of the ālaya-vijñāna], the distinction (*viśeṣa*) between the receptacle-world (*bhājanaloka*) and world of animate beings (*sattvaloka*) would be impossible."

6 Marlya Falk makes this point: "In its original use the *plural* term *dhammā* meant, in fact, nothing else but the changeful elements of experience, the contents of the function of *manas* (see e.g. *Dhammapada*, 1), and in this acceptance covered the whole range of the notion of contingent reality, both in its sensuous and in its unsensuous aspects. This outlook, in which reality is, first and last, merely the content of experience – and thus of psychic essence throughout – is in conformity with the point of view underlying the ṣaḍdhātu climax, in which sensuous existence appears as only a secondary derived aspect of reality, whose primary aspect is unsensuous, psychic" (1943: 63 f.).

7 See, for example, Collins (1982: 44–9) for the early Vedic and Upanishadic sense of *loka* as a multidimensional "world" constructed by human, particularly ritual, action.

8 Johansson (1979: 28 f.) has collected numerous passages from early Pāli texts to this effect. SN 169: "The world (*loka*) has arisen through the six, it gives rise to knowledge through the six; building on the six, the world (*loka*) is destroyed in the six." "Six" refers here to the six groups of cognitive awareness: their objects, respective faculties and the modes of cognitive awareness they give rise to.

A IV 430. "These five love-objects (*kāmaguṇā*) are called the world (*loka*) in the code of the noble one. What five? Forms, cognized by the eye, longed for, alluring, pleasurable, lovely, bound up with passion and desire, sounds ... smells ..., tastes ..., contacts ..."

S I 39. "The world is brought up by the mind, swept away by the mind" (*cittena nīyati loko, cittena parikissati*). A II 49: "there is no release from suffering without reaching the end of the world" (*na ca appatvā lokantaṃ dukkhā atthi pamocanaṃ*).

9 A II 48; IV 45, #60 in Nyanaponika (1999: 90).

10 Johansson similarly concludes that in early Buddhism "there is no independently existing world. The world is a dynamic process, constantly being produced and deliberately constructed by our senses, our thoughts, and our desires. ... This does not mean that we and the world are unreal or a mere illusion. The objects are there but our perceptions of them are constituent and essential parts of them ... all our ideations (*saññā*, i.e. perceptions and images) are true processes, and it is extremely difficult to control them or become independent of them. The achievement of independence, 'destruction of the world,' is the same as the achievement of nibbāna and is possible through meditation and understanding (*paññā*). In order to understand this view correctly we must not forget that it is not mere subjectiveness. It is only that the cleavage into 'objective' and 'subjective' was never made; the subjective process of image-formation was thought to be part of the object itself" (1979: 28f.).

11 M I 295. "These five faculties, each having a separate field, a separate domain, not experiencing each other's field and domain, have mind as their resort, and mind experiences their fields and domains" (Ñāṇamoli, 1995: 391). See also Ch. 1, n. 47.

12 SN 834 speaks of thinking on the views in the *manas* (*manasā diṭṭhigatāni cintayanto*) and S I 207 of the "reflective thoughts of *mano*" (*manovitakkā*) (Johansson, 1965: 183, 186). Ñāṇananda: "[C]onceptual activity presupposes language, so much so that thought itself may be regarded as a form of sub-vocal speech" (1976: 5).

This bears comparison with modern accounts of the role of linguistic use in human cognitive processes, as for example in the following: "There are thus two basic levels of knowledge and understanding in Karmiloff-Smith's model. First is the kind of knowledge that humans share with other animals. ... The second level derives from a representational redescription of this procedural knowledge. ... Systems of thought emerge from this reflexive activity because self-observation employs all of the categorization and analytic skills that are employed in perceiving, understanding, and categorizing the outside world – in effect the subject perceives, understands, and categorizes her own cognition facilitated by the fact that it is expressed externally in language" (Tomasello, 1999: 195).

13 Language is thus a constituent part of all mental cognitive awareness, if not of sensory cognitive awareness as well. One canonical passage states that both verbal and sensual contact are necessary for the arising of name-and-form: "'That name-and-form conditions contact should be understood in the following way. If, Ānanda, those modes, characteristics, signs, indications by which the name-group (*nāma-kāya*) is manifested were absent, would there be the manifestation of verbal contact (*adhivacana-samphassa*) in the form-group (*rūpa-kāya*)?' 'There would not, venerable sir.' 'If, Ānanda, those modes, characteristics, signs, indications by which the form-group (*rūpa-kāya*) is manifested were absent, would there be the manifestation of sensual contact (*paṭigha-samphassa*) in the name-group (*nāma-kāya*)?' 'There would not, venerable sir'" (D II 62; Reat, 1990: 311).

Reat concludes from these passages that both sensual and verbal contact are necessary since name-and-form "refers to both the appearance and the conceptualization of a given object of consciousness" (Reat, 1990: 306). Sensual and verbal contact correspond to the form- and name-aspect, respectively, which are also the respective functions of sensual cognitive faculties and mind (*manas*). Thus, "the term *manasikāra*, often translated as 'attention,' but meaning literally 'making or doing in the mind,' apparently refers to the specific functioning of *manas* in perceiving the conceptual (*nāma*) aspect of a given object (*rūpa*). It will be noted as well that since *vedanā* [feeling] and *saññā* [apperception] are invariably aspects of the arising of consciousness, *there can be no actual instance of consciousness of a form without an accompanying verbal/conceptual content*. In other words, there is no *rūpa* without a *nāma*. This is reflected no doubt in the status of *manas* [mind] as *sensus communis*. The five empirical senses 'resort to' *manas*, not only in the sense that the mind as *sensus communis* sorts and arranges the information they convey. They also resort to *manas* in the sense that, as the faculty responsible for *adhivacana-samphassa* (verbal/conceptual contact), *manas* supplies the *nāma*, partly on the basis of previous consciousness, for the *rūpa* conveyed by the five senses" (1990: 317, emphasis added).

14 This view is by no means limited to Buddhist or even Indian thought. Michael Tomasello, who studies communication among both primates and human children, states in his *The Cultural Origins of Human Cognition* that "the uniquely human forms of thinking... do not just depend on, but in fact derive from, perhaps even are constituted by, the interactive discourse that takes place through the medium of intersubjective and perspectival linguistic symbols, constructions, and discourse patterns" (1999: 215).

15 Again, there are strong similarities between this notion of *prapañca* and the view of language articulated in modern linguistics, particularly in semiotic theory. As classificatory, symbolic systems based upon terms that are mutually yet disjunctively defined, languages are only meaningful when they are organized according to systemic rules of combination, that is, grammar. Language is thus the mode of reference which Deacon, a neurophysiologist working with the semiotic model developed by Charles Peirce, defines as *symbolic*, in his masterful book *The Symbolic Species: The Co-evolution of Language and the Brain*:

> Because symbols do not directly refer to things in the world, but indirectly refer to them by virtue of referring to other symbols, they are implicitly combinatorial entities whose referential powers are derived by virtue of occupying determinate positions in an organized system of other symbols.
> (Deacon, 1997: 99)

In other words, just as searching for the meaning of a word in a dictionary leads only to yet other words, so the meaning of a term in any linguistic system necessarily keeps deferring to other terms, never directly to "things themselves." This give rises to an endless recursivity: "[S]ymbolically mediated models of things...," Deacon notes, "exhibit complicated nonlinearity and recursive structure as well as nearly infinite flexibility and capacity for novelty due to their combinatorial nature" (ibid.: 434).

16 Ñāṇamoli, 1995: 203. "Perception" has been modified to "apperception" for terminological consistency.

17 M I 293. "Feeling, apperception, and cognitive awareness – these factors are conjoined, not disjoined, and it is impossible to separate each of these states from the others in order to describe the difference between them. For what one feels, that one apperceives; and what one apperceives, that one cognizes."

18 "It is a final irony," Deacon observes, "that it is the virtual, not actual, reference that symbols provide, which gives rise to this experience of self. This most undeniably real experience is a *virtual* reality... its virtual nature notwithstanding, it is the symbolic realm of consciousness that we most identify with and from which our sense of agency and self-control originate" (1997: 452, emphasis in original).

19 The idea that the world or environment does not refer to some objective reality existing independently of cognizing organisms is also shared by some streams of modern scientific thinking. As the geneticist, Richard Lewontin (1983) defines it, "the environment is not a structure imposed on living beings from the outside but is in fact … a reflection of the biology of the species" (cited in Varela *et al.*, 1991: 198). Also: "An *environment* is something that surrounds or encircles, but for there to be a surrounding there must be something at the center to be surrounded. The environment of an organism is the penumbra of external conditions that are relevant to it because it has effective interactions with those aspects of the outer world" (Lewontin, 2000: 48).

20 AKBh *ad* IV 1.a; Shastri: 567; Poussin: 1 (*sattvabhājanalokasya bahudhā vaicitryamuktaṃ tat kena kṛtam? … sattvānāṃ karmajaṃ lokavaicitryam*). See AKBh *ad* V 1a (Ch. 2, n. 66), *ad* II 56b, 57b (Schmithausen, 1987: 203).

21 Asanga's *Abhidharma-samuccaya* (T 31.679b24–7, P 102b6–8 f.: *las thun mong ba zhes kyang 'byung/las thun mong ma yin pa zhes kyang 'byung /… thun mong ba gang zhe na/gang snod kyi 'jig rten rnam par 'byed pa'o//thun mong ma yin pa gang zhe na/gang sems can gyi 'jig rten rnam par 'byed pa'o*). The *Ālaya Treatise* (I.5.b)A.1–3, also mentions the ālaya-vijñāna as the root of the inanimate and animate worlds coming into existence (*nivṛtti*). See Schmithausen, 1987: 491–2, n. 1302 f.

22 For "cause" (*kāraṇa-hetu*) Tib. has *byed rgyu*, but Ch. only *yin*. For "representations" (*vijñapti*) Ch. reads merely *shih*, "vijñāna." For "force" (*adhipatibala*), Ch. has *tseng shang li*, though Tib. has only *dbang*, **bala*. For "similar" (*sādharmya*) Ch. reads *hsiang ssu*. (U 397c12 f.; u 267a8–268a1: *de la thun mong ni snod kyi 'jig rten gyi sa bon gang yin pa'o//zhes bya ba ni snod kyi 'jig rten du snang ba'i rnam par rig pa rnams kyi byed rgyu'o//thun mong ba ni rang gi las dang mthun pa'i rnam par smin pa'i dbang gis de la spyod pa po thams cad la der snang ba'i rnam par rig pa skye ba'i phyir ro*).

23 In (some strands of) biological thinking, an organism's "world" is also defined by what it responds to: "Living organisms respond to only a small fraction of the stimuli impinging on them. … In this way each living system builds up its own distinctive world according to its own distinctive structure. … The range of interactions a living system can have with its environment defines its 'cognitive domain.' … cognition is not a representation of an independent, pregiven world, but rather a bringing forth of a world. … not *the* world, but *a* world, one that is always dependent upon the organism's structure. Since individual organisms within a species have more or less the same structure, they bring forth similar worlds" (Capra, 1996: 269 f.).

24 According to Tomasello: "The consequences of learning to use linguistic symbols and other symbolic artifacts are multifarious. … The symbolic representations that children learn in their social interactions with other persons are special because they are (a) intersubjective, in the sense that a symbol is socially 'shared' with other persons; and (b) perspectival, in the sense that each symbol picks out a particular way of viewing some phenomenon (categorization being a special case of this process). The central theoretical point is that linguistic symbols embody the myriad ways of construing the world intersubjectively that have accumulated in a culture over historical time, and the process of acquiring the conventional use of these symbol artifacts, and so internalizing these construals, fundamentally transforms the nature of children's cognitive representations" (1999: 95).

25 Tomasello: "Social and cultural processes during ontogeny do not create basic cognitive skills. What they do is turn basic cognitive skills into extremely complex and sophisticated cognitive skills. … their continuing use of the language conventional in their culture leads children to construe the world in terms of the categories and perspectives and relational analogies embodied in that language" (1999: 189).

26 That the arising of consciousness, and the train of responses that follow, occur in similar patterns is not only the gist of the formula of dependent arising in general, but also of the arising of the latent dispositions in particular (M I 303: "The underlying

tendency to lust underlies pleasant feeling…to aversion underlies unpleasant feeling," etc.).

27 "Brain-language co-evolution has significantly restructured cognition from the top-down…", Deacon argues, such that "*its secondary effects have also ramified to influence the whole of human cognition.* Human beings approach the world of sensory stimuli and motor demands differently from other species…even when our symbolic-linguistic abilities are uninvolved" (1997: 417, emphasis added).

28 Maturana and Varela make a remarkably similar point: "Through language we interact in a domain of *descriptions* within which we necessarily remain even when we make assertions about the universe or about our knowledge of it. This domain is both bounded and infinite; bounded because everything we say is a *description*, and infinite because every *description* constitutes in us the basis for new orienting interactions, and hence, for new *descriptions*. From this process of recursive application of *descriptions* self-consciousness emerges as a new phenomenon in a domain of self-description, with no other neurophysiological substratum than the neurophysiological substratum of orienting behavior itself. The domain of self-consciousness as a domain of recursive self-descriptions is thus also bounded and infinite" (1980: 50, emphasis in original).

29 As the linguists/cognitive scientists Lakoff and Johnson point out, "the categories we form are *part of our experience*! They are the structures that differentiate aspects of our experience into discernible kinds. Categorization is thus not a purely intellectual matter, occurring after the fact of experience. Rather, the formation and use of categories is the stuff of experience" (1999: 18f, emphasis in original).

30 Vasubandhu's Bhāṣya *ad* MSg I.58, cited earlier in this chapter.

31 We are indebted to Professor Odani of Otani University for pointing out the significance of this passage in this context.

32 According to Deacon: "It is simply not possible to understand human anatomy, human neurobiology, or human psychology without recognizing that they have all been shaped by something that could best be described as an idea: the idea of symbolic reference" i.e. language (1997: 409f.).

33 We have explored these, and related themes, at more depth in Waldron (2002).

34 U 398a10f.; u 268a2f.

APPENDIX II INDEX OF RELATED CONTROVERSIES

1 Otherwise, a strict determinism and an infinite regress would follow. For example, *Kathāvatthu*, XVII.3 rightly rejects the thesis that everything, even karmic action itself, is due to (previous) karma (*sabbaṃ idaṃ kammato ti kathā*), while VII.10 rejects that idea that results (*vipāka*) themselves entail further results (*vipāko vipākadhammadhammo ti*).

2 The diversity of positions taken by the various schools testifies to the universality of these questions within the Abhidharma traditions, as well as to the relative inability to resolve them within the prevailing presuppositions.

Many of these issues appear in rudimentary form in such early texts as the *Kathāvatthu* and Vasumitra's *Samayabhedoparacanacakra*. The most thorough edition of the latter is that of Teramoto and Hiramatsu (1935), which includes three Chinese and one Tibetan texts, Japanese translations of the commentaries by Bhavya and Vinītadeva, and indices and comparative charts. These issues were much more developed by the time of the Sarvāstivādin literature and the *Abhidharma-kośa*, much of which was contemporaneous with the Yogācāra school.

The similarity in terminology used in discussing these issues also illustrates the commonality between the Yogācāra and other schools of the period, warranting our continued reference to Abhidharma literature. No one has more clearly demonstrated this doctrinal and terminological commonality between the various Abhidharma schools of this formative period than Bareau (1955), who has collected and collated references to the doctrinal positions of all the traditional eighteen schools, including their various sub-sects and splinter-groups, and from whom we have heavily drawn below. He draws chiefly upon the *Kathāvatthu*, the above-mentioned texts of Vasumitra *et al.*, the *Vijñapti-mātratā-siddhi* (La Vallée Poussin, 1928), and several Chinese commentaries. These materials, however, differ greatly in their original dates, their proximity to their sources, their sectarian perspectives, and thus in their ultimate reliability; we thus use them with due caution. The sectarian affiliations of the views disputed in the *Kathāvatthu*, for example, derive only from the much later commentary. Dube (1980) has also compiled and discussed many of these issues, based upon much the same sources, in a more accessible thematic and narrative format.

Due to limitations of space we will merely register the positions of the different sects on each issue in the notes that follow, with few comments and no attempt to standardize the Sanskrit and Pāli terminology.

3 *Kathāvatthu*, XV.11: Andhakas and Sammatīyas assent; Theravādins dissent.

4 *Kathāvatthu*, XV.11: Andhakas and Sammatīyas assent; Theravādins dissent.

5 *Kathāvatthu*, XIV.5: Andhakas assent; Theravādins dissent. Bareau: Mahāsāṃghikas (1955: 70, thesis 63), Vibhajyavādins (177, thesis 38), and Mahīśāsakas (183, thesis 4) assent; Theravādins dissent (230, thesis 139).

6 *Kathāvatthu*, IX.4; XI.1; XIV.5: Mahāsaṃghikas and Sammatīyas assent; Theravādins dissent. Bareau: Bahuśrutīyas reject either alternative (1955: 83, thesis 11); Andhakas (95, thesis 47), Sammatīyas (125, thesis 17), Vibhajyavādins (177, thesis 39), Mahīśāsakas (183, thesis 3), Dharmaguptakas (194, thesis 5: both *anuśaya* and *kleśa* are *viprayukta*), Uttarāpathakas (249, thesis 13), and Vātsīputrīyas assent, though the latter claim that *anuśaya* pertain to the *pudgala*, the "person" (120, 118, theses 37, 18); Sarvāstivādins (142, theses 26, 27) and Theravādins (226, 230, theses 108, 140) dissent.

Kathāvatthu, XIV.6 relates the position of the Andhakas that even the outbursts of the afflictions (*pariyuṭṭhāna*) are disjoined from mind (*citta-vippayutta*).

7 *Kathāvatthu*, IX 4; XI.1: Andhakas, Mahāsāṃghikas and Sammatīyas assent; Theravādins dissent.

8 Bareau: Sarvāstivādins assent (1955: 148, thesis 85). See AKBh *ad* V 19.

9 Bareau: Mahāsāṃghikas (1955: 68, thesis 46), Sautrāntikas (157, thesis 12), Vibhajyavādins (177, thesis 38), and a Mahīśāsaka subsect (188, thesis 10) assent; Theravādins dissent (240, thesis 222).

10 *Kathāvatthu*, I.2; III 5: Theravādins dissent.

11 This controversy concerns the attainment, or predicted future attainment, of fruits of the path either in the present or in future lifetimes. It is discussed in various regards in *Kathāvatthu*, I.5; V.2, 4, 10; VI.1; XII.5; XIX.7 (Dube, 1980: 180–3). Assurance of entering the path (*sammattaniyāmāvakkanti*) is mentioned in S I 196; S III 225; SN 55, 371; A I 121; and *Kathāvatthu*, V.4, VI.1, XIII.4; AKBh *ad* VI 26a.

12 Bareau: Sautrāntikas (1955: 159, thesis 29), Dārṣṭāntikas (165, thesis 58), and Vibhajyavādins (172, theses 5, 6) assent. Bareau states the Theravādins (1955: 240, thesis 217) assert a subtle mental-consciousness (*sūkṣma-manovijñāna*) which is present in the attainment of cessation, citing the Siddhi (pp. 142, 202–3, 207); this however is contradicted by Collins (1982: 245 f.). See discussion in text.

13 Bareau: Mahāsāṃghikas (1955: 72, thesis 78) posit a root-consciousness (*mūla-vijñāna*) which underlies and supports (*āśraya*) the discrete forms of sensory awareness; a Mahāsāṃghika subsect (74, thesis 8) asserts a subtle mental-consciousness (*sūkṣma-manovijñāna*) that pervades the entire body; Mahīśāsakas posit an aggregate which lasts as long as samsara (*saṃsāra-koṭiniṣṭha-skandha*) (187, thesis 37); Theravādins posit a *bhavaṅga-citta*, a mind (*citta*) which is a constituent (*aṅga*) of

existence (*bhava*), that is, the cause of existence and the unity of diverse successive existences (240, thesis 219). See discussion in Chs. 2 and 4.

14 The Theravādins (Bareau, 1955: 240, thesis 218) assert a certain mental-consciousness that exists at the moment of rebirth. The Sautrāntikas and Sarvāstivādins also consider it to be a moment of mental-consciousness (*mano-vijñāna*; AKBh III 42b–c).

15 Bareau: Sautrāntikas assent, and claim mind (*citta*) and body (*kāya*) can seed each other (1955: 158, thesis 18) and that ordinary *vijñāna* arises from seeds (159, thesis 28); Mahāsāṃghikas dissent (72, thesis 79).

16 Bareau: Mahāsāṃghikas (1955: 72, thesis 78) assent; Sautrāntikas dissent (159, thesis 30); a Mahīśāsaka subsect asserts that *anuśaya* and *bīja* reside perpetually in the present from where they exclusively produce other dharmas (188, theses 9, 10).

17 *Kathāvatthu*, XVI.4: Theravādins dissent. Bareau: Mahāsāṃghikas assent (1955: 72, thesis 79).

APPENDIX III TRANSLATION: THE *PRAVṚTTI* AND *NIVṚTTI* PORTIONS OF THE *VINIŚCAYASAṂGRAHAṆĪ* OF THE *YOGĀCĀRABHŪMI*

1 No single translation of *pravṛtti* can satisfactorily convey its multiple meanings of "to come forth, issue, originate, arise, be produced, result, occur, happen, take place, commence, continue, etc." (SED 693). This emphasizes not only that the ālaya-vijñāna arises moment to moment in conjunction with its objective supports and mental factors, etc. but that its perpetuation is also the perpetuation of samsaric existence. This contrasts with *nivṛtti*, "to turn back, cease, disappear," and thus, "the cessation" of samsaric existence. The theme of this text is thus how the ālaya-vijñāna comes forth, continues, and prolongs such existence, and, conversely, how it is abandoned through the cessation, the *nivṛtti*, of the ālaya-vijñāna.

2 This entire passage is paralleled in the TrBh, 19. 5 f.: *ālaya-vijñānaṃ dvidhā pravartate/ adhyātmam upādānavijñaptito bahirdhā 'paricchinnākāra-bhājana-vijñaptitaś ca.* Also, ASBh, 21.9 f.: *asaṃviditavijñaptiḥ bhājanavijñaptiḥ, sarvakālamaparicchinnākāratvāt.* See Ch. 3, n. 46, for further references.

3 There is a parallel Sanskrit passage referring to these two objective supports for the arising of ālaya-vijñāna in the TrBh, 19. 7 f.: *tatrādhyātman upādānaṃ parikalpita-svabhāvābhiniveśa vāsanā sādhiṣṭhanam indriya-rūpaṃ nāma ca.* The objective supports of ālaya-vijñāna here are thus the impressions gained from past experience, knowledge, etc., and the bodily processes. These, together with the next objective support, the receptacle world, make up the three objective supports which instigate the arising of ālaya-vijñāna, namely past experience and knowledge, bodily sensations, and the receptacle world.

4 This passage emphasizes not only the cognitive functions of the ālaya-vijñāna but also that its perception of the receptacle world depends upon its inner appropriation, that is, the impressions (*vāsanā*) and the body.

5 *Ekarasa*, according to the SED, means "having (always) the same object of affection, unchangeable" (SED 229). However, this term has deeper, more metaphysical nuances from the *Upaniṣadic* tradition. See Falk, 1943: 135.

6 Hakamaya (1979: 55) has reconstructed this phrase as **kṣaṇika-srotaḥ-saṃtāna-vartin.*

7 T 30.580a18. Hsüan Tsang: *fei i fei ch'ang.*

8 Schmithausen (1987: 393, nn. 647, 653) argues for *upādāna* here based on occurrences of *rgyu* and *len rgyu* for *upādāna in* MSg I.5 and Y zi 189b4 f.

9 These passages closely follow those found in the *Saṃdhinirmocana Sūtra*, VIII, 37.1.3–7. See also Schmithausen, 1987: 383 f., 392.

10 The point here is that just as the material sense-faculties are the simultaneous support (*sahabhū-āśraya*) of the sensory forms of cognitive awareness, *ālaya-vijñāna* is the

simultaneous support of *manas* and *mano-vijñāna*. Cf. MSg I.7a.2 where *kliṣṭa-manas* is the support of *mano-vijñāna*. Hsüan Tsang's translation here (580b13–17) states that *ālaya-vijñāna* is the support of *manas*, which in turn is the support of the *mano-vijñāna*. See also Siddhi: 235, 240. See Schmithausen, 1987: 326, n. 358.

For purposes of clarity I have divided this sentence into two. More literally it reads: "when there is *ālaya-vijñāna*, which is the support of the mind (*manas*) and mental cognitive awareness (*mano-vijñāna*), mind and mental cognitive awareness will also arise, but not when there is not" (D. 5a2 f.: *yid dang yid kyi rnam par shes pa'i gnas kun gzhi rnam par shes pa yod na/yid dang yid kyi rnam par shes pa yang 'byung bar 'gyur gyi med na ni ma yin no*).

11 Schmithausen states that the pronoun *tad* (Tib.: *de*), in the expression "**tad-abhinirvṛtti* clearly stands for *ālayavijñānābhinirvṛtti*" (1987: 60, 562, 564). D. 5a4: *tshe phyi ma la* de *mngon par 'grub pa'i sa bon yongs su 'dzin pa skyed par byed pas so.*

12 This passage is also opaque. Schmithausen states that "it is clear … that the [Result-of-]Maturation (*vipāka*) to be taken possession of is the new *ālaya-vijñāna*" (1987: 564, n. 1477).

13 *Sahabhāva* more literally means "co-existence." In Abhidharma doctrine this term, with its nuances of "simultaneity, concurrence or concomitance," is distinguished from *saṃprayoga*, "association, conjoined." *Saṃprayoga* refers to the relationship in which the certain mental factors (*caitta-dharma*) are associated closely enough with one's overall state of mind (*citta*) at any given moment that they invariably color or condition the karmic nature of that moment of mind. Factors which are "concurrent, co-existent or simultaneous," on the other hand, have no such influence and hence can persist in the mental stream without impeding the karmic quality of each moment of mind. On the definitions and differences of these two relationships, see Ch. 2, nn. 34, 35, above. On Yogācāra understanding of "co-existence," see Ch. 3, n. 52.

14 This highly significant passage describes what will later be called the afflicted-mind (*kliṣṭa-manas*). Interestingly, it is here considered one of the *pravṛtti-vijñānas*. We follow Schmithausen (1987: 444) in taking **manyanā* as a verb related to *ahaṃkāra* and *asmimāna*, as is quite clear in H 580c3. Schmithausen states that this passage has "good chances of being the oldest occurrence of the new *manas*" (ibid.: 149 f.).

15 Both "simultaneous" or "concurrent" are translated from *lhan cig*.

16 This passage follows the Chinese (H 580c9 f.) more closely than the Tibetan (D. 5b4: *yid kyi rnam par shes pa de ni yid la brten pa zhes bya ste/rgyu mtshan gyi yid ma 'gags na rnam par rig pa'i 'ching* ba mi 'grol la/'gags na ni de 'grol ba'i phyir ro*). Schmithausen (1987: 202, nn. 1293–8) discusses it at some length. Discrimination of putative entities will remain as long as the sense "I am" accompanies *manas*. To the extent that they are accompanied by such deep-seated, unconscious self-centeredness, no moments of mind will ever be entirely free from the bonds of perceiving all phenomena in terms of subject and object, self and other.

17 That is, if the feeling of the six forms of arising cognitive awareness (*pravṛtti-vijñāna*) are *duḥkha*, then the ālaya-vijñāna arises mingled with *duḥkha*. The relationship between the ālaya-vijñāna and *duḥkha*, however, is simultaneous (*sahabhū*) not associated (*saṃprayukta*), in contrast to that between the six *pravṛtti-vijñāna* and *duḥkha*, which is *saṃprayukta*. Accordingly, the occurrence of that state of suffering, of *duḥkha*, is dependent upon the *pravṛtti-vijñānas*. See Hakamaya (1979: 75, n. 43).

18 *Caitasika* in H 580c27.

19 See n. 13. This important passage states that the ālaya-vijñāna is not directly related to the overt processes of mind, but rather constitutes a distinct stream of consciousness, a position Vasubandhu explicitly states in the *Karmasiddhiprakaraṇa*, # 38 (*'o na de lta na ni rnam par shes pa'i rgyun rnam par smin pa'i rnam par shes pa dang/gzhan dang gnyis cig car 'byung bar 'gyur ro zhe na/de lta yin na ci nyes*). Lamotte, 1935–36.

20 This passage reads *chos mtshungs pa 'gas tshul de bzhin du blta bar bya'o*, supported by H: *i shao fen hsiang ssu tao li.*
21 *Virodha* conveys the sense of "obstruction, incompatibility, conflict, contradiction, impediment." *A-virodha* denotes their absence.
22 See *Saṃdhinirmocana Sūtra*, V.5, Ch. 3, p. 97, above.
23 Following Pek. 7b5: *dper na lus kyi rnam par shes* pas *reg bya'i dngos po gcig la res 'ga' ni reg bya rigs gcig pa sna tshogs ma yin pa 'dzin par byed la*). D. 6b3 has *pa'i* instead of *pas*.
24 Words in parentheses following H 581a16f.
25 Following H 581a18. (D. 6b5: *kun nas nyon mongs*).
26 "Indeterminate" means that these particular afflictions are karmically neutral, that is, they do not instigate actions that incur a specific kind of result. See discussion in Ch. 2, n. 38, concerning this distinction between *satkāyadṛṣṭi* and *antagrāhadṛṣṭi* in AKBh II 30a–b, and *ad* V 19d. This position also has several parallels in Yogācāra literature. In the Siddhi (2a12ff.), for example, as Schmithausen points out, "the continuous, subliminal *sahaja ātmagrāhaḥ* of *manas* (which has ālaya-vijñāna as its object) is distinguished from a sporadic *sahaja ātmagrāhaḥ* on the supraliminal level of *manovijñāna*, which has five skandhas as its object" (1987: 447, n. 953).
27 *Nivṛtti*, the antonym of *pravṛtti*, has all the meanings implied in its literal sense of "to turn back," that is, "to retreat, escape, get rid of, cease, end, disappear, give up, abandon, remove." (SED 560).
28 *Bhājana-loka* literally means "recipient, receptacle or vessel."
29 The ālaya-vijñāna contains the seeds of karma, and it is karma that, according to the both the *Abhidharma-kośa* and the *Abhidharma-samuccaya*, ultimately creates the variety of both the animate and inanimate worlds (see Ch. 5, nn. 20 and 21).
30 Following Schmithausen (1987: 491, n. 1303), who suggests **itaretarādhipatyāt*.
31 Since *ālaya-vijñāna* results from past *saṃskārās*, it is comprised within *saṃskāra-duḥkhatā*, the *duḥkha* inherent in the conditionality of things. It is that which receives the seeds of *karma* to be experienced in the future, as well as the support and seed of present states.
32 This parable is also mentioned in the Siddhi (Poussin: 102; T. 31.8b). In the *Yogācārabhūmi*, *dhatu* is given as one of the synonyms of *bīja* (Y 26, 18–19: *bījaparyāyāḥ punardhāturgotraṃ prakṛtirhetuḥ*).
33 Concluding that the three previous paragraphs are "heterogenous elements, and are suspect of having been added after the composition of the nuclear text including the final resumé" (1987: 221f.), Schmithausen suggests that this phrase refers to and continues the summary at (5.b)A.5. Based on these arguments, we have altered Hakamaya's outline (1979) by putting this paragraph, (5.b)B.2., into the next section. All of the seemingly interpolated material is thus confined to (5.b)B.1.
34 Schmithausen reconstructs the Sanskrit as *samyaktvaniyāmam avakrānta*, the "guarantee of salvation" (1987: 197).
35 We have drawn heavily on Schmithausen (1987: 198) to make sense out of these, and the last several, difficult passages. These two types of bondage, the *nimitta-bandhana* and the *dauṣṭhulya-bandhana*, are said to be removed by *śamatha* and *vipaśyanā*, calming and insight meditation, respectively (*Saṃdhinirmocana Sūtra*, VIII 32).
36 Hakamaya (1979: 78, n. 71) points out a Sanskrit parallel to this passage, albeit in a different context, in ASBh, 121.29f.: *ekadhyam a[bhi]saṃkṣipyaikaṃ bhāgaṃ karoty ekaṃ piṇḍam ekaṃ puñjam ekaṃ rāśiṃ karoty ekaṃ kṛtvā.*
37 This closely follows Hsüan Tsang's Chinese. The Tibetan says literally: "one should know that the basis, *ālaya-vijñāna*, is revolved (*vivartita*) by [its] antidote, [its] enemy" (D. 8a4: *kun gzhi rnam par shes pa de'i gnas ni/gnyen po dang/dgra bos bsgyur bar rig par bya'o.*) Throughout this short section ((5.b)C.2.), Paramārtha (T 30.1020b11–19) has consistently translated *āśraya-parivṛtti*, the revolution of the basis, as *amala-vijñāna*, "pure-consciousness." The term *āśraya-parivṛtti* is one of the central terms in

Yogācāra soteriology. The *āśraya*, the basis or support, refers to *ālaya-vijñāna* and its transformation or revolution is understood here as the transformation of the very basis of personal existence, from afflicted self-centeredness to the state of perfect enlightenment and wisdom. The theme of transformation in Yogācāra, in its many dimensions, is the topic of Ronald Davidson's (1985) "Buddhist Systems of Transformation: Āśraya-parivṛtti/parāvṛtti Among the Yogācāra."

38 Paramārtha (1020b13) translates these antonyms as *sāsrava* and *anāsrava-dharma*, the latter referring to *amala-vijñāna*.

39 Schmithausen (1987: 499, n. 1337) suggests that this passage too is heterogeneous.

40 Following H 581c21. See Schmithausen, 1987: 365, n. 555.

41 Schmithausen (1987: 499, n. 1337). Paramārtha (1020b23 f.) adds "due to the cause of *amala-vijñāna*."

42 These three abandonments correspond to the elimination of suffering in the future, the elimination of the origin of suffering in this life, and elimination of suffering in this life, the three aspects presented in (5.b)A.4.a–c.

43 Schmithausen (1987: 208–9) points out that these correspond to the Preparatory Path (*prayoga-mārga*), the Path of Seeing (*darśana-mārga*), and the Path of Cultivation (*bhāvanā-mārga*), respectively.

44 The *manas* is not considered here at all. This contrasts with MSg 1.7.4–5 (cited in our text) which argues that the notion of unconscious mentation is necessary in order to distinguish these two types of attainment, that is, it must be present in the *asaṃjñī-samāpatti*. Schmithausen thus suggests that "the new *manas* is not taken into account because it had not yet been introduced when the above statement was formulated" (1987: 481, n. 1232).

BIBLIOGRAPHY OF WORKS CITED

List of texts and abbreviations

A — *Aṅguttara-nikāya*. Nyanaponika Thera and Bhikkhu Bodhi (trans.) (1999), *Numerical Discourses of the Buddha: An Anthology of Suttas from the Anguttara Nikāya*, Walnut Creek, Cal.: AltaMira Press
Aṅguttara Nikāya. F. L. Woodward and E. M. Hare (trans.) (1885–1910; 1932–6), *The Book of the Gradual Sayings*, London: Pali Text Society

Abhidhammattha-sangaha — See *Compendium*

Abhidharmadīpa — P. S. Jaini (ed.) (1959; 2nd edn, 1977), Patna: K. P. Jayaswal Research Institute

Abhidharmasamuccaya — W. Rahula (trans.) (1980), *Le Compendium de la super-doctrine (philosophie) (Abhidharmasamuccaya) d'Asanga*, Paris: École Française d'Extrême Orient

AKBh — *Abhidharmakośa-bhāṣya*. S. D. Shastri (ed.) (1981), Varanasi: Bauddha Bharati Series; L. de La Vallée Poussin (trans.) (1971), *L'Abhidharmakośa de Vasubandhu*, Bruxelles: Institut Belge des Hautes Études Chinoises; L. Pruden (trans.) (1988), *Abhidharmakośabhāṣyam*, Berkeley: Asian Humanities Press. Cited by chapter, verse, and page number

Ālaya Treatise — A section of the *Yogācārabhūmi-Viniścayasaṃgrahaṇī* comprised of the *Proof Portion* and the *Pravṛtti* and *Nivṛtti Portions*
Proof Portion: The *Proof Portion* is in substantial agreement with corresponding passages in the ASBh, 11.9–13.20, still extant in Sanskrit. Hsüan Tsang's Chinese translation: T. 31.1606.701b4–702a5
Tibetan Peking edn.: #5554. Si. 12a2–13b5; Derge edn.: #4053 Li. 9b7–11a5. See Hakamaya (1978); Griffiths (1986)
Pravṛtti and *Nivṛtti Portions* in the *Yogācārabhūmi*: Hsüan-Tsang's Chinese: T. 30.1579.579c23–582a28. Tibetan Peking edn. #5539 Zi. 4a5–11a8; Derge edn, #4038. Shi. 3b4–9b3. See Hakamaya (1978, 1979)

ASBh — *Abhidharmasamuccaya-bhāṣyam*. N. Tatia (ed.) (1976), Patna: K. P. Jayaswal Research Institute, TSWS 17

Bh — Hsüan Tsang's Chinese trans. of Vasubandhu's *Mahāyāna-saṃgraha-bhāṣya*, T. 1597

bh. — Tibetan translation of Vasubandhu's *Mahāyāna-saṃgraha-bhāṣya*, P. #5551

BHSD — *Buddhist Hybrid Sanskrit Grammar and Dictionary*. F. Edgerton (1953; rep. 1985), Kyoto: Rinsen Book Co.

Bodhisattvabhūmi — U. Wogihara (ed.) (1971), Tōkyō: Sankibō Busshorin

Compendium — *Compendium of Philosophy* (*Abhidhammattha-sangaha*). S. Z. Aung (trans.) (1979), London: Pali Text Society. Also: Nārada (trans.), Bhikkhu Bodhi (rev.) (1993), *A Comprehensive Manual of Abhidhamma*, Kandy: Buddhist Publication Society

D — L. Walshe (trans.) (1987), *Thus Have I Heard*, Boston: Wisdom Books. *Dīgha Nikāya* (1890–1911), T. W. Rhys-Davids and C. A. F. Rhys-Davids (trans.) (1899–1921), *Dialogues of the Buddha*, London: Pali Text Society

D. — Derge edition of the Tibetan Tripitaka

Dhammasangaṇi — *A Buddhist Manual of Psychological Ethics*. C. A. F. Rhys-Davids (trans.) (1974), London: Pali Text Society

H — Hsüan Tsang's Chinese translation of the *Mahāyāna-saṃgraha* (MSg), T. 1594

I Pu Tsung Lun Lun — Teramoto Enga and Hiramatsu Y. Kokusho (ed.) (1975), Tōkyō: Kankōkai

Kathāvatthu — (1979) London: Pali Text Society

Karmasiddhiprakaraṇa — E. Lamotte (ed. and trans.) (1935–6), *Mélanges Chinois et Bouddhiques* 4. English translation from the French in L. Pruden (1988), *Karmasiddhiprakaraṇa: Treatise on Action by Vasubandhu*, Berkeley: Asian Humanities Press. See also Muroji (1985), Anacker (1984)

Kośa — *Abhidharmakośa-bhāṣyam*. See AKBh

M — Ñāṅamoli (1995), *The Middle Length Discourses of the Buddha*, Boston: Wisdom. *Majjhima Nikāya* (1948–51), I. B. Horner (trans.) (1954–9), *Middle Length Sayings*, London: Pali Text Society

Miln. — *Milinda's Questions*. I. B. Horner (trans.) (1963–4), London: Pali Text Society

MSg — *Mahāyāna-saṃgraha*, T. 1594; P. 5549; D. 4048. Cited by chapter numbers and section. See Griffiths *et al.* (1989)

MVBh — *Madhyāntavibhāga-bhāṣya of Vasubandhu*. G. Nagao (ed.) (1964), Tōkyō: Suzuki Research Foundation

Nivṛtti Portion — See *Ālaya Treatise*

P — Paramārtha's Chinese translation of MSg. T. 1593

P. — Peking edition of the Tibetan Tripitaka

PED — *Pāli–English Dictionary*, T. W. Rhys-Davids and W. Stede (eds) (1979), London: Pali Text Society

Poussin — See AKBh

Pravṛtti Portion	See *Ālaya Treatise*
Proof Portion	See *Ālaya Treatise*
S	*The Connected Discourses of the Buddha*. Bhikkhu Bodhi (trans.) (2000), Somerville: Wisdom. *Saṃyutta Nikāya* (1894–1904), C. A. F. Rhys-Davids and F. L. Woodward (trans.) (1917–30), *The Book of the Kindred Sayings*, London: Pali Text Society
Saṃdhi	É. Lamotte (ed. and trans.) (1935), *Saṃdhinirmocana Sūtra. L'Explication des mystères*. Louvain. Cited by chapter and section
SED	*Sanskrit–English Dictionary*, M. W. Monier-Williams (ed.) (rep. 1986), Tōkyō: Meicho Fukyukai
Shastri	*Abhidharmakośa-bhāṣya*. See AKBh
Siddhi	*Vijñaptimātratāsiddhi*, L. de La Vallée Poussin (trans.) (1928), Paris: Libraire Orientaliste, Paul Geuthner. French translation of Hsüan Tsang's Chinese translation (T. 1585) of Dharmapala's commentary on Vasubandhu's *Triṃśikā*
SN	*Sutta-nipāta* (1948), London: Pali Text Society; Saddhatissa (trans.) (1985), London: Curzon Press
T	*Taishō* edition of the Chinese Tripiṭaka
TrBh	*Triṃśikā-bhāṣya of Sthiramati*. S. Levi (ed.) (1925), *Vijñaptimātratāsiddhi*, Paris: Librairie Ancienne Honoré Champion
U	Hsüan Tsang's Chinese translation of Asvabhāva's *Mahāyāna-saṃgraha-upanibandhana*. T. 1598
u.	Tibetan translation of Asvabhāva's *Mahāyāna-saṃgraha-upanibandhana* P. #5552
Vibhanga	*Vibhanga*, T. W. Rhys-Davids (ed.) (1904), London: Pali Text Society
VGPVy	**Vivṛtagūḍhārtha-piṇḍavyākhyā*. P. #5553. Tibetan commentary on MSg I.1–49
Visuddhimagga	*The Path of Purification* by Buddhaghosa. Ñāṇamoli (trans.) (1976), Berkeley: Shambala. Cited by chapter and paragraph
Vyākhyā	*Abhidharmakośa-vyākhyā*. Yaśomitra's commentary on AKBh in Shastri
Y	*Yogācārabhūmi of Asanga*. Bhattacharya (ed.) (1957), Calcutta: University of Calcutta
Y-C	Hsüan Tsang's Chinese translation of *Yogācārabhūmi*. T. 1579

Dictionaries and reference works

Apte, V. S. (1986), *The Practical Sanskrit–English Dictionary*, Kyoto: Rinsen Book Co.

Bukkyō Gaku Jiten (1986), Kyoto: Hōzōkan.

Childers, R. C. (1979), *A Dictionary of the Pali Language*, New Delhi: Cosmo Publications.

Chandra, L. (1982), *Tibetan–Sanskrit Dictionary*, Kyoto: Rinsen Book Co.

Chu Fei Huang (1988), *Fa-hsiang Tai Tz'u-tien*, Taipei: Hsin Wen Li Kung-Ssu Chupan Yin-hsing.

Concise Oxford English Dictionary (1976), 6th edn, Oxford: Oxford University Press.
Das, S. C. (1981), *Tibetan–English Dictionary*, Kyoto: Rinsen Books Co.
Hirakawa, A. *et al.* (1973, 1977, 1978), *Index to the Abhidharmakośa*, Tōkyō: Daizō Shuppan Kabushikikaisha.
Jaschke, H. A. (1985), *A Tibetan–English Dictionary*, Kyoto: Rinsen Book Co.
Matthew, R. H. (1952), *Chinese–English Dictionary*, Cambridge: Harvard University Press.
Mizuno, K. (1987), *Pāli-go Jiten*, Tōkyō: Shunjūkai.
Nakamura, H. (1986), *Bukkyō-go Daijiten*, Tōkyō: Tōkyō shōseki.
Nelson, A. N. (1982), *Japanese–English Character Dictionary*, Rutland: Charles E. Tuttle Co.
Nyanatiloka (1980), *Buddhist Dictionary: Manual of Buddhist Terms and Doctrines*, Colombo: Frewin & Co. Ltd. Reprint: (1977), San Francisco: Chinese Materials Center, Inc.

Secondary works cited

Anacker, S. (1972), "Vasubandhu's *Karmasiddhi-prakaraṇa* and the Problem of the Highest Meditations," *Philosophy East–West*, 22 (3): 247–58.
—— (1984), *Seven Works of Vasubandhu*, New Delhi: Motilal Banarsidass.
Aramaki, N. (1985), "The Short Prose Pratītyasamutpāda," *Buddhism and its Relation to Other Religions*, Kyoto: Heirakuji Shoten: 87–121.
Archard, D. (1984), *Consciousness and Unconsciousness*, London: Hutchinson & Co.
Barash, D. (1979), *The Whisperings Within: Evolution and the Origin of Human Nature*, New York: Harper & Row.
Bareau, A. (1955), *Les Sectes Bouddhiques du Petit Vèhicule*, Paris: École Française d'Extrême-Orient.
Bateson, G. (1979), *Mind and Nature: A Necessary Unity*, New York: Bantam Books.
Becker, E. (1973), *Denial of Death*, New York: The Free Press.
—— (1975), *Escape from Evil*, New York: The Free Press.
Buswell, R. and Gimello, R. (1992), *Paths to Liberation: The Marga and its Transformations in Buddist Thought*, Honolulu: University of Hawai Press.
Capra, F. (1996), *The Web of Life*, New York: Anchor Books.
Chaudhuri, S. (1983), *Analytical Study of the Abhidharmakośa*, Calcutta: Firma KLM Ltd.
Collins, S. (1982), *Selfless Persons: Imagery and Thought in Theravāda Buddhism*, Cambridge: Cambridge University Press.
Conze, E. (1973), *Buddhist Thought in India*, Ann Arbor: University of Michigan Press.
Cousins, L. S. (1981), "The Paṭṭhāna and the Development of the Theravādin Abhidhamma," *Journal of the Pali Text Society*, 9: 22–46.
Cox, C. (1995), *Disputed Dharmas: Early Buddhist Theories of Existence*, Tokyo: International Institute for Buddhist Studies. Studia Philologica Buddhica. Monograph Series XI.
Davidson, R. M. (1985), "*Buddhist Systems of Transformation: Āśraya-parivṛtti/parāvṛtti Among the Yogācāra*," unpublished Ph.D. dissertation, Univ. of California (University Microfilms #8609992).
Deacon, T. W. (1997), *The Symbolic Species: The Co-evolution of Language and the Brain*, New York: W. W. Norton & Co.
Dube, S. N. (1980), *Cross Currents in Early Buddhism*, New Delhi: Manohar Publications.
Dutt, N. (1960), *Early Monastic Buddhism*, Calcutta.
Eliade, M. (1973), *Yoga: Immortality and Freedom*, Princeton: Princeton University Press.
Falk, M. (1943), *Nāma-rūpa and Dharma-rūpa*, Calcutta: University of Calcutta.

Flanagan, O. (1992), *Consciousness Reconsidered*, Cambridge, Mass.: MIT Press.
Frauwallner, E. (1995), *Studies in Abhidharma*, Albany: SUNY.
Freud, S. (1965), *New Introductory Lectures on Psychoanalysis*, New York: W. W. Norton & Co.
—— (1984), *On Metapsychology: The Theory of Psychoanalysis*, "Papers On Metapsychology" (1915); "The Unconscious" (1915). Pelican Freud Library, Harmondsworth: Penguin Books.
Gazzaniga, M. (1998), *The Mind's Past*, Berkeley: University of California Press.
Govinda, A. (1969), *Psychological Attitude of Early Buddhist Philosophy*, London: Rider & Co.
Griffiths, P. J. (1986), *On Being Mindless*, La Salle, Ill.: Open Court.
—— and Hakamaya, N., Keenan, J., and Swanson, P. (1989), *The Realm of Awakening: A Translation and Study of the Tenth Chapter of Asanga's Mahāyānasaṃgraha*, New York: Oxford University Press.
Guenther, H. V. (1959), *Philosophy and Psychology in the Abhidharma*, Delhi: Motilal Banarsidass.
—— (1989), *From Reductionism to Creativity*, Boston: Shambala.
Hakamaya, N. (1978), "Araya-shiki sonzai no hachi-ronshō ni kansuru shobunken," *Kamazawa Daigaku Bukkyō-gakubu Kenkyū-kiyō*, 16: 1–26.
—— (1978a), "Mahāyāna-saṃgraha ni okeru shinishiki-setsu," *Tōyō Bunka Kenkyūjo Kiyō*, 76: 197–309.
—— (1979), "Viniścayasaṃgrahaṇī ni okeru āraya-shiki no kitei," *Tōyōbunka-kenkyūjo-kiyō*, 79: 1–79.
Hall, Calvin S. (1954), *A Primer of Freudian Psychology*, New York: Mentor Book.
Harland, R. (1987), *Superstructuralism*, London: Routledge.
Harvey, P. (1995), *The Selfless Mind*, London: Curzon Press.
Hoagland, M. and Dodson, B. (1995), *The Way Life Works*, New York: Times Books.
Hocart, A. M. (1927, repr. 1969), *Kingship*, London: Oxford University Press.
Jackson, R. (1993), *Is Enlightenment Possible?* Ithaca, New York: Snow Lion.
Jaini, P. S. (1959), "The Sautrāntika Theory of Bīja," *Bulletin of the School of Oriental and African Studies*, 22 (2): 236–49.
—— (1959a), "The Development of the Theory of Viprayukta-saṃskāras," *Bulletin of the School of Oriental and African Studies*, 22 (2): 531–47.
—— (1959b), "The Vaibhāṣika Theory of Words and Meanings," *Bulletin of the School of Oriental and African Studies*, 22: 95–107.
Jayatilleke, K. N. (1963), *Early Buddhist Theory of Knowledge*, Delhi: Motilal Banarsidass.
Johansson, R. E. A. (1965), "Citta, Mano, Viññāṇa – A Psychosemantic Investigation," *University of Ceylon Review*, 23 (1, 2): 165–215.
—— (1970), *The Psychology of Nirvana*, Garden City: Anchor Books.
—— (1979), *The Dynamic Psychology of Early Buddhism*, London: Curzon Press.
Keenan, J. P. (1982), "Original Purity and the Focus of Early Yogācāra," *Journal of the International Association of Buddhist Studies*, 5 (1): 7–18.
—— (2000), *The Scripture on the Explication of Underlying Meaning*, Berkeley: Numata Center for Buddhist Translation and Research.
Kihlstrom, J. F. (1987), "The Cognitive Unconscious," *Science*, 237: 1445–52.
Kritzer, R. (1999), *Rebirth and Causation in the Yogācāra Abhidharma*, Vienna: Arbeitskreis für Tibetische und Buddhistische Studien Universität Wien.
Kuhn, Thomas S. (1970), *The Structure of Scientific Revolutions*, Chicago: University of Chicago Press.

Lakoff, G. and Johnson, M. (1999), *Philosophy in the Flesh: The Embodied Mind and its Challenge to Western Thought*, New York: Basic Books.
Lamotte, E. (1935), "L'Ālayavijñāna (Réceptacle) dans la Mahāyānasaṃgraha (Chapter II)," *Mélanges Chinois et Bouddhiques*, 3: 169–255.
—— (ed. and trans.) (1935), *Saṃdhinirmocana Sūtra. L'Explication des mystères*. Louvain.
—— (ed. and trans.) (1935–6), *Karmasiddhiprakaraṇa Mélanges Chinois et Bouddhiques* 4. English translation from the French in Pruden, L. (1988), *Karmasiddhiprakaraṇa: Treatise on Action by Vasubandhu*, Berkeley: Asian Humanities Press.
—— (1973), *La Somme du Grand Véhicle d'Asanga (Mahāyāna-saṃgraha)*, Université de Louvain, Institut Orientaliste Louvain-la-Neuve.
La Vallée Poussin, L. de (1913), *Théorie des Douze Causes*, Gand: Université de Gand.
—— (1935), "Notes sur l'ālayavijñāna," *Mélanges Chinois et Bouddhiques*, 3: 145–68.
—— (1937a), "Documents d'Abhidharma," *Mélanges Chinois et Bouddhiques*, 5: 7–158.
—— (1937b), "Le Bouddhisme et le Yoga de Patañjali," *Mélanges Chinois et Bouddhiques*, 5: 223–42.
Lewontin, R. (1983), "The Organism as the Subject and Object of Evolution," *Scientia*, 118: 63–82.
—— (2000), *The Triple Helix: Genes, Organism, Environment*, Cambridge, Mass.: Harvard University Press.
Luckmann, T. (1967), *The Invisible Religion: The Problem of Religion in Modern Society*, New York: MacMillan.
Matthews, B. (1983), *Craving and Salvation: A Study in Buddhist Soteriology*, Waterloo, Ontario: Wilfrid Laurier University Press.
Maturana, H. and Franciesco Varela (1980), *Autopoiesis and Cognition: The Realization of the Living*, Dordrecht, Holland: D. Reidel Pub.
Mitchell, S. (1993), *Hope and Dread in Psychoanalysis*, New York: Basic Books.
Mizuno, K. (1978), *Pāli Bukkyō o chūshin to shita Bukkyō no shinishiki-ron*, Tōkyō: Piṭaka Press.
Muroji, G. (1985), *The Tibetan Text of the Karma-siddhi-prakaraṇa of Vasubandhu with Reference to the Abhidharma-kośa-bhāṣya and the Pratītya-samutpāda-vyākhyā*, Kyoto (privately published).
Nagao, G. (1982), *Shōdaijōron: Wayaku to Chūkai*, Tokyo: Kodansha. Japanese translation and commentary of the MSg with Sanskrit reconstruction by N. Aramaki.
—— (1985), *Chūgan to Yuishiki*, Tōkyō: Iwanami Shōten.
—— (1991), *Madhyamika and Yogacara* (trans. and ed.), L. Kawamura, Albany: SUNY.
Ñāṇananda, Bhikkhu (1976), *Concept and Reality in Early Buddhist Thought*, 2nd edn, Kandy: Buddhist Publication Society.
Nyanaponika, Thera (1976), *Abhidhamma Studies*, 3rd edn, Kandy: Buddhist Publication Society.
—— (1986), *The Vision of Dharma*, York Beach, Maine: Samuel Weiser.
Nyanatiloka, Mahathera (1983), *Guide through the Abhidhamma-pitaka*, 4th edn, Kandy: Buddhist Publication Society.
Odani, N. (2001), *Shôdaijôronkôkyū*, Kyoto: Shinshū-ôtaniha-shūmusho Shuppanbu.
Paden, W. (1992), *Interpreting the Sacred*, Boston: Beacon Press.
Piatigorksy, A. (1984), *The Buddhist Philosophy of Thought*, London: Curzon Press.
Powers, J. (1995), Wisdom of Buddha: *The Saṃdhinirmocana Mahāyāna Sūtra*, Berkeley: Dharma Publising.

Puhakka, K. (1987), "The Doctrine of Karma and Contemporary Western Psychology," *The Dimensions of Karma*, Delhi: Chanakya Publications.
Rahula, W. (1959), *What the Buddha Taught*, New York: Grove Books.
Reat, N. R. (1990), *Origins of Indian Psychology*, Berkeley: Asian Humanities Press.
Saussure, F. (1959), *General Course in Linguistics*, New York: The Philosophical Library.
Schmithausen, L. (1985), 'Once Again Mahāyānasaṃgraha I. 8,' *Buddhism and Its Relation to Other Religions*, Kyōto: Heirakuji Shoten, 139–60.
—— (1987), *Ālayavijñāna*, Tōkyō: International Institute for Buddhist Studies.
Silva, P. de (1972), *Buddhist and Freudian Psychology*, Colombo: Lake House Investment, Ltd.
—— (1979), *An Introduction to Buddhist Psychology*, London: Macmillan Press.
Sopa, Geshe Lhundup (1986), "The Special Theory of Pratityasamutpada: The Cycle of Dependent Origination," *Journal of the International Association of Buddhist Studies*, (9)1: 105–19.
Sparham, G. (1993), *Ocean of Eloquence*, Albany: SUNY.
Sparkes, A. W. (1991), *Talking Philosophy: A Wordbook*, London: Routledge.
Sponberg, A. (1979), "Dynamic Liberation in Yogācāra Buddhism," *Journal of the International Association of Buddhist Studies*, 2 (1): 44–64.
Stcherbatsky, T. (1956), *The Central Conception of Buddhism*, Calcutta: Susil Gupta Ltd.
—— (1976), *The Soul Theory of the Buddhists*, Delhi: Bharatiya Vidya Prakashan.
—— (1977), *Madhyānta-vibhāga, Discourse on the Discrimination Between Middle and Extremes*, Tōkyō: Meicho-fukyū-kai.
Stern, D. G. (1995), *Wittgenstein on Mind and Language*, New York: Oxford University Press.
Tanaka, K. (1985) "Simultaneous Relation (Sahabhū-hetu): A Study in Buddhist Theory of Causation," *Journal of the International Association of Buddhist Studies*, (8) 1: 91–111.
Tomasello, M. (1999), *The Cultural Origins of Human Cognition*, Cambridge, Mass.: Harvard University Press.
Varela, F., Thompson, E., and Rosch, E. (1991), *The Embodied Mind: Cognitive Science and Human Experience*, Cambridge, Mass.: MIT Press.
Verdu, A. (1985), *Early Buddhist Philosophy: In the Light of the Four Truths*, Delhi: Motilal Banarsidass.
Waldron, W. (1994), "How Innovative is the *Ālayavijñāna?*" *Journal of Indian Philosophy* Part I: 22: 199–258; Part II: (1995) 23: 9–51.
—— (2000), "Beyond Nature/Nurture: Buddhism and Biology on Interdependence" *Contemporary Buddhism*, 1. 2: 199–226.
—— (2002), "Buddhist Steps to an Ecology of Mind: Thinking about 'Thoughts without a Thinker,'" *Eastern Buddhist*, 34.1: 1–52.
Whyte, L. L. (1978), *The Unconscious Before Freud*, London: Julian Friedmann Publishers.
Wijesekera, O. H. de A. (1964), "The Concept of Viññāṇa in Theravāda Buddhism," *Journal of the American Oriental Society*, 84 (3): 254–9.
Williams, D. W. (1974), "Translation and Interpretation of the Twelve Terms in the Paṭiccasamuppāda," *Numen*, 21 (1): 35–63.
Williams, Paul (1981), "On the Abhidharma Ontology," *Journal of Indian Philosophy*, 9: 227–57.
Yūki, R. (1935), *Shinishiki-ron yori mitaru Yuishiki Shisōshi*, Tōkyō: Tōhō Bunka Gakuin. Tōkyō: Kenkyūjo-kan.

INDEX OF TEXTS QUOTED

Cited by title, volume (where applicable), page of text, followed by page or note where cited.

Sanskrit Compositions

INDEX

Pāli terms are found under their Sanskrit forms. Material from appendices is not included.

Abhidharma: as phenomenology 51, 53, 161; ultimate aim of 46, 50, 124, 201 n. 2, 202 n. 13, 228 n. 78; as ultimate discourse 67, 86, 209 n. 61, 216 n. 129, *see also dharma*, as ultimate discourse; Yogācāra as 49, 237 n. 4; *Pravṛtti Portion* example of 107, exceeding limits of 111

Abhidharma Problematic 56, 63, *see also dharma, dharmic* discourse, and mental stream, as diachronic discourse; assumptions of leading to (singularity and transparency of mind) 123, 138; as common framework 60, 86; *vijñāna* central in 57, 87; Western parallels to 204 n. 28, n. 29

Abhidharma Problematic, as addressed in Msg. 129: afflictions 144f; karma 140f; path of purification 150, 236 n. 57

Abhidharma Problematic, concerning diachronic continuity: of karmic potential 63, 65, 142f; of latent afflictive potential 56, 65, 117f, 149, in *Kathāvatthu* 60; in mindless (*acitta*) states 144, *see also* attainment of cessation

Abhidharma Problematic, raised by gradual purification on the path 61, 66, 146, 150f, 157, 236 n. 57: attainments on the path 66, 151, 209 n. 60, *see also niyāma*; backsliding of Aryan 61, 73, 207 n. 50, *see also* Aryan

Abhidharma Problematic, regarding synchronic compatibility between latent and manifest aspects 55: during antidote (*pratipakṣa*) 145f; of karmic potential 59, 65, 209 n. 59; of latent afflictive potential 61, 65, 118, 147; during supramundane attainments 154

Abhidharma Problematic, responses to 66: *ālaya-vijñāna* (*ā.v.*) model as 67, 91, 102, 108, 139; *kliṣṭa-manas* (afflictive mentation) as 149; mentation (*manas*) as 121; need to reconcile both discourses as 78, 94, 216 n. 127; possession (*prāpti*) as 72f, 118, *see also* possession; as questioning assumptions 124, but still limited by 139, 157; seed (*bīja*) as 73f, 118, *see also* seed

abhisaṃkhāra-viññāṇa (construction consciousness) 220 n. 27

ādāna-vijñāna see appropriating consciousness

adventitious (*āgantuka*) 154, feelings of *ā.v.*, 235 n. 51; *see also* originally luminous mind

afflicted mentation *see kliṣṭa-manas*

afflictions (*kleśa*) 4, 25, 46, 208 n. 53; *ā.v.* as root and cause of 125; distinction between latent and manifest 12, 39f, 200 n. 79, 207 n. 48, n. 49, n. 50, *see also* latent tendencies; elimination of 69, 117, 122, 207 n. 50, 210 n. 72, n. 73, 225 n. 59, as destruction of seeds 75, 212 n. 92, 236 n. 58; as perpetuating samsaric existence 67, 101, 117, 146, 210 n. 66; as persisting until far along path 37, 61, 73, 118, 207 n. 50, 225 n. 59, *see also* Aryan

aggregates of grasping (*upādāna-skandha*, P. *-kkhandha*) 10, 32, 120

as dependent upon diachronic discourse 63; result of as karmically indeterminate 64; as temporally separated 64, 208 n. 56; in tension with *samanantara-pratyaya* 64; *see also* karma
mental cognitive awareness (*mano-vijñāna*, P. *-viññāṇa*): with (*kliṣṭa-*)*manas* as basis 122, 163, 227 n. 72, n. 73, n. 74, as bound by 122, 167; and language 37, 163, 167; as needing *ā.v.* for clarity 105; and rebirth 81, 141, 215 n. 118, 232 n. 24, 233 n. 28; *see also vijñāna, viññāṇa*
metaphorical notion (*prajñapti-dharma*) 71, 73
mentation *see* manas
mental stream (*citta-santāna*, or *-santati*) 56, 99f, 149f, 208 n. 53, 212 n. 94, 213 n. 104; as continuity of cause and effect as karmic formations (*saṃskāra*) 74; as continuity of *citta* 75; as continuity of *vijñāna* 213 n. 97, 216 n. 131; as diachronic discourse 55, 63; as necessary to distinguish 'own stream' (*svasantāna*) of possession 72, 211 n. 81; as necessary for karma to work 63f, 72, 85, 87; problems entailed by interruption of 78, 214 n. 113, 214 n. 108; in relation to seeds (*bīja*) 74; *see also santati-pariṇāma-viśeṣa*
mind *see citta* or *manas*
mindless states (*acitta*) 79, 92, 121, 144, 149, 214 n. 113, 222 n. 26, 234 n. 43; *see also* attainment of cessation and non-apperception
Mitchell, S. A. 128
mokṣa-bīja (seeds of liberation) 154; perceived only by a Buddha 235 n. 52
mūla-vijñāna (root-consciousness; synonym of *ā.v.*) 131

Nagao, G. 233 n. 30, 236 n. 55
name-and-form (*nāma-rūpa*) 14, 132; and language 238 n. 13; in relation to seeds 74, 85; in reciprocal relation with *vijñāna* 132f, 229 n. 7
nāma-rūpa see name-and-form
Ñāṇamoli 199 n. 77, 200 n. 80
Ñāṇananda, Bhikkhu 38, 162, 164, 198 n. 67, 199 n. 71, n. 73, 238 n. 12
nimitta (image), Schmithausen's definition of 219 n. 18
nirodha-samāpatti see attainment of cessation
niyāma (or *niyata*) 209 n. 60; assurance of liberation (*samyaktva-niyāmam*) 126
nominal entity (*prajñapti-dharma*) 71
non-abiding liberation (*apratiṣṭhita-nirvāṇa*, P. *apatiṭṭhita-viññāṇa*) 194 n. 36
Nyanaponika 86, 216 n. 129
Nyanatiloka 82, 191 n. 14, 203 n. 18, 208 n. 53

Odani, N. 241 n. 31
originally luminous mind (*prakṛti-prabhāsvara-citta*) 154, 235 n. 51, n. 53; *see also* adventitious
outbursts (of the afflictions) (*paryavasthāna*, P. *pariyuṭṭhāna*) 12, 40, 61, 71, 119, 199 n. 79, 210 n. 76, n. 77, 212 n. 87; dharma that evokes, of sensual desire (*kāmarāga-paryavasthānīya-dharma*) 69, 74, 210 n. 69

Paden, W. 158, 168
parallel processing 106, 222 n. 35; *see also* simultaneity
paramārtha (ultimate discourse) *see* Abhidharma, *dharma*
Paramārtha-śūnyatā-sūtra (*Samyukta* 13, 22) 204 n. 24
paribhāvita see infused
paryavasthāna (P. *pariyuṭṭhāna*) *see* outbursts
perfect view (*samyag-dṛṣṭi*) 152; as arising from the perfectly pure *dharma-dhātu* 155
Piatigorksy, A. 52, 53, 56, 192 n. 19, 203 n. 22, 207 n. 51, 216 n. 130
possession (*prāpti*) 72f 118, 211 n. 81, n. 94; as dissociated from mind (*citta-viprayukta*) 72, 216 n. 127; as distinguishing Aryan 73; as euphemism for person 212 n. 87; in mindless attainments 79
Poussin, L. 215 n. 117
power *see śakti*
prajñapti-dharma, nominal or metaphorical entity 71, 73
prapañca (P. *papañca*) *see* conceptual proliferation
pratipakṣa see antidote
pratisandhi-citta see (mind at) rebirth
pratītya-samutpāda (P. *paṭicca-samuppāda*) *see* dependent arising

Printed in the United States
116139LV00001B/397-398/A

9 780415 406079